NAPLES
1944

NAPLES
1944

War, Liberation and Chaos

Keith Lowe

WILLIAM COLLINS

William Collins
An imprint of HarperCollins*Publishers*
1 London Bridge Street
London SE1 9GF

WilliamCollinsBooks.com

HarperCollins*Publishers*
Macken House, 39/40 Mayor Street Upper
Dublin 1, D01 C9W8, Ireland

First published in Great Britain in 2024 by William Collins

1

A catalogue record for this book is
available from the British Library

HB ISBN 978-0-00-833959-3
TPB ISBN 978-0-00-833960-9

Maps by Martin Brown

Set in Adobe Garamond Pro
Printed and bound in the UK using 100%
renewable electricity at CPI Group (UK) Ltd

To the 'Fazzoletti in Testa' Club

Contents

PART II – Uprising

PART III – Compromises and Betrayals

Maps

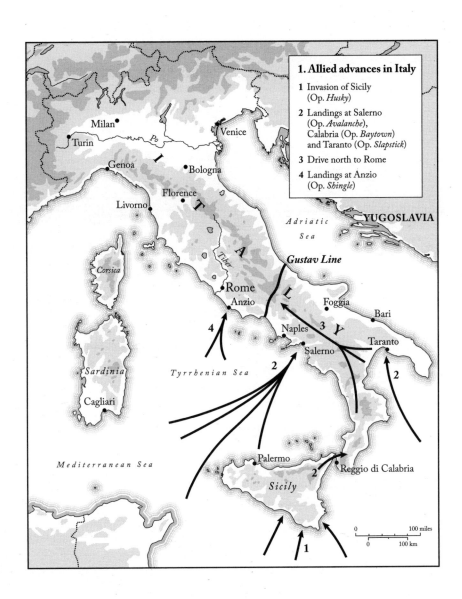

1. Allied advances in Italy

1 Invasion of Sicily
(Op. *Husky*)

2 Landings at Salerno
(Op. *Avalanche*),
Calabria (Op. *Baytown*)
and Taranto (Op. *Slapstick*)

3 Drive north to Rome

4 Landings at Anzio
(Op. *Shingle*)

Milan
Turin
Venice
Po
Genoa
Bologna
I
Florence
Livorno
T
*Adriatic
Sea*
YUGOSLAVIA
Corsica
A
Gustav Line
Tiber
L
Rome
Anzio
Foggia
Bari
4
Y
Naples
3
Taranto
Sardinia
Salerno
2
2
Tyrrhenian Sea
2
Cagliari
Mediterranean Sea
Palermo
2
Reggio di Calabria
Sicily

1

0   100 miles
0   100 km

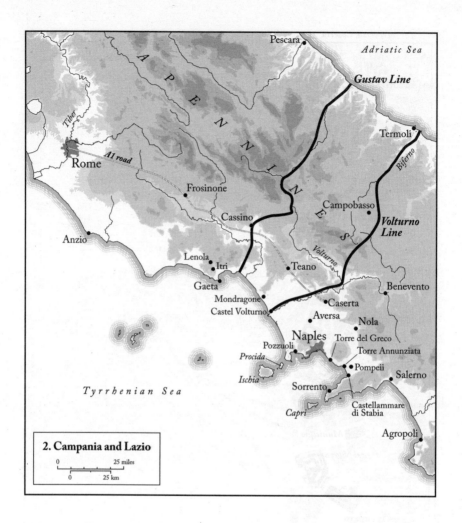

Adriatic Sea

Gustav Line

Pescara

Termoli

APENNINES

Biferno

Rome

Tiber

A1 road

Frosinone

Campobasso

Volturno
Line

Cassino

Volturno

Anzio

Lenola

Itri

Teano

Benevento

Gaeta

Mondragone

Caserta

Castel Volturno

Aversa

Nola

Naples

Torre del Greco

Pozzuoli

Torre Annunziata

Procida

Pompeii

Salerno

Ischia

Sorrento

Tyrrhenian Sea

Castellammare
di Stabia

Capri

Agropoli

2. Campania and Lazio

| 0 | | 25 miles |
| 0 | | 25 km |

to Aversa, Caserta

to Capodichino

to Nola

to Torre del Greco, Salerno

to Bagnoli, Pozzuoli

PIAZZA
CARLO III

MATERDEI

RIONE
SANITÀ

VIA S. TERESA
DEGLI SCALZI

VIA FORIA

CORSO GARIBALDI

VIA CASANOVA

National Museum

PIAZZA CAVOUR

VIA CARBONARA

VASTO
(INDUSTRIAL AREA)

Incurabili
Hospital

VIA DEI TRIBUNALI

Cathedral

Castel
Capuano

Main
Station

ANCIENT
CENTRE

VIA DEL DUOMO

PIAZZA
GARIBALDI

PIAZZA
DANTE

VIA S. BIAGGIO AI LIBRAI
(SPACCANAPOLI)

VIA
FORCELLA

INDUSTRIAL
AREA

University

VIA DUOMO (RETTIFILO)

PIAZZA DEL
MERCATO

Santa Chiara

VIA MONTEOLIVETO

CORSO UMBERTO I

VIA NUOVA MARINA

Post
Office

SPANISH
QUARTER

VIA ROMA (TOLEDO)

Municipio

Castel Nuovo

Palazzo Reale

VIA CHIAIA

PIAZZA
DEL PLEBISCITO

3. Naples city centre

0   1000 yards

0   500 m

4. Principal sites of fighting during the Four Days

Scenes of heavy fighting

Introduction

The Second World War destroyed countless cities in Europe and Asia. This is the story of one such city. It describes not only what happened to Naples when the scourge of war lashed down upon it, but also, crucially, what happened next. The aftermath of the Second World War was often just as dramatic, exhilarating and traumatic as the war itself; and yet it is rarely written about by historians, and almost never acknowledged in our public memory of the war.

Naples, which at the time was still the most populous city in Italy, was the first major metropolis in the whole of mainland Europe to be liberated by the Western Allies. When the British and American armies first entered the city on 1 October 1943, they found it in a state of absolute crisis. All stores of food and fuel had been comprehensively looted, leaving hundreds of thousands of people on the brink of starvation. Law and order was virtually non-existent. Much of the city was in ruins – not only because of the destruction caused by years of Allied bombardment, but also because the German army had tried to destroy everything that they could not take with them. The final days before the Allies arrived had been particularly devastating, when the Germans had performed dozens of massacres and atrocities as their final farewell.

At the end of that year, the city's first Allied governor, Colonel Edgar Erskine Hume, wrote a lengthy report describing the conditions that he and his staff had been forced to cope with:

At the time of our arrival the city was in darkness. There was no
electric power, gas, sewage disposal, means of collecting refuse,
facilities to bury the dead, air raid signals, telephones,
ambulance service, fire protection, telegraphs, postal service,
street cars, buses, taxis, funiculars, railways, or regular water
supply. Police organization had broken down and after days of
terror there was almost a state of anarchy … No schools were
open. Courts were not functioning. The great port, second
largest in Italy, had been almost wholly destroyed. All banks
were closed and the city's financial system was at a standstill.
There was filth in the streets and all shops were closed. Food
was practically unobtainable and people were starving … All
these things were added to the widespread destructions of public
and private buildings. Despair was everywhere.[1]

Unfortunately, things would get worse before they got any better. In
the following months Naples would suffer one catastrophe after
another: there was an economic crisis, a typhus epidemic, widespread
starvation and increasing demonstrations of social unrest. An almost
unprecedented crime wave also struck the city, with outbreaks of
murder, theft and rioting, a burgeoning black market and a sudden
resurgence of Mafia activity. As if that were not enough, in March
1944 Vesuvius erupted, sending rivers of lava towards the sea and
clouds of ash over the entire city. And all the while the war continued,
with huge and brutal battles taking place less than 100 km away on the
borders of Campania.

For Allied observers arriving in the city for the first time, what they
found here was a lesson in moral degradation. Norman Lewis, a British
intelligence officer, later wrote an extraordinarily vivid memoir of his
time here that has been quoted and requoted by countless historians of
the war in Italy. He described a world where 'ordinary well-washed
respectable' housewives were forced to offer their bodies to queues of
Allied soldiers in return for a few tins of food; where desperate old
ladies touted the services of their pre-pubescent granddaughters; and
where even aristocrats begged to be allowed to work in Allied brothels
in the hope of a meal.[2]

The Australian war reporter Alan Moorehead was another observer who spent time here, and who has been quoted by numerous historians of the war. He was even more shocked by what he saw:

> Children of ten and twelve were being offered in the brothels ... Six-year-old boys were pressed into the business of selling obscene postcards, of selling their sisters, themselves, anything. Army cigarettes and chocolates were stolen by the hundredweight and resold at fantastic prices ... Knifing skirmishes in the back streets became a nightly affair. In the whole list of sordid human vices none I think were overlooked in Naples during those first few months. What we were witnessing in fact was the moral collapse of a people.[3]

American observers were just as horrified, and just as poetic in their horror. The novelist John Horne Burns, who served as a US intelligence officer in Naples, described a city in ruins, where the only preoccupation of the Allied soldiers who came here on leave was to get as drunk as possible, and where the only preoccupation of the locals was to relieve them of as much money as possible. 'Civilization was already dead,' he wrote, 'but nobody bothered to admit this to himself.'[4] The Hollywood film director John Huston, who came here with the Signal Corps in 1944 to shoot propaganda films, was even more brutal in his assessment. 'Naples was like a whore suffering from the beating of a brute: teeth knocked out, eyes blackened, nose broken, smelling of filth and vomit ... The souls of the people had been raped. It was indeed an unholy city.'[5]

Even the Italians themselves could not contain their disgust at some of the things they saw here. Curzio Malaparte wrote one of his most famous novels about the city and its wholesale corruption, which, in his description, took place at every level of Neapolitan society. The men here 'spat on their own country's flag and publicly sold their own wives, daughters and mothers'; meanwhile, the women danced with drunken Allied soldiers 'amid the frightful stench that emanated from the countless hundreds of corpses buried beneath the ruins'. In Malaparte's imagination, the corruption of Naples in the aftermath of the liberation was like a 'plague' that infected every man, woman and child in the city.[6]

Eyewitness testimonies like these provide a compelling portrait of the city centre in the last few years of the war, but they do not tell the whole story. For decades, British and American military historians have relied far too heavily on just a handful of such accounts – particularly Norman Lewis's memoir – without thinking to dig any further. Few, if any, stop to ask *why* the food crisis was so bad in Naples and the surrounding area, or what was driving the economic crisis, or who was responsible for all the civil unrest. The black market in Naples would never have existed without someone to supply it; and the astonishingly widespread prostitution here would never have existed without the equally widespread demand for it. For all their good intentions, the Allies bear a good deal of responsibility for the chaos that engulfed the city while they were supposed to be governing it.

The failure of English-speaking historians to engage with these subjects is partly due to a lack of language skills – which have put Italian accounts of what happened in Naples beyond their reach – but it is mostly due to a lack of curiosity. It is not actually very difficult to find information about these subjects if one only cares to look. The National Archives in both London and Washington contain tens of thousands of documents about each of these topics and more – the vast majority of them in English – and yet very few of them have even been consulted by British and American historians, let alone published in their books. There is also a huge, untapped wealth of eyewitness testimony from these times in museums and archives on both sides of the Atlantic.

To my knowledge, this book is the first major history of wartime Naples to appear in the English language. Its purpose is to fill a glaring gap in the British and American historiography of the war, and to share a hoard of new stories – some of them truly shocking – that have never yet been published in any language.

This ancient city was never merely the colourful background to the big set-piece battles that took place further north: it was the hub around which much of the war in Italy was organized. By putting Naples centre stage, I hope to shine a light on aspects of the war that many readers might never have considered before, such as the vast logistical systems that supply any army, the vast corruption that accompanies them and the utter powerlessness of any civilian population that finds itself caught beneath the wheels of the military juggernaut. I also hope to extend their understanding of what war does to a society, how it distorts as well as liberates, and how even a peaceful occupation can have devastating repercussions for decades to come. What happened in Naples in 1944 set a template for the rest of Italy in the years that followed, and also, to a certain degree, for Europe more widely.

If the history of post-liberation Naples is underappreciated, then so is the history of the city before the Allies arrived there. Long before the Allied tanks rolled down the Via Roma, the population had become accustomed to living semi-permanently in the ancient caves and catacombs that riddle the ground like a labyrinth beneath the city streets. They hid here to escape the bombs: Naples was the most heavily bombed city in the whole of Italy, and at least 6,000 people lost their lives here in 1943 alone.

Unrest also simmered just beneath the surface. Even at the height of Fascist power, all the repressive organs of the state could not prevent Communists from handing out anti-Fascist leaflets, and students raising banners in public spaces proclaiming 'Death to Mussolini'.

But the defining moment of Naples' wartime history came when the Germans took control of the city in September 1943. In three weeks of astonishing violence, German soldiers blew up large parts of the port and its surrounding neighbourhoods, committed wholesale atrocities and attempted to seize tens of thousands of Neapolitan men for use as slave labour. The people of Naples reacted by rising up as one and driving the Germans out of their city. The 'Four Days of Naples' was one of the most heroic episodes of the war: apart from the Jewish ghetto uprisings in Poland, it was the first revolt against the Germans in all Europe. It was also one of the few to succeed. Had the people of Naples been left at this point to organize their own affairs, the history of the city, the region, and indeed the whole country might have been very different. But the arrival of the Allies immediately snatched the opportunity – and the responsibility – from their hands.

This history is not well known outside Italy. More surprisingly, it is not particularly well known within Italy either. This, again, is not for a lack of publicly available information. The wartime history of Naples has been told brilliantly and exhaustively by Neapolitan journalists and historians – Aldo De Jaco, Aldo Stefanile, Guido D'Agostino, Paolo De Marco, Gabriella Gribaudi, Giuseppe Aragno, to name but a few – but it has somehow failed to make its way into the national story. In the popular Italian consciousness, if such a thing can be said to exist, the Neapolitan experience of the war remains a blind spot.

The main purpose of this book, therefore, is to place Naples right at the heart of Italian history. What happened in this city was not a mere sideshow to bigger events taking place further north, it was central to the story of the country as a whole. Neapolitans resisted Fascism just as the Florentines, the Bolognese and the Milanese did. They suffered just as northerners did, and they longed as much for constitutional rebirth. The heroism and sacrifice that took place here were harbingers of what would later happen throughout Italy – as were the compromise and corruption of ideals that came after the Allies took control. The Neapolitan story *is* the Italian story.

And yet there are undeniably aspects of this history that are uniquely Neapolitan – that, indeed, could not have taken place anywhere else. For all its similarities to other cities in Italy and the wider continent, Naples is quite unlike any other place in Europe. With 3,000 years of history behind it, the city stands both literally and metaphorically at the centre of the Mediterranean world. It is impossible to write about Naples without acknowledging its legendary contrasts of beauty and squalor, of passion and corruption, of violent crime and extraordinary kindness. For centuries it has been the subject of all kinds of myths and stereotypes, many of which will appear in the following pages.

For some Neapolitan readers, particularly those with family members who lived through these times, some of the descriptions of squalor and crime might make difficult reading. These years, for many, were years of trauma.

Or there may be other reasons to feel uncomfortable. For at least the last two hundred years, southern Italy has been characterized as the

'Africa' of Europe – with all the racist connotations that the term implies. Naples, as the capital of the south, is also the capital of the 'southern problem': the term that northerners have always used to describe the supposedly endemic poverty, sickness, superstition and crime that is found here. To this day, when the Napoli football team play in other parts of Italy, they are routinely greeted with the mocking chant, 'Napoli merda, Napoli colera: Sei la vergogna dell'Italia intera' ('Naples shit, Naples cholera; you're the shame of the whole of Italy.') As a summary of prejudices about the south, it is pretty succinct.

In the eighteenth and nineteenth centuries, travellers from around Europe marvelled at the city's beauty, its extraordinary natural setting, its delightful songs and exquisite food; but also bemoaned its poverty, its promiscuity, its appalling hygiene and its crime. How could such a magnificent country be home to such a squalid people? It was 'a paradise', they were fond of saying, but one that was 'inhabited by devils'.[7]

These myths and stereotypes found new life during the Second World War, and became inextricably intertwined with both Allied and Italian memories of the chaos that came next. It is impossible to write about the history of the war without confronting these myths, celebrating them when possible and debunking them when necessary.

I am acutely aware that I am just another outsider with the audacity to write about this city – God knows Naples has had enough of those over the centuries – but I console myself with the thought that it is a city I have known and loved since I was a child, and which my parents knew and loved even before I was born. And, besides, sometimes an outsider's point of view can also be helpful. If nothing else, I hope that my deep affection for the city and its people shines through in this book.

With this in mind I would like to thank the many people and institutions in Naples, and indeed elsewhere in Italy, who helped me with my research. They are too numerous to mention individually here, though I will try to do so in the acknowledgements. But special mention must go to Sara De Carlo and Valeria Di Gennaro, volunteers at the Istituto Campano per la Storia della Resistenza in Naples, who spent several days helping me with the archives and showing me round Second World War sites across the city when I was in the early stages of my research. Their generosity, sense of humour and passion for history were a perfect reminder of all the reasons why I fell in love with this remarkable city in the first place.

PART I

Beautiful Monsters

CHAPTER 1

Dreams of Naples

At the beginning of September 1943, the editor of the *Stars and Stripes* in North Africa asked one of his staff to write a feature describing what American troops could expect when they finally reached Naples. Staff Sergeant Ralph G. Martin was based in Algiers and had never himself been to the city. He openly admitted in his article that he was basing it on the images he had seen in a cinema travelogue before the war, and on the opinions of 'a friend of mine who has been there and done things'. As a description of the realities of Naples life in 1943 it is next to useless; nevertheless, it gives a good idea of the preconceptions held by Allied soldiers in the days immediately before they first arrived in the city.

'Naples,' wrote Martin, '… is one of the original "pleasure cities" of Europe. It's not exactly as wide-open a town as Las Vegas, Nevada, but the people who live there have the crazy idea that everybody should have a lot of fun out of life. So they do. They run around the streets singing "Santa Lucia" and "Funiculi funicula" at the drop of a hat or a lire, and they go fishing and sailing and drink their vino and leisurely act as tour guides for curious tourists.'

He went on to describe the incredible view across the city from the top of the hill at Vomero, the wonders of Capri, the Amalfi coast ('one of the most spectacular stretches of scenery in the world'), and the archaeological site at Pompeii. It was only towards the end of the article that he gave the all-important caveat: 'Of course, all this was Naples before our bombers came over. Nobody is exactly sure just how much of it is left now ...'[1]

Martin's article merely echoed what journalists, artists and poets have been writing about this city since time immemorial. In the popular imagination, Naples occupies one of the most beautiful natural settings in the world: it is as close as one can come to an earthly paradise. Virgil compared this landscape to Arcadia – a mythical place peopled by shepherds and shepherdesses who had no need of wealth or power because of all the natural riches that surrounded them. The Renaissance Neapolitan poet Jacopo Sannazaro did likewise, waxing lyrical about 'the delights of the bay, the marvellous and great buildings, the pleasant lakes, the enjoyable and beautiful islands, the sulphurous mountains, and the happy coastline of Posillipo with its grotto, inhabited by delightful villas, and softly bathed by salty waves'.[2]

But the image of the city expressed by Martin was really born in the eighteenth and nineteenth centuries, when tourists first began to flock here from northern Europe, often as the final stop on the Grand Tour. The French novelist Stendhal came here in 1817 and declared it 'without comparison the most beautiful city in the universe'.[3] Jean-Jacques Rousseau also visited, as did the Romantic poets Byron and Shelley, who called it an 'Elysian city', the metropolis of 'Paradise'.[4] According to such people, a visit to this beautiful landscape was all that one needed to make one's life complete: it was around this time that the city gained its unofficial motto: *Vedi Napoli, e poi muori* – 'See Naples and die'.

There was plenty to entertain tourists in the eighteenth and nineteenth centuries. They could rest, bathe and enjoy the sunshine. They could visit the ancient sites of Pompeii and Herculaneum, which were rediscovered in the 1750s, along with a vast and unparalleled collection of ancient art and sculpture. They could stroll down the Via Toledo, the 'most crowded and gayest street' in Europe.[5] They could buy all kinds of souvenirs, from ornate ceramics manufactured by the king's factory at Capodimonte to miniature gouache paintings of Arcadian scenes around Vesuvius, or cameos – exquisite pictures carved into shells by artisans at Torre del Greco. All of these things became the clichés of Neapolitan tourism, and were very much alive when Allied soldiers arrived here in 1943.

Perhaps the most famous tourist during this so-called 'golden age' was the German writer Johann Wolfgang von Goethe, who visited many Italian cities between 1786 and 1788 – but it was in Naples that he found his earthly paradise. His evocation of the carefree poor of Naples – the *lazzaroni*, as they were known, after the biblical beggar Lazarus – has since become famous:

> Here the ragged man is not naked. Anyone who has neither home nor lodging, but who spends summer nights under the projecting roof of a doorway to a palazzo, church or public building, and finds a bed for a small fee when the weather is bad, is not a wretched outcast. A man here is not poor if he has no provisions for the next day. If one only considers the mass of fish and seafood offered by the richness of the sea (of whose products the people of these parts are required to eat so many days a week); how an abundance of fruit and garden crops are to be had at all seasons of the year, how the country in which Naples lies goes by the name of *Terra di Lavoro* (the land, not of *work*, but of *cultivation*), and how for centuries the whole province has been distinguished as the 'happy land' (*Campagna felice*); then one gets an idea of how easy life is here.[6]

For Goethe, this was a city of 'universal gaiety', where even the poor could afford to give themselves up to the delights of sensual pleasure. He imagined himself surrounded by people who had nothing to do but enjoy themselves: 'Naples is a Paradise; everyone lives in a sort of intoxicated self-forgetfulness. It is even so with me; I scarcely know myself – I seem quite an altered man ...'[7]

The more educated soldiers and administrators who arrived here in 1943 would have been familiar with such texts, but even those who had never heard of Goethe or Stendhal would have come across the Arcadian daydreams they espoused – not only from newspaper articles like Ralph Martin's, but also from the tourist brochures of the 1930s, from images in newsreels and feature films, or from some of the more sentimental Neapolitan songs made famous by singers like Enrico Caruso.

The idea of a paradise filled with sunshine, song and carefree pleasure must have been a welcome distraction for the frightened, homesick young soldiers who were disembarking in the Mediterranean for the first time. It must have appealed even more to the exhausted troops who had already spent three years fighting their way across the deserts of North Africa and the battlefields of Sicily. The headline of Martin's article spoke volumes about the hopes and dreams of the average soldier: 'See Naples and Live, That's How This Reporter Heard It'.

But first of all they had to get there.

CHAPTER 2

Salerno

'Italy is like a boot,' claimed Napoleon towards the end of the eighteenth century; 'you must, like Hannibal, enter it from the top.'[1]

Of all the many invaders who have conquered parts of Italy over the past 2,500 years, the vast majority have done so from the north. The Goths and the Lombards, Charlemagne and Frederick Barbarossa, the Bourbons and the Habsburgs: all began their conquests by crossing the Alps, before their armies swept across the vast flat plains of the Po Valley, taking its great cities along the way. Those who crossed the Apennines towards Florence found themselves on equally easy ground: they could manoeuvre their armies with relative ease across the rolling hills of Tuscany and the flat lands of the Papal States all the way down to Rome.

For any invader who came this far, Naples was the last stop. For most of its history, Naples has been Italy's most populous city, and capital of its largest kingdom, which for hundreds of years encompassed the whole of the Mezzogiorno. Beyond Naples there were no great cities to be conquered, no riches to be looted, no great stores of agricultural or industrial wealth. Everything south of here was, in the characterization of the great travellers of the eighteenth and nineteenth centuries, merely mountains and brigands.[2]

In the summer of 1943, the Allies did not follow the example of Hannibal or Napoleon. Instead they followed that of Giuseppe

Garibaldi, one of the few commanders to have successfully invaded
Italy from the south.

Almost exactly eighty-three years earlier, Garibaldi had landed in
Sicily with a force of just 1,000 red-shirted volunteers. After a three-
month campaign, gathering thousands more supporters along the way,
he crossed the Strait of Messina onto the toe of Italy. The journey
northwards from here offered none of the wide-open spaces enjoyed by
those who came down from the Alps. Instead, he had had to negotiate
a landscape of winding roads and narrow mountain passes, where
hidden defenders threatened to ambush him at every turn. A series of
rivers running down from the mountains to the coast formed another
set of barriers. Nevertheless, Garibaldi encountered little resistance. He
arrived in the city of Salerno at the beginning of September 1860.
From here he boarded a train to Naples, his ultimate goal, where he
received a rapturous welcome from the local population.

During the Second World War, the Allies planned to follow a similar route. In July 1943, they too landed on the shores of Sicily, only this
time with a much larger force than Garibaldi could ever have dreamed
of. After eight weeks of fierce fighting, the island was finally secured.
Then, like Garibaldi, the British general Bernard Montgomery led an
invasion force across the Messina Strait onto the Italian mainland. A
few days later, on the night of 8–9 September, a second invasion force,
led by the American general Mark Clark, would land further up the
coast at Salerno – that same city from which Garibaldi had boarded his
historic train. From here it was just over 30 miles (50 km) to Naples,
where Clark hoped to receive a similarly rapturous reception from the
liberated Italian people.

Unfortunately, this was where the similarities ended. Garibaldi had
not had to fight his way into Naples: he had arrived unopposed, armed
only with a single powerful idea – that of Italian unification. Alexandre
Dumas, who had followed Garibaldi to Italy, later wrote of the crowds
of people who came out onto the streets to welcome the general:

> The whole of Naples followed him from the sea fort to the
> cathedral and from the cathedral to the palace. An immense
> shout, which sounded as if from the throats of five hundred

thousand inhabitants of Naples, burst forth towards heaven …
it was the hosanna of gratitude for the liberator: 'Evviva
Garibaldi!' The general was forced to show himself at the
window. The shouts then redoubled; hats and bouquets were
then thrown into the air. At every window looking on the palace
the women waved handkerchiefs, leaning out at the risk of
falling into the streets. The revolution was accomplished, and,
as I had promised Garibaldi, without shedding a drop of blood.[3]

The Allies also came armed with a set of powerful ideas: liberation
from Fascist tyranny, an end to the war, freedom from fear and freedom from want. By this time the Italians were so demoralized by
their experience of war that they would happily have allowed the
Allies to march into Naples and Rome unopposed. In preparation,
they had already ousted Benito Mussolini, their dictator of twenty
years, and had entered into secret negotiations for an armistice with
the Allies.

But Germany, their Axis partner, would never allow such an even-
tuality. Over the previous months, German troops had been pouring
into the country to shore up its defences. Those German troops had no
loyalty to the Italian people, and no emotional attachment to its towns
and villages: they were only here to fight a war. As soon as they heard
of the Italian armistice, they seized power throughout the country.
They brutally disarmed the nation's army, seized all its weapons and
stores and massacred anyone who dared to resist them.

Unlike the Italians, the Germans drew up plans to vigorously defend
every riverbank and every mountain pass between Salerno and the
Alps. There would be no triumphant entry into Naples without a fight.

The Landings

As night fell on 8 September 1943, a vast armada of more than 600
Allied ships headed towards Salerno Bay. On board were some 55,000
assault troops of Mark Clark's Fifth Army, followed by a similar
number of reinforcements and support troops.[4] They brought with
them all the impedimenta of an invading army: weapons, munitions,

army vehicles, medical supplies, food, water, petrol – the British contingent even brought a grand piano for use in the officers' mess.[5]

As they neared the coast towards midnight, those on the northern-most flotilla could see the faint red glow of Vesuvius ahead of them off the port bow. The island of Capri rose like a distant shadow – as the US official naval history put it, 'swimming in a silver sea'. Beyond lay the Bay of Naples, 'redolent with history, beauty and romance': this was the timeless coastline where Sirens had once tempted Odysseus and his men with their enchanting song, and where the waves still whispered with memories of the fleets of ancient Rome, of Normans and Saracens, of the exploits and treacheries of the eighteenth-century admirals Nelson and Caracciolo.[6]

On board the ships, the thousands of waiting soldiers were mostly quiet. Earlier in the evening, when the announcement of the Italian armistice had been broadcast on Radio Algiers, there had been scenes of wild excitement. Those on board HMS *Hilary* had leapt and danced on the steel decks with cries of 'The Eyeties have jagged it in!', and on some of the ships the rumour had quickly spread that the whole of the war in the Mediterranean was now over.[7] 'I never again expect to witness such scenes of sheer joy …' wrote Clark's aide-de-camp. 'We would dock in Naples harbor unopposed, with an olive branch in one hand and an opera ticket in the other.'[8] But by now a slightly more sober sense of reality had returned. Those who had enthusiastically thrown aside their ammunition with cries that they would not need it now gathered it up again and readied themselves for the battle that lay ahead of them in the midnight surf: the Italians might have surren-dered, but nobody knew how the Germans would react.

Around midnight, as the moon was setting, the lead ships of the armada reached the 100-fathom mark, and gradually drifted to a halt. Anchors were dropped, followed by the sound of winches lowering landing craft into the water. These huge warships could not proceed any closer to the coastline until minesweepers had cleared a path for them through the shallows. From here, the invading armies would have to proceed on shallow-draft Higgins boats, armour-clad assault barges known as LCAs ('Landing Craft Assault'), and amphibious DUKWs that could drive straight out of the surf and up onto the beach. Cargo nets were dropped over the sides of the ships so that men laden with all their kit could climb down into the boats below – an exercise that one soldier compared to 'crawling down a ten-story building on a mesh ladder with a file cabinet on your back'.[9]

According to General Clark's plan, the troops would come ashore in three distinct prongs of attack. At the northwestern end of the bay, at Maiori and Vietri, a small force of US Rangers and British Commandos would scramble ashore and make their way into the mountains to secure the passes that led through to the wide open spaces of the Neapolitan plain.

Around Salerno itself, and on the beach that stretched for miles to the south of it, the British 46th and 56th Divisions would land, protected by a massive barrage of naval fire aimed at German positions in the hills that overlooked the coastline.

The third prong of attack would land south of the River Sele, which disgorged itself into the Tyrrhenian Sea about two-thirds of the way along the beach. Here the US 36th Division would come ashore and drive inland to secure the invasion's southern flank. Unlike the British troops further north, they would land without an initial bombardment from the powerful naval guns 12 miles out to sea. 'I see no point to killing a lot of peaceful Italians and destroying their homes,' declared their leader, Major General Fred Walker, arguing that if they sneaked ashore quietly they might be able to take the Germans by surprise.[10]

Such illusions evaporated when the first wave of American troops finally arrived at the beach near the ruins of ancient Paestum. While tracers split the darkness to the north of them, accompanied by the muffled thumping of the naval bombardment around Salerno, here there was little but the sound of surf and the low hum of the engines driving the landing craft up to the shore. But as the boats finally hit the sand at 3.30 a.m. the silence was broken by what sounded like a public address system cutting through the darkness telling them all, in English, to surrender. Moments later, a flurry of silver flares appeared in the skies above them illuminating the beach, and the German guns opened up with a roar.[11]

No account of the following two hours could do justice to the chaos that engulfed the beaches around Paestum. Machine guns raked the

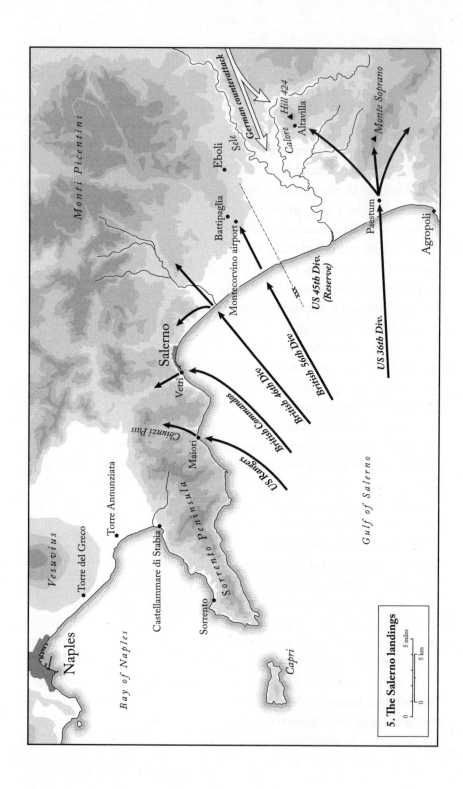

5. The Salerno landings

water, and shell fragments sprayed the landing craft with a sound like 'spring rain on a taxi window'.[12] Several landing craft were blown apart by tank shells, or by artillery shells tearing into them from the invisible mountainsides up ahead. 'Shells were *wopping* in all around us,' recalled one soldier in the third wave. 'We knew that when the ramp fell those red and yellow tracers would eat right into us.'[13]

The American official history describes burning landing craft drifting helplessly in the surf, and men losing their heavy equipment and weapons in the water, or swimming ashore as the boats sank under them. Those who reached the shore faced other hazards: tripwires, machine-gun nests, barbed wire and Teller mines that tore through the wheels of the first jeeps to drive up the beach, spraying all around them in great fountains of sand and shrapnel. 'Scared, tense, excited, some soldiers blundered across the loose sand. Others ran for cover across the open ground to the dunes. Some threw themselves into shallow irrigation ditches or huddled behind rock walls in the fields. Still others sought the scant protection afforded by scattered patches of scrub.'[14]

As dawn approached, isolated pockets of men found themselves in a twilight landscape of sand dunes, watermelon fields and olive groves, scattered with various buildings left behind by more than 2,000 years of history. One artillery unit found itself nestled beside the ancient Greek temples to Neptune and Ceres at the foot of Monte Soprano. Others found themselves under fire from the walls of an ancient Etruscan city; others still from a medieval tower built centuries earlier to watch for Saracen pirates.[15]

With daylight came new dangers. That morning German panzers began roving beyond the dunes, firing on any groups of American infantrymen they came across.[16] They were followed shortly afterwards by German planes that strafed and bombed the invaders in 'the heaviest aerial resistance ever encountered during the war in the Mediterranean'.[17] The picture was fairly similar all along the coast. Further north, the British had got onto the beaches more easily, but then found themselves pinned down in the narrow exits to the hinterland that lay beyond.[18] According to the plan for Operation Avalanche, the first waves of attackers should have been a couple of miles inland by now – but in some areas they had barely made it 400 yards.[19]

In the grand scheme of things, casualties were still relatively light at this point, but that was not how the soldiers themselves experienced it. On the beaches, and in the fields that lay just beyond them, corpses lay in lines, 'shoulder to shoulder … as if about to present arms'; others had been propped up into sitting positions 'so it wouldn't look so bad to the troops coming in'.[20] It did not bode well for the days that lay ahead.

The German Reaction

The Germans had known for several days that the Allies were coming. German reconnaissance planes had spotted the vast armada of ships on the morning of 8 September as it hovered off the Italian coast. The German Commander-in-Chief, Albert Kesselring, knew that the Allies would have to land soon, and when he heard the news that the Italians had signed an armistice it was not difficult to guess what was coming next.

He also had a pretty good idea *where* they would land. There were only a few suitable places to land such a large invasion force. The perfect place was the Gulf of Gaeta, to the north of Naples, where mile upon mile of wide sandy beaches gave easy access to the roads that led north towards Rome. But since this was too far away from the airfields in northern Sicily for Allied planes to provide effective fighter cover, it seemed likely that the Allies would strike south of Naples instead. Salerno was 'the most obvious, indeed uniquely suitable place to land'.[21]

Kesselring had instructed one of his most trusted generals, Heinrich von Vietinghoff, to set up his defences at Salerno accordingly. Mines had been laid both in the sea and in the ground along the coastal strip. Artillery was placed in the hills overlooking the beach and the coastal plain, and a network of machine-gun nests arranged around the plain itself. Salerno was already garrisoned with one of the strongest German units in Italy, the Sixteenth Panzer Division – 100 tanks and 17,000 veterans of the Russian Front – who had had plenty of time to rehearse anti-invasion exercises on this very beach. Two further armoured divisions were waiting not far away at Caserta and Gaeta, ready to be called into action as soon as the Allies landed, and a further two were already on their way from the deep south, retreating before a second invasion force that had landed a few days earlier in Calabria.[22]

The first few days of the battle were bloody and brutal. As thousands of men scrambled ashore in wave after wave, they were pounded mercilessly by German artillery that had been trained on the beach long before they arrived. And yet still they came. Huge piles of stores and equipment began to pile up on the beach.

If the Allies were hoping for a swift, decisive victory, what they got was an uncertain, drawn-out battle of attrition – as one American GI described it, 'a nightmare of exploding shells, of moving here and digging in, then suddenly up and moving again, and doing that over and over again'.[23] The only troops who had made it to their initial objectives with relative ease were those who landed at the northwestern end of the bay: the US Rangers and British Commandos quickly managed to seize the mountain passes across the Sorrento Peninsula, but then found themselves dangerously isolated as the main force failed to link up with them. The key to winning this battle was to break out of this narrow pocket of coastland to the north, but the whole of the rest of the invasion found itself pinned down by the well-organized German defences. By the time the Fifth Army commander, General Mark Clark, came ashore three days after the initial attack, the whole operation looked as though it had become bogged down in a bloody stalemate.

Then came the inevitable German counterattack. At Battipaglia, Tiger tanks broke through the overstretched Allied lines, creating panic among the British troops. Soon, according to one officer of the Grenadier Guards, 'the small roads were full of frightened soldiers, many retiring pell-mell regardless of officers'. Trucks hurtled back towards the beaches overloaded with Guardsmen yelling, 'They're coming! They're through!' – before calmer heads prevailed and the lines were stiffened once again.[24]

The following day the same thing happened to the Americas around Altavilla and Persano. A withering artillery barrage from the mountains ahead of them shredded their forward troops, before a major counterattack by German Panzergrenadiers drove them off the high ground.

Soon, groups of shell-shocked, disoriented soldiers were scrambling back down the hillsides in disarray.

These men were not seasoned soldiers like the British troops further along the beach, let alone like the battle-hardened Germans they were facing. The 36th Infantry Division was made up entirely of new recruits, fresh off the boat from America. Some of their leaders were equally inexperienced. The commander of the US VI Corps, Major General Ernest J. Dawley, had never yet held a combat role. The same was true of General Clark himself. The only US troops in this part of the beachhead with any experience of combat were elements of the 45th Division, who had already seen action in Sicily. These troops had been brought onto the beaches on the first day to bolster the American attack – but since they had landed on the other side of the Sele river, they were unable to come to the aid of their Texan comrades. As any more experienced commander might have predicted, this river had become a dangerous obstacle, cutting off the southern invasion force from any kind of reinforcement.[25]

The inexperience of the Americans showed itself in many ways, not least in the barely suppressed sense of dread that seemed to permeate the higher levels of command. After the setback at Altavilla, General Clark briefly considered burning the vast piles of supplies he had amassed on the beach to make sure they didn't fall into enemy hands – but quickly dismissed the idea for fear of destroying his troops' already fragile morale. He hastily put together plans to evacuate his command post from this part of the beachhead, and even to evacuate larger numbers of troops by sea and move them further along the coast – but, again, abandoned these ideas as impractical. In the end his decision to stand and fight was the correct one, but to those around him these vital moments of confusion and indecision had the distinct whiff of panic.[26]

The following day, what had begun as a setback for the Americans suddenly began to look like a rout. On the afternoon of Monday 13 September, the Germans attacked in force. Thousands of infantry and dozens of German tanks descended from the high ground and stormed along the banks of the Sele river towards the coast, destroying ill-sited American positions along the way. In one fell swoop they drove a wedge between the 36th Division and the rest of the Allied invasion force. Stunned by the fury of the attack, hundreds of American soldiers were forced to surrender, while hundreds of others turned and fled. American losses were devastating: one battalion of 36th Division lost all but sixty of its men; a second lost 508 officers and men; and, on the other side of the Sele river, another battalion of the 45th Division had also been virtually annihilated.[27] Within a few hours the Germans had forced their way to within a couple of miles of the Fifth Army headquarters, and were threatening to push the whole invasion force back into the sea.

The confusion that seized officers and men that afternoon defies description. Norman Lewis, a British field security officer attached to the American HQ at Paestum, later wrote about how he witnessed officers abandoning their men, leaderless soldiers firing 'at anything that moved' and a 'rabble of shocked and demoralised soldiery' retreating headlong towards the beach. At one point the soldiers all around him became gripped with outright panic. 'In the belief that our position had been infiltrated by German infantry they began to shoot each other, and there were blood-chilling screams from men hit by the bullets.'[28]

One artillery gunner described the chaos that gripped his unit when a bullet pierced a drum of lime on one of their trucks. 'Someone smelled the lime and not knowing what it was hollered "Gas".' His fellow gunners immediately grabbed their gas masks, but forgot that the intake canisters had been taped up to keep them waterproof during the landings: many found themselves unable to breathe, but were terrified of removing the masks for fear of inhaling the imaginary gas. 'One soldier had lost his gas mask and he kept walking in a circle saying "They got me, I'm f___ed, they got me I'm f___ed."' The panic did not subside until someone from another gun section walked over and asked them why they were all wearing masks.[29]

Norman Lewis also witnessed 'frantic figures wearing gas masks running in all directions', men 'wandering about' looking for their officers, and American anti-aircraft gunners shooting down British Spitfires by mistake. His final word on the scene was characteristically withering: 'What we saw was ineptitude and cowardice spreading down from the command, and this resulted in chaos. What I shall never understand is what stopped the Germans from finishing us off.'[30]

Even Mark Clark himself, a man never exactly shy about blowing his own trumpet, admitted in his memoirs that his troops were 'at the mercy of Kesselring'. In a desperate phone conversation that afternoon with his subordinate, Major General Ernest J. Dawley, he asked the VI Corps commander what he intended to do to stop the rout. 'Nothing,' Dawley replied. 'I've no reserves. All I've got is a prayer.'[31]

To this day, it is not entirely clear why Kesselring's troops did not push home their advantage and finish the Americans off. There was certainly some valiant last-ditch defence, particularly by two battalions of field artillery – the 158th and the 189th – who refused to join the rout. By the end of that desperate afternoon they were the only units standing between the German attack and Fifth Army's headquarters, but they held the line by rallying a rag-tag group of retreating soldiers, mechanics and truck drivers and thrusting guns into their hands.

The Germans also made some fundamental errors. At key points they ended up using tanks in a piecemeal fashion rather than concentrating them to punch through the American lines. They also lost momentum by driving their tanks into a cul-de-sac at the confluence of the Calore and Sele rivers. But even here they might have broken through if they had realized how weak the American lines really were. As one soldier put it, 'the enemy could have thrown the crushing blow and destroyed us. But for some unknown reason they let up on their fighting.'[32]

Hubris may also have played a part in the failure to finish the Americans off. That evening, the German commander of the Salerno sector, Heinrich von Vietinghoff, signalled to Kesselring that he was about 'to throw the enemy back into the sea'.[33] In Berlin, radio stations even announced that 'the Anglo-US invasion of the Gulf of Salerno has collapsed', and that 'victory in the battle for Naples goes to German arms'.[34]

In the end such reports were premature. That night Clark's beleaguered men were reinforced by paratroopers from the 82nd Airborne Division: bolstered with these troops, the Americans quickly regained their confidence. In the following days more reinforcements arrived, and a new assault by Allied bombers and naval gunfire brought an end to any German hopes of an outright victory.

Nevertheless, British and American troops remained bogged down in and around Salerno for another week before they were finally able to break out towards Naples. The whole operation had been characterized from the start by poor planning, inadequate resources, inexperienced leadership and disorganization: at one point there was even a mutiny by several hundred British troops orphaned from their division.[35]

It was also a costly operation. By the end of the month, BBC Radio was reporting the loss of 5,211 men killed, missing or wounded among British troops alone.[36] Even Clark himself admitted that over 3,500 Allied soldiers had been killed or wounded within the first week.[37] In the end, the official figures listed around 9,000 casualties – 5,500 British and 3,500 American. The Germans had suffered only around a third of those losses.[38]

The American general had been no match for his German counterparts, and had only managed to avoid defeat with the help of the powerful guns of the British and US navies. When it was all over Clark tried to deflect attention from his own failings by sacking his VI Corps commander, General Dawley, but by now it was beginning to look like the pattern for whole of the Italian campaign had been set. As one British artillery officer remarked in his diary at the time, it was 'one hell of a shambles'.[39]

Scorched Earth

The Allies took more than ten days to break out of their beachhead at Salerno, and another week to fight their way through the narrow mountain passes of the Sorrento Peninsula. Once through the mountains, the vast Neapolitan plain spread out before them, broken only by the looming presence of Vesuvius – which smoked ominously throughout the battle – but even here they found themselves constantly delayed by a complex terrain of canals, irrigation ditches, blown bridges and narrow village roads blocked with rubble. The main force took a route around the north of the volcano, liberating San Giuseppe, Nola and Pomigliano d'Arco as they went. A second thrust skirted the volcano to the south, along the coast, through Pompeii and Torre Annunziata. They did not reach the outskirts of Naples until 30 September.

For the city of Naples, the consequences of this faltering Allied advance were dire. Kesselring did not need to push the Allies back into the sea at Salerno – all he really needed to do was to delay them, and in this he was supremely successful. The Germans were merely buying time to allow themselves to set up their next line of defence, along the River Volturno north of Naples. This in turn would hold up the Allies long enough for them to complete an even more impregnable line of defence further north still, in the mountains around Cassino. The Germans would continue in the same vein for the next two years, step-by-step, all the way up the Italian peninsula.

As they retreated, Kesselring issued orders for his men to strip the country of anything of military or economic value. Whatever could not be moved was 'to be destroyed together with the territory being abandoned'.[40] As a consequence the countryside south of Naples was systematically stripped of food stores, fuel, livestock, farm equipment, trucks, cars, bicycles and any other modes of transport at all. Every bridge was blown up after the Germans had crossed it. The shelf-roads cut into the mountainsides were destroyed, and all other roads and railway tracks were sown with mines and booby traps.

In the cities they pursued an even more ruthless 'scorched earth' policy. German sappers set about destroying not only military installations and transport infrastructure, but also electricity stations, telephone exchanges, gas pipelines, sewers and aqueducts, factories of every size and description along with their machinery, and even hotels. All of the industrial towns around the Bay of Naples were treated the same way – Castellammare di Stabia, Torre Annunziata, Torre del Greco – as were those further inland on the Neapolitan plain – Nola, Acerra, Aversa and Caserta. But it was Naples itself, as the main industrial and economic hub of the whole region, that was their main target.

This was precisely what the Allies had hoped to avoid. Throughout the planning of Operation Avalanche, generals and staff officers alike had stressed the need to get to Naples as quickly as possible in order to prevent its destruction by the Germans. In particular they wanted to save its port, the second largest in the whole of Italy. Clark and his colleagues had contemplated all kinds of short cuts to Naples, including parachute drops around the city, and even a second amphibious landing in the Bay of Naples itself, but they were all considered too risky or impractical.[41] Even according to the plan they eventually settled on, it was hoped that they might reach the city by D+13, or 23 September – a week before they actually did.

In the end the Germans were so skilful at delaying them that they were forced to watch from a distance as the city was methodically destroyed. 'We could hear loud explosions at fairly frequent intervals and at night flashes of flame were often visible,' wrote Colonel Edgar Erskine Hume, the future head of the Allied Military Government (AMG) in Naples. 'Stragglers said that not only was the port being wrecked, but that public utilities, hospitals, and factories were being systematically destroyed by the Germans. We heard likewise that the University had been burned. Unfortunately, most of these statements were found to be true.' By this point, parties of AMG officers had already moved forward to Amalfi, Gragnano and Castellammare, ready to head straight to Naples as soon as it was captured – but it was beginning to look as though there would not be much left of the city by the time they arrived.[42]

As the month drew to a close, the reports became ever gloomier. 'Last night, throughout the night there were anywhere from eight to 20 large fires blazing in the city,' wrote one journalist from the *Stars and Stripes* on 26 September. 'The Germans appear to be following in Naples the scorched city policy which they have also pursued in Russia.'[43] A reporter from *The Times* concurred. 'For many days Naples has lain under a black cloud of smoke, the index of systematic destruction on a vast and merciless scale. It may be taken as certain that the whole of the harbour installations has been smashed.'[44]

The Germans did not finally vacate the city until the night of 30 September. As they pulled out, retreating troops were able to report that they had managed 'to blow up all set objectives' in Naples. They were confident that they had destroyed everything that might be of worth to the Allies.[45]

CHAPTER 3

Liberation

Among the first members of the Allied forces to enter Naples were two photographers with the British Army Film and Photographic Unit – Stanley Gladstone and his colleague, 'an impetuous, adventurous man' named Ackland. On the evening of 30 September 1943, Gladstone and Ackland ignored orders to wait on the outskirts of the city, and pressed ahead in search of the scoop. 'I suppose it was Ackland determined to have a go at something,' Gladstone later remembered. 'We found a way, a road which took us right into Naples. And we found ourselves alone.'[1]

The pair were taking an enormous risk. German troops were still in Naples at this point, although they were in the process of evacuating, and some parts of the city still had Fascist snipers on the rooftops. Only a few days before, three similarly adventurous newspaper correspondents had been blown to pieces by a German tank during the liberation of Scafati, near Pompeii. By this point in the war almost 150 Allied journalists had already become casualties – 35 of them killed, 45 wounded, 19 missing and 50 captured or interned – and many more would follow in the years to come.[2]

Fortunately, on this occasion the risk paid off. Over the next twenty-four hours Gladstone and Ackland took some of the most iconic photographs of the liberation of Naples, which were reproduced in newspapers all over the world.

We got some magnificent pictures being welcomed by the Italian people, who did make us welcome – there was no question at all that we were enemies ... [T]hat night in Naples was a very memorable one because although there was some sort of blackout operating, a good many windows were open wide, and wherever we went in Naples that night we walked through the streets and we heard all the Neapolitan songs coming out of the windows. It was a pure film set-up, and quite a magical evening.[3]

The official liberation of the city did not take place until the next morning, at 9.30, when the King's Dragoon Guards, a British unit, drove into the city centre from the northwest.[4] They, too, were accompanied by journalists, whose reports of the utter joy they witnessed were wired to London and New York in time to make the following day's newspapers:

We drove in ahead of the British and American patrols who were waiting outside the city, and as we reached the centre of the city thousands of shouting, hysterical people ran up to us, pulled us from the jeep, and smothered us with embraces. The crowds grew until fully 20,000 people were around our jeep, and we could do nothing but submit to the howling, cheering, weeping mob, and had to stay jammed in until the arrival of the first patrol cars claimed the crowd's attention.[5]

As the main column overtook the stranded journalists' jeep and made its way down the Via Roma towards the Palazzo Reale, the rapture of the crowd engulfed it. Thousands swarmed around the tanks and armoured cars with cries of 'Liberty!' and 'Long live Britain and America!' Allied soldiers found themselves being showered with offerings, both by those in the streets and by people in the windows up above: as the local newspaper *Roma* reported the following day, 'The Anglo-American vanguard entered Naples on tanks covered with flowers ... literally covered with leaves and flowers'.[6]

For the Allied soldiers who found themselves caught up in the celebrations, the whole experience was quite bewildering. '[T]here was the

wildest excitement in the streets,' recorded Colonel Hume, who was
about to take charge of the city as head of its military government.

> People on all sides were laughing, weeping, cheering, praying,
> and in every possible way showing their happiness at their
> deliverance from the Germans. Our officers were called
> 'deliverers' and 'liberators', and their cars could hardly pass
> through the streets for hysterical multitudes. They were pelted
> with flowers and attempts made on all sides to touch them, kiss
> their hands, and receive their benedictions.[7]

Such scenes would become common in the months to come, not only
in Italy but also in France, Belgium and the Netherlands. Allied troops
were often treated as heroes, saints, even as 'messiahs' when they first
entered a newly liberated city. But Naples was the first, and the experience was unlike anything the Allies had encountered before.[8]

The rapturous reception of the Allies in Naples has become one of the
most important motifs of the Italian liberation. It is mentioned in
virtually all of the most important histories of the era, not only those
written by British and American historians, but also some of those by
Italians, too. Rick Atkinson's magisterial history of the war in Italy, for
example, describes people 'weeping and genuflecting' and even flinging
themselves to the ground to kiss the boots of Allied soldiers.[9] The
Italian journalist Aldo De Jaco, who wrote one of the seminal works on
this period of Neapolitan history, described the Allies being welcomed
by huge crowds of men and women 'who shouted and cried with joy
for the end of the terror'.[10]

However, it is important to remember that joy was not the only
emotion on the streets of Naples that morning, and that the streets
themselves were not all overflowing with jubilant crowds. While thousands did indeed gather along the Via Roma, outside the Municipio
and in Piazza del Plebiscito, in the east of the city another, far less
enthusiastic scenario was playing itself out.

Shortly after the British tanks entered Naples from the northwest,
the main column of Americans arrived in the east of the city at Piazza

Garibaldi, near the main station. They were led by soldiers from the US 82nd Airborne Division, with General Clark himself riding at their head. Clark's intention had been to stage-manage a triumphant entry into the city. The symbolism of arriving in Piazza Garibaldi was part of the spectacle: this was where the last great liberator of Naples had made his own victorious entry into the city eighty-three years earlier, heralding the victory of the Risorgimento and the birth of Italy as a unified nation.

The historical parallels between the Allies and Garibaldi's red-shirted volunteers would not have been lost on Clark and his staff. But while Garibaldi had been met at the station by rapturous crowds waving handkerchiefs and throwing their hats into the air, Clark was greeted with silence. According to his war diary, 'The streets were practically empty of civilians', so much so that his diarist imagined that the entire city had been evacuated.[11] Later, in his memoirs, Clark himself had a different explanation. He remembered glimpsing people peeping at him from behind the closed shutters of the houses all around him: 'I had a feeling that I had been seen by millions of persons, although I hardly glimpsed a civilian during the entire trip. It was an eerie sensation.'[12]

Some other Allied commentators reported these scenes in Piazza Garibaldi with a keen sense of *Schadenfreude*. Clark was a notoriously vain general, not much liked by his subordinates, and the failure of his attempts to stage-manage a 'triumphant entry' into Naples was the source of much glee. As one officer who was there that day commented, the fact that the real party was happening on the other side of the city – where 'Conquerors were traditionally received' – filled many of them with a sense of 'pleasant irony'.[13]

But leaving aside the personal dramas of generals and their vanity, there was a serious side to this story that should not be missed. Not everyone was pleased to see the British and Americans. And neither were the people of Naples necessarily the happy, welcoming singers and revellers of Allied fantasy. Many of them were mourning friends and family who had only recently been killed beneath Allied bombs. And large parts of their city had been utterly destroyed, first by the Allies and then by the departing Germans. What reason did these people have to rejoice?

Complicated feelings like these were just as much a part of the liberation of Naples as any of the celebrations that took place alongside them. Some of the more astute observers among the Allied soldiers and journalists could not help noticing that there were darker scenes beyond the celebrations. The crowds were all 'shouting and waving', remembers Private Ronald Hickman, a British soldier who entered Naples with the Sherwood Foresters: 'But it was a complete mess. We went down by the dock area and there were ships scuttled in the docks so they couldn't be used. The Germans had blown up all the sewers and the water supply ... It was quite horrendous.'[14]

Alan Moorehead, working for the London *Daily Express*, saw straight away that the cheering crowds were hoping for more than just an end to the German occupation. 'They screamed in relief and in pure hysteria,' he wrote shortly after the war. 'When we stopped the jeep we were immediately surrounded and overwhelmed. Thrusting hands plucked at our clothing. *Pane. Biscotti. Sigarette.* In every direction there was a wall of emaciated, hungry, dirty faces.'[15]

For General Fred Walker, whose 36th Infantry Division had been so badly mauled at Salerno just two weeks earlier, the main characteristic of the people he saw in Naples that day was not their joy at liberation, but how stunned they all looked. 'The sight of a great city like Naples with wrecked buildings, deserted streets and bewildered people was very depressing.'[16]

Elements of the US 82nd Airborne division had been assigned the role of policing the streets on that first day and in the following few weeks: the first thing mentioned in their after-action report is not the rapturous reception received by the Allied troops, but the landscape of devastation that formed the backdrop. 'The city was a scene of ruin, starvation, and general wretchedness,' it reads. 'Bombed buildings were to be seen everywhere and the streets were littered with an accumulation of rubble piled by months of bombing. The public utilities – water, gas and electricity – had each been carefully and systematically destroyed by the enemy on the eve of his departure from the city.'[17]

One of the most interesting newspaper reports written that day is an account by John O'Reilly, war correspondent for the *New York Herald Tribune*, which has been almost totally overlooked by historians of the war. O'Reilly's report describes many of the themes above – the wild celebrations, the air of desperation that shone through them and the poignant scene of a city in ruins. What really shines through, however, is the reporter's own misgivings about the place he has found himself in, which from the very start seems alien, unintelligible and darkly threatening.

'I entered Naples in the wake of the first British armored patrols,' he wrote. 'It was hard to believe even when we had reached the central part that this was one of the world's famous cities. An atmosphere of wholesale tragedy seemed to penetrate the place from the time we entered it.'

He went on to describe the 'smoldering ruins', the 'hulks of merchant vessels and warships' that lay half submerged in the harbour, the refugees who had fled the city, and the 'yells of armed mobs' who roamed the streets. At one point he came across the carcass of a dead horse lying in the street with its head blown off – a picture that seemed somehow symbolic of the city as a whole. Later, on the outskirts of the city, he saw columns of confused-looking refugees wandering in every direction, dragging all their worldly belongings on carts behind them. Such scenes were 'as horrible as anything since the beginning of the war', and were being reproduced all across the continent of Europe.[18]

At various points O'Reilly's article demonstrates as much prejudice as it does sympathy, and shows how little the Allies really knew about the city they were entering. Like most other correspondents of the day, he repeatedly describes the people here as 'hysterical'. He recounts how 'One old hag, bare-footed and with flying gray hair' ran alongside his jeep 'screaming unintelligibly until she was out of breath and had to fall by the wayside'. She was probably just delighted to see him. He also describes seeing a crowd of several hundred armed men and women grouped around a couple of British armoured cars 'yelling and gesticulating with their rifles and hand grenades'. The handful of British soldiers, he writes, 'gripped their tommy guns and tried to keep the mob at arm's length'. In reality there was probably nothing threatening about these happy, jubilant people at all. They, too, had spent the previous days fighting a desperate battle against the Germans, and were probably greeting the British as allies, or even saviours.

These were just some of the misunderstandings that occurred between the Allies and the Neapolitans that day: there would be many more in the weeks to come. The British and Americans had come here armed with fantasies about a city devoted to pleasure, beauty and song. What they discovered instead was something much more tragic, and much more complicated, than any of them had imagined.

CHAPTER 4

The Destruction

On the day Naples was liberated the Allied Commander-in-Chief, General Eisenhower, sent an urgent message to General Alexander, the head of the Allied forces in Italy, requesting a survey of all the recent damage that had been done to the city.[1] The reply, which came just a few days later, makes grim reading. Before evacuating, the Germans had destroyed the main aqueduct leading into the city at seven different points, causing a 'critical water shortage' and an 'acute sewage disposal problem'. Without any water in their homes, the inhabitants of Naples were now facing the 'peril of severe epidemics', particularly of typhoid fever and dysentery. All major power plants had been deliberately demolished, leaving the entire city without light or power. This was a particular problem for essential pumping plants, but also for flour mills, without which the production of bread was impossible. All the major telephone exchanges had been demolished, the principal hotels had all been burned and 'all motor transportation essential to operation of city utilities' had been removed. All these actions could be 'partly justified' by military necessity. But there were also 'Uninvestigated reports of acts of violence on individuals', and evidence that the prisons had been thrown open and notorious criminals deliberately freed.[2]

In the following days, one report after another came in listing more and more damage all around the city. The worst of it was in the port, where all the cranes and most of the port structures had been demolished. The destruction of the quays was so bad that 'On some quays it was almost impossible to walk over the debris.' All warehouses had been rendered useless: indeed, according to the initial report by the new port commandant, 'The only building in the whole dock area which is useable (Ground floor only), is the Port Offices.'[3]

Another set of reports highlighted the sheer number of vessels that had been sunk in order to choke up the harbour: over 300 craft, including destroyers, tankers, tugs, sloops, corvettes, trawlers, floating cranes, barges and a hospital ship.[4] There was a grudging admiration for the way the Germans had achieved all this, particularly in one of the British reports. 'The wreckage of these vessels had obviously been supervised by an expert with a knowledge of salvage, for each vessel had been systematically destroyed internally' to prevent them being refloated, and a 'super-tangle of obstructions' had been created over the top of them in order to hamper any diving operations. Similar damage had been done to the other significant port towns in the bay, Castellammare di Stabia, Torre Annunziata, Torre del Greco and Pozzuoli. 'Never in history,' claimed the report, 'has such an unprecedented task of rehabilitating captured ports fallen upon its Naval and Allied Task Force Commanders as that undertaken at Naples and its satellite ports.'[5]

The damage continued further inland, particularly to the roads and transport systems, some of which had already been partially destroyed by Allied bombing before the Germans tried to finish the job. Yet another report at the end of October explained that many of the roads around Naples had been deliberately blocked by felling trees or pulling down buildings to create piles of rubble – but that the biggest problem was the demolition of major bridges, '75% being destroyed'. In Avellino province alone, which lay to the north of Naples, some 700 bridges had been blown up. Within the city itself, out of the 2,500 trucks that had once distributed goods around Naples, only 300 were left; and 90 per cent of the city's buses and trams had been removed or destroyed.[6]

It was a similar picture on the railways. According to one British report, 'Railway track and bridge destruction varies from 20% to 100%, averaging 50%.' The main line between Naples and Torre

Annunziata was 90 per cent destroyed, and three-quarters of the rolling stock had been put out of action. Several road and rail tunnels had also been blown up, including the railway tunnel that linked Naples to Bagnoli further west along the coast.[7]

There were mines and booby traps everywhere. On the beaches around Bagnoli, for example, 500 Teller mines and twenty-nine 'S' mines had to be dug carefully out of the ground – that was around two mines for every yard of seafront. It was the US 504th Combat Regiment that conducted this hazardous task, and which later reported it as 'the most difficult minefield it ever encountered'.[8]

All the industrial areas were comprehensively destroyed. Descriptions of the oil refinery in the east of the city show once again how thorough the Germans had been. Before the war, the vast Società Raffineria di Napoli had been capable of refining 210,000 tons of crude oil every year, and stored around 180,000 cubic metres of oil in 140 huge tanks at the edge of Naples' industrial district.[9] But by the time American engineers arrived here, the entire site had been destroyed:

> German demolition teams had blown in the sides of the tanks, had blasted away suction and discharge outlet plates, and had raised some tank bottoms off their foundations. Sections of the intra-terminal dock lines had been blown out and pumps and machinery had been either removed or completely wrecked. At the terminal, the repair crews found many unexploded bombs, demolition charges, booby-trapped cans, drums, and fittings, and mountains of debris. Everything in the terminal was covered with a tarry residue from the burned crude and fuel oil formerly stored there.[10]

Similar reports were made about the steelworks and the ore piers at Bagnoli, where each of the vast 284-ton cranes that had once loaded steel onto ships had been toppled, their huge legs 'twisted and severed'; and also the electricity station here, 'which had been blown apart methodically'.[11]

Cultural Destruction

As General Alexander had already made clear to Eisenhower, almost all of this destruction could be justified to some degree by military necessity. Even the destruction of the sewers and aqueducts, cruel though it was on the local population, could be justified to some extent, because it tied up Allied engineers who might otherwise have been at the front line repairing roads and bridges for the next push northwards.

There were other demolitions, however, that had no military purpose whatsoever, and were quite obviously vindictive. Principal among these was the massive and deliberate damage that was done to Neapolitan history and culture. In mid-September, German forces had intentionally set fire to parts of the university, and to various historic libraries in the city. Countless works of art were stolen and taken north, supposedly for 'safekeeping', while others had simply been burned or blown up.

The first stories about these events appeared in the international press not long after Naples was liberated;[12] but in October and November the Allied governments released much more detailed information about them.[13] At the beginning of February the British War Office then capitalized on this by releasing a comprehensive document describing exactly what the Germans had done, as well as what had been lost. On each occasion, the story was covered in the press: tragic events they may be, but they were also a good opportunity for propaganda.[14]

One of the worst cases of 'German vandalism' was the destruction of the Library of the Royal Society: around 200,000 volumes were lost in a raging fire that burned for days, including a priceless collection of rare books and periodicals. The National Library was similarly ravaged. Before the Germans burned it, it had contained a unique collection of Greek and Roman papyri from Herculaneum and a collection of more than 4,000 of the very earliest printed books in Europe. There were also 10,000 manuscripts, and more than 11,000 autographs and autograph letters from famous people. As *The Times* reported in November 1943, 'the Germans carried off as booty whatever appealed to them most. The remainder they burned.'[15]

But perhaps the most vicious and pointless attack of all was the destruction of the State Archives of the Kingdom of Naples. These had been deemed so precious that the Italian government had moved them outside the city to the Villa Montesano in Livardi, a small village to the northwest of Naples near Nola. The priceless artworks of the Filangieri Museum were also stored here for the same reason.

On 30 September a detachment of German soldiers passed through here and set fire to it all. There was no reason for them to do this: indeed, it was contrary to their own orders.[16] According to the report released by the British War Office, the caretaker of the collection had tried to reason with them, pointing out that many of the treasures were as important to Germany as they were to Naples, but he was ignored. Among the items lost were documents and registers from the time when Frederick Barbarossa had ruled Naples as part of his Germanic empire, as well as a collection of civic and monastic charters dating back 1,400 years. Documents like these from the depths of the Dark Ages were irreplaceable: their destruction was a loss of global significance.[17]

There were other cultural losses, too, which the Allies did not advertise quite so strongly. The medieval monastery complex of Santa Chiara, which stands in the centre of Naples, was badly hit by Allied bombs in the summer of 1943, and the church at its heart completely gutted. All of its Angevin monuments and artworks were destroyed. Some Allied newspaper articles spread the story that it was the Germans who had brought this destruction upon the city, by deliberately placing anti-aircraft guns in the vicinity – Allied aircraft, they suggested, had only ever been trying to hit these guns, which were a legitimate war target. In the case of Santa Chiara, this was not true: along with several other churches in Naples, the destruction had simply been the result of Allied carelessness.[18]

The same was true for hundreds upon hundreds of residential buildings throughout the city. Before their bombardments, the Allied air forces had produced aerial maps with the different regions of the city clearly delineated: air crews were briefed to drop bombs over the railway, the port areas and the industrial zone in the east and south of the city, but to leave the densely populated centre alone. Nevertheless,

mistakes were inevitably made. Residential areas near the port especially were hit – but in fact stray bombs fell all over the city. The Allies
did not know exactly how bad this problem was because they never
compiled statistics about it – this fact alone speaks volumes about their
priorities. Over the coming months, as people returned to Naples from
the surrounding countryside, the lack of housing in the city would lead
to a crisis that the Allies never properly understood, and never got to
grips with.

Crisis Management by the Armed Forces

The multiple crises facing Naples were immediately obvious to all the
armed forces arriving in the city for the first time. For the sake of the
war effort – not to mention the people of Naples – it was essential to
get the city back up and running again as soon as possible. Various
teams of Allied experts were immediately dispatched across the city in
order to get a clear idea of the damage and, more importantly, what to
do about it.

American engineers arrived in the port on 2 October and began
clearing the roads and passageways to the piers around noon.[19] The
following morning a fleet of minesweepers, salvage vessels and tugs
appeared to begin the work of clearing the water of obstacles – 'An
army of ants,' as the head of the British naval team colourfully put it,
ready 'to eat their way into the wreckage and clear away the mark of
the Hun.' The sight of the salvage vessels on the horizon – 'a forest of
masts' rising out of the sea – put him in mind of an earlier fleet, sailing
into Naples under the command of Lord Nelson in 1798.[20]

The US Navy took responsibility for the eastern end of the port,
including the dry docks, while the British Royal Navy took responsibility for the western end. One by one, wrecks were lifted from the sea
floor and towed away to be dumped in a 'graveyard' away from the
main piers. In one or two areas they were obliged to blow up bits of
wreckage in order to clear it, but in the deeper approaches into the
harbour it was deemed quicker and simpler just to lift the wrecks
whole. Their work was hampered by a thick layer of fuel oil on the
surface of the water, which covered navy divers as they climbed in and

out of the water. It posed a serious danger to the whole clear-up operation: any incendiary dropped from a German plane could easily have turned the whole port into a blazing inferno.[21]

'At the back of all our minds was the question of the weather,' wrote the chairman of the hastily established Port Control Committee, Rear Admiral J. A. V. Morse. With winter approaching, conditions in the Mediterranean were already beginning to worsen. This put a strain on the clean-up operation – but, more importantly, it was already beginning to affect the flow of troops and supplies landing on the Italian mainland. Just a few days earlier a violent electrical storm had stopped all beach operations at Salerno. Huge waves had stranded several coastal ships and Rhino ferries on the beach, and at one point a tornado had ripped along the coast, destroying a field hospital as it did so. If the Allies were to avoid such conditions affecting their supply lines, the port of Naples had to be put back into operation as soon as possible.[22]

Miraculously, engineers in the British sector managed to clear berths for four landing craft within just a few days of their arrival. For larger ships, a different solution was found. Rather than clearing away the wrecks from the quayside, Allied engineers decided to leave them where they were and simply built walkways across the top of them. In this way, the first Liberty ship was able to dock at Pier A as early as 4 October, just three days after the arrival of the Allies in the city.[23] In the coming months, the one thing that troops most remembered about arriving in Naples was the experience of disembarking from their ships and walking across the tops of the submerged hulks to the quayside. 'They had planks from one ship to another,' remembers one GI who disembarked here shortly after Naples was liberated. 'We must have walked at least two blocks across [sunken] ships before we got to land.'[24]

The speed of the clear-up operation in the port was astonishing. Within just a month of its liberation, the port of Naples was capable of processing 10,000 tons of shipping per day, with a further capacity of 3,000 tons in the various satellite ports nearby.[25] Within three months Naples was handling more tonnage than New York, and required an army of 20,000 port workers. It was already by far the biggest cargo port in the world.[26] Naval chiefs immediately hailed the reconstruction as a 'tremendous undertaking' on a par with any of the recent victories in battle. It was a brilliant example of what could be achieved through Anglo-American cooperation.[27]

Similar miracles were performed in the reconstruction of roads, bridges and railways in and around the city. Between the beginning of October and the beginning of May, US engineers maintained almost 1,000 miles of major roads, and carried out repairs on a combined total of 10 miles of roadway that had been destroyed by bombing and shelling. Two hundred and fifty-one bridges were built in the same time. In Naples alone, major obstructions were cleared from the streets at over 200 separate locations.[28]

It must be stressed that all these miracles were strictly *military* miracles: the needs of civilians were necessarily pushed to the back of the queue. What mattered first and foremost was always the war. For example, the roads and bridges being reconstructed were for military use only: to prevent civilians from blocking them up any Italian wishing to travel more than 10 km from Naples had to acquire a special permit.[29] The railways were similarly repaired – and similarly restricted: in fact, the main state railway was taken over completely by the army, and was reserved almost exclusively for transporting troops and their materiel and supplies.[30] A rudimentary new telephone exchange was constructed in a little butcher's shop next to the central telephone office that had been blown up by the Germans; but once again it was almost exclusively for military use.[31]

The same pattern quickly established itself in every area of Neapolitan life. The Allied armies could perform miracles of reconstruction, but would only do so if it served their own purely military needs. The only priority was the war: everything else had to take second place. Thus the ships that arrived in the newly rebuilt port were all military ships carrying military supplies: civilian cargo, even essential food supplies, fell to the bottom of the list of priorities. Houses were requisitioned as officers' billets. Schools could not reopen because almost all of them had been requisitioned as a military barracks. Overcrowding in prisons reached dangerous levels because some of the buildings were also full of Allied troops. Palaces, museums, art galleries, newspaper offices were all taken over for military use. Civilians were even cleared out of the Naples hospitals to make way for military patients.[32]

But there was one civilian issue that was so pressing that it simply could not be ignored. The lack of water in the city was so universal, and so dangerous, that even the most hard-hearted of military tacticians could see that it needed to be addressed urgently. If the water was not switched back on soon, the Allies would have a humanitarian disaster on their hands.

The Water Crisis

When war correspondent John O'Reilly toured Naples on the day of its liberation, one of the most distressing sights he witnessed was that of women and children carrying empty bottles through the streets in search of water. At one point he saw 'three women and some children dipping the water and filling their bottles from a sewer which had been opened by an exploding bomb'.[33] O'Reilly was not the only person to witness scenes like this. Stanley Fennell, a British sapper with the Royal Engineers, also saw people 'drinking sewage ... literally. We tried to stop them ... Our officers used to go round and say to them, "Don't do that", but they still did.'[34] According to other British reports, 'Civilians were forming queues to collect drinking water from the sewers.'[35] For those in desperate need, it seemed as if they had no alternative.

For several days the city was almost completely without water. The Serino aqueduct that led into Naples from the north had been blown up in several places, and the Germans had also laid mines in the sewers at key points around the city. Once again, this demolition job had been approached with disturbing efficiency. The Germans had not simply blown up stretches of the pipeline: in addition they had targeted key points such as the bridge that took the aqueduct over the valley between Capodimonte and the north of the city, and the junctions where the water branched off to different suburbs: 'Complicated control chambers ... had charges so placed that all valves and connections were totally destroyed.' Outside the city, in the hills between

Pannarano and Avellino, they had also tried to destroy several reservoirs.[36]

At the beginning of the crisis the majority of the local population was forced to rely on bottled water, supplies of which very quickly ran out. 'We discovered several depots,' remembers one British soldier, that 'had been broken into by the local populace, and they were just taking these cartons of water. We wondered at first what they were after, because we had no water problems ourselves of course. But it was really obviously a big problem for the local people.'[37]

As an emergency measure, the Allies hurriedly set up five water points at strategic sites around Naples. Two of them were supplied by a US Water Supply Battalion, which began hauling water in canvas tanks, 3,000 gallons at a time, from a nearby industrial aqueduct that remained undamaged. To make sure that the water was drinkable, it had to be chlorinated by hand. The other three main water points were supplied by temporary pipelines from the Cancello reservoir. After a while, sixty more water points were also set up at artesian wells around the city.[38] Water for washing or cooking had to be found elsewhere: according to Norman Lewis, people often resorted to using sea water.[39]

Drinking water at this time was so precious that people waiting in long queues were only allowed to fill two bottles each for personal consumption. Unfortunately, desperation occasionally got the better of them. Fights and arguments inevitably broke out as some people tried to jump the queue. One British engineer on water duty came away with a very poor opinion of Neapolitans. 'You couldn't help them very much. They used to cut holes in the hoses because they wouldn't stand in a queue to take a water ration. They'd see the long trail of snaking hose and they knew the water was in there, so whilst you weren't looking they'd cut a hole further down and take some water. And then the pressure would die away ... in that way they didn't help themselves at all.'[40]

While these temporary measures were in place, other groups set about repairing the aqueduct. Allied officers met with Italian officials of the water company, and an international assortment of engineers, military and civilian, made their way to the fringes of the city to assess the damage. They finally got to work on repairs just a couple of days later, military engineers working alongside a force of 500 Italian labourers. In just four days, the worst of the damage was patched up: the aqueduct was flowing again by 11 October.[41]

There was still a problem with pumping water to the high parts of the city, because the whole of Naples was still without electricity. But this problem was quickly solved by the foresight of Rear Admiral Morse, who, on same day he arrived in Naples, requested that some submarines be brought in to supply electrical power. On 7 October, four Italian submarines arrived in the port and, by using their engines and batteries as a kind of mobile electricity generator, soon the pumps were working again – a fact that 'had a very great bearing on sanitary conditions'.[42]

At the same time, repairs were made to the sewers, which had major breaks in forty-one different locations, and hundreds of smaller breaks all around the city. By the end of the month 80 per cent of these had been repaired.[43]

The speed with which this crisis was handled was yet another seemingly miraculous feat, and the Allies were rightly very proud of the achievement. By the end of October, 75 per cent of the destroyed water mains had been repaired; and by the end of the year the headquarters of the new Allied Military Government were able to report that 'As a result of the work from October 2nd to December, the water system was adequate for wartime Naples.'[44]

The water crisis was only the first of many, many emergencies that would strike the city in the months to come. That it was tackled so efficiently is a testament to what could be achieved using Allied resources if the political will was there to make it happen. Unfortunately, the problems to come would not receive nearly the same level of commitment or resources. As the Allies repeatedly made clear, they were not here to help rehabilitate the city. They were only here to win a war.

CHAPTER 5

Underground

Naples is one of the oldest cities in the Mediterranean. According to local tradition it was founded almost 3,000 years ago when the body of Parthenope washed up on the beach here. Parthenope was a Siren – a beautiful monster, half virgin, half bird, who used her enchanting voice to lure passing sailors onto the rocks of Capri. She and her sisters had tried to ensnare Odysseus and his men, but Odysseus had been forewarned: he lashed himself to the mast of his ship so that he could hear their song without being led to his destruction. Distraught by her failure to seduce him, Parthenope threw herself into the sea and drowned. When her body appeared on the shore of Megaride, a small island that sits hard by the headland that dominates this part of the bay, a group of Greek settlers found her. They carried her up to the Pizzofalcone hill on the headland and buried her. They named their colony 'Parthenope' in her honour. It remains an alternative name for the city to this day.

Archaeologists have never discovered the bones of any demi-god buried here, but they have uncovered evidence of a Greek settlement dating back to the ninth or eighth centuries BCE. There were already several Greek colonies along this stretch of coast, particularly on Ischia, and at Cumae on the mainland nearby. 'Parthenope' was originally set up as a trading post deeper in the bay. It was founded on the headland, which was easy to defend, and which dominated the approaches to the coastline on either side. But after a successful war against the Etruscans,

the city fathers felt confident enough to move their settlement a kilometre or so to the east, on flatter ground, where there was more room
to expand. They called their new colony, rather less imaginatively, *nea
polis* – the 'new city'.

In the centuries since then Naples has been ruled in turn by the
ancient Romans, the Ostrogoths, the Byzantines, the Normans, the
Hohenstaufens, the Angevins, the Aragonese, the Spanish viceroys, the
Austrian viceroys, Napoleon's marshals, the Bourbons and finally, after
1860, by the Italians. Each one of these dynasties has left its mark upon
the city. But despite this, the street plan of the ancient centre remains
largely unchanged.

Two parallel streets – the Spaccanapoli and the Via dei Tribunali –
form the east–west axes around which the rest of the city is arranged
(see map on p. xi). When viewed from the hill, these two long, straight
streets look like narrow canyons slicing through the centre of the city.
Each is wide enough only for a horse and cart, and is flanked on either
side by tall houses. Leading off these streets is a labyrinth of alleyways
where the houses are packed so close together that daylight barely
penetrates to the bottom, even in the height of summer. Only the
occasional courtyard, or the piazza of one of city's myriad churches,
provides any kind of oasis of light and fresh air.

In ancient times these bustling alleyways stretched all the way down
to the shoreline. Naples has always been a port city, with facilities that
expanded from the original trading post on the headland all the way
round to San Giovanni a Teduccio in the southeast. Under the ancient
Romans this port became an important military base during the
conquest of Sicily and North Africa – a history that would have deliberate echoes when the Fascists came to power in the twentieth century.
It was vibrant and teeming with life, but also filthy and cramped: by
the Middle Ages it was already one of the most densely populated cities
in the world.[1] As the city expanded up the sides of the hills to the north
and west, it did so along the same lines, with houses and people piling
on top of one another in layers.

The sheer density of housing in this city was the single most
important factor in the events that took place here in 1943. Naples
was a labyrinth of alleys and courtyards, with intricate, close-knit

communities born of constant overcrowding. Without an intimate knowledge of its people and its streets, outsiders found it virtually impossible to negotiate their way around the obstacles that the city constantly threw in their way. This was one of the main reasons why the Germans found Naples so difficult to subdue in 1943, and why the Allies, in their turn, also found it so difficult to govern.

The Subterranean City

As the city grew over the next thousand years, and the buildings began to pile up on one another, a parallel world also started to form below ground. Naples is built on a bed of tuff, a kind of rock made of compressed ash laid down over the ages by countless volcanic eruptions. It is a relatively soft rock, easy to cut and quarry. Almost all the ancient buildings in the historic centre (*centro storico*) are built of this stone, which was dug from the ground beneath where they stand: Naples is a city honeycombed with ancient tunnels, caverns and channels, many of them dating back to the time when it was founded nearly 3,000 years ago.

The ancient Greeks put these underground spaces to good use. Since the city had been built using stone excavated from the ground beneath it, each group of dwellings effectively had its own cistern below it, which could be used for storing rainwater. The genius of the Greeks was to carve channels between each of these underground chambers and link them to a water source from Mount Vesuvius. In this way the cisterns were made into wells continually replenished with fresh water. There are an estimated 12,000 of these wells in the city centre alone: if the terrain could be seen from above it would resemble a vast sieve. The main aqueduct ran beneath Via dei Tribunali, with side channels that led to other parts of the city. This water system was later expanded by the ancient Romans to serve all the towns along this stretch of coastline, and was further augmented by the Spanish in the seventeenth century.[2]

As the city grew, new quarries were dug in the hills around Naples in order to supply the building materials. Long tunnels followed the layers of tuff, forming great catacombs around and beneath the city.

Wherever large deposits were found, larger caves were excavated, some of them vast in size. The Carafa quarry, for example, which lies beneath the Pizzofalcone hill on the headland, has a floor area of over 3,000 square metres, and a ceiling that rises 35 metres high.[3] In the Fontanelle Valley, about a mile outside the ancient city walls, are a whole series of cavernous chambers, some of them almost twice as big as the Carafa cave.[4]

Some of these caves and tunnels have a long and fascinating history of their own. The Crypta Neapolitana, for example, was originally excavated by the ancient Romans as a road tunnel to link Naples to the towns of Posillipo and Pozzuoli. In Roman times it was used at night by devotees of a secret cult devoted to Priapus, the Greek fertility god: childless women would come here to participate in obscene rituals in the hope of sparking their unrealized fertility. The tunnel's association with fertility continued at least until the nineteenth century, when young wives continued to make nocturnal pilgrimages here to pray to the Madonna for numerous and healthy children. The poet Virgil is buried near the entrance at Mergellina, and perhaps for this reason a legend grew up during the Middle Ages that Virgil himself had built the tunnel single-handedly.[5]

During the Second World War, the Crypta Neapolitana was converted into an air raid shelter, so that local people would have somewhere to go when British and American aeroplanes began bombing the city. As the war dragged on, it also became a refuge for those people whose homes had already been destroyed: there were still people living in the tunnel on a semi-permanent basis long after the war was over.

Naples in the 1940s was full of such places. Beneath the Via dei Tribunali, the tunnels and cisterns that had once made up the ancient water system were also converted into air raid shelters. Beneath the Spanish Quarter and the Pizzofalcone hill the same thing was done to the old Spanish underground water cisterns; as it was to some of the larger quarried caves north and west of the ancient centre. When the air raid sirens sounded, people hurried down long spiral staircases into the depths of the ground, where they would spend interminable hours waiting for the 'all clear' protected by 40 metres of solid rock above their heads.

Many of the old caves and water chambers have multiple entrances from the surface – a fact that became invaluable when they were used as air raid shelters during the Allied bombing campaign – but they also gave rise to myths of secret doorways to underground temples, haunted chambers and smugglers' caves full of hidden treasure. Such myths were built on folk memories and echoes from a half-forgotten past. For example, the familiar spirit of the city is the *monaciello* – the 'little monk' – who can appear from underground in any house at any time. According to folklorists, the *monaciello* takes the form of 'a child dressed in white when he brings luck, and dressed in red when he brings misfortune' – a possible reference to the different coloured habits worn by workers in the water system, who occasionally frightened Neapolitan residents when they popped their heads out of wells or basement cisterns.[6]

Such dreams and apparitions are manifestations of Naples' subconscious, and continue to form part of the city's folklore even today.[7] They were certainly still alive during the Second World War, when the population lived in daily proximity to death and misfortune, and had become more familiar with the underground world than ever before.

Fears of an unseen danger lurking underground were given a new twist in the aftermath of the liberation. In mid-October, rumours began to circulate about a crack SS squad hiding in the tunnels, who had stayed behind to continue sabotaging the city. Mysterious knocking sounds had been heard coming from various places around some of the northern suburbs, and it was said that these soldiers had got lost underground and were trying to find their way back out.

At first, the Allies did not take these rumours seriously. Allied officers had become used to Neapolitan gossip about spies and saboteurs, and had investigated dozens of people, denounced by their neighbours for hiding caches of arms in their basements or transmitting radio messages to the Germans 50 km away. The vast majority of these supposed enemy agents turned out to be harmless eccentrics, or simply ordinary people going about their everyday lives. Occasionally neighbours would denounce one another as Fascists for malicious reasons that had little or nothing to do with the war.[8]

This rumour, however, was slightly different. According to Norman Lewis, who by this time was already working in the Allied Military Government in Naples, the Italian police forces were taking these strange noises very seriously. One such force, the Pubblica Sicurezza, had already gathered a whole file of evidence on the subject, some of it from quite credible sources: indeed, one of their own senior officers had himself heard these mysterious knockings.

The sounds were coming from various locations in the Rione Sanità, just north of the ancient city walls, where the hills were honeycombed with tunnels and catacombs. Some of the tunnels in this area date back at least 2,000 years. In Roman times this was where the early Christians had hidden from persecution. They had also held their religious rites and buried their dead, laying their bodies out on shelves carved into the tunnel walls. Between the fourteenth and seventeenth centuries, when various waves of plague swept through the city, some of the caves here and in the Fontanelle Valley had become vast charnel houses choked with the bones and bodies of the dead. There are at least four levels of tunnels, each one deeper than the last, stretching out in all directions. It is impossible to know how far the tunnels reach, but there are well-documented stories of explorers entering the San Gennaro catacombs and emerging again through the San Severo cata- combs in the Rione Sanità half a mile away.[9] If a team of German saboteurs had indeed entered this underground world it was more than possible that they had got lost among the labyrinthine avenues of the dead.

To discover who or what was making these mysterious underground sounds, the Public Security section of AMG assembled a team of about fifty men, including Italian policemen and American Counter- Intelligence officers, and set off to investigate. One morning, shortly after dawn, they ascended to the church of San Gennaro fuori le mura – the ancient church that guards the catacombs where San Gennaro, the patron saint of Naples, had once been buried. A dozen jeeps pulled up outside the church and the party entered the tunnels to begin their search. One of the monks tried to bar their way, claiming that their search amounted to the desecration of a holy place. He had to be forci- bly removed.

According to Lewis, the search party first passed through a series of anterooms, many of them painted with 1,600-year-old frescoes, before passing into the galleries lined with the skeletons of the dead. 'It soon became clear that we were looking for a needle in a haystack,' he wrote.

> We were in narrow, bone-choked streets, with innumerable side-turnings to be explored, each with its many dark chambers in any one of which our quarry could have hidden, or from which they could have suddenly sprung out to ambush us, if they were still alive. These men, had they gone into the catacombs – and we were all still convinced they had – must have been in the darkness for nearly a fortnight since their torch batteries had finally given out. After which, groping their way, or crawling about among the bones, they would have encountered terrible hazards. Even in the second gallery we came suddenly to a black chasm. In the depths of this, where the whole roadway from wall to wall had caved in, the lights showed us a pile of dust from which protruded a few ancient rib-bones. We dangled a microphone into this pit and listened … but the silence was absolute.

In the end they were forced to give up their search and return to the surface. After a few days the mysterious underground knocking sounds ceased. The authorities never discovered what had been causing them.[10]

Not all these fears of sabotage were entirely fanciful. There was indeed a danger lurking underground, but it did not come from any crack squad of SS troops. Rather, it came from something else that the Germans had left behind: delayed-action mines hidden in the sewers and basements beneath the city streets.

The first of these went off less than a week after the arrival of the Allies. It blew apart the central post office building in Piazza Duca D'Aosta,* which stood opposite the provincial council building where

---

* Piazza Duca D'Aosta was renamed Piazza Giacomo Matteotti in 1944, in honour of the anti-Fascist politician assassinated at the beginning of Mussolini's reign.

the Allied Military Government was busy setting up offices. The post office had only been opened in 1936, and was one of the landmarks of Mussolini's new, modern Naples. It was the only major public building left intact by the Germans: as an icon of Fascist architecture, it was thought to have been spared the general destruction. Unbeknown to the people of Naples, several tons of explosive had been left in the basement of the building; and on Thursday 7 October at 2.30 p.m., one of the busiest times of day, the bomb went off.

The explosion was massive, and instantly devastating. According to a special correspondent for *The Times*, the whole pavement of Via Armando Diaz was 'flung into the air'. Almost everyone on the ground floor of the post office was killed or severely injured, as well as many civilians walking in the street a block away. 'The most appalling aspect of the explosion was the number of children killed,' reported Noel Monks, a correspondent for the London *Daily Mail*. 'One moment they were playing in the street – the next they were mere ribbons of flesh. I visited the scene within a few minutes of the explosion and counted the torn bodies of 15 children. A woman walking around the corner on the Via Roma, 150 yards from the post office, had her head blown off.'[11]

British and American Red Cross workers hurried to the scene straight away and began tending to the wounded – both in the building itself, a large chunk of which had collapsed, and on the street, where there was now a crater '60 feet in diameter'. One American sergeant standing a hundred yards away was knocked flat by the blast. As he was recovering one of the passing emergency responders instructed him to get his gas mask and come quickly to help. All he could hear, he said, was 'the screams of the victims trapped in the debris'.[12] Italian firemen also hurried to the scene, but a lack of equipment such as slings and stretchers meant that they were forced to use whatever methods they could in the rescue. In some cases, claimed one report, 'badly wounded and shocked men were hoisted two floors from a sub-basement by ropes tied around their waists'.[13]

In the days that followed, wild claims were made, with several newspapers asserting that 'hundreds' had been killed – the true number was later revised down to about fifty killed and a hundred injured.

Historians in recent years have revised this down again to 'at least 30 killed and 84 gravely injured' – a horrific death toll nevertheless.[14] The outrage this caused among ordinary Neapolitans was understandably fierce: *The Times* reported, rather condescendingly, that 'hundreds of people worked themselves into hysteria calling for vengeance against their former allies' – but since the Germans had long since moved on there would be no opportunity for any kind of justice.[15]

Unfortunately, the post office bomb was not the only delayed-action mine to go off in Naples during those first few weeks after the liberation. Four days later, on 11 October, another mine exploded on the other side of the city centre, killing at least twelve and wounding eighteen. According to the *New York Times* the bomb exploded in yet another underground space – this time a sewer – wrecking a building near the cathedral. What the article neglected to mention, presumably because it was militarily sensitive information, was that the bomb had gone off in a barracks, and most of the dead were US engineers. The whole of the southern end of the building was destroyed, and rescue workers spent the next eight days searching for bodies in the rubble. By the time they were finished, the official casualty toll was 23 dead and 22 wounded, 16 of them seriously.[16]

Five days later, another delayed-action mine went off in Santa Lucia district, killing five and wounding another thirty. Then, four days after that, on 20 October, yet another bomb went off, in an office building next to the US consulate. According to the United Press report the following day, the bodies of ten Italians were recovered, but there were probably many more still buried inside.[17]

In total, five delayed-action mines went off in buildings around the city in the month after it was liberated.[18] Some of them had been placed underground, in hidden spaces beneath people's feet – but others had been cleverly concealed among the normal furniture of the buildings. British and American engineers found some of these booby traps and defused them – for example, in the Hotel Parker on the Corso Vittorio Emanuele II, which had served as the German headquarters in the final days before they left.[19] But they were severely criticized for those they missed. 'The charges were so large and so pre-fabricated that they looked like filing cabinets,' explained one British sapper, years later.

'Our engineers until that time hadn't seen such large charges so prepared. And they must have passed them by and they didn't realise they were explosive charges, you see. They looked so beautifully made – green painted and so on – that they thought they were part of the equipment of the buildings.'[20]

At the beginning of November, yet another underground danger threatened Naples. For over a month the city had been without power or light, because of the huge damage done to all the electricity plants in this part of the country. Italian and Allied engineers worked together to try to repair the damage to the power grid, and to reroute electricity supplies from hydro-electric plants further south. However, when they were finally ready to switch the lights back on, they were forced to hesitate. According to reports received by AMG, the Germans might have rigged up a series of mines to go off as soon as the current was turned back on. 'This information was not of the usual "Neapolitan type of gossip",' AMG's public works chief stressed, 'but rather from respectable, rational sources, such as business executives and directors of Naples Public Utilities, obviously men of judgement and sobriety.'[21]

For three weeks, army engineers checked every inch of exposed cable for signs of tampering. They found nothing suspicious, but were acutely aware that there were also miles of cable underground that could not be properly checked. To be completely safe, therefore, it was decided that they would have to evacuate the whole of the city centre before switching on the power. Notices were posted on the walls, and articles placed in the city's only Italian newspaper at this time, *Risorgimento*, instructing everyone to leave the city by 10 a.m. on 1 November.

So it was that, on that Monday morning, 400,000 civilians left their homes and walked up into the hills around Naples. Some people treated it as a day out, an excuse to have a rudimentary picnic in one of the parks or terraces overlooking the city. Others were more anxious about what might be about to happen to their homes down below. For the old or infirm it was stressful for other reasons: those who could not walk had to be carried – on chairs, on hand carts, or on the backs of younger, stronger family or friends. Even the hospitals had to be evacuated, just in case. Army vehicles patrolled the area equipped with public address systems borrowed from the Psychological Warfare Branch, encouraging the crowds to keep moving. The fire services were put on alert, along with rescue services and two Red Cross ambulances.[22]

At noon the first switch was thrown – but nothing happened. While army patrols and Italian policemen kept guard, electricians and care-takers entered building after building, turning on thousands of household switches. For a few hours lights were switched on and off while hundreds of thousands of people watched from the nearby hills, waiting for explosions that did not come.

Norman Lewis was among the crowds who climbed to the hilltop suburb of Vomero that morning:

All Naples lay spread out beneath us like an antique map, on which the artist had drawn with almost exaggerated care the many gardens, the castles, the towers and the cupolas. For the first time, awaiting the cataclysm, I appreciated the magnificence of this city, seen at a distance which cleansed it of its wartime tegument and grime, and for the first time I realised how un-European, how oriental it was. Nothing moved but a distant floating confetti of doves. A great silence had fallen and we looked down and awaited the moment of devastation. At about four o'clock the order came for everyone to go home.[23]

*

The threat of hidden mines and booby traps remained a problem for months after the liberation, not only in Naples itself but also in the surrounding province.[24] The sheer scale of the problem, the lack of trained engineers, and the vast number of other tasks that engineers were also expected to do, meant that much unexploded ordnance went undiscovered or neglected until well into 1944. At one point Fifth Army tried to wash its hands of the problem and pass responsibility on to AMG staff. The head of Public Safety in Naples, Lieutenant Colonel Francis, resisted this strenuously. 'I do not have any civilian mine disposal unit, and I do not consider it possible to organise such a unit in a satisfactory way,' he told his Fifth Army counterparts, pointedly.[25]

It has to be stressed that it was not only the Germans who hid explosives in the caves and passages that honeycombed the hills in and around the city. The Allies also used many of these underground spaces as stores for hazardous material, some of which posed just as much of a threat to the local population as anything the Germans had left behind.

In the Fontanelle Valley, for example, alongside the catacombs, was a large grotto that was used as a store by the US Army Chemical Warfare Branch. Towards the end of the year a fire broke out here, and the whole area had to be evacuated. The fire brigade was called to the scene immediately, but the sound of small explosions repeatedly going off inside the cave kept them from entering. Since no one was exactly sure what was being stored here it was decided to withdraw everyone to a distance of 150 yards while one of the AMG Civil Defence Officers, Captain Glenn Griswold, inched forward towards the cave mouth to see if he could assess exactly how bad the fire was. At this point, unfortunately, an almighty explosion blew out of the opening, killing him.

The explosion caused considerable damage to the houses on top of the hill above the grotto, and Allied officials began to worry that a second even bigger explosion might cause their collapse. The following morning 8,000 people were evacuated from the entire area within half a mile of the cave. They were not allowed back until the fire had burned itself out, and civil engineers had had the chance to inspect their houses to make sure they were still structurally sound.[26]

Events like this were a constant reminder to the people of Naples that, although the war had moved on, they were still not entirely safe: danger could still be lurking, unseen, in the ground beneath their feet. And it was a reminder to the Allies that, no matter how much they liked to believe themselves in control of Naples, they could never truly be sure of what dangers were still lying in wait for them beneath the surface of the city. Over the coming months they would find themselves repeatedly surprised by forces and events that they had never foreseen and never prepared for: random underground explosions would be the least of their worries.

CHAPTER 6

Allied Military Government

The liberation of a city is never a simple matter. It necessarily involves the sweeping away of old power structures and the imposition of new ones – presenting all kinds of dangers and opportunities for anyone with an interest in exercising authority.

In the first few days after the liberation of Naples, when everything was still in flux, several different groups tried to impose themselves as leaders in the city. Fascists and former Fascists tried desperately to cling onto their positions in the local administration (some of them, as we shall see later, quite successfully). Representatives of the central Italian government also arrived to stake their claim to power. Anti-Fascist politicians emerged from their hiding places and hastily began publishing their manifestos. And armed revolutionaries stepped forward to remind everyone that, as the only Italians who had actively fought against the Germans in the days before the Allies arrived, they had also earned the right to a say in how their city was run.

But in reality the only group with any real power in October 1943 was the Allies themselves. In the early days of the liberation, it was the fighting armies who took control of the city. While essential repairs were being carried out by combat engineers, the US 82nd Airborne Division assumed police control. A series of military proclamations were made: declaring Mark Clark the military governor of the city, declaring the institution of military courts, announcing a curfew, and so on. It quickly became obvious that the city was to be reorganized according to Allied military needs.

The Consequences of Poor Preparation

With the war still waging further north, General Clark had better things to think about than the everyday affairs of civil administration. He and his staff soon moved out of Naples to a new headquarters at Caserta, and left the city in the hands of specially trained officers. These were the men of Allied Military Government – a group of officials with a background in management, finance, medicine, law and other civil affairs. Although AMG would rely heavily on Italian officials and administrators, it was these Allied officers who were now exclusively responsible for governing Naples and its surrounding provinces.

During the first few months of the liberation, the head of AMG in Naples was an American medical officer named Colonel Edgar Erskine Hume. From an Allied point of view he was an ideal man for the job. He had already had extensive experience of disaster management during and after the First World War: in 1915 Hume had been the director of American relief expedition to Italy after the 1915 Avezzano earthquake, before going on to lead American Red Cross efforts in war-torn areas of the Balkans. With the coming of the Second World War he had been brought to Naples as the Regional Civil Affairs Officer in charge of governing all the areas currently being liberated by Mark Clark's Fifth Army.[1]

Hume was one of the first Allied officers to arrive in the city on 1 October. His presence at the spearhead of the troops was not an accident: as he himself made clear, it was a deliberate policy to 'set up military government as early as practicable, because it has been found that any delay results in looting and other lawlessness'.[2] At around the same time that Mark Clark was making his 'triumphant entry' into Piazza Garibaldi, Hume and three other senior civil affairs officers drove into Naples in two jeeps. The first thing they did was to go to the Municipio (City Hall) to meet the acting mayor and take formal possession of the city. They then proceeded to the Prefettura (the

Prefecture building) in Piazza del Plebiscito to meet with representatives of the Italian central government and the various opposition parties. It was vital to gain the support of local political leaders in order to ensure a smooth handover of power: the last thing the Allies wanted was a power struggle behind their front lines. Hume's time in Naples therefore began with a charm offensive: he shook hands with all the local dignitaries, smiled – but also made sure that everyone was aware of the weight of Allied armour and manpower he had behind him – and then sat down with them all for a formal lunch.[3]

In the following days, more AMG officials arrived and began setting up their various departments. One by one, they began calling in their Italian counterparts for conferences. First to be summoned were the various police chiefs in Naples, who were given instructions by the new Commissioner of Public Safety, Lieutenant Colonel Wilson. Law and order was the top priority, and Allied officials were acutely aware that their own military police did not know the city, its people or the language: if they were to have any hope of governing Naples effectively, they would need substantial help from the local police forces. Similarly, the new Chief Finance Officer, Lieutenant Colonel David Nielson, met with bankers; the new head of Public Health, Colonel Crichton, met with hospital directors; and so on with the new heads of justice, agriculture, labour, public works and utilities, education, industry and commerce, and economic supply.

In theory, this should have laid the foundations for mutual cooperation and understanding, and a seamless transition of power. In practice, however, there was a great deal of confusion. This was partly because of the chaotic state of the city, which would have presented a challenge to even the most competent and well-equipped of administrations. But it was also because the Allied officials who turned up with the first wave did not seem to appreciate exactly what they were getting themselves into. Even those who had previous experience with disaster zones did not properly understand the Italian system, let alone the particular problems of a city like Naples.

Among the first people to meet Hume and his staff were representatives of the main Italian opposition parties, who had already formed themselves into a unified 'Committee of National Liberation'

(*Comitato di Liberazione Nazionale*, or CLN). The Allies did not take them seriously at first, and dismissed them as a group of 'ineffective theorists' full of 'hot air'.[4] But the feeling was quite mutual. On the day of their first meeting, one of the leaders of the CLN described Hume as 'intelligent and full of honest good will, but totally unaware of the problems he is preparing to face'. In his opinion, none of the Allied officers had the faintest idea what they were up against: 'The questions they ask are sometimes acute, but more often naive.'[5]

To be fair to them, most of the Allied officials also understood very quickly that they were out of their depth. It was not only that conditions in Italy were so much worse than they had been expecting; it was also that the entire political landscape had changed. Few had predicted that the Fascist government, which had ruled the country for more than twenty years, would collapse even before the Allies arrived on the mainland. Nor had they foreseen that Mussolini's replacement would so quickly enter into an agreement with the Allies, effectively making them co-belligerents. In a matter of weeks, all their assumptions about Italy had been turned on their head.

Theodore Shannon, who worked as a Civil Affairs Officer in both Sicily and mainland Italy in 1943, remembered many of the training lectures he received being nothing but 'pie in the sky'. 'Back in Michigan,' he claimed years later, 'when these young officers were trying to tell us what we were going to find, they had no idea.' Even after he arrived in North Africa and started receiving more specialist training from supposed experts, 'much of it was speculative'. Worryingly, there were other, even more basic failures in their training. For example, very few of those arriving in Italy for the first time spoke any Italian: according to Shannon, not one of his fellow officers spoke more than a few words of Italian before they arrived in the country.[6]

Other former AMG officers agree. According to Thomas Fisher, who saw every level of the Allied administration of Italy over three years, the training most officers received was 'totally useless'. Most AMG officers had no interest in politics – indeed, they regarded it as 'distasteful' – but more crucially, 'They did not know, nor did they ever learn, the Italian language. They knew little if anything of Italian culture and less about Italian psychology.'[7]

Not only was Allied Military Government unprepared, it was also understaffed, under-financed and under-equipped. At the end of the year, the Senior Civil Affairs Officer for Naples province, Colonel James Kincaid, wrote a report that outlined how his staff had been forced to work 'with an absolute minimum of officers and enlisted personnel, with the woeful lack of proper military transport and with no office and stationery supplies'. At one point, for example, 'only one officer was available for assignment in an area covering 27 communes with a combined population of 500,000'. In such conditions 'adequate control and supervision' was simply not possible. He recommended that in future 'at least twice the officer personnel and three times the enlisted personnel ... should be made available to meet similar conditions'.[8]

Similar problems occurred across the board. For example, the new regional head of public security, Lieutenant Colonel Francis, complained that it was 'impossible to effectively carry out the duties which devolve on us' because of the chronic lack of staff.[9]

'The eternal struggle for transport' was what most angered Colonel W. H. Crichton, Naples' new regional health chief. 'In a city in which every means of public conveyance, except a few decrepit taxis and some flea-infested horse drawn vehicles, is out of action, it is literally impossible for any efficient work to be done by the staff of this Division unless adequate transport is made available.'[10] Meanwhile, his counterpart at the central AMG headquarters was complaining that the medical price lists they were all working with were 'worthless', and that the Naples warehouse where they stored all the medical supplies for the region could not even be locked, and had a badly leaking roof.[11]

Such conditions were multiplied across the whole breadth of Allied Military Government, not only in Naples but across the south. As a consequence it was plain to everyone, Allies and Italians alike, that the new administration was going to struggle.

Light-Touch Government

At the root of all these problems was the underlying principle upon which the whole of the Allied Military Government was based. The Allies did not want to govern Italy at all, only to supervise the Italians to govern themselves. This was partly for idealistic reasons: the Allies were not there to colonize Italy, and now that Mussolini had been ousted it was only right that Italians should be allowed to govern their own affairs. But it was mostly for pragmatic reasons: the fewer resources they spent on governing the people, the more they could direct towards fighting the war. In Hume's own words, the only purpose of AMG was 'to aid the army in its advance'. If they could do this simply by maintaining law and order in the rear areas, and by directing as many Italian resources as possible towards the war effort, then anything more was superfluous. Ideally, Italian political and administrative life would simply continue as before, and the Allies would just get on with winning the war.

There are all kinds of arguments as to why this light-touch principle was morally and politically misguided, most of which will become obvious as events unfold in the following chapters. But more important than any of them is the simple observation that, in a city as comprehensively destroyed as Naples, a light touch could not possibly work. As the water crisis had shown, the only way to bring such a situation under control was through a massive combined effort, and through the immediate allocation of precious Allied resources. But the water crisis was just one among many. In the autumn of 1943, the whole of Italian society was in disarray: the infrastructure had been destroyed, the administrative systems were fragmented, the economy had collapsed and people were on the edge of starvation. None of these were situations that required a light touch.

To their credit, the AMG officials who arrived here in October recognized this straight away, and did everything they could to divert more Allied resources into restoring normal life in the city. Many of them routinely put in sixteen-hour days: 'Even mediocre administrators tried to alleviate the sufferings of their communities.'[12] But no amount of hard work and good intentions could make up for the lack of resources that

AMG had at their disposal. It was this lack of resources that would quickly turn a critical situation in Naples into a full-blown emergency.

Administrative Chaos

There was one other major factor that played into the looming crisis, and that was the structure of Allied Military Government itself, which was needlessly complicated. At the city level, the relationships were relatively simple. Naples city and Naples province each had separate jurisdictions, just as they had done under Fascist rule, but both were part of what was now being called 'Region III' (i.e. the region of Campania). Region III contained three other provinces besides Naples – those of Benevento, Avellino and Salerno – and, as the Regional Civil Affairs Officer, Colonel Hume was responsible for them all.

Although nominally in charge of Naples, Hume and his administration had no control over the port and the huge supply base that would quickly grow up around it. This was the domain of Fifth Army Base Section – a unit that would soon change its name to Peninsula Base Section, or PBS. Relations between AMG and PBS were not always good. PBS officers regularly requisitioned apartments, buildings, and sometimes whole areas of town without clearing it first with AMG, who were left to deal with the consequences.

It was above Hume's level where things started to become almost Byzantine in their complexity. As a military government officer, Hume was answerable to the central Allied Military Government of Occupied Territories (AMGOT), whose headquarters was in Palermo, in Sicily.* However, since Hume's region was still a combat zone, his first loyalty was actually to the commander of Fifth Army, Mark Clark, in Caserta. Allied officials often had to drive back and forth between Caserta and Naples in order to conduct their business, a journey that was tiring and time-consuming, but necessary because communications were notoriously bad.

---

* AMGOT would officially simplify its name to 'Allied Military Government' (AMG) on 24 October, after which time it gradually merged with the Allied Control Commission.

A new layer of complication was added towards the end of October, when all of those parts of the region that were not directly involved in the fighting were transferred to a different army command – that of Fifteenth Army Group. Their headquarters were on the other side of the country, in Bari. Whenever conflicts of interest arose between Fifth Army and Fifteenth Army Group, the matter had to be referred back to Allied Forces Headquarters (AFHQ). This was further away still, all the way back in Algiers, in North Africa. Officials at the higher levels of government had to fly between Algiers, Palermo, Naples and Bari on a regular basis in order to negotiate a system that had quickly turned into an 'administrative nightmare'.[13]

As if this were not confusing enough, there were also the remnants of the Italian government to deal with. This was based in yet another city – Brindisi, in the heel of Italy – which was where the king and his prime minister, Pietro Badoglio, had fled at the beginning of September when they had left Rome in order to avoid being captured by the Germans.

By the time Naples was liberated Badoglio's government was only in charge of a small part of southeast Italy. However, as was demonstrated by the presence of central government representatives in the Naples Prefettura, including the Minister for Commerce and Industry, Badoglio's administration still considered itself the official government of the whole country. Italian ministers were certainly not shy about issuing proclamations to the people of Naples and elsewhere in the south.

Since the Allies did not trust Badoglio's government to act in the Allied interest, they hastily set up a new organization to oversee it – the Allied Control Commission, or ACC – which became yet another player in the government of the country. This massive, bloated, ineffi- cient organization came into being on 10 November and immediately made everyone's lives more much difficult. It was staffed by men with little or no experience of civil administration, and an almost complete ignorance of conditions in Italy. In order to ensure parity between Americans and British officers, there were often two people doing the same job at every level. In addition, since the other Allies also wanted to have their say, an advisory council was set up that included Soviet and French representatives, and later on Greek and Yugoslavian ones, too. As a consequence the ACC was horrendously slow at coming up with coherent policies, and wasted far too much time liaising with London and Washington – and sometimes also Moscow.

This plethora of different authorities in different parts of the world caused all kinds of muddles in the early days of the Allied occupation of Italy. For example, nobody seemed to understand whether AMGOT in Palermo or AMG Region 3 was responsible for looking after monuments and museums; AMGOT and AFHQ set up rival schemes for issuing vehicle permits; the Badoglio government appointed school directors who were different from those appointed by AMG officials; and the various Allied armies requisitioned civilian buildings everywhere, seemingly without authorization from anyone. When each of these separate entities issued conflicting orders and proclamations, which one took priority? The whole situation was a mess.[14]

To complete the chaos, the demands of the war meant that boundaries kept changing, and headquarters kept moving. It was not only the spearhead formations of the army that moved as the front was pushed forward. The Badoglio government also moved from Brindisi to Salerno, in preparation for a final move back to Rome if and when the time came. And just before Christmas AMG headquarters itself moved from Palermo to Naples, with all kinds of disruption. Files got lost, staff found themselves without offices – at one point an entire subcommission found itself without access even to a typewriter.[15]

In the light of all this chaos it is hard not to be critical of Allied Military Government in all its forms. There were certainly plenty of critics at the time. Harold Macmillan, Britain's most senior political representative in the region, singled out the Allied Control Commission especially as 'ill-conceived, ill-staffed and ill-equipped for its purpose'.[16] Some American politicians were equally critical. At the beginning of 1944, the US government sent an economic mission to Italy headed by the future governor of Illinois, Adlai Stevenson. According to Stevenson, the ACC was too military, too short-term in its thinking and lacked any appreciation for the very real needs of civilians. Its inability to come up with any long-term policy objectives was 'uneconomic and embarrassing': 'Time and energy are wasted; hopes are aroused and frustrated; and uncertainty, indecision and confusion in the field are the result.'[17]

The lower levels of Allied Military Government also came in for a great deal of criticism. In the aftermath of the war, two former AMG officials wrote a damning essay on the shortcomings of the organization they had both worked for. They described a lack of expertise at every level: 'Only one regional commissioner had had any important political or administrative experience prior to joining military government.' They wrote of 'ignorance of internal conditions', 'lack of preparation', 'faulty planning' and 'vacillating policy'. Worst of all, they claimed that the Allies were slow to learn from their mistakes, leaving civilians to suffocate under the failures of management 'that covered the entire career of AMG in Italy like a slow and steady rain of ash'.[18]

The Allied administration of Naples in particular came in for the worst criticism. According to another former AMG officer, the city was run by well-meaning mediocrities with no political experience, no clear plan and no proper direction from above. They were only ever given proper guidance 'long after problems had arisen', and were otherwise left to 'the painful process of learning by mistakes'. Other regions suffered under the same circumstances but, as the first major city to be liberated on mainland Italy, it was in Naples that all the major mistakes were first made. In the winter of 1943–4, 'Naples was probably the worst-governed city in the Western world, and it was not much better a year later'.[19]

Such judgements are perhaps a little harsh, especially when made by those who have nothing but praise for the regular army. As we shall see, some of the worst problems that arose in Naples were caused by the behaviour of Allied troops, and by the indifference of their British, American and French officers: their presence in Naples alone had a very real effect on the economic and political life of the city. Nevertheless, the inability of AMG to rein in some of the worst excesses of the Allied soldiers who came through the city, let alone to mitigate the more general effects of their presence, would cause untold misery for tens of thousands of ordinary Neapolitans.

CHAPTER 7

City of Pleasure

While Neapolitan life slowly tried to get back to normal, the war continued. In the days after Naples was first liberated, the fighting coalesced along the Volturno river about 25 miles (40 km) to the north of the city. These were ancient battlegrounds. Hannibal had repeatedly clashed with ancient Roman forces along this same river in 212 and 211 BCE near Capua. Garibaldi had also fought here in 1860: it was where he had finally faced and defeated the troops of the Neapolitan king, Francis II, in his campaign to unite Italy.

In October 1943 the Germans built a line of defence along this river and delayed the Allied advance for another a couple of weeks. The river was so swollen by days of torrential rain that in some places it was almost 100 metres wide. Some units, like the US 34th Division, had to cross and recross the river several times as it wound back and forth across the plain, causing at least one GI to wonder aloud why 'every durn river in the fool country is named Volturno'.[1]

A few weeks later the fighting moved further north to the next major river, the Garigliano. Again, this was a battlefield with a long history: it was where, at the end of 1503, the Spanish and French armies had met in the climax of one of their many wars for control of different parts of Italy. On that occasion the Spanish had taken advantage of the terrible weather conditions and crossed the river in secret, taking the French by surprise: their victory had paved the way for a further 200 years of Spanish rule in Naples.

At the end of 1943 the weather was just as bad, the rivers just as swollen. Allied troops found themselves mired in fields of mud. Vehicles got stuck, and had to be pulled out of the quagmire with donkeys or pack horses, or sometimes even by hand. British troops in particular, some of whom were still wearing the same kit they had worn in the deserts of North Africa, often found themselves floundering with equipment that was ill-suited to the terrible conditions.[2] 'There is nothing glamorous about this campaign,' admitted the American forces newspaper the *Stars and Stripes*. 'It is dirty, uncomfortable and dangerous.'[3]

Worse than the rivers were the mountains. Allied soldiers repeatedly found themselves facing an entrenched enemy who was firing down at them from the hilltops. They had no choice but to attack uphill, often arriving to find that the Germans had simply moved on to the next hill, which was even better defended than the first. 'It is this constant plugging that characterises the campaign here,' wrote one war reporter. 'It is being won by men who are worn thin from fatigue and over-exposure, who go up to the snow line and down across the cold valley stream, pushing forward, always dreaming of the warm bed and the steak the size of your arm; and pushing, always pushing forward.'[4]

Eventually the Allies reached the Winter Line, a string of German defences 10 miles deep that stretched from one side of the country to the other. The fortifications were at their strongest around the town of Cassino, some 60 miles (100 km) north of Naples, which guarded the entrance to the only viable route north toward Rome; and it was here that the Allies finally stalled. They would not manage to break through for a full six months, by which time the whole focus of the war had moved away from Italy to other parts of Europe.

Trouble in Paradise

A 'warm bed and a steak the size of your arm' were not the only things that soldiers on the front line longed for. The chance to have a drink with friends, to enjoy some female company, to put on clean clothes and get away from the boredom and constant stress of army life – these were universal daydreams in the winter and early spring of 1944.

'When men are undergoing a great strain, and it begins to wear them down, they must have a moon to reach for,' wrote Fred Majdalany, a British officer who spent weeks on the wet, snowy mountainsides opposite the German lines at Cassino. 'This need was fulfilled by the city of Naples. Naples was the nearest embodiment of the Other World. It became the symbol of every man's immediate aspirations … To go to Naples was the most wonderful thing that could happen to you.'[5]

In the minds of soldiers exhausted by weeks of mud, blood and squalor, the old clichés about Naples as a place where tourists could relax and enjoy the pleasures of the senses became magnified beyond all proportion. For men who had become used to washing and shaving from a helmet full of water, the idea of a hot shower in a Naples rest camp seemed like a vision of paradise. One GI claimed that the first thing he did when he got a five-day leave to Naples was to spend a full hour in the shower: 'I felt so good that if General Clark came around, I would have kissed him on both cheeks.'[6] Others dreamed of the food they would find there: fresh eggs, fresh meat and fish, fresh fruit and vegetables, fresh pastries, doughnuts and real coffee. 'In Naples you could buy things in the shops; you could get drunk; you could have a woman; you could hear music.' It was 'a fairyland of silver and gold and great happiness'.[7]

There was no way that a city could live up to such expectations, especially one that had been as heavily destroyed as Naples. Nevertheless, the Allies did their best to make their soldiers' dreams come true. Almost all the hotels around the bay and on the Sorrento Peninsula were requisitioned for use by Allied personnel. A whole succession of rest camps were constructed in and around the city, each one capable of accommodating upwards of 800 men at a time. Here, soldiers could get a change of clothes, a haircut for 6 lire, and a shave for only four. They could sleep, read magazines and play cards. They could listen to music on the radio or the phonograph, watch movies, or enjoy the shows put on by military bands and USO entertainers. But the real attraction was always Naples itself. 'After one good night's sleep, practically nobody stays around the rest camp much,' noted one reporter. 'They've all got some drinking to do, some sightseeing, some shopping, and maybe some pretty signorina with whom they want to discuss the world situation.'[8]

The army recognized this and did little to discourage it. Indeed, the officers who met the battle-weary men as they climbed out of the trucks, bearded and exhausted, often greeted them with a promise of pleasure: 'We want you to enjoy yourselves. Naples is yours ...'[9]

By this point in the war, thousands of Allied servicemen were descending upon Naples every day. All the main thoroughfares teemed with men in Allied uniform: not only soldiers from the front lines, but also sailors and airmen, and those who were stationed in Naples more permanently – anti-aircraft gunners, engineers, port workers, supply staff from the Peninsula Base Section, and so on. There were plenty of women in uniform, too: WACs and WAAFs and 'Wrens', women representing the Red Cross or the United Nations Relief and Rehabilitation Administration (UNRRA); not to mention the hundreds of British or American nurses who worked in various hospitals in and around Naples. Nevertheless, the majority of those wandering up and down the Via Roma looking for a good time were men. They congregated in the many Allied service clubs that had been set up along this street and its close environs. Or they went drinking in one of the many bars and restaurants close by.

A favourite haunt for soldiers on leave was the Galleria Umberto I – a huge covered arcade close to the Royal Palace and the seafront, whose grandeur had somewhat faded since all the glass had been blown out of its roof by Allied bombs. This gallery was the setting for John Horne Burns' classic wartime novel about Naples. There were dozens of bars and clubs in and around this building, some of them of a more dubious nature than others, and the gallery itself frequently played host to drunken brawls between men from rival services.

For a significant proportion of soldiers out on the town, the main preoccupation was always where to buy alcohol. When the Allies first arrived in October, this was not a problem: wine was quite plentiful, and you could buy a whole bottle for only 4 lire – the equivalent of 4 cents in American currency, or just a few pence if you were British. As a consequence, while the Italians celebrated the liberation by parading in the streets and singing songs, the Allies celebrated by getting drunk.

After a while, however, they seemed to drink the city dry. Within three months of their arrival even the official price of a bottle of wine had more than trebled to 14 lire; while on the black market the same bottle now cost at least 25 lire. By March the price had gone up to 45 lire – more than eleven times what it had cost when the Allies first arrived.[10]

In order to keep up with the seemingly insatiable demand, unscrupulous bar owners began creating their own 'cognac' out of surgical or industrial alcohol, much to the concern of the Allied authorities. The after-action report of the US 82nd Airborne Division, which provided a makeshift police force for the city in these early days, describes the whole process as it happened:

> These were happy days; duty was light, wine, women and song were the order of the day, and with each passing week Naples could be seen to progress another degree towards business and life as usual. Shops and cafes opened gradually in spite of the scars of war. Then came inflation – everything doubled, then tripled in price; champagne, wine and cognac disappeared in favour of a new and more deadly beverage – 'ten-minute' cognac. Pure medicinal alcohol, with sugar and water added, and primed with a few drops of the essence of cognac, was bottled, labelled, aged, and sold on the streets within a matter of minutes.[11]

Allied servicemen were simply not accustomed to this kind of alcohol. Most of them were young and inexperienced, and were not familiar with drinking strong spirits: even wine was much stronger than the beer they were used to drinking back home. As one Royal Navy engineer put it, candidly, whenever he came to the city 'you were drinking wine as if it were beer, and nine times out of ten I was sick afterwards'.[12] In the coming months, the Americans would set up their own brewery for this very reason – it was deemed safer to let their men drink beer rather than allow them to head into the city in search of stronger alcohol. When supplies were low, they even began to use valuable shipping space to import beer all the way from the USA.[13]

After their initial entry into Naples, when they were universally welcomed, Allied servicemen very quickly won themselves a reputation for public drunkenness. Report after report rolled in, as the local police struggled to cope with the sheer number of inebriated soldiers roaming the streets and causing mischief after curfew. Some of their behaviour was quite serious. At the beginning of October 1943, for example, just a week after the liberation, the owner of the Hotel Vomero in Via Bonito reported night after night of American soldiers coming in drunk, sometimes with women, one of them even 'brandishing a gun'. The translation of the police report made by AMG officials says blandly that the soldier with the gun threatened people 'without any reason'; but the original Italian makes it clear that he fired it at a boy, fortunately without hitting him.[14]

The following month, the manager of the Hotel Sirena in Piazza Garibaldi, who was himself an Allied soldier, felt obliged to complain of 'the outrageous treatment of his staff and general atrocious conduct of American troops especially colored ones. These incidents usually occur during Curfew hours in the region of 10 to 11 p.m.'[15] (It is perhaps worth mentioning here that Piazza Garibaldi was an area of Naples where many of the all-black American support troops were billeted, which might account for the disproportionate number of instances involving black GIs.)

At the beginning of December, a man who lived just off the Via Roma reported that his upstairs neighbour was routinely selling black market alcohol in vast quantities. 'There is a big traffic of Allied soldiers who come to drink wines and liquors,' he wrote. 'The soldiers get drunk and create a lot of disturbances and furthermore dirty the staircase in every way, sometimes by vomiting etc.' When this man warned his neighbour that what he was doing was illegal, his neighbour 'replied that in his house he is going to do as he pleases'.[16]

Some of the more public displays of drunkenness caused almost as much consternation among the Allied authorities as they did among the local population. There were regular street fights between drunken groups of British and Americans, sometimes involving guns, but more often just brawling.[17] A typical instance occurred in the Galleria Umberto I in April 1944 when a group of American paratroopers were passing through the arcade early one evening, 'shouting and staggering from side to side'. For no apparent reason one of them started assaulting random passers-by. A report received by the Psychological Warfare Branch describes what happened next:

> One of them, who was tall and fair, stopped several people walking in the opposite direction, seized hold of them by the collar, shook them and then laid them out with a blow of his fist. When these unfortunate persons were picked up by people nearby they were half unconscious and one of them was bleeding from the mouth. As if this spectacle was not sufficient, two English soldiers, stretched out on the ground, shouted to the Americans, and the latter hurled themselves to the ground, forming a confused heap of humanity.

Eventually a couple of MPs arrived to arrest them all, and disperse the large crowd of disapproving Neapolitans that had gathered to watch their unseemly display.[18]

Such behaviour was by no means confined to Naples. All of the towns nearby reported similar instances of drunken behaviour, often accompanied by violence, thefts, robbery and the sexual harassment of local women. It was difficult to know who were the worst offenders. In Avellino, American troops were blamed, particularly black troops – that is, until a large contingent of Canadians arrived and 'troubles rapidly increased'.[19] In Miano, just north of Naples, black American troops were once again singled out for their poor behaviour.[20] Negative reports about black soldiers figure disproportionately in the police files – perhaps because the local police, who had rarely ever seen black people before, were more likely to complain about them than they were about their white counterparts. There is also anecdotal evidence to suggest that some of the Allied MPs, who were mostly white Americans, treated black soldiers much more harshly – sometimes even brutally – than they did white soldiers who were guilty of the same offences.[21]

In the end, just about the only group of soldiers who were not criticized for drunken behaviour were the French. Again, it is difficult to know precisely why this should be. Perhaps it was because there were fewer of them; or perhaps it was because they were more used to drinking wine than their Anglo-American allies. It is also true that most of the French colonial troops in the city – the Moroccan *goumiers* and Algerian *tirailleurs* – were Muslims, and so the vast majority of them did not drink at all. Whatever the reason, according to the Psychological Warfare Branch, 'They are considered to be the best behaved of all the Allied soldiers in Naples; it is rare to see a French soldier drunk.'[22]

How to Manage Anti-Social Behaviour

It did not take long for the Allied Military Government to get wind of what was happening on the streets of Naples. Throughout October and November, report after report came in listing the bad behaviour of Allied troops, whose 'chief source is drink'.[23] In December, things became even worse. In the course of just five days, the Neapolitan police reported twenty-six incidents of drunken soldiers beating and robbing policemen, breaking and entering private houses, assaulting women, refusing to pay their bills in restaurants, and even smashing up a local hospital.[24] 'It can be said at once,' wrote the Commissioner for Public Safety at the turn of the year, 'that the discipline and behaviour of Allied troops, particularly in Naples, was bad. Instances of drunkenness, assault, looting and rowdyism were continually being reported.'[25]

In an attempt to crack down on behaviour like this, several measures were put in place – none of which made much difference. The principal measure was the 7 p.m. curfew, which was widely ignored by everyone, soldiers and civilians alike. Military policemen would occasionally scoop up some hapless soldier staggering home along one of the main thoroughfares late at night – but MPs could not be everywhere at once, and what went on in the smaller streets away from their regular routes of patrol was largely a mystery to them.

The most notorious areas were in the maze of alleyways that led off the Via Roma on both sides of the road, but particularly in the area known as the 'Spanish Quarter'. In order to keep servicemen away from these parts of the city they were declared 'Off Limits', and signs were painted on the street corners making this clear – one or two of which are still visible today. But once again the restrictions were widely ignored: as soon as word got round that a particular brothel or drinking den was open after hours, soldiers flocked to it, safe in the knowledge that the MPs rarely ventured into the more densely packed parts of the city.

At the beginning of December the Allies announced a crackdown on adulterated alcohol, and made several arrests that were widely publicized in the press. In a surprise raid in the suburb of Portici, a 'poison liquor' plant was raided and over 3,000 bottles of 'cognac', 'vermouth' and 'cherry brandy' seized. When tested, the bottles were actually found to contain solidified fuel alcohol, which had been melted down and mixed with water and fruit juice.[26] A few days later another bootlegger was arrested in Via Mezzocannone selling bottles of 'cognac' made from methylated spirits; and two days after that another four stills were shut down and fifty street touts arrested.[27] But for every Neapolitan bootlegger who was caught there was always another ready to take his place: demand for all types of alcohol among the troops was so high that there were enormous profits to be made.

Among the troops themselves, feelings about this anti-alcohol campaign were mixed at best. Almost everyone approved of the arrest of the worst of the bootleggers, but there was less support for the efforts of MPs to crack down on drinking more generally. Some soldiers in the rear echelons freely admitted that their principal form of entertainment was to 'get drunk and fight', and they resented anyone who tried to stop them.[28] Among front-line troops, meanwhile, there was a feeling that they had earned the right to a couple of nights out in Naples, and that they should be free to celebrate them however they chose. The letters section of the *Stars and Stripes* was littered with complaints about overzealous MPs arresting GIs over some technicality or another, or otherwise getting in between them and a good time.[29]

Bill Mauldin, the cartoonist who became famous for his depictions of wry, unkempt GIs, wrote passionately in his memoirs about the typical front-line soldier who came to Naples on a four-day leave:

Naturally, when he arrived in Naples he was a mess. His shoes were muddy, his clothes were filthy, torn, and often bloody, he needed a shave and a haircut, and you could smell him a block away. He also needed to get drunk and get laid. The dogface seldom achieved these last two aims. The general of Naples had worked out a neat scheme for keeping these apparitions from the front off his orderly streets. His MPs met them as they entered town and hauled them off to jail, where they learned that the sentence for wearing unshined shoes, unpressed trousers, unbuttoned shirts, beards, or long hair, or any combination of these things was exactly four days in jail. Having paid their debt to society, they were shaved, showered, and released to return to their foxholes.[30]

"Th' hell with it, sir. Let's go back to th' front."

He was exaggerating, of course. Thousands of combat troops on leave
came through Naples, and many of them refused to abide by the rules.
The attitude of the US 504th Parachute Infantry Regiment was probably typical. This regiment had been among the first troops in Naples
when it was liberated, before going on to fight the Germans along the
Winter Line further north. When they returned in January 1944, they
were told that the whole of Naples was officially off limits to them.
'But then who were they – the victors of Altavilla, the assaulters of Mt
Sammucro, and the participants of a hundred other engagements – to
suddenly become impotent at the flicker of a PBS directive; besides,
hadn't they taken the town four months before?' Armed with this sense
of entitlement, the whole regimental combat team ignored the rules,
and 'Naples was retaken by mass infiltration'.[31]

The other approach used by the Allies to rein in their soldiers was to
try to provide them with alternative, more wholesome entertainment.
One of the many things that the Allies did when they first arrived in
Naples was to requisition properties that could be used for the recreation of their troops. The British set up their Army and Navy Club at
no. 343 Via Roma, for example, and another club specifically for
NCOs on the same street at no. 405. The American Red Cross (ARC)
set up a club for GIs on Via Armando Diaz, and an Officers' Club in
Piazza Carità. Then there was the American Merchant Seamen's Club
in Piazza San Ferdinando, the ARC Liberty Club in Via Milano (no.
104), the Christian Science Service Centre at 64 Via Santa Brigida …
the list went on. Some of these clubs had dormitories and showers, and
almost all of them had games rooms where servicemen could play
cards, ping-pong and billiards. They also had reading lounges, writing
rooms, barber shops and even 'symphony rooms' where servicemen
could listen to music. And then there was the food. While most of
Naples was going hungry, Allied servicemen were guaranteed an
endless supply of fruit and pastries at their snack bars and cafeterias,
often provided free of charge.

The grandeur of some of these buildings was sometimes beyond
anything that these soldiers and other Allied officials had ever dreamed
of. For example, the British set up a NAAFI (Navy, Army and Air

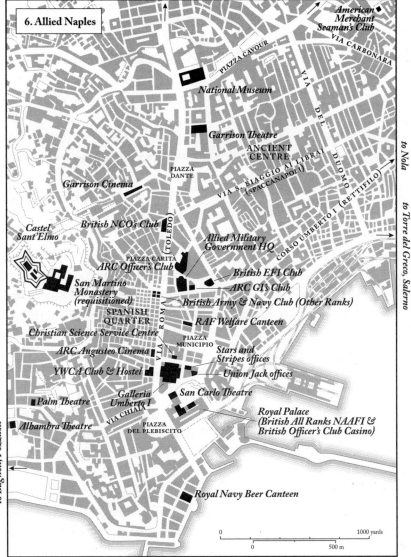

6. Allied Naples

to Aversa, Caserta

to Capodichino

American
Merchant
Seaman's Club

VIA CARBONARA

PIAZZA CAVOUR

National Museum

VIA DEL DUOMO

Garrison Theatre

ANCIENT
CENTRE

to Nola

VIA S. BIAGGIO AI LIBRAI
(SPACCANAPOLI)

PIAZZA
DANTE

Garrison Cinema

to Torre del Greco, Salerno

CORSO UMBERTO I (RETTIFILO)

*Castel
Sant'Elmo*

British NCO's Club

(TOLEDO)

*Allied Military
Government HQ*

PIAZZA CARITÀ
ARC Officer's Club

British EFI Club

*San Martino
Monastery
(requisitioned)*

ARC GI's Club

British Army & Navy Club (Other Ranks)

SPANISH
QUARTER

RAF Welfare Canteen

Christian Science Service Centre

VIA ROMA

PIAZZA
MUNICIPIO

ARC Augusteo Cinema

*Stars and
Stripes offices*

YWCA Club & Hostel

Union Jack offices

Palm Theatre

*Galleria
Umberto I*

San Carlo Theatre

VIA CHIAIA

*Royal Palace
(British All Ranks NAAFI &
British Officer's Club Casino)*

Alhambra Theatre

PIAZZA
DEL PLEBISCITO

to Bagnoli, Pozzuoli

Royal Navy Beer Canteen

0   1000 yards

0   500 m

Force Institute) in the Royal Palace that welcomed servicemen of all ranks. 'It was one of the poshest NAAFIs I've ever been in,' remembered one private soldier with the Black Watch Battalion. 'It overlooked the Bay of Naples. You could go in there and have a haircut and a shower and a shave, and they had a restaurant up on one of the balconies ... And every day the singers from the opera next door would come and sing Neapolitan arias.'[32]

Another British soldier remembers entering this palace as if in a dream. Wilfred Beeson, an NCO with the Royal Army Ordnance Corps, had been captured at Dunkirk at the beginning of the war, had escaped from a German prisoner-of-war camp, and fought with the French Resistance throughout 1943. Eventually he made his way to Corsica, and from there to Naples to be repatriated. On his first day in the city he was taken to the all-ranks NAAFI in the Royal Palace: he walked up the gigantic marble staircase and into the huge salon, and found himself confronted with a string orchestra playing 'Come Back to Sorrento'. The whole experience was overwhelming: 'There was a beautiful restaurant, beautiful food. There was wine. There was always a show going on ... I spent my first day there. Every time I hear "Come Back to Sorrento" today I always shed tears.'[33]

Alongside the service clubs, the Allies set up other entertainment venues, such as the San Carlo Theatre, which sat between the Royal Palace and the Galleria Umberto I. The San Carlo Theatre had been the centre of musical culture in the city ever since it was first opened in 1737. Unfortunately it had been considerably damaged during Allied bombing earlier in the year, including the destruction of many of the dressing rooms and the entire foyer. Peter Francis, a British artillery officer and theatre-lover, found himself organizing its restoration. With permission from his brigade commander, he gathered a small team of people to do essential repairs to the building and see if he could get the opera back up and running again. 'We worked day and night to get it going,' he explained in an interview sixty years later. 'Luckily one of the tenors was married to an English woman, and he spoke English quite well ... We just got the orchestra together, got the stage staff together, and started to work ... Once it got round that the theatre was reopening, they came.'[34] Recognizing the value of what they were doing, the British Army diverted enough resources to help with the repairs. They managed to source some timber and some canvas for scenery, and by the middle of November they were ready to put on their first show: a revue show full of scantily clad dancing girls, and renditions of English and Italian popular songs. Over the following month they staged vaudeville acts, symphonies and selections of songs from various famous operas, all accompanied by a seventy-two-piece orchestra. Finally, in December, a new opera season began with a performance of Donizetti's *Lucia di Lammermoor*.[35]

The San Carlo was not the only musical venue open for Allied entertainment. The Palm Theatre in Chiaia, on the other side of the headland, also put on opera for the troops, as well as swing bands, singers and music groups. At the top of the Via Roma the Augusteo Theatre, run by the Red Cross, used to put on swing bands and live magic shows, as well as movies fresh from Hollywood; and the Garrison Theatre in Piazza Dante boasted classical concerts conducted by a 'former school friend of Enrico Caruso', as well as specially adapted plays, such as Louis Verneuil's *Jealousy*.[36]

As time went on, the entertainment multiplied. English-language movies appeared in all the service clubs, as well as at many of the Italian commercial cinemas. Sometimes Allied soldiers even got to see new films before their friends and families back home: the world premiere of Bing Crosby's *Going My Way*, for example, was shown at the Palm Theatre on the Via Dei Mille.[37] Film stars like Marlene Dietrich, Humphrey Bogart and Gracie Fields came to Naples to entertain the troops.[38] There were talent shows, book groups and art appreciation societies.[39] And then there was sport. In March 1944 a huge basketball tournament began in venues all around Naples, with 224 American teams taking part.[40] Football matches were organized between British and Italians, and boxing matches between the various services, British and American.[41]

Finally, there was conventional tourism. Soldiers on leave could take guided tours around the city, or visit the world-famous aquarium in Chiaia for 20 lire. Special tours were laid on for visits to the ancient ruins at Herculaneum and Pompeii, and boat trips to the island of Capri and its famous blue grotto. Once the local trains were working again, servicemen could also travel westwards towards Pozzuoli to visit the monastery of San Gennaro, the patron saint of Naples, who was beheaded here in the year 305 CE. They could see the Solfatara volcano, the smoking Phlegraean Fields, or the caves at Avernus where, according to Virgil's *Aeneid*, the Cumaean Sibyl had once guarded the entrance to Hades.

Or they could visit Vesuvius itself. In January 1944, when the funicular railway began running again, hundreds of Allied servicemen made the journey up to the summit of Vesuvius each day. From up here they could enjoy views over the Bay of Naples, from the Sorrento Peninsula and the island of Capri to the south, to the islands of Procida and Ischia in the distance, beyond the city of Naples itself. And they could stand on platforms to view the molten lava, and 'see huge boulders thrown into the air like pebbles'.[42]

Not everyone was enthusiastic about the experience. For one early visitor there was something disturbing, even 'demoniacal', about this ancient volcano. By its very nature it seemed to invite parallels with the violent war that was still raging nearby: 'It was a good lesson in humility,' wrote the *New York Times* reporter Herbert Matthews; 'for who could hang on to the edge of the crater peering fearfully into the seething, glowing mass below that every few seconds exploded molten lava into the air and not think what puny forces 4000-pound block-busters unleash as compared to this monstrosity of nature?'[43]

The Cost of Pleasure

The attempt by the Allied armies to harness the energies and passions of their young men was very important in the winter of 1943–4. Front-line soldiers in particular needed a chance to relax and to blow off steam, and opportunities for them to do so had to be created if they were to be able to continue fighting effectively. In this respect, the Naples rest-area programme that was set up that autumn of 1943 was very successful. But it was not without consequences. With so many resources being directed towards entertaining the troops, there was much less available for the genuine and quite urgent needs of local people – which, as we shall see in the following chapters, were quite substantial. Furthermore, local people began to feel alienated in their own city. Day by day Naples seemed to be turning into little more than a playground for Allied troops.

What happened on the island of Capri is a good example of the tensions that arose. Capri was used to catering to foreigners. Before the war, tourists and expatriates had come here from all over the world, making it a truly 'international society'.[44] Italian nobles and British film stars had built extravagant villas on the dramatic coastline, with views across the bay towards Naples and Ischia. The war did not seem to have touched Capri at all. Not a single bomb had dropped on the island, and its anti-aircraft batteries had only ever opened up twice. It was dubbed 'the isle the war forgot' by Alexander Clifford of the *Daily Mail*: when the Allies first arrived here in 1943 there were still English illustrated society magazines from the 1930s stacked up in the hotel lounges.[45] Alan Moorehead called it 'a curious little nodule of lotus-eating', worn out but unchanged, 'as though someone had placed a glass bowl over the whole confection in 1939' and was only now lifting it off again.[46]

When the flocks of Allied soldier-tourists first started to visit the island, the local people opened their arms enthusiastically to them, hoping to regain some of the prosperity that they had enjoyed before the war. But the experience soon turned sour. The bars began to fill up with drunken soldiers on leave, who would regularly collapse on the street or harass the local women with loud whistling and crude sugges-tions. One sergeant got so drunk that he fell off an 800-foot cliff into the sea – his body washed up on the rocks below like a grotesque parody of the Parthenope myth in Homer's *Odyssey*. Meanwhile, the Allied authorities requisitioned all the best hotels, bathing beaches and bars for their own exclusive use, and sacked the local staff, claiming that they were 'unclean'. As one British report later remarked, 'the proprietors and waiters, now unemployed, claim that they have been serving drinks for many years and are just as clean as the monopolised military bar now instituted'. Needless to say, the initial enthusiasm shown by the local people for the return of tourism to the island 'soon waned'.[47]

The story was slightly different in Naples itself, but nevertheless attracted a similar feeling of resentment. Here, the Allies increasingly treated the local population like a colonized people, imposing all kinds of rules upon them that they did not always understand and had little opportunity to challenge. It did not escape attention that all the old symbols of power had been occupied – such as the Castel Nuovo, the ancient seat of the Angevin kings, which was used to accommodate the Royal Navy. Likewise the monastery of San Martino, which commanded a view of the entire city from where it sat at the top of the Vomero, was requisitioned by British soldiers belonging to an anti-aircraft battery.[48]

High and low culture alike were completely hijacked by the Allies. The San Carlo Theatre, once the city's pride and joy, was now reserved almost exclusively for the use of Allied soldiers and personnel. As if to underline this fact, the national anthems of Britain, the USA and France were played every evening before each opera began, but, despite regular complaints from Italian guests and even from Allied officers, the British area commander steadfastly refused permission for any Italian anthem to be played alongside them.[49] Likewise, ordinary cinemas were also taken over, causing great resentment everywhere. In Salerno, for example, so many cinemas were reserved for Allied use that the local population complained that 'there is little room for the Italians'. Even in Naples it could be difficult for locals to buy a ticket to the cinema. The films they got to see were always in English, but they did not always have Italian subtitles.[50]

Some Allied soldiers seemed to delight in humiliating local people. In mid-November, for example, five drunk soldiers – both British and American – stopped a car belonging to the acting mayor and demanded that the driver take them around town. For the next few hours he was forced against his will to ferry them about Naples like a tour guide. He did not manage to escape until they left him alone for a few minutes towards the end of the day: they had taken the car keys with them, but the resourceful driver managed to start the vehicle with his penknife and drive away.[51]

At the end of March, another incident occurred that seemed painfully emblematic. In Piazza del Gesù Nuovo, in the ancient centre, two American soldiers from the 1002 Fire Station Engineers Company rigged up a practical joke to play on passers-by. One of them offered pieces of candy to passing Italians – but the candy was wired up to a 'telephonic generator of electricity' that his friend had hidden around his neck. 'As soon as someone touched the toffees, the first soldier turned on the current and caused the person to receive a slight electric shock, making him look like a fool, amidst the laughter of the surrounding soldiers and Italian onlookers.'

Unfortunately, what started out as a relatively harmless prank soon turned ugly. 'Some girls who refused to take the toffees were forced to do so, and two women students who were treated in this way had all their books and personal belongings fall into the mud. Several young men who warned passers-by not to touch the toffees were seized and given a series of electric shocks.' Recognizing that things had gone too far, some of the observers asked a group of American MPs to intervene, but they refused to do so and simply 'joined in the fun'.

Episodes like this were extremely damaging for the Allied cause. These soldiers were treating the Italians as playthings, to be used and laughed at – and to be intimidated if they refused to play along. As a report of the time points out, the original joke itself was in bad taste because 'it derides the present misery of the people of Naples': American candy was a luxury few people in Naples could afford, and to have their desperation exploited in this way was unbearably humiliating. But the aggression that followed, and the complicity of the Allied military police, was even worse, leaving some observers with the impression that 'the Allies despise the Italians and regard them as a conquered people and a race inferior to themselves'.[52]

It was for just such reasons that the Neapolitan people slowly began to fall out of love with the Allies. It was one thing to have their public buildings requisitioned, their public parks filled with the tents of an occupying army, their bars and restaurants taken over by foreign soldiers and their language made redundant by powerful people who refused to speak anything but English – such things could be justified by the war and its immediate needs. Besides, most people agreed that the Allies were at least better than the Germans had been in such respects. But the personal nature of the everyday insults and humiliations that so many Neapolitan people were forced to endure was much more difficult to accept.

In Curzio Malaparte's novel about Naples during this time, the Allies are presented as a kind of 'plague', unwittingly corrupting everything they touch despite all their good intentions. 'I preferred the war to the "plague",' he wrote, 'which, after the liberation, had defiled, corrupted and humiliated us all – men, women and children.'[53] Many Neapolitans, alienated in their own city, ashamed at constantly having to kowtow to foreigners, began to feel something similar.

That is, until another, more literal kind of plague began to stalk their streets, and those same foreigners once again stepped up and showed their worth.

CHAPTER 8

Epidemic

The Allies were not completely insensitive to the effect their presence was having on the local population. When they first arrived in Naples, they knew that they would be obliged to requisition offices and accommodation for their troops, but they did not want to impose themselves too heavily on the city. This was just a matter of common sense: requisitioning is never popular, and without the willing cooperation of the Neapolitan people the flow of troops and supplies to the battlefields further north would undoubtedly suffer.

With this in mind, an order was issued to both American and British forces to keep requisitioning to an absolute minimum. Wherever possible, troops were told to set up camp in public parks, gardens and on wasteland. They could be housed in public buildings, hotels, schools and other institutions, even museums – but only in private homes as a last resort. This order was disseminated on 29 September, two days before they entered the city.[1]

As thousands of Allied troops flooded into Naples, they did their best to stick to these rules. Troops established camps in the Villa Floridiana and the Parco di Capodimonte, just as their German counterparts had done before them. The site of the Mostra d'Oltremare in Fuorigrotta – Mussolini's pre-war attempt at a 'World's Fair' – was converted into a hospital complex for wounded soldiers returning from the front. The Palazzo Reale was requisitioned, as was the world-famous National Museum of Antiquities, much to the dismay of its curator. The British even requisitioned parts of the Poggioreale prison as accommodation.[2]

Unfortunately, there were only so many parks and public buildings to go round: inevitably, private dwellings were also requisitioned. As more and more Allied officials arrived over the coming months – government staff, intelligence officers, logistics experts and port managers – all of the best apartments were quickly taken over. By the end of the war some 35,000 dwellings had been requisitioned for Allied use – their previous owners and tenants had simply been forced to make way.[3]

What the Allies failed to take into account was the seriousness of the accommodation situation in Naples, which had been in crisis even before their arrival. The destruction caused by three years of bombing and three weeks of deliberate demolition by the Germans had left tens of thousands of Neapolitans homeless. According to Allied engineers, around 10 per cent of the housing stock had been destroyed, and a further 14 per cent very heavily damaged.[4] Some of these buildings were so structurally unsound that over the coming months the sudden collapse of buildings would become a regular feature of city life.[5]

Even those buildings that had only been lightly damaged – about 43 per cent of the total – were still not comfortable to live in. October and November 1943 proved to be exceptionally wet months, and in December the cold really set in, with temperatures sometimes close to freezing.[6] Allied troops often made wry jokes about 'sunny Italy' – where 'One day it rains, one day it snows, and the third day there is a doubleheader.'[7] Countless Italian families, living in semi-ruined buildings with no windows and leaking roofs, would have sympathized.

It was not until the end of the year that Allied health officials finally began to worry about what housing shortages might mean for the people of Naples. In his monthly report for December, the head of the Public Health and Welfare Division, Colonel Crichton, warned his superiors that 'Private houses are … filled to capacity' and that 'those who have been rendered homeless by the air raids or by military requisitions have not been provided with alternative accommodation'.[8]

With nowhere else to go, thousands of people were moving into the only places they knew to be dry and secure: the underground bomb shelters. These places already had a semi-permanent population living in them – not only the homeless, but also many ordinary families who felt it was safer to stay here than to risk the continued dangers of bombing on the surface. Old people especially, and some mothers with small children, sometimes felt that it was easier to stay down here than to make the daily journeys up and down the steep spiral staircases when the air raid alarms went off.

By the winter of 1943 there were at least 12,000 people living in caves and tunnels underground.[9] Some estimates went as high as 30,000 – but the truth is that nobody knew the real numbers, because the population was always shifting.[10] What everyone agreed on, however, was that conditions down here were appalling: the deep level caves especially were dark, damp, cold and 'indescribably filthy'.[11]

History of Overcrowding

One of the main reasons why the Allies did not take the accommodation crisis seriously at first is that they did not think it had anything to do with them. Overcrowding was not exactly a new problem in Naples. The Allies were here to win a war, not to tackle social and structural inequalities that had their roots deep in the city's history.

Naples is one of the most densely populated cities in Europe, and has been so for centuries. Indeed, in many ways overcrowding has *shaped* Naples. During the seventeenth century, the city's Spanish rulers introduced a ban on new building in order to discourage immigration from the provinces. Neapolitans reacted by simply extending their houses upwards: at a time when residential buildings in most European cities were rarely higher than two or three storeys, in Naples they were routinely between four and seven storeys high, packed into alleyways so narrow that those who lived on the higher floors could reach out of their windows and touch each other across the divide. By the late nineteenth century, the average population density in the ancient centre was ten times that of Victorian London, with almost half a million people crammed into just a few square kilometres of space. Even today it remains the most overcrowded city in Italy.[12]

During the golden age of the eighteenth and early nineteenth centuries it was possible to ignore the terrible conditions that existed in the darker quarters: tourists like Goethe and Stendhal were blinded by the bright lights of Via Toledo and rarely ventured into the alleyways beyond. But after the Risorgimento, when Naples lost its status as the capital city of a great kingdom, it became notorious as one of the poorest, most squalid cities in all Europe. Entire families lived in single-room apartments known as *bassi* – ground-floor or basement rooms with no windows and a door leading directly out onto the street – where they cooked, ate, slept and made love with virtually no privacy at all. There was no plumbing, so household waste was simply thrown out onto the street, and sanitary conditions were appalling. In a letter to the prefecture in September 1885, local tenants described themselves as being 'forced to live in the actual inside of a sewer', since the nearby cesspool frequently overflowed into their courtyards and through their front doors.[13]

Even worse were the *fondaci* – tenement buildings in which tiers of single, windowless rooms rose high above a tiny, damp courtyard, almost like the inside of a dovecote. In 1884, when the Swedish doctor Axel Munthe worked in Naples, he made health visits to dozens of these notorious buildings, which he called 'the most ghastly human habitations on the face of the earth'. The tiny courtyards that sat in the centre of these miserable dwellings were so deep that they were permanently dark; they acted simultaneously as rubbish tip, latrine, playground and kitchen for the dozens of families that shared them. According to statistics of the time, between 30,000 and 90,000 people lived in these places. The discrepancy between these two figures tells a story in its own right: the authorities had no idea how to keep track of the population, most of whom lived their lives without ever coming into contact with any state institution. It was a similar state of affairs in 1943, regarding the population who lived in the underground air raid shelters.[14]

When once writers and poets had flocked here to marvel at a Neapolitan 'paradise', now they came to witness a kind of hell. The English author Jessie White Mario, who had made her home here, wrote an impassioned study of conditions in the city in the 1870s: 'See misery in Naples,' she wrote, 'to learn what misery means.'[15] Pasquale Villari, writing in 1875, described a city filled with crumbling houses and filthy, cave-like dwellings and a complete lack of any functioning institutions.[16] But perhaps the most famous description of the Naples slums was by the local journalist Matilde Serao, who wrote a book in 1884, aptly titled *Il ventre di Napoli* ('The Bowels of Naples'). Serao passionately lamented the abject squalor in which so many Neapolitans were forced to live, and berated the Italian authorities for allowing it to continue:

> Surely you cannot leave standing houses that are cracked by damp, where there's mud on the ground floor and the top floor burns in summer and freezes in winter; where the stairs are garbage receptacles; in which the wells, from which water is so agonizingly drawn, get filled with every kind of human refuse and every kind of dead animal; and which all have a melting pot, a so-called *vinella*, an internal courtyard into which everything is thrown; whose latrine system, where there is one, resists any disinfection.[17]

In the following years, several attempts were made to solve the city's centuries-old housing crisis, most famously the slum clearances along the Neapolitan shoreline at the end of the nineteenth century – the 'disembowelment' of Naples, as it came to be known. New housing projects were planned by the Liberals at the beginning of the twentieth century, and eventually brought to fruition under the Fascists in the 1920s and 1930s. But much of the old city remained untouched. In 1910, there were still 126,000 people living in *bassi* – almost a fifth of the total population.[18] Long after the Second World War, Italian Communists were still writing about the appalling conditions in the *bassi* of Naples, where 'space is so restricted that people are born and die there side by side; the toilet, with a flowered curtain around it, is right next to the stove and pans, and the floor is made of paving stones, exactly the same ones you find in the streets'. As late as 1967, according to Catholic sociologists, some 200,000 people were still living in 50,000 *bassi*.[19]

In such conditions, epidemics became commonplace. Outbreaks of the plague killed hundreds of thousands of people here in the fourteenth and fifteenth centuries, and again in 1656, when communal graves became so glutted that the people resorted to burning corpses or throwing them into the sea. On one particularly gruesome occasion, the drains beneath Via Toledo became blocked with dead bodies thrown into the sewers by unscrupulous grave diggers. During a sudden downpour, the road flooded and the cadavers began to float up into the basements of the houses on either side, and eventually into the street itself. 'I saw with my own eyes,' wrote one witness a few years later, 'this street of Toledo where I used to live so paved with cadavers that some carriages going to the palace could not run anywhere but over baptised flesh.' It is estimated that more than half of Naples' population died from plague that year.[20]

During the nineteenth century there were at least twelve major epidemics – four of typhoid and eight of cholera. Perhaps the worst of these occurred in 1884, when some 8,400 people died of cholera in Naples, mostly in the old city and the port area.[21] According to a local health officer, Federico Sirignano, such outbreaks were entirely predictable, owing to the location of public and domestic latrines right next to the wells where people drew their drinking water. In an attempt to tackle such problems, 300 wells were immediately closed down.[22] The eventual draining of the ancient water system in the city left a series of empty underground cisterns – some of the very spaces that would be converted into air raid shelters in the run-up to the Second World War.

In the twentieth century public health certainly improved, but there were still some major outbreaks of disease. In 1910, cholera returned to the city and claimed around 3,000 lives.[23] In 1919, in the wake of the First World War, an outbreak of typhus hit the city – a disease transmitted by lice living in people's hair and clothing. A second outbreak of typhus hit the city in 1926. In a city as overcrowded as Naples the spread of infected lice was seemingly unstoppable.

This was the disease that returned in 1943, causing a crisis for both the people of Naples and the Allied armies. That it should find its incubation nucleus in the overcrowded underground shelters was no surprise to anyone who had seen conditions there. In the words of the cartoonist Bill Mauldin, down here 'A louse could walk miles over warm bodies without having to touch the ground.' It was a disaster waiting to happen.[24]

The Epidemic Begins

Typhus first arrived in the region in the spring and early summer of 1943, a few months before the Allies invaded. Several cases of the disease were recorded in towns around Naples, particularly Castellammare, Casalnuovo, Aversa and Pozzuoli. The worst outbreak occurred in Pozzuoli prison, where six people died of the disease. Unfortunately, as the Neapolitan prefect admitted at the beginning of September, several inmates had escaped from the prison during the outbreak, and could not be traced. It was suspected that they were hiding out in the air raid shelters – particularly in the Galleria IX Maggio, one of the tunnels that linked Pozzuoli to Naples – where several people sheltering from the bombs came down with typhus in August and September.[25]

Within Naples itself, five cases of the disease had been recorded in July in a building near the port where Serbian prisoners of war were housed. When the building was hit by Allied bombs in early August, these prisoners were dispersed to various locations around the city, taking their sickness with them. Soon new foci for the disease began popping up in various places around Naples, such as bath-houses frequented by Italian soldiers. Before the arrival of the Allies, the Neapolitan authorities had done their best to control these outbreaks, in particular with 'measures taken all over and about the City to get rid of body lice, but this was too difficult to control due to the congestion of people living in Shelters'.[26] Conditions in the Poggioreale prison were also pretty dire. During the Allied bombing campaign the prison's bathing facilities had been destroyed, leaving prisoners with no way of washing: 'The inmates were almost all louse infested, so that conditions for the transmission of typhus were ideal.'[27] When the departing Germans threw open the doors of the prisons at the end of September, they also unwittingly released another source of infection into the civil population.

The Allies were not aware of any of this when they first arrived. According to the Allies' chief medical specialist in Naples at the time 'no accurate picture could be obtained as to the incidence of infectious disease' because 'the Public Health Service was barely functioning'.[28] Despite this, on the day after their arrival senior AMGOT officials were confidently reporting back to the Combined Chiefs of Staff that 'there was no cholera or typhus' in Naples. A statement to that effect was even released to the British press a few days later.[29]

This rather complacent attitude continued throughout October: there were so many problems to be attended to that the seemingly remote probability of a typhus outbreak did not register as much of a priority. In later days, the head of civil affairs for the region, Colonel Hume, would blame poor communications between the hospitals and the AMG public health officials, 'which interfered with reporting of new cases'.[30]

It was not until the second week of November, when the Italian Director of Public Health reported eight new cases of suspected typhus among the civilian population, that alarm bells finally began to ring. Most of these new cases had been registered at the ironically named Incurabili Hospital in the ancient city centre. The following week another seven cases were reported. It immediately became obvious that something had to be done to stop the disease from spreading: the Incurabili Hospital had around 750 patients, and three-quarters of them were already reported to be infested with lice.[31]

On 24 November an emergency conference on typhus was called, and all the senior public health officials in the city attended. According to the minutes of this conference, everyone agreed that 'the most energetic, and, if necessary, drastic action should be taken immediately'. A special Typhus Committee was set up, and two of the Italian members – Professor Marinelli and Professor Ninni – were nominated to investigate exactly how bad this new outbreak really was. The complete disinfestation of the Incurabili Hospital was ordered at once, and plans were drawn up in case the outbreak spread to the civil population at large.

At the time, the Allies simply did not have the resources to deal with any large-scale epidemic. The traditional way of disinfesting people's clothing of lice was to steam-clean them, but with fuel so short in the city this was simply impossible: in fact, the disinfestor at the Incurabili Hospital itself had been out of action for some time. Normal standards of hygiene were also impossible, because soap was completely unavailable to most civilians in Naples.[32] There were some stores of insecticide powder in army warehouses, but not nearly enough to delouse an entire city. The same was true of vaccine stores.

The Allies' greatest worry was that an epidemic might spread to the army, putting their operations on the front line at risk. Orders were therefore issued to vaccinate troops and all medical staff, and to issue all units with stores of anti-louse powder, especially those who had regular contact with civilians. As a precaution, 10 tons of DDT powder was ordered from America, with a request that the shipment be made 'on highest priority'.[33]

Over the following weeks, the situation escalated rapidly. Reports of new cases started coming in from all over the city, but with communications as bad as they were it was impossible to get a proper understanding of the true scope of the problem.[34] Subsequent investigations showed how rapidly the situation was degenerating. In the last week of November, the number of new cases suddenly doubled. Four weeks later they doubled again, and then again two weeks after that. The disease was spreading exponentially.[35]

It did not take long for the medics on the Typhus Committee to realize that they were out of their depth. Early in December they called in a pair of experts from the Rockefeller Foundation who had recently conducted a study on the control of typhus in North Africa. The first thing this group did was to try to make sure that the disease was contained within Naples, and didn't spread to outlying towns. On 15 December it was made compulsory for anyone leaving the city to be dusted with anti-louse powder before they were allowed to board a train. The following day the Rockefeller team began tracing the family and contacts of all known typhus sufferers so that they, too, could be dusted. Any contacts who showed signs of infection were immediately taken into hospital. However, the main nucleus of the disease – the air raid shelters – was for the moment left alone. It was decided that it was probably safer to keep the people who lived down here all in one place, 'rather than to scatter the lice with them'.[36]

And yet still the statistics kept rising. The AMG Typhus Committee finally realized that much more drastic measures were needed. They decided that a civilian mission like the Rockefeller team would not have the authority to carry such measures out, so they finally called in the US Army's Typhus Commission to come and help.

The head of the Commission, Brigadier General Fox, arrived in Naples on 21 December to find the epidemic already raging out of control. On Christmas Day, he addressed an emergency meeting of senior army medics, where he gave a terrifying summary of the situation:

> Naples, a city of over 800,000 inhabitants, has hundreds of
> thousands of refugees added to normal population. Economic
> conditions are bad, malnourishment is general, soap and fuel are
> not available and overcrowding is severe. Population has not
> had contact with epidemic typhus for several generations and
> may be regarded as non-immune … Situation is desperate, and
> outlook is grave for civil population … AMG should have called
> for help 60 days ago.[37]

From now on, Fox's commission would take charge. It seized control from the AMG Typhus Committee, and took the Rockefeller team under its wing. Over the following weeks the Allies would fight what came to be known as 'the second battle of Naples', with General Fox as their temporary Commander-in-Chief.

The Course of the Disease

Typhus is a particularly nasty disease, which begins with a vivid skin rash, first on a person's trunk but then spreading to their limbs. It can cause nausea and vomiting, headaches and fever, but in particularly bad cases it can affect the heart and other internal organs, and eventually lead to death. In Naples, the mortality rate was about 25 per cent, but in the over-fifties it killed half of all people who contracted it.[38]

The disease is transmitted by infected lice, whose faeces contain the bacteria. When a louse-ridden person scratches his or her bites, they unwittingly rub the infected faeces into their punctured skin. The spread of the disease can be prevented by regular washing with soap and hot water, which kills the bacteria and cleans away both the lice and their faeces; and likewise with the regular washing of clothes and bed linen. But the only way to ensure that it is dealt with definitively is to eradicate the lice altogether. This can be done by shaving people's hair and steam-cleaning their clothing, or by dusting them with an insecticide powder. In 1943 there were three different powders in common use by the Allies. The British used AL-63, while the Americans used MYL powder – but a new powder called DDT had recently become available, which had the added advantage of lingering in people's clothes, keeping them more or less sterile for around seven days after application.

In an overcrowded city like Naples there was no point in treating people individually, because as soon as they returned to their crowded homes or entered one of the busy air raid shelters they would almost certainly become reinfested. The only way to stop a major outbreak of the disease was to treat the whole population simultaneously. This had been tried successfully in North Africa, but only ever on small, contained populations – in prisons, for example, or in small villages. It had never been tried before on a mass scale. Naples would be the first major city anywhere in the world to experience a programme of mass disinfestation with the use of DDT powder: it would become the model for similar programmes throughout Europe during the rest of the war and its aftermath.

Considering that the Allies were in the midst of fighting a war, the resources that they poured into defeating the typhus outbreak in Naples were phenomenal. Until now AMG had been extremely reluctant to put any kind of lockdown in place, because the city was so important not only as an essential transport and supply hub, but also as a centre of rest and recreation for their troops. But on 27 December an order went out locally making most of the city off limits to anyone who did not have specific duties there; a more general order to the same effect was disseminated throughout the region ten days later. For the next two months, no Allied personnel were allowed in the city without a pass signed by their commanding officer stating exactly what

their business was and how long it would last. All troops, including
those with legitimate duties, were specifically instructed not to use any
form of public transport, or to enter any local cafés, restaurants or
places of entertainment. They were banned from giving lifts to civilians
in their vehicles, and strongly reminded not to consort with 'louse-
ridden' prostitutes. And most of all they were banned from entering
the air raid shelters, 'which are universally infested with lice'.[39]

The lockdown did not apply to Neapolitans themselves, who were
mostly allowed to carry on their daily activities as normal, except that
they were banned from entering any buildings in use by the Allies
unless they specifically worked there. Halfway through January, cinemas and theatres were shut down – supposedly just for two weeks, but
in the end they would not open again until mid-March.[40]

At the same time, an attempt was made to massively improve hospital facilities throughout the city. In order to cope with the sudden
influx of new patients, a new emergency treatment centre was set up in
the 'poor house' – the Albergo dei Poveri – in the northeast of the city.
Another emergency centre was set up at the Cotugno Hospital for
Infectious Diseases. This had been badly bombed earlier in the war,
and parts of it were being used as accommodation by Allied troops.
These troops were moved out, new equipment was ordered, including
new linen and new blankets, and the windows were finally replaced
with a valuable consignment of new glass. These were all measures that
should have been taken in October, but which were only now being
done because the epidemic had suddenly made them a priority.[41]

The most urgent need at the end of December was that for insecticide powder. The Surgeon's Office immediately released 20,000 tins of
MYL powder from army stores, and its counterpart in North Africa
authorized the transport of a further 500,000 (there were two ounces
of MYL powder in each tin). Four tons of AL-63 powder was also
shipped to Naples from British sources, and 400 pounds of concentrated DDT was immediately flown over. Eventually a shipment of 10
tons of concentrated DDT would arrive in the port, and from 1 January
onwards the treatment of civilians would be carried out exclusively
with this powder. Hundreds of dusting guns also had to be shipped to
Naples.[42]

Large numbers of medical staff were urgently assembled, including local nurses and physicians, volunteers, Allied medics, and the Malaria Control Sections, who were retrained in methods of administering the powders effectively. They were given thirty-two vehicles – a huge luxury in a city almost entirely devoid of transport – and organized into teams of twelve or thirteen. The campaign to dust everyone in the city began on 27 December 1943, when six of these dusting teams descended into several of the air raid shelters in the city centre armed with hundreds of tins of MYL powder. The operation was carried out between 6 p.m. and midnight when they knew the shelters would be at their fullest. Over the next few months these teams would visit each of the eighty or ninety shelters in the city once every seven days to dust everyone they found there.

The following day, the first two mass dusting stations were opened for walk-in visitors. The one in the Ascalesi Hospital in one of the poorest parts of the ancient centre began by bringing in children from the street to be dusted. On the first day only 107 people were treated, but by the end of the week they were dusting over 1,600 people each day. The second dusting station, in the Anguili Elementary School just north of the city centre, treated 837 people on its first day, and over 3,500 per day by the end of the week. Two more stations were opened in other parts of the city on 30 December, and a fifth opened on New Year's Day. Eventually there would be fifty stations all over Naples, capable of dealing with 100,000 people a day.[43]

While all this was going on, other teams were targeting individual blocks that were known to have had concentrated outbreaks of the disease, or which were particularly infested with lice. The problem with the walk-in stations was that not everyone could be bothered to visit them. By targeting the specific areas where cases were clustered, the teams could make sure that the disease was eradicated at source. In addition special 'flying squads' were set up to make trips outside Naples to the surrounding towns and villages to make sure that the epidemic did not spread. There were particular worries about Salerno, where several cases had been recorded, but which lacked many of the facilities of Naples. Captain Crichton Jones, the Public Health Officer here, described Salerno as 'a culture bed' just waiting to be infected.[44]

All of this imposed an enormous strain on the health system in Naples, particularly on those health workers who were dealing with the sick. John Miles, a member of the Friends Ambulance Unit, worked night and day in a typhus ward for what he remembered as 'three hectic months of non-stop life and death work'. Since there was no accommodation in the hospital, he and his fellow staff had to sleep in a building nearby whose windows and doors had all been blown out. In the absence of antibiotics, the only way of treating patients was by keeping them hydrated until they stabilized: Miles later recalled that his duties consisted mainly of 'the feeding of five pints of liquid per day to each patient'. Unfortunately, he added, 'During a period of delirium typhus patients are incontinent and uncooperative, so our work was pretty grim ...'[45]

Medical staff like Miles ran a high risk of becoming infected themselves, so they were among the few people in the city to be offered typhus vaccinations. Most people accepted this gratefully – but in the febrile atmosphere of Naples during the epidemic, vaccine scepticism quickly grew up, even among medical staff. The reason for this was an unfortunate event in the Incurabili Hospital. One of the nurses there had died from a heart attack not long after being vaccinated, and some of her fellow workers began spreading the rumour that her death was not just a coincidence. As a consequence, uptake of the vaccine among medical staff was painfully slow, and in the following weeks at least eighteen hospital attendants and nurses became infected with typhus, along with two doctors. In the end the Italian head of provincial medicine, Professor G. Beneduce, issued instructions to all hospital staff informing them that vaccination was now compulsory: any member of staff who refused to be vaccinated would lose their job.[46]

There was a similar reluctance among some parts of the general population when it came to being dusted with this new, mysterious powder. In some cases it was just a matter of embarrassment. Being dusted was quite an intimate procedure, which involved opening your shirt and your underwear so that medical staff could pump powder beneath your clothes. Pubic hair had to be treated as well as the hair on people's heads. This was not something that everyone was comfortable with, especially in public: women and men had to be treated separately by teams of the same sex. Then there were those who were too proud to be dusted: for those of the middle and upper classes, it was humiliating to admit that they were just as susceptible to lice as anyone else, but once they emerged from a treatment centre covered in white powder there was no hiding it.[47]

Inevitably there were also those who did not trust the powder itself. DDT was considered completely safe for humans at the time, but some people were still worried about using it. Just as physicians had reassured patients during the cholera epidemic of 1884 by demonstrating their medicines on themselves first, so too did physicians in 1944. One medical officer is even reputed to have convinced sceptics by sprinkling DDT powder on his food and eating it. Whatever the dangers of insecticides, the dangers of typhus were considered far, far worse.[48]

The conquest of the typhus epidemic in Naples was one of the greatest successes of the Allied occupation of Italy and, according to an UNRRA observer mission, 'one of the major medical triumphs of the war'.[49] Between January and May 1944, more than three million applications of DDT powder were carried out in Naples, and a further 211,000 in the towns and villages around the city. As a result of this and other measures, the epidemic was stopped in its tracks. The peak of the crisis came in mid-January, when 261 new cases were reported in a single week, but after that the number rapidly began to decline. By mid-March there were only a handful of new cases in the city, and by May the disease had been eradicated altogether. A few cases continued to appear in the provinces outside Naples, but soon they, too, had been snuffed out.[50] In the words of Major General Cowell, the Chief Surgeon at Allied Forces Headquarters, it was 'the best organized and equipped anti-typhus campaign the world has ever seen'.[51]

All of this was achieved through unprecedented cooperation between Italians, British and Americans at every level of the administration: it was this unity of purpose that most defined the anti-typhus campaign. As with the water crisis, the Allies had shown that when they truly put their minds to something, and backed it up with proper resources, they were capable of extraordinary things.

Nevertheless, the crisis also highlighted some serious shortcomings in the Allied administration of the city. As one of the senior British medical officers suggested towards the end of the epidemic, one of the reasons why this had happened in the first place was because AMG had failed to re-establish any kind of bathing and washing facilities in the city: 'DDT is undoubtedly a gift from heaven, but it does not supersede the use of soap.'[52] Everybody knew that soap was almost impossible to buy in Naples – it is repeatedly mentioned in report after report – and yet nothing was done to rectify the situation for the best part of a year. As late as August 1944, Allied officials were still complaining of a lack of soap, which had led to a new epidemic, this time of scabies.[53]

If the Allies were able to mobilize such huge resources at such short notice, why were they so seemingly incapable of providing even basic necessities of everyday life? It was not just soap that was missing from the shelves in Neapolitan shops and stores: medicines of all kinds were in particularly short supply. According to the Psychological Warfare Branch, in the summer of 1944 hospitals and pharmacies were missing even the most basic supplies of vitamins, rubber gloves, gauze and bicarbonate of soda, let alone vaccines and life-saving medicines such as insulin: 'The doctors are at a loss what to prescribe for their patients.'[54] There was a similar lack of building materials that would allow Neapolitans to repair their homes. Nor were there any clothes to buy, nor shoes – at least, not from legitimate sources.

Worse than all of this, however, was the lack of food. One report after another highlighted the serious deficiencies in the Neapolitan diet, especially a chronic shortage of fats and proteins. Even more worryingly, Neapolitans were missing the most basic commodity of all – bread. To put it bluntly, they were starving.

At the height of the epidemic, this was the one problem that most worried Allied medical staff in Naples. 'Until the food question could be satisfactorily solved,' they claimed, 'it was impossible to hope for any further appreciable amelioration of the typhus epidemic. It is the most pressing and serious problem of the day.'[55] Unfortunately, it was also a problem that went far beyond the walls of the hospitals and underground shelters. That winter, hunger spread to every level of Neapolitan society: it was to become the single issue that would most undermine support for the Allies during the course of 1944.

CHAPTER 9

Hunger

W ar and hunger have always walked hand in hand. Sometimes hunger is an active weapon of war; sometimes it is merely a symptom of the conditions of wartime, which make food production and distribution immensely more difficult. In Naples in 1943 and 1944 both things were true.

During the twentieth century, governments around the world put a great deal of thought into the problem of food during wartime. How many calories did each individual need in order to thrive? What types of food were essential for a healthy diet? How could this information be scaled up in order to ensure that the needs of an entire army, or an entire society, could be met? And, most importantly, what sort of distribution system was necessary to ensure that everybody got their fair share?

Towards the end of the First World War, the American nutritionist Graham Lusk published a scientific pamphlet about the food needs of both soldiers and civilians during wartime. According to Lusk, an average man weighing 156 pounds (70 kilograms) would need to consume 2,400 calories a day in order to carry out a sedentary job like working as a tailor or a bookbinder. A man doing more physical labour, like a carpenter or a painter, would need around 3,000 calories a day; while a soldier on the march would need more than 4,000 calories. Women doing similar work apparently needed slightly less food than men did – just over nine-tenths of the amount.[1]

At the outbreak of the Second World War, calorie scales like this came into use all over the world as governments everywhere tried to plan out how they would feed their populations during the conflict. As international trade became much more limited, ration programmes were introduced almost everywhere. The most complete system was set up by Britain, where 'rationing schemes covered so many foodstuffs that they amounted to a comprehensive system of food control'.[2] Shipping, road and rail transport were also tightly controlled, to ensure efficiency of distribution; and a propaganda campaign called 'Dig for Britain' encouraged people to turn their gardens, local parks and all kinds of disused bits of land into allotments for growing vegetables. In the end the system was so successful that general levels of health actually *improved* during the war. The average British person's calorie consumption was maintained at around 3,000 calories per day all the way through to 1945.[3]

The schemes that were set up in other countries were not quite so comprehensive. Some nations, like the United States, did not feel they needed such strict controls: food was more plentiful here, and international trade with its neighbours largely uninterrupted. In other nations strict control was impossible because there was not enough public support for it. In occupied Europe, for example, the black market burgeoned because farmers and traders were reluctant to stick to rules imposed upon them by their German enemy.

In theory, the Italian government should have been in a position to impose food controls every bit as comprehensive as those in Britain. The one-party state had already been conducting a 'Battle for Wheat' ever since the 1920s, and had successfully pushed through land reclamation projects all over the country, including the draining of the Pontine Marshes between Rome and Naples. But support for the war was never as strong here as it was in Britain – indeed, many people questioned why Italy should get involved in the war at all. Neither did Italy have the same kind of resources and infrastructure that Britain did. More importantly, support for the regime was never quite as strong as Mussolini liked to pretend it was: few people trusted the fantastically corrupt Fascist institutions to administer any kind of rationing system fairly.

Rationing was introduced at the beginning of 1940, nearly five months before Italy formally entered the war. In Naples one of the local newspapers, *Il Mattino*, immediately tried to bully its readers into understanding why rationing was necessary:

> We dedicate this note to all those hard-brained people who still
> have not understood an elementary truth: which is to say that
> the ration card is an initiative taken by the regime only to
> defend the people from the idiotic and criminal greed of
> hoarders and speculators. In a time of emergency like today,
> rationing prevents frightened, alarmist people of little faith,
> typically the middle classes, from filling their pantries at the
> expense of the majority of workers, employees and labourers
> who have neither the means nor the inclination to do the same.
> Instead, everyone can be fed sufficiently in the same way, and
> every inequality artificially created by money can be prevented.
> Is that clear?[4]

Unfortunately, Mussolini's government proved singularly inept at administering such a system. According to an Allied report conducted shortly after their arrival the official structures for food distribution in Italy were not only 'rotten in politics' but also 'very inefficient in their operations'. For example, prices for agricultural products were always set centrally, but always much too low, because the Fascists wanted to keep up the pretence that food was more abundant than it really was. Since everyone knew that these prices were unachievable, producers universally preferred to sell their food on the black market instead, creating an unofficial food distribution system that was completely unregulated. In short 'the whole scheme was a *failure*'.[5]

Until the summer of 1943, the official ration in Italy was enough to provide normal consumers with around 1,500 calories each per day.[6] They were expected to make up the difference in their diet by buying food, either on the open market at fixed prices, or on the black market. Despite the faults with the system, it functioned well enough to provide most people with what they needed. According to the historian Paolo De Marco, the average Italian consumed just under 2,600 calories per day in 1940, just under 2,300 the following year and a little over 2,200 in 1942.[7] Italians were hungry, but not disastrously so.

But everything changed after the Allies invaded. All of a sudden the south of Italy found itself engulfed in a savage war. The retreating Germans requisitioned all the food and livestock they came across, and destroyed whatever they could not take with them. With the utter devastation of all the transport systems the vital links between city and countryside were broken, cutting off city dwellers from their main sources of food. The severing of links between different provinces and regions was just as serious: when the battle lines were drawn across the middle of the country, for example, the south found itself completely cut off from the wheat-producing areas of the north. By the time the Allies had taken control of Naples, all the 'normal channels of food-marketing' had 'practically completely broken down': the whole distribution system was 'in complete chaos'.[8]

The consequences of all this were immediate. Almost overnight, the black market price of pasta doubled, and the price of sugar trebled. Other essential foods, like bread, milk, eggs and olive oil, rose in price by 60 to 70 per cent.[9] Massive inflation like this, within a very short space of time, had a disastrous effect on the local economy. Those who could afford it immediately began to hoard all the food they could: any shops and stores that had not already been looted by the Germans were now emptied by panic buyers. Those who arrived too late, or who could not afford the new prices, were forced to go without. Food shortages had always been a concern; now, suddenly, they were an emergency.

Allied soldiers watched this unfold before their very eyes. Allied veterans of the war in Italy have often spoken of the damage and destruction they witnessed in the autumn and winter of 1943 – the small towns and villages around Naples that were reduced to 'absolute heaps of rubble' by Allied bombardments.[10] Some have described the shock of civilians caught in the crossfire, and their own discomfort at having to deal with traumatized refugees. But the most common images are those of poverty and deprivation. Luther E. Hall, an American soldier who fought with the segregated African American 370th Infantry Regiment, gave a typical description during an interview with the Indiana Historical Society in 1993:

There's something else I want to mention. I just want to mention how poor the place is over there … These people had *nothing*. The store on the corner – you could walk in the store and there was not a thing on the shelf. Nothing … And the farmers out there, they didn't have any tractors, and they would be farming land with the battle going on. They had no horses, and the women would be pulling the ploughs, walking barefooted over the dirt. I stopped one day and I said, 'Man, I can't *believe* that!' The man walking behind was holding the plough, and two women, or three women, or four women with straps over their shoulders were pulling the plough. It was horrible.[11]

According to Hall, the field kitchens often did not bother with garbage cans, because a long queue of Italians were willing to eat whatever food the GIs did not want. Such impressions are recorded again and again in the memoirs and recollections of Allied veterans. Leonard Neely, who fought with an anti-tank company in the US 45th Infantry Division, described scenes in which starving Italians had been reduced by their hunger to behaving almost like animals:

The whistle blows for chow, and all the G.I.s rush for the kitchen area to form that famous chow line … By the time the first G.I. is through the line and ready to eat, he is surrounded by hungry people. They are silently begging for his food; some come right out and ask for it. The guard comes up and tries to run them off, but they know the guard will not shoot; so they only walk away and turn and come back again. It is hard to eat with hungry people looking on, staring like hungry wolves. I picture my little brother and sister begging for food, or my mother. I can hardly swallow …

As most people know, the Army can't give food away to civilians; so if there are seconds, the G.I.s, including myself, will make the line again and then walk directly to the garbage can where the Italians fight like dogs and cats for the extra food or scraps from the mess kits. They stand there and gulp it down from their filthy pails – like hogs feeding from a trough. When they have feasted, they will try to scrape out some more for the next meal, or for a sick relative.[12]

British accounts of conditions in southern Italy in the early days of the liberation are very similar. Henry Moore, a gunner with the Royal Artillery, recounted stories of hungry Neapolitans fighting one another over the rubbish thrown out by his battery cookhouse, 'to see if they could lick a tin'.[13] Norman Lewis described women and children gathering dandelions by the roadside, or prising limpets off the rocks by the seafront at Santa Lucia, out of desperation for something to eat: 'Nothing, absolutely nothing that can be tackled by the human digestive system is wasted in Naples.'[14] Others concurred. Any kind of meat at all – chicken heads, bits of offal, 'horrible pieces of straggly, scraggy meat, hanging on hooks with flies swarming all around them' – was sold in the street markets for eye-watering prices.[15]

Those whom the soldiers felt most sorry for were the children. One US artillery technician described the daily trial of eating his food with groups of 7-year-old 'street urchins' staring at him. 'A couple of soldiers really couldn't take it. They just gave their meals to the kids.'[16] 'I felt bad for the kids,' remembered another technician from the 45th Infantry Division. 'Well, I felt bad for all of them really, but the children in particular. You hate to see kids eat garbage.'[17]

Some soldiers felt compelled to do something to alleviate their suffering. In the run-up to Christmas 1943, for example, one army cook organized a giveaway of surplus candy bars for the local children. Unfortunately, when he opened the doors to the mess hall a riot broke out as hundreds of children rushed into the building: 'they had the chocolate scattered all over the floor, and a lot of them didn't get a thing because there just wasn't that much to go round'.[18] Another GI in one of the combat engineer battalions was so upset by the children who used to gather around his mess tent, 'with their hands so chapped that they were bleeding open … and their little legs blue with cold', that he helped to organize some of the local women to sew clothes for them. Bloody blankets from the field hospitals, that would otherwise have been thrown away, were gathered up, washed and sewn into 'little winter suits'.[19]

Children across southern Italy received such gifts with gratitude, but in reality the problems they faced were much too broad to be solved by individual acts of kindness. As that winter progressed, it became obvious that yet another humanitarian crisis was looming. Unless the Allies could come up with a proper plan to feed liberated Italy the whole region would be plunged into famine.

Myths and Preconceptions

The Allies might have foreseen conditions like these, but they didn't. Their plans for government had never envisaged a divided, war-torn Italy; instead they had assumed that the country would carry on functioning more or less as it had done before their invasion, only now with the Allies supervising things from above. With this in mind, they had drawn up proclamations instructing the Italians to continue with the same rationing system, the same wages and the same maximum food prices.[20] Their agricultural plan stated, rather optimistically: 'It will be the objective of AMGOT to make the occupied territory self-supporting in food production to the maximum extent possible.'[21] Such ambitions were shown to be misguided almost as soon as the Allies first set foot on Sicily; and yet they continued to stick doggedly to their original plans. When the opportunity arose to modify these policies before the invasion of the mainland, they kept them just as they were.[22]

When it came to southern Italy, Allied planners were blinded by all kinds of prejudices and preconceptions about the people and the land. For example, the well-known poverty of the region – which had been referred to in Italy as the 'southern problem' ever since the Risorgimento – was a cliché that could easily be used as an excuse not to do anything to help. One pre-invasion study implied that wartime food shortages would not be a problem in the south because 'the population is used to a frugal diet'.[23] Those at the highest levels made a point of emphasizing the fact that they were coming to Italy only to liberate it, not to save it from poverty. 'Churchill has made it abundantly clear,' claimed one high-level document, 'that Britain is not fighting this war in order to engage freely hereafter in a vast humanitarian campaign to transfer into the farthermost places an Anglo-American standard of living. Neither

is the United States, despite the slogans of wartime.'[24] Statements like
these normalized the starvation conditions in southern Italy even
before the Allies arrived.

The idea of southern poverty was not the only stereotype that the
Allies carried with them to Naples. So, too, was the idea of Campania
as a pastoral idyll where even the humble *lazzaroni* could provide for
themselves. The series of studies into the land and economy of
Campania, conducted by Allied planners on the eve of the invasion,
might have been written by Virgil or Goethe, such were their evoca-
tions of a land of plenty. The district around Naples, they enthused,
was not only 'some of the richest land in Italy', but 'one of the most
fertile regions in the world': almost anything could grow in its 'fine
volcanic' soil. 'Irrigation is easy, rainfall is adequate, and temperature
during the coldest months of the year rarely falls beneath 10°C (50°F).'
As a consequence, the vineyards and tomato farms in Campania
produced 'the highest yield in Italy', and the rest of the countryside
produced 'very high yields' in just about everything else, including 'the
largest production of fruit ... and nuts on the Italian mainland'.
Furthermore, the sea was almost as abundant as the land: along with its
satellite towns along the bay, Naples was 'the most important of Italian
fishing centres'. The only shortages highlighted in any of these reports
were those of wheat and sugar, but only as an aside: the main impression was one of abundance and self-sufficiency.[25]

Unfortunately, by the time British and American troops had fought
their way to Naples, almost all the assumptions that Allied planners
had made were already redundant. The abundance of fish in the sea
was immediately made irrelevant when the Allied navies banned all
night-time fishing along the coast. Many of the fertile fields and
orchards had been turned into battlefields: in the worst affected areas,
vineyards and olive groves were so damaged that their yield was reduced
by 30 per cent.[26] A series of storms and downpours in September and
October made a mockery of Allied notions that Campania had a mild
and gentle climate, and the snows that followed completely contradicted the idea that the temperature would not fall below 10°C. Because
of conditions like these, and wartime shortages of both manpower and
fertilizer, the harvest in 1943 was not nearly as good as expected. When

the Allied officials arrived in Salerno in September they made a hasty
survey of the wheat situation: 'it was quite obvious that the harvest had
been an extremely poor one and that the outlook for feeding Campania
... was very poor indeed.'[27] And yet, even after such reports were circulated, the Allies did nothing to modify their original plans. The
assumption that Naples would be able to feed itself remained, and no
attempt to bring in substantial supplementary supplies was made until
long after the region's fabled wealth of fruit and vegetables had all been
consumed.

A faulty plan, prejudices and misconceptions, a mythological idea of
Campania's agricultural riches – all of this might have been forgiven if
the Allies had radically changed their policies once they had arrived
and discovered that the reality in and around Naples looked nothing
like their preconceived ideas. For a while it seemed as if they would do
exactly that. According to Colonel Hume, as the Allies approached
Naples they began to receive intelligence 'that there was a most serious
shortage of food in the city'. General Clark's first instinct was to
manage the situation in the same way that his men would manage the
other humanitarian emergencies they encountered: by throwing
resources behind it. Before entering the city, Allied aircraft dropped
propaganda leaflets in Clark's name promising that food and medicines would soon be on their way. 'To the people of Naples,' the leaflet
began: 'A ship has arrived in the Gulf of Salerno, loaded with food
ordered by me for the people of Naples ... This ship is but the beginning. I have ordered that provisions be sent in at regular intervals.' The
leaflet went on to list all the riches that were coming to the city: 'Bread
for the hungry, milk for babies, medicines for the sick and wounded.'
It ended with a plea for the people to rise up against the Germans, and
help the 'Rebirth of Italy' to begin.[28]
    There is no reason to suppose that Clark did not mean every word
of this; but it required much more than fine words to make such promises come to fruition, and neither he nor his staff did anything to follow
them up. The Allies entered Naples on 1 October. The first ship
docked in the harbour on 4 October, but it was not Clark's fabled ship
full of supplies. In fact, according to a report by the Economics and

Civilian Supply Division of AMG, the first shipment of flour for civilian use did not arrive until 8 October, and the first bread ration was not distributed until two days later. Rather than rushing to feed the people of Naples, therefore, the Allies had largely left them to their own devices for ten days. 'Fortunately,' the report went on, 'fruit and vegetables started to come into Naples almost immediately after the occupation and this supply together with hoarded supplies in the hands of consumers saved the day.'[29]

In the following weeks, Allied supplies of food trickled into the port at a rate that made their promises of feeding the population almost impossible. Four more shipments of food arrived in Naples in November, including 12,367 tons of flour – but since the city of Naples alone required 600 tons of flour each day just to fulfil the requirements of bread rationing, these shipments were barely enough to feed the people for more than a couple of weeks.[30] In December, to everyone's dismay, shipments massively *decreased*. AMG officials complained that of the 20,417 metric tons of supplies that they had requested, only 3,823 tons – less than a fifth – actually arrived.[31]

As a consequence of these continued shortages, the rations issued by the Allies during the first three months of their administration were meagre to say the least. The daily bread ration in the city was just 100 grams per person, and in the province a mere 50 grams per person – less than two slices of a standard American loaf.[32] Even Mussolini had managed to give the people a minimum of 150 grams of bread per day.

Other rationed items, such as cheese, olive oil and sugar, were hardly generous either. According to a report made by the Office of Strategic Services, even after the bread ration had been raised slightly, 'the standard ration amounted to 615 calories a day, which is less than a third of what is needed by the human body at rest'.[33] According to the Allied plan for Italy, rations were supposed to remain unchanged after the arrival of the Allied armies. In reality, the people were being offered less than half the calories they were used to under the Fascists. They were expected to make up the shortfall by buying food on the free market, but by now food prices were so high that few could afford them.

Eventually the bakeries began to run out of bread altogether: angry demonstrations broke out in half a dozen towns around Naples at the beginning of December because food deliveries had failed to material-ize.[34] The Allied rationing system was beginning to break down.

By this time the head of the Public Health and Welfare Division in Naples, Colonel Crichton, was so concerned that he felt compelled to write at length about the severity of the crisis he was witnessing. Many essential foods, he explained, had become completely unavailable anywhere but the black market. Olive oil, despite being reasonably abundant, was unobtainable unless you were willing to spend 200 lire for a litre. Milk was 'obtainable if one can afford to pay the price', but 'the vast majority cannot do so'. He continued: 'The humble bean, for generations scorned by everybody but the lowest classes, has risen to a delicacy which can only be afforded by the rich.' Fish, meanwhile, was 'beyond the dreams of avarice'.[35]

Allied officials did not generally see people dying of hunger in the streets because, as the Communist Mario Palermo angrily told one Englishman, the average Neapolitan 'preferred to die of starvation in his own home'.[36] But Crichton had direct contact with all the hospitals in the city, and probably saw for himself the effects that the lack of food was having on the poorer people in the city. As yet, there had been no reported cases of severe vitamin deficiency, 'but the pinched and miserable appearance of the poorer population affords ample evidence of malnutrition even to the layman'. With conditions like these the norm throughout Campania, he concluded, 'Malnutrition in the urban areas' had now become 'rife'.[37]

Unfortunately, those at the highest levels of military government refused to believe there was a problem. Even as Crichton was writing the above report, the head of the regional AMG for Campania, Colonel Hulme, was reassuring London and Washington that 'the average worker is able now, as he was in the past, to purchase his minimum needs of rationed goods'.[38] At a national level, the Allied Control Commission was just as complacent. As one officer in Sicily put it, 'In direct contrast to the confirmed opinion of the Prefects and the public, ACC authorities repeatedly state that the food situation is far from grave.'[39]

The final link in the chain of command was Allied Forces Headquarters in Algiers, which was responsible for allocating shipping space in the Mediterranean. Naturally they always prioritized the needs of their own fighting men over those of Italian civilians: there was always a reason why space for civilian food could not be found in the ships bound for Naples. Without a specific office dedicated to civilian supply there was no one to champion the needs of starving Italians, and it was not until the very end of the year that AFHQ finally got round to appointing a dedicated Food Controller for Italy. As a consequence, the Allies did not begin to ship larger quantities of flour and other essential foodstuffs to Naples until January 1944 – four months after the food crisis had begun. By their own admission, this was 'probably too late to stop the continual increase in prices'.[40]

Without the active support of the Fifth Army, AFHQ or even their own superiors, AMG officials in the field were all but powerless to stop the crisis that was unfolding before them. The only course of action open to them was to try to coax more food out of the Italian supply chain, just as the original Italy plan suggested. But to expect inexperienced Allied officers to be able to do this was hopelessly optimistic. Few of them could speak the language, and they had little knowledge of the arcane Italian distribution systems: indeed, quite early on they were forced to admit: 'We seem to have had considerable difficulty in our efforts to learn just what agencies formerly existed for control of foodstuffs, and the part which each played.'[41] They had neither the staff nor the resources to set up an alternative system that made more sense to them, let alone to police it.

Some of the descriptions of Allied attempts to reorganize the food distribution system in Naples would make comical reading had the consequences not been so dire. For example, attempts to get cattle to an improvised meat market almost ended in disaster when cattle trucks were held up for two days at a station near Eboli because someone had forgotten to pay one of the local transport fees. The fee only amounted to 90 lire – less than a single US dollar – but as a consequence the cattle were left without food or water for several days. In the end 'these animals did not arrive in Naples for over a week, in, as to be expected, a most shocking condition'.[42]

Allied attempts at restarting milk sales were just as unsuccessful. AMG officials held a series of conferences with Italian officials and farmers and agreed a fair price of around 4 lire per litre; they restarted the *Centrale del Latte* organization to oversee distribution; and, 'after much difficulty', they even laid on transport to ensure the fresh milk made it to market. 'However, on zero day, not one litre of milk appeared.' It turned out that, despite agreeing a price, none of the producers was willing to sell their milk for 4 lire per litre when they could make it into cheese and sell it for 150 lire per kilogram on the black market.[43]

After fiascos like these, AMG did not even bother trying to set up a system for amassing and distributing beans and pulses because 'it was felt that attempts would probably result in failure'.[44]

AMG officials did their best to solve the many problems that were piling up before them, but without the resources and the authority to back them up it was always going to be a losing battle. Their activity reports for the month of December were particularly gloomy. They reported 'negligible' success in amassing olive oil, 'No solution' to the shortage of meat and 'No solution yet to fresh milk problem'. As a consequence, there was 'a serious shortage of basic food items', and prices 'were approximately double the prices of the previous year'.[45] According to one report, even the hospitals were struggling to get hold of enough food to feed their patients. The food crisis was fast becoming a public health matter almost as serious as the typhus epidemic itself.[46]

In the end, the Allies had no choice but to abandon the city to the black market. In the words of one Allied official, at least 'the black market ... *brought food into Naples*', which was better than nothing.[47] It was a humiliating defeat, especially since the Fascists – whom the Allies had criticized so roundly for their inefficiency – had never capitulated to market forces so completely. But the people who really suffered were the Neapolitans, who were now effectively cast adrift on a rising tide of black market prices.

Inflation and Its Consequences

If the higher levels of AMG were complacent about food supplies, they were equally complacent about keeping prices down. Given the short- age in food supplies, close control of prices was essential – but the Allies had neither the staff nor the expertise to do what needed to be done. At a national level the ACC did not set up an anti-inflation committee until May 1944, seven or eight months after the problem had first spiralled out of control. At a local level AMG was no better. After the Allies arrived in Naples, 'no prices were posted and no discernible effort was made to control prices until the area had been occupied for about three months'. Even after price lists were published, little was done to enforce them.[48]

AMG's record on keeping wages down was just as bad. Their proc- lamation that wages would be frozen was widely ignored by their own officers, as well as the rest of the Allied forces and agencies, whose only concern was to attract civilian staff quickly. As one Neapolitan woman later explained, 'When the Americans came, they paid twice as much. So I quit my job and applied at the American embassy.'[49] This attitude was very common, as different military units began to compete with one another for the best workers, espe- cially those who could speak a little English. The conditions for a classic wage–price spiral were built into the Allied occupation from the moment of their arrival.[50]

Perhaps the most disastrous Allied policy was the way they abused the currency. On their arrival in Italy, the Allies introduced a new form of money – the Allied Military Lira, which was equivalent to the normal Italian lira – and proclaimed a new exchange rate of 100 lire to the dollar. This represented a massive devaluation of the Italian currency, which even Washington believed should probably have been valued at 50 lire to the dollar.

Such a high exchange rate suited the Allied armies because it imme- diately gave them more buying power – but it was disastrous for the local economy. Shopkeepers felt justified in doubling their prices on the grounds that the lira was now worth half of its former value. The unfortunate parity of one cent to one lira also encouraged American

GIs to think of the two currencies as equivalent, and to pay American prices for Italian goods – thus driving up the prices for everyone.[51]

However, what really supercharged inflation in Naples was the presence of the Allies themselves. It was not only a lack of supply that kept prices rising all the way into the summer of 1944, but a surfeit of demand. Hundreds of thousands of Allied servicemen passed through Naples during the first year of the occupation, none of whom had any use for the official channels of food distribution. They had no need for ration cards, because all their essential needs had already been met. Whatever they bought was paid for in straight cash – which they had in abundance. Allied soldiers, and particularly American soldiers, were fabulously wealthy compared to the local population in Naples. While the British and Canadian armies tried to limit soldiers' spending by withholding a portion of their pay, the US Army made no such move. As a consequence, according to one former military government officer, the lowliest American private soldier 'could draw and spend in Italy as much money as an Italian prefect received'.[52]

From the moment they arrived in Naples, the Allies embarked on a massive spending spree: 'They See Naples and Buy', as the London *Daily Mail* put it at the end of November 1943.[53] Soldiers bought souvenirs and gifts for their parents or girlfriends. They paid for personal services, like a visit to the barbers or one of the ubiquitous shoeshine boys along the Via Roma. And, crucially, they went to restaurants and bars. To soldiers on leave, who had plenty of money and only a limited time in which to spend it, price was rarely an obstacle: in the words of one GI, if things were costly, 'Who cared? You weren't going to need the money anyway.'[54]

This was a boom time for shopkeepers selling cameos and other tourist knick-knacks, but it was a disaster for ordinary people who were just trying to feed their families. In a city where food was already desperately scarce, the arrival of tens of thousands of wealthy, hungry GIs drove black market prices into the stratosphere. 'As soon as the big spending GIs hit town inflation really took over,' remembers one American artilleryman. 'From twenty five Lire (25 cents), the price of a bottle of wine jumped to 150 Lire in two weeks.'[55] The same thing happened to food prices. By the spring of 1944 Naples was full of restaurants charging 'fantastic prices' to military personnel.[56] When AMG belatedly tried to ban Allied soldiers from visiting local restaurants, the rule was widely ignored. Besides, it was not only restaurants that served food to GIs: private homes also offered soldiers home-cooked food for a fee. This carried on all over Naples, even when the whole city was supposed to be out of bounds because of typhus restrictions.[57]

Allied soldiers had no concept of the disastrous effects they were having on the local economy. Julian Philips, a junior officer in the US 143rd Infantry Regiment, later described how a Neapolitan barber called Giuseppe, whom he visited every time he came to the city, gave him a valuable lesson in occupation economics:

> As I settled into the chair I felt some relief that I was away from all the hawkers for at least an hour. I turned to the barber, whom I had become friends with, and asked him why every Italian was on the take. I told him it seemed to get worse every time we came to Naples and I asked if all Italians were that way. It seems everyone is out to take the Americans for a few bucks.
>
> As Joseppi straightened the cloth around my neck he said, 'It's all because of the Americans.' I jumped out of the chair jerking the cloth from around my neck, threw it on the floor as I yelled, 'How in the hell can you blame anything on the Americans; they are the most generous people in the world. The British didn't give you anything but a kick in the ass. The French … and Senegalese, steal, rape and kill anyone that gets in their way. The Poles don't have anything to give – they are supplied by the British. The Sikhs, Gurks, Aussies and New Zealand troops are also supplied by the British and they remember when the Italians were in Hitler's camp. How can you still blame the conditions in Italy on the Americans?'
>
> My voice was back to normal and he had eased me back into the chair. He put the cloth around my neck and as he began to cut my hair he spoke. 'Lt. Philips, when you Americans landed at Salerno on 9 Sept. 1943 the average wage here in Naples was thirty five cents per day.' He hesitated, 'Today thirty five cents

won't buy one loaf of bread, so if we aren't into something else we will starve.' I came right back, 'And you blame this on the Americans?' He said, 'Yes sir, but let me give you an example. I cut from twelve to eighteen heads of hair every day. Today you will be in my chair for one and a half hours. You will receive a haircut, shampoo, shave, and a facial to include a mud pack and the price is three cents. When you first came into my shop you asked what the cost was and my answer was, 'Joe, pay what you want' and you gave me a dollar and a half. You don't ask any more but you usually give me two dollars. I try to please, I put you ahead of Italians and I treat you as a preferred customer. Lt. Philips, there isn't one American that will get up out of my chair in one and a half hours and give me three cents. You Americans are the most generous people in the world but you have ruined the Italian economy. I no longer can feed my family on thirty five cents a day the way I could last September.'

It had never dawned on me that our free spending, giving and generous hearts could ruin another country's economy, to the point where everyone was on the take. We saw it happen in Italy in 1943–1944.[58]

With the arrival of the Allies in the autumn of 1943, the entire economy of Naples changed practically overnight. Rather than serving the needs of the people who lived here, it reoriented itself towards serving the needs of the Allies. Tens of thousands of Neapolitans began working for the Americans, who paid wages that were far higher than anything most Italian employers could afford: at the beginning of 1944, there were 45,000 people officially on the Allied payroll – and closer to 161,000 when those working directly for individual Allied units were also taken into consideration.[59] Tens of thousands more, like Julian Philips' barber, refocused their businesses towards tending to the needs of British and American servicemen. Those who could not change jobs, or otherwise gain access to this fabulous new source of money, quickly found themselves left behind.

Prices of everything, but particularly food prices, began to spiral out of control. In December 1943 the official price for a kilogram of bread was 3.60 lire, but on the black market the same kilogram of bread cost 130 lire – more than thirty-six times its official price. A kilo of pasta, which cost 5 lire on the official market, could cost as much as 220 lire on the black market.[60] Such prices were way beyond what most ordinary people could afford. The average unskilled labourer, for example, earned less than 50 lire per day. The lowest-ranking policemen in Naples were paid just 30 lire per day. For people like this, a single kilo of pasta could cost a full week's wages.[61]

What was more, these prices continued to rise throughout the first half of 1944. A kilogram of rice, for example, which had cost 30 lire on the black market before the invasion, doubled in price after it. By December the price had risen to 170 lire, by March 1944 it was 290 lire, and by June it was 355 lire – almost twelve times its pre-invasion price. It was not until July that the price finally began to drop a little.

The suffering this caused to ordinary Neapolitans was enough to melt even the hardest of Allied hearts. Maurice Crowther, a British soldier who worked for the Army Post Office, was used to thinking of the Italians as enemies when he first arrived in Naples, but as part of his work he had to supervise civilian labourers who had been employed to carry bags of mail.

> I hated their guts at first … Then I began to feel sorry for them.
> They had nothing. The Allies weren't interested in keeping them
> alive … I was always having to keep on at them, saying 'Wake up
> and let's have some work out of you!' We found out that the
> bulk of them were working on night shift for the Army Post
> Office, and then during the day they were driving the trams in
> Naples. So they could hardly keep awake. And the total earnings
> of two shifts wouldn't buy their kiddies a pair of shoes.[62]

Another British worker, whose job involved unloading Liberty ships in Naples harbour, was so appalled by the state of the Neapolitan stevedores working alongside him that he took it upon himself to smuggle food to them. 'They were so weak that they were obviously having great difficulty working', so he used to steal tinned food 'in large quantities and give it away to these Neapolitans'.[63]

ITEM	Unit	June '43		Sept '43		Dec '43		Mar '44		Jun '44	
		Official	B M	Official	B M	Official	B M	Official	B M	Official	B M
Bread	Kg	2.50	50.00	2.50	85.00	3.60	130.00	3.60	130.00	3.60	161.00
Flour	Kg	2.30	55.00	2.30	70.00	4.10	150.00	3.60	190.00	3.60	214.00
Flour (corn)	Kg	1.80	25.00	1.80	40.00	3.75	110.00	3.75	145.00	3.75	–
Rice	Kg	3.45	30.00	3.45	60.00	4.00	170.00	4.00	290.00	4.00	355.00
Potatoes	Kg	4.00	6.00	4.00	7.00	7.00	17.00	12.00	37.00	12.00	–
Dry Figs	Kg	–	36.00	–	40.00	27.00	65.00	31.00	78.00	40.00	98.00
Pasta	Kg	3.10	35.00	3.10	70.00	5.00	220.00	5.10	250.00	5.50	300.00
Sugar	Kg	7.65	40.00	9.10	120.00	15.00	180.00	15.00	310.00	15.30	282.00
Wine	Lt	4.00	6.50	4.00	10.00	14.00	25.00	14.00	45.00	22.50	–
Barley	Kg	–	20.00	–	27.00	–	90.00	–	120.00	–	92.00
Milk	Lt	2.60	8.00	2.60	11.00	7.00	25.00	13.00	35.00	15.00	–
Beans	Kg	6.15	28.00	6.15	38.00	11.00	150.00	13.00	190.00	75.00	187.50
Beef	Kg	18.50	70.00	32.00	90.00	34.00	120.00	34.00	270.00	220.00	–
Eggs	Each	1.80	5.00	2.00	10.00	4.00	20.00	4.00	22.00	15.00	18.33
Cheese	Kg	24.10	120.00	24.85	130.00	35.00	220.00	96.00	420.00	88.00	363.00
Coffee	Kg	–	700.00	–	1000.00	–	1300.00	–	1100.00	–	650.00
Butter	Kg	27.50	110.00	27.50	150.00	–	220.00	–	350.00	170.00	259.00
Olive Oil	Lt	14.75	90.00	14.75	150.00	25.00	165.00	25.00	270.00	29.00	249.00

Official and black market prices in Naples, mid-1943 to mid-1944[64]

It was not long before people simply stopped showing up for work. In January 1944, Rear Admiral Morse wrote to Eisenhower complaining that all the best Italian workers were leaving the port because they could no longer afford to feed their families on the wages that the Allies were paying them. Those who stayed were forced to supplement their wages by stealing, or by dabbling in the black market.[65] The head of Labor Supply in AMG concurred, warning his superiors that it was 'more desirable to a Neapolitan to stay at home and run a small-time black market than to work at an entirely unrealistic wage for the Allies'.[66]

Unfortunately, the first instinct of the Allies was not to raise wages or improve conditions for workers, but to introduce draconian measures against them. In the towns around the periphery of Naples, manual labour was forcibly conscripted among the local population. Anyone who did not turn up for work had their ration cards taken away 'until they have a change of heart'.[67] In the following months, Allied officers in Naples briefly considered making 'forced employment' their default policy before, thankfully, wiser heads prevailed. In the end, all it took to get people to turn up to work was the introduction of a free meal at lunchtime.[68]

In the meantime, it was not only manual workers who were suffering. According to a report by the Psychological Warfare Branch, 'The worst sufferers are not to be found among the working classes who have been able to find employment with the Allies at greatly increased wages ... but among the employees of the State and the local administration.' These white-collar workers had fixed incomes that were completely wiped out as soon as prices started to rise. Those on monthly salaries often found that they had run out of money even before the middle of the month.[69]

Another report in July 1944 compared the income of the middle classes against their outgoings, and found that a typical family of three had a monthly income of just 2,200 lire, but outgoings of 6,817 lire. Such a balance sheet was unsustainable over the long term: 'this class is suffering in the extreme, sacrificing its small savings, its family treasures and even its household belongings in the fight for existence.'[70] All over Naples, members of the middle classes could be seen hawking personal possessions of all kinds – jewellery, old books, clothing, even furniture – in order to make enough money to feed their families.

And when all that was gone, there was only one thing left to sell.

Changes in Relationship

The Allies had much to be proud of during their first few months administering Naples. In his report at the end of December 1943, Colonel Hume listed many of their achievements: the return of power and water, the restoration of some telephone services, the reopening of the banks, the return of some kind of law and order, and so on. 'Naples is well on the way to reassuming its traditional air of gaiety,' he claimed.[71]

But the chronic inability to provide the city with even basic food supplies threatened to undermine all these successes. In his rather rosy and self-serving report, Hume claimed that 'We are supplying food to the people daily', but this was not the experience of tens of thousands of people in and around the city. The protests against food shortages, which began in various towns around Naples towards the end of the year, only accelerated at the beginning of 1944. Demonstrations against rising food prices and failures in food distribution took place not only in Naples itself, but in Trentola, Afragola, Pastorano, Torre del Greco and Saviano. In Villamaina, in Avellino province, an angry mob prevented the authorities from requisitioning their stores of grain – the police had to fire into the air to prevent the demonstration from turning into a riot. In Paduli, in Benevento province, 200 angry farmers attacked police officers with pitchforks when they came to requisition food stores – two policemen and one of the farmers were severely injured.[72]

Hume might not have been able to see the dangers in events like this, but others could. In a note to the Combined Chiefs of Staff in Washington, written at about the same time that Hume was writing his report, AFHQ warned that 'Conditions in Southern Italy and Sicily are such that unless reasonable quantities of food are supplied very promptly, we will experience sabotage, unrest and a complete cessation of those activities necessary to our advance.'[73] By the middle of 1944 it was obvious to everyone that the food shortages threatened to become both a military and political disaster. In the words of the American Consulate General in Naples in June 1944, 'shortages are so acute that, without manifesting its resentment, no modern people could be expected to support them long'.[74] Unfortunately, the crisis would continue in many parts of the country right up until the end of the war.

The shortage of food, and the resentment that came with it, caused a significant shift in the relationship between the Allies and the people of Naples. The contrasts in physical appearance between local people and Allied soldiers were becoming impossible to ignore. While Neapolitans were increasingly shabby and emaciated, the 'Tommies' and 'Jimmies' who paraded up and down the Via Roma in their uniforms remained strong, healthy and well fed. While local people were forced to sell their most precious belongings on the street, GIs spent lavishly in bars and restaurants, and bought up family heirlooms as trinkets and souvenirs to send back to their folks in America. And, most tellingly, while Neapolitan women were forced to prostitute themselves for food, the Allies became their main customers. They increasingly treated the women here like objects to be bought and sold just like everything else.

It was the massive rise in prostitution, brought on by the food crisis, that was perhaps most symbolic of the new relationship between the Allies and the people of Naples. In his memoir, Norman Lewis estimated that around a quarter of the young, female population of Naples were forced to sell their bodies on a regular basis.[75] In 1944 it was virtually impossible to walk along the Via Roma without being accosted by child pimps offering up their sisters or their mothers for sex – indeed, it was a phenomenon that almost every Allied serviceman who passed through the city felt compelled to comment on.

CHAPTER 10

Prostitution

Naples has always been considered a female entity. In ancient times the fertile landscape around the city was associated with Demeter, the Greek goddess of agriculture, and her daughter Persephone, a fertility goddess. A temple to Aphrodite Euploia, the goddess of safe voyages, once stood on the headland so that sailors could see it as they headed out to sea. But the figure most closely linked with the city is Parthenope, the Siren, whose intentions were rather less benign. Mesmerizing, irresistible, she lured men to their deaths on the rocks as they were drawn towards her haunting song.[1]

The myth of Parthenope has resurfaced many times in the history of Naples. In the aftermath of the Second World War, Curzio Malaparte made use of it in his great novel about life in the city under the Allied occupation. In *The Skin*, he describes a banquet held by General Cork – a caricature of Mark Clark, whom Malaparte had come across in real life. The general, he explains, frequently holds banquets for visiting dignitaries, and likes to serve fish: but since fishing has been banned by the Allied navies, he is reduced to raiding fish from the world-famous Naples Aquarium instead. When Eisenhower visits, for example, they all dine on the aquarium's giant octopus; Churchill is served its electric torpedo fish; and the Soviet diplomat Andrey Vyshinsky is honoured with the aquarium's valuable Arabian pearl oysters. Soon the aquarium is emptied of everything except its most precious animal – the manatee, 'a very rare example of that species of "sirenoids" which, because of their almost human form, gave rise to the ancient legend about the Sirens'.[2] In Malaparte's banquet scene, this is the dish that is served up to honour the arrival in Naples of a matronly WAC officer called Mrs Flat. When it arrives on a huge silver platter, all the guests are pale with horror, because it looks so much like the body of a young girl. 'Are you sure it's a fish – a *real* fish?' asks the general; and Malaparte's narrator reassures him that it is indeed a fish: 'It's the famous Siren from the Aquarium.'[3]

Since 1943, the serving of a manatee at General Mark Clark's banquet has become something of an urban myth in Naples. Norman Lewis mentions it in his memoir of the war, stating boldly, 'All Neapolitans believe that at the banquet offered to welcome General Mark Clark … the principal course was a baby manatee – the most prized item of the aquarium's collection – which was boiled and served with a garlic sauce.'[4] In Lewis's account, the story is symbolic of the desperate shortage of food that gripped the city in the autumn and winter of 1943–4. But in Malaparte's hands, the myth is something much more disturbing. The manatee is not merely the last item of food available in an already exhausted city: it is a 'Siren', the ancient symbol of Naples itself, which is about to be ritually consumed by the American military.

Just as significantly, Malaparte's Siren takes the form not of a powerful and dangerous demi-god, capable of luring soldiers to their death, as she was in the Homeric original. Instead she is a helpless little girl:

> She was naked; but her dark, shining skin … was exactly like a well-filled dress in the way in which it outlined her still callow yet already well-proportioned form, the gentle curve of her hips, her slightly protruding belly, her little virginal breasts, and her broad, plump shoulders. She might have been not more than eight or ten years old, though at first sight, owing to the precocious development of her body, which was that of a grown woman, she looked fifteen … It was the first time I had ever seen a little girl who had been cooked, a little girl who had been boiled; and I was silent, gripped by a holy fear.[5]

The sexualized depiction of a little girl served up on a silver platter for American soldiers to eat is just one of the many grotesque images in a book that is packed with similarly disturbing scenes.

This story is significant for two reasons. Firstly, it is a perfect demonstration of how myth and reality become inextricably entangled with one another in people's memories of wartime, particularly in a city like Naples. In Norman Lewis's memoir of the war, he mentions that 'most Neapolitans' believe the story of the manatee to be true – but he also asserts as a fact the disappearance of all the other fish, which were stolen to be eaten by hungry Neapolitans. Taking him at his word, many historians have repeated this claim. Rick Atkinson, for example, states in his history of the Italian war that 'All the tropical fish in the municipal aquarium were devoured.'[6] I myself made the same mistake in my 2012 history of Europe in the aftermath of the liberation.[7] And yet, just a quick glance at the Allied newspapers of the time shows the story to be untrue: the aquarium stayed open after the Allies arrived, and continued to charge soldier-tourists 20 lire to come and marvel at the fish, which were all still very much alive. Lewis, who wrote his memoirs in the 1970s, seems to have absorbed the story as a memory of his own, despite the fact that it never happened. Such is the process by which fiction becomes myth, myth becomes recollection and recollection becomes history.

Secondly, it gives us an insight into the Neapolitan sense of victimhood, which has echoes in many other parts of its history and mythology. Malaparte's purpose, and perhaps also Lewis's, was not to present a documentary truth, but to convey the emotional truth of what it felt like to be an Italian in Naples during that extraordinary time: defeated by a former enemy, yet grateful for that defeat; enamoured of their new occupiers, yet also resentful of them; liberated but not yet free. Malaparte was also aware, much more than Lewis, of the echoes of former defeats and occupations suffered by Naples over its long and painful past. In a time of such confusing and heightened emotions, it is no wonder that fictions and myths become entangled with layers of history until it is no longer entirely clear what is true or not.

The Allies had no concept of this complex tangle of emotions – indeed, they still struggle to understand it today. Neither Britain nor

America was ever forced to suffer the indignity of defeat as Italy did, or to switch sides during the conflict, or to endure multiple occupations by opposing armies. In most of the English-speaking world the Second World War was, and remains, a war of moral certainty: it was the 'Good War', fought by a generation of heroes against the forces of tyranny.[8]

The vast majority of soldiers who passed through Naples between 1943 and 1945 had no idea of the effect they were having on the city. It was this juxtaposition of heroism, corruption and innocent ignorance that was the defining irony of the Allied occupation. 'If ever it was an honour to lose a war,' wrote Malaparte, 'it was certainly a great honour for the people of Naples, and for all the other conquered peoples of Europe, to have lost this one to soldiers who were so courteous, elegant and neatly dressed, so good hearted and generous. And yet everything that these magnificent soldiers touched was at once corrupted.'[9]

Erotic Daydreams

Naples came as a surprise to most of the soldiers who arrived here during the Second World War. The young men arriving from Britain, America and other parts of the English-speaking world had been led to believe that it was some kind of paradise, a place of moonlight, and song, and love. It was strongly associated with the female aspect of life – 'bella Napoli' in the feminine – as the novelist John Horne Burns put it, 'Huge and inscrutable as the feminine Idea.'[10] The reality, however, was something much more broken and shabby. 'In the winter of 1943–44 it was beautiful only from a distance,' wrote one American port worker. 'Close in, it was a stinking, rotten, diseased, revolting mess.' As an afterthought, he added, 'Yet, from stinking messes beautiful things sometimes emerge.'[11]

Many Allied soldiers had dreamed about the famously beautiful Neapolitan women – especially those soldiers who had spent the last year in the deserts of North Africa 'where you saw no women at all'.[12] But they, too, turned out to be different from what the men expected. Unlike the women in Britain and America, they did not shave their legs and armpits: 'I remember the glistening damp under-arm hair when the Neapolitan women put up a hand to their heads,' wrote John Horne Burns, 'and their legs, which seemed often to be skinned in dewy feathers.'[13] They smelled different, too. In a city utterly devoid of soap, both men and women had a sour, animal odour, suggestive and repulsive in equal measure.[14]

Many Neapolitan women seemed utterly unselfconscious about their bodies, particularly in the summer months when, as one observer put it, they were so lightly clad 'that no effort of imagination is needed to follow the forms begun in naked arms and legs and neck'.[15] They appeared equally relaxed about male bodies, and indeed their bodily functions. In the countryside around Naples, for example, the women made a habit of approaching GIs while they were squatting over make-shift latrines and trying to sell them oranges, walnuts or wine. According to one artillery soldier, they had worked out that this was where the men were most vulnerable: 'The women, who were never embarrassed, would stand there and haggle until the poor GIs would buy something just to get the women to go away.'[16]

One young corporal in a US ordnance maintenance company tells the story of being approached by a group of young women while he was taking a shower in an olive grove. Shy about his nakedness, he immediately scrambled to get his clothes on. One of the women came closer. 'She took out her boob: she'd been pregnant and had milk in her boob, and she was squirting at me with it.' Bewildered, he simply put on his clothes and hurried away.

Such stories have a timeless quality. The woman in the olive grove might have been a tree nymph from ancient myth. But even the truth – that this was just a mischievous woman amusing herself at his embar-rassment – was impossibly exotic to a naive young man from Cleveland, Ohio.[17]

At the other end of the spectrum were women who seemed utterly untouchable – the daughters of the wealthy middle classes, virginal students and intellectuals, the wives of Fascist hierarchs, the occasional *contessa*. And, of course, there was also every other kind of woman in between: 'the women and girls of Naples,' as one American intelligence officer put it, 'stood for all the women and girls of the world.'[18] In the minds of the soldiers they were all exotic, fascinating, desirable.[19]

The fascination was often entirely mutual. To a certain degree, the women of Naples had also been starved of men. So many had been swallowed up by the army, lost in the battles of North Africa, or taken prisoner by the Allies or by the Germans – and those who were left behind were just as poor, just as hungry and ragged, and smelled just as much of sweat and stale clothing as the women themselves did. Compared to Italian men, the clean, strong, well-fed Allies were undeniably attractive. They were also fabulously wealthy. 'A British private, wretchedly paid as he is, earns more than a foreman at the Navale Meccanica,' wrote Norman Lewis, 'while an American private – who can shower cigarettes, sweets, and even silk stockings in all directions – has a higher income than any Italian employee in Naples.' The local boys simply could not compete.[20]

It did not take long for soldiers and other Allied servicemen to make friends with Italian women, and indeed their families. Their motivations were not just sexual. These men had mothers and sisters back home, and many of them desperately missed female company. They also missed the easy intimacy of normal family life. When a soldier was invited home to dinner with a local family, he generally accepted enthusiastically in the hope of a home-cooked meal, a little mothering and the chance to flirt with girls his own age. In return he would bring gifts – candy, cigarettes, some of his army rations – to be shared among the family (or, more likely, sold on the black market at a later date).

Many genuine and lasting friendships were forged in this way; and also romances, some of which ended in marriage. Nevertheless, there was always an element of transaction involved, particularly at the start. 'The GI was happy to be part of a family again and the family was grateful to receive whatever rations he could supply,' explained Paul Brown, an American NCO in one of the port battalions. 'The local people generally made the soldiers welcome, but I could never decide how much was innate hospitality and how much was thanks for the rations. At least it was a symbiotic relationship.'[21]

Neither could Neapolitans be entirely sure of the intentions of the men they let into their homes. Families who became reliant on soldiers' gifts often ended up tolerating behaviour that would never be allowed in normal times: lascivious glances at their daughters, open flirtations, even unchaperoned meetings. Women in particular sensed intuitively that gifts of food and cigarettes often came with strings attached. One 19-year-old Neapolitan woman, who met her future husband while working in an American officers' club, repeatedly turned down his offers of food, despite the fact that she was starving. 'I hadn't eaten in three days …' remembered Eva Erminia Denson, 'but I was so afraid that if I ate, he would expect something in return.' When he took her to the kitchen of the club and offered her lobster and T-bone steak, she told him simply that she was not hungry. One night he walked her home and gave her a whole box of Hershey chocolate bars at her door. Reluctantly she accepted them, and hurried inside. Alone at last, she began ravenously eating the chocolate bars until they were finished. 'I was sick all night long,' she remembered, but also grateful that her suitor had not tried to come inside. She decided to trust him, and after a two-year courtship they finally married in 1946.[22]

Inevitably, many Allied soldiers were not content with such ambiguous and long-term arrangements. And neither did every Neapolitan women have Eva Denson's willpower: they were starving, and so were their families. Some were forced into the cold realization that, if they were to ensure a steady supply of Allied rations, they would have to offer solid reasons for soldiers to visit them.

In this way, some of the homely family meals described above very quickly became corrupted into something a little more sordid. 'At any hour of the day on the main streets, small boys try to entice Allied officers and men into the side streets for a meal "en famille",' explained one British intelligence report from September 1944. The meal, if indeed there ever was one, was, 'usually followed by the head of the family selling his wife or daughter to their guest.'[23]

Few Allied soldiers admit to having taken advantage of such arrangements, but those who did were almost always disappointed by the experience. They were pursuing a fantasy of love, in homely surroundings – but the reality inevitably punctured their daydreams. 'I went to a few of those homes,' wrote Paul Brown, 'and found the scene not just sordid, but very sad, with family members in one room and a girl or woman in another room in a dirty bed, often with an infant in the corner. A couple of times I followed a *scugniz* [street urchin] up the stairs and entered a dingy apartment with erotic anticipation (I wouldn't have been there if I hadn't been horny), but I was never able to proceed ... The squalid environment and the obvious sadness of the woman (or her total resignation) was not conducive to pleasure.' Unable to go through with his intentions, Brown simply handed over some money and 'fled the scene feeling uncomfortable and embarrassed'.[24]

Norman Lewis describes a similar scenario, although he had less of an idea of what he was getting himself into. Enticed by a 'pleasant-faced old lady' to come to her home, he found himself led to a 'single windowless room' where a 13-year-old girl was standing in a corner. 'Many soldiers, it seems, will pay for sexual activity less than full intercourse, and she had a revolting scale of fees for these services.' Appalled, Lewis threatened to call the police, 'but it was an empty threat and she knew it ... There are no police to deal with the thousands of squalid little crimes like this committed every day in the city.'[25]

The Exploitation of Women and Girls

There was nothing new about the sex trade in Naples in 1943. Prostitution has always been a feature of life here, particularly in the poorer areas around the ancient centre and the port. In the early seventeenth century the English diarist John Evelyn claimed that there were as many as 30,000 registered courtesans in the city, each of them paying tax to the Spanish treasury.[26] At the end of the nineteenth century, when the Italian government carried out a forced 'disembowelling' of the worst slum districts, it was hoped that prostitution would likewise be swept away – but all that happened was the creation of new red-light areas around the city's central station.[27]

The scale of the sex trade during the Second World War dwarfed anything that had gone before. At this time Italy had a system of licensed brothels, and these were allowed to continue after the Allies arrived. Ostensibly they were off limits to Allied soldiers and officers, but in reality this rule was not enforced with any kind of vigour: 'The majority of licenced padronas freely admit that they cannot make a living from civilians,' reported the office of the Provost Marshal in

Naples. As a consequence they 'rely on Allied troops', who more than made up for the lack of trade from Neapolitan men.[28] As more and more troops poured into the city, business began to boom. New brothels sprang up everywhere, almost all of them unlicensed. In addition, more and more women took up occasional prostitution on their own – again, on an entirely unofficial basis. To give some idea of the scale of the trade, in 1945 the local police reported that in the fifteen months between the liberation and the end of 1944 some 1,874 illicit brothels had been closed down, and over 14,000 unlicensed prostitutes arrested. And this was just the tip of the iceberg.[29]

In 1944, according to British documents, there were probably around 40,000 women engaged in prostitution on a regular or occasional basis, or around 10 per cent of the entire female population of Naples.[30] If such figures are correct, it means that around one in five women between the ages 16 and 50 years old were prostituting themselves. 'It seemed that the war and devastation and hunger had transformed every female in Naples over the age of ten into a whore,' wrote Paul Brown. 'At least, that's the way it seemed to this naïve GI.'[31] Or, as another British report put it, prostitution was 'possibly the most thriving business in the city'.[32]

No matter how many women took it up, demand always outstripped supply. Before the Allies arrived in Naples, the fixed price for a date in a licensed brothel ranged between 10 and 50 lire; a year later those fees had increased tenfold.[33] On the street, and in unlicensed brothels, the price for Allied troops could be higher still. According to prostitutes interviewed by intelligence officers in the autumn of 1944, they tended to charge British soldiers between 200 and 500 lire per date. American GIs, who were much wealthier, were charged between 500 and 1,000 lire. The normal rate for black soldiers, no matter their nationality, was 1,000 lire or more. Meanwhile, a soldier who wanted a woman for the whole night could expect to pay up to 3,000 lire. That was far more than any woman in a conventional job could expect to earn in a whole month.[34]

Such prices meant nothing to most Allied servicemen. At the beginning of the occupation they were usually able to pay with items from their standard army rations: a tin of food or a packet of cigarettes could be worth more than the asking fee on the black market, and Allied soldiers had a plentiful supply of both. 'I think the going rate for a woman was a tin of bully beef,' remembers one British artillery gunner.[35] Laurence Rector, a New Yorker who fought with the 45th Division, remembers that 'a piece of soap would get you anything you wanted from the women'.[36] But if cash was what was required, that was fine, too. Soldiers on leave from the front especially reasoned that there was no point in saving up their pay – and what else could they spend it on? As Paul Brown crudely put it, 'They were lusty men who wanted to fuck before they died.'[37]

The main centres of prostitution were the poorest areas to the west of Via Roma, especially the narrow alleys of the Spanish Quarter. Away from the city centre, the factory area around Fuorigrotta and the port area of Bagnoli were also notorious hotspots.[38] It soon became impossible for an Allied soldier to walk through the streets without being continually accosted by child pimps. 'The place was absolutely a ruin,' remembers one Royal Navy signaller who came ashore early after the liberation. 'There was nothing you could buy. Nothing. All you got was little boys trying to sell their sisters to earn a few bob. You got pestered with that the whole time. You couldn't help but feel sorry for them because they were in really dire straits there.'[39]

Others were not quite so sympathetic. Julian Philips was sickened by the thought of children selling their mothers, or husbands their wives. 'I thought I'd seen it all,' he wrote later, but this was 'one thing I just couldn't accept.'[40] His compatriot Bill Harr got so tired of being accosted by pimps every few yards that he hung a sign round his neck saying, simply, 'NO'.[41] 'I was terribly sorry for them,' said British NCO Wilfred Beeson. 'But I don't know why they should have sunk so low as to send their children out to become touts for prostitution ... Animals don't sink as low as that. But there you are. It happens. That's war, I suppose.'[42]

The shock of witnessing such things for the first time is a constant theme in the memoirs and recollections of veterans. Norman Lewis wrote with disgust at the 'perfunctory jogging of the haunches' he witnessed in a municipal building just outside Naples, where queues of soldiers were lined up to take their turn, quite publicly, with one of the local housewives.[43] Another British officer vividly remembered giving away his rations to a hungry crowd, only to be scolded by a fellow officer: 'What a waste ... Don't you know that you could have had the best looking woman down there for just a couple of those tins?'[44] Vere L. Williams, a soldier with the 45th Division, remembers seeing 'a line of 60 or 70 men' waiting to have sex. At the head of the queue was a man taking money, and a single woman lying on a mattress, servicing the soldiers one by one.[45]

Attitudes inevitably hardened with familiarity. Men who might never have approached a prostitute on their own found the excuse to do so when egged on by their comrades. What mattered was not necessarily the act of sex itself, but the communal experience of visiting a brothel together – in other words, it was sometimes just as much an exercise in male bonding as it was a matter of personal gratification. Men on leave would visit a bar together, go on to a brothel together, and then brag about it together afterwards. The women, much like the alcohol, were only incidental to what was otherwise an all-male experience. It was one big bachelor party.

In 2005, Elvin E. Thomas gave an extraordinarily frank interview to the American Veterans History Project that demonstrates this perfectly. Thomas was one of the Tuskegee Airmen, an all-black unit of fighter pilots who were based for a while at Capodichino airport in 1944. One day, during a period of leave at a Sorrento hotel, he heard laughter coming from one of the other rooms. On investigating, he found a group of his fellow airmen standing in the doorway watching another man lying on the bed with a woman. 'These guys, they had gotten together with one of the maids, and agreed that they would pay her so much money for one of the guys, and everybody could look at it.' Unfortunately, the young airman they had selected to have sex with this girl was unable to perform. He had evidently been put off by being watched by half a dozen of his comrades, and now they were all laughing at him and chanting, 'You can't do it! You can't do it!' Eventually the maid was allowed to go, and the airman rejoined his friends, disappointed and embarrassed.[46]

The way Thomas tells it, the maid herself is almost irrelevant in this story. We know nothing about her circumstances, or how she felt about being surrounded on the bed by men shouting and laughing in a foreign language. All that matters to Thomas's friends was the fun that they were having together as a group. Naples was their playground, and its women their entertainment.

In the minds of some servicemen, the women of Naples became completely dehumanized: they were not people, but merely things to be used and then discarded. They were even given a generic name: Maria. Soldiers who expected sex would show up at brothels or people's houses and simply ask for 'Maria'.[47] Even some of the unit histories occasionally refer to 'Maria' as a shorthand for all the women of Naples.[48]

'Maria' could be any shape or size, or indeed any age. Vere Williams tells the story of a group of women who came to his camp when he was close to the front lines. They set up some canvas to provide them with shade, and a couple of beds underneath it. 'One of the girls had an 11-year-old sister and she would perform fellatio and only got half as much as the girls got for intercourse. She wanted more money, so the girls told her what she had to do. When she serviced the 6th man she passed out.' Rather than take pity on this young girl, the men in the camp appeared to view her simply as a curiosity. 'A buddy and I went to see her,' remembers Williams. 'A man was on her and she didn't even move. The man said that she was really tight but it was like jacking off.'[49]

This little girl was just one child of hundreds who were involved in the sex trade in and around Naples during the war. The men who used them saw no reason to hide the fact; and their comrades did not seem to feel the need to intervene when they did. Williams himself admitted to having sex with girls as young as 12 as well as women in their sixties: his only comment on the matter was that the older women were better because they 'had more experience'.[50]

Thus it was not only young women who found themselves caught up in the communal degradation that arrived in Naples alongside the liberation, but also pre-pubescent girls – each of them 'consumed' by Allied soldiers, much like the 'Siren' at Malaparte's banquet. In August 1944 Ovidio Serafini, the director of a local charity devoted to young girls, painted a dark picture of the unfolding tragedy. Around half of the patients admitted to the Pace hospital for women with venereal disease, he claimed, were minors. 'There is the same proportion in all the other hospitals of the Province and in the Region.'[51]

His numbers were not quite right. The true figures were much less than 50 per cent, but nevertheless quite shocking. Out of the 756 women admitted to the Pace hospital the following month, seven were under the age of 14. Another eighty-two were aged between 15 and 18 – around 11 per cent of the total.[52] But, as everyone knew, these girls were just a small sample of the hundreds, perhaps thousands, who were never discovered by the local police forces. 'There is sadness,' wrote Serafini, 'in seeing little girls ill and pregnant; at 13 and even 12 years of age unconscious of their condition and who continue to play with dolls, ignorant of their state and their ruined future.'[53]

The picture that emerges from all of this would become depressingly familiar over the following years: if Naples was a city under Allied occupation, then the most visible symbol of that occupation was the wholesale exploitation of the city's women. The same scenario would be reproduced all over Italy, and indeed all over Europe, right up until the end of the 1940s. It may have been men who bore the brunt of the violence during battle; but it was almost always women and girls who bore the brunt of the exploitation and retribution that came after the battles had moved on.[54]

I am aware that any discussion of this subject is necessarily problematic. To explore it properly, one must include the voices of those at the very heart of it – the Neapolitan women themselves – and yet these are the very voices that have so far been missing. Prostitution is still a taboo subject in Italy: those who engaged in sex work during the war years have been understandably reluctant to speak about their experiences, especially in any way that is likely to be made public. During the research for this book I have been unable to find any detailed accounts by women involved in prostitution. It seems that no one has been willing to speak openly about sleeping with Allied soldiers for money, or about how doing so affected their lives and their families – for better or for worse. (As a male historian, and a foreigner, I did not even consider the possibility of interviewing Neapolitan women about such a delicate subject myself.)

The unfortunate consequence of this is that almost all the accounts and documents referred to above – some of which are reproduced here for the very first time – were produced by men. Most of them are by men in various positions of power – government officials, army officers, doctors, policemen and so on. But some of them are by ordinary soldiers who themselves used prostitutes, and who, unlike the women they slept with, seem quite happy to admit to it. In other words, throughout these pages it is the occupiers, not the occupied, who get to speak. This is plainly problematic. It is my sincere hope that new research will be forthcoming that redresses the balance, before the voices of this group of Neapolitan women are gone forever.

The 'VD scourge'

The Allied armies did not really care about whether their soldiers had sex with local women or not, even if money changed hands. They did not even particularly seem to care whether their men had sex with underage girls, as long as the fact did not become too public. In all the AMG files I have scoured, I have found no reference to this as a special problem, despite the fact that everyone in Naples knew it was going on: the exploitation of children was treated merely as another form of prostitution.

Each of the different forces had its own way of turning a blind eye. The French had perhaps the most honest and practical policies: they took the view that if their men were going to use prostitutes, the practice should at least be regulated. France had long had a system similar to that in Italy, whereby prostitution was legal as long as it was licensed by the state. In September 1944, just a couple of months after their arrival in Naples, the French opened three official army brothels for white and black troops. Women were recruited locally, and inspected medically three times a week. 'In view of the many criticisms of Allied troops, particularly the Moroccans, accosting women,' noted British observers, 'this move by the French has been well received.'[55]

Constrained by public opinion at home, the British and American armies held a slightly more complicated stance towards prostitution. For the British, brothels were officially out of bounds from the outset

– but, unofficially, many British officers were willing merely to give their men a wink and a nod when they broke the rules. The US Army, meanwhile, remained largely silent on the issue of prostitution. They did not institute official brothels like the French, but neither did they follow the British and prohibit their men from visiting Italian ones. Throughout Europe, according to American historian Mary Louise Roberts, the American policy was one of 'condoning it privately while condemning it publicly'.[56] Thus, while American propagandists were busy painting a picture of their soldiers as pure, clean-cut boys, the army itself did nothing much to ensure that the reality matched the myth. Indeed, some of the more colourful army commanders openly encouraged their men to find sex wherever they could, on the grounds that it would make them better soldiers: 'if they don't fuck, they don't fight', as General Patton famously put it.[57]

Taking their lead from the American combat forces, AMG seemed equally prepared to leave Allied servicemen to their own devices. During the first three months of their administration very little was done to suppress prostitution in Naples: it was considered a matter for the local police to manage under existing Italian law. Thus, despite the usual handful of arrests, on the whole pimps and prostitutes were left to ply their trade up and down the Via Roma, and Allied soldiers on leave were free to wander into the Neapolitan backstreets without hindrance. Virtually the only measure put in place by AMG that might have impeded servicemen in their quest for illicit sex was the 7 p.m. curfew – which, as we have already see in Chapter 7, was widely ignored by everyone.

As the desperation of the people grew, and the demand for women boomed, prostitution began to spill out of the supervised brothels and onto the unregulated streets. The consequences of this did not take long to appear. By the end of the year, rates of venereal disease among Allied troops had become 'alarmingly and disgracefully high'.[58] In the US 82nd Airborne Division, which prided itself on its devotion to 'wine, women and song', almost one in every seven men had contracted VD. In the US 1st Armored Division the figure was almost one in five.[59] By April, the VD rate for all American troops in Italy was running at 168 cases per 1,000 men – more than five times the rate that the US War Department considered acceptable.[60] The problem was not quite so widespread in the British Army, but was nevertheless alarming: British soldiers in Italy were almost twice as likely to end up in hospital with VD compared with those back in the UK, and almost three times as likely as those stationed in the Middle East.[61] Naples was at the heart of this crisis. When the Fifth Army interviewed a sample of 338 soldiers with VD, they discovered that 75 per cent of them had picked up their diseases in Naples.[62]

This was an issue that the Allies could not afford to take lightly: VD was a serious problem that affected a soldier's ability to fight. If left untreated, gonorrhoea could lead to inflammation of the testicles and fevers. Syphilis caused skin lesions, fevers, headaches and a whole host of other symptoms, and could be deadly. High rates of such diseases were potentially disastrous. On average, before the advent of penicillin, a soldier with VD could expect to spend three weeks in hospital: when multiplied by the tens of thousands of cases each year in Italy, this added up to a serious manpower problem.[63] In the words of the regional AMG report for December 1943, 'Venereal disease, next to typhus, provides the most serious problem affecting the health of the troops.'[64]

So it was that at the end of the year the Allied authorities in Naples finally began to take action against the VD crisis. A specialist adviser on VD was appointed – an American medical officer, Major John A. Lewis. From 31 December, brothels were finally declared out of bounds to all Allied soldiers. Shortly afterwards the densely packed residential areas around the Via Roma, where most of the clandestine prostitution took place, were also put off limits. The measure was designed to kill two birds with one stone: 'These areas,' wrote the provost marshal's office, '… are indescribably squalid, and have no shops or anything which could possibly be of interest to troops except for the purpose of having sexual intercourse.'[65]

In the minds of those tasked with dealing with this crisis, local women were to blame. In some army documents, women are described as if they were locusts who 'descended' on Allied camps 'by the hundreds'.[66] Troops were reminded that 'Prostitutes, most of whom were lice-ridden, are particularly dangerous', and that typhus was effectively another form of VD.[67]

Posters in Italian began to appear in Naples and the surrounding towns inviting women to register themselves officially as prostitutes; but at the same time posters in English warned Allied servicemen to avoid those prostitutes at all costs.[68] Even the local people began to warn soldiers, 'Don't go out with the girls here in Naples, they're all sick.'[69] Neapolitan women were portrayed simultaneously as the objects of desire and disgust: they were beautiful temptresses who would lead you to your death – much like the Sirens of ancient myth.

During the course of 1944, AMG waged a campaign that looked less like a war against VD than one against the women of Naples. A conference of VD specialists from every level of the army and AMG urged that all suspected prostitutes 'should be handled on a criminal basis rather than solely as a medical problem'.[70] The provost marshal's office wanted to go even further and 'make sexual intercourse with a local civilian a military crime'; but since this was not possible it recommended the contraction of VD should be made a crime instead. In the meantime, they also suggested a series of draconian measures that targeted women directly: the immediate arrest of all prostitutes, minimum sentences of six months for a first offence, indefinite imprisonment for any woman found to be infected with VD and punitive reformatories for 'child offenders'. The health of the army should be protected at all costs, claimed the deputy provost marshal: 'The campaign against V.D. must be waged just as ruthlessly as that against any other form of sabotage.'[71]

A special vice squad was set up, and a series of sweeps carried out throughout the city. Arrests ballooned. In the first two months of the Allied occupation there had been only a few dozen arrests for clandestine prostitution; but in the three weeks around and after Christmas more than 600 women were arrested, and 230 of them forcibly hospitalized.[72] In February the campaign intensified: 1,413 suspected prostitutes were arrested, 510 of whom were found to be diseased.[73]

The problem with such sweeping arrests was that no distinction was made between professional prostitutes, women who were having legitimate relationships with Allied soldiers and other women who just happened to be in the wrong place at the wrong time. In October, for example, over 1,000 women were arrested, but more than half of them were almost immediately freed again for lack of any evidence of wrong-doing. This 'over-enthusiasm', as the subsequent inquest called it, so offended local women that the Allies were forced to issue new orders to 'only arrest a woman if she is a notorious harlot visibly bearing signs of venereal disease or surprised in the act'.[74] Many Allied soldiers resented the assumption that their local sweethearts were prostitutes, and actively resisted any attempts to arrest them – indeed, local police forces had to be bolstered with Allied MPs to stop fights from breaking out.[75]

The picture that emerges is one in which *every* woman in Naples was assumed to be a prostitute unless proved otherwise. In his role as an intelligence officer, Norman Lewis witnessed many women being treated this way, including one episode where dozens of ordinary housewives, 'some with their shopping bags on their arms', were rounded up and forced to undergo humiliating VD inspections. According to Lewis, many genuine romances between British soldiers and local women were strenuously opposed on the grounds of the supposed dubious moral character of Neapolitan women.[76] The same was true for American soldiers: according to American historian Susan Zeiger, their local romances were deliberately hindered by the US Army, which similarly assumed all Italian women to be prostitutes.[77]

While the Allies were busy stigmatizing Italian women, they still had to deal with their own soldiers. Despite repeated warnings, lectures and educational films about VD, the vast majority of Allied soldiers contin-ued to consort with local women. According to soldiers' surveys carried out by the Americans in 1945, 74 per cent of white GIs and 96 per cent of black GIs admitted to sleeping with women in Italy – and the vast majority of them also admitted to paying for the experience.[78]

Such large numbers of servicemen could not be meaningfully punished without jeopardizing the war effort, so instead the Allies treated the issue like a public health problem. In 1944 they set up 'Prophylaxis Stations' around Naples, where soldiers who had just had sex could disinfect themselves: an uncomfortable process that involved several stages, including the insertion of a pipette into the end of the penis to flush the urethra with iodine solution. In addition, all troops were regularly subjected to 'short-arm inspections' ('short arm' being an army euphemism for a soldier's penis) by their medical officers, who were obliged to report any abnormalities they found. Anyone who showed symptoms of VD was sent to the specialist hospital in Bagnoli, where he received shots of penicillin. This was no picnic: soldiers being treated for syphilis had to endure a punishing schedule of injections every three hours, day and night, for eight days. Nevertheless, this was a great improvement on the drugs on offer before penicillin had become widely available to the army in 1944: earlier treatments with the more primitive sulphonamide drugs had taken weeks, not days, to have any effect. (Penicillin, much like DDT, was one of the miracle substances that saw its first mass use in the treatment of disease in Naples – but unlike DDT it was only available to infected Allied soldiers, not Italian civilians.)

Once a soldier's treatment was over, he was sent back his unit. His only real punishment consisted of an automatic demotion. Inevitably, rates of reoffending and reinfection were high.[79]

Long-Term Consequences

The social consequences of so much prostitution, exploitation and objectification of women were huge. When the Allies first arrived in Naples they were welcomed as liberators, but within a few weeks they were already being regarded as occupiers. The way that they treated women was emblematic of that occupation.

In his memoirs, Norman Lewis recalls with shame the sense of entitlement his fellow soldiers appeared to feel towards the women of Naples. On one occasion, while he was driving through the city with a young American soldier, the GI asked him to stop the car, declaring that he felt like finding himself a woman. Lewis watched as he knocked on the door of a random house, showed them the cans of meat he was carrying in his knapsack and disappeared inside. This was not an uncommon practice. Police and AMG documents from the time show that soldiers throughout the city felt they could knock on any door and demand sex with whichever woman happened to be living there. The

women of Naples, hungry and with families to feed, often felt they had
no choice but to accept such offers and make the best of it; while the
men of the city had no choice but to stand by and watch the exploitation of their womenfolk. As Lewis noted, the old traditions of
Neapolitan courtship had suddenly been replaced by a brutal, wordless
approach, and a crude act of purchase: 'One wonders how long it will
take the young of Naples, after we have gone, to recover from the
bitterness of the experience.'[80]

As 1944 progressed, the behaviour of Allied troops became more
brazen, often taking place in daylight, and in public. In May, for example, an American soldier tried to snatch away a woman who was out
walking with an Italian in the city centre. She resisted, as did the man
who was with her, but eventually the soldier and his buddies had to be
driven away by an angry crowd of Italians 'amidst boos and threats'.
Such behaviour, which was as common in the suburbs as it was in the
city centre, caused a 'high feeling of resentment' everywhere.[81]

In some instances local people took the law into their own hands –
although, once again, it was often the women who bore the brunt of
their anger. In July an American soldier was crossing Piazza Dante with
two Italian women when a large group of local men, led by some
Italian sailors, seized the women and dragged them into a doorway,
where they proceeded to cut off their hair. The GI ran off to get the
military police to intervene, at which point a street fight broke out.
The Allied report of the incident stressed the indignation of the Italian
men, who 'considered that they had a right to safeguard their national
honour'.[82] The shaving of women's heads would become common
practice not only in Italy but throughout Europe in the months to
come, as young, resentful men, who had been more or less powerless
against the might of the German and Allied armies, vented their frustrations instead on the women they felt had betrayed them.[83]

Traumatic events like these had a huge effect on the city of Naples
that would be felt for decades to come. A whole generation of women
were treated as commodities to be bought and sold. Even those women
who were never prostitutes were often assumed to be, not only by
Allied servicemen, but also by the military government and sometimes
by their own countrymen.

The Allied landings at Salerno. *Above*: The battle in the Italian skies was almost as ferocious as that on the ground. (NARA) *Below*: Allied troops and equipment pour off the LSTs and onto the beaches. (NARA)

In defiance of orders, British Army photographer Sgt Stanley Gladstone entered Naples ahead of the troops on 30 September to take some of the very first pictures of the liberation. These two photos appeared in *The Times* (London) a week later. *Above*: 'Hysterical' crowds run to welcome the Allies. *Below*: General Mark Clark, expecting a hero's welcome, arrives to rather less enthusiasm in the east of the city. (IWM)

A combination of Allied bombing and the German scorched earth strategy left large stretches of the Naples waterfront utterly devastated. This photograph was taken the day after the Allies arrived. (NARA)

A sunken hospital ship in Naples harbour. So many vessels were sunk by the departing Germans that Allied engineers built walkways over the top of them and used them as quays. (IWM)

In the early days of the liberation, Naples suffered one humanitarian crisis after another. An acute water crisis, caused by the German destruction of the water mains, was later followed by chronic shortages of all foods. *Above*: A soldier shares his food with Neapolitan children. *Below*: Families queue for water from a broken main in Piazza Mazzini. (NARA)

After their homes had been destroyed, thousands of Neapolitans took up residence in caves and quarries like this one (*above*). Sanitary conditions were appalling, and the crowded conditions provided a perfect incubation ground for the typhus epidemic that gripped the city in the winter of 1943–44. (NARA) *Below*: In the world's first mass anti-typhus campaign, almost a million Neapolitans were dusted with insecticide powder. (NARA)

The infamous *scugnizzi* of Naples are mentioned by almost every serviceman who visited Naples during the war. These young street kids became notorious for acting as pimps and runners for unofficial brothels in the out-of-bounds areas of the city. (NARA)

Spiralling food prices gave many women in Naples little choice but to sell their bodies to Allied servicemen. *Top*: An American sailor takes advantage of the local girls. (ICSR) *Middle*: American soldiers queue up outside a Neapolitan brothel. Official brothels were off limits to British troops. (NARA) *Bottom*: One of the thousands of ordinary women rounded up by police for a compulsory VD examination. Privacy was never a priority. (NARA)

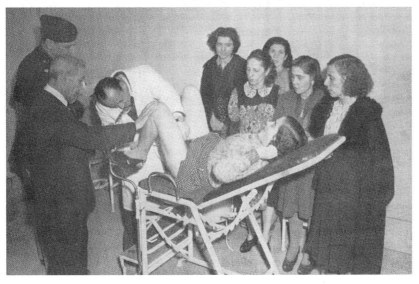

Some Italians began to grumble that they had been reduced from a nation of conquerors to a people who were only fit to clean the boots of their Allied occupiers. In Naples, shoe-shine stations like this one were everywhere. (NARA)

Allied soldiers relax in the palatial setting of the American Red Cross's Continental Club. In contrast to the poverty and squalor that most Neapolitans had to endure, Allied soldiers and staff lived like kings. (NARA)

Nor were women the only victims of this wave of exploitation. Children, too, were caught up in the business of prostitution, not only as child prostitutes themselves, but also as child pimps selling the services of their mothers and sisters. These young boys, the infamous *scugnizzi* of Naples, are mentioned by just about every serviceman who visited Naples during these years. A whole generation of children were exposed to obscenity and exploitation on a scale never before known in the history of the city.

And finally there were the thousands of illegitimate children born during and after the war, who had to live with the stigma for the rest of their lives – particularly those children of black soldiers, who could not even hide their illegitimacy.[84] This, too, would become a feature of the whole country, and indeed the whole of Europe, in the years to come.[85]

CHAPTER 11

Africans

The people of Naples and the south have never been regarded as an integral part of the Italian family, let alone the European community. In the writings of tourists and statesmen they were always treated as a race apart – unpredictable and exotic, charming and terrifying, like the beautiful monsters of ancient legend. In the western imagination, the 'happy *lazzaroni*' of Naples are like the 'noble savages' of the New World: they live in a Garden of Eden, close to nature, untainted by original sin and therefore able without guilt to enjoy the simple pleasures of life – good food, sunshine, sex and song. The price of this primeval joy is to live in poverty and squalor: happy they may be, but they are also poor, uncivilized, unsophisticated – inferior.

The myth of the Neapolitan 'savage' was yet another ancient stereotype that gained currency during the course of the nineteenth century. Alexandre Dumas, celebrated author of *The Three Musketeers*, compared Neapolitans to the 'red Indians' of the American Wild West, claiming that progress frightened them and that they were 'withdrawing before the approach of civilization'.[1] Others likened them to Africans – a comparison that, during the age of empires, inevitably had pejorative connotations. Klemens von Metternich, for example, called Neapolitans 'A half-barbarous people, utterly ignorant, superstitious beyond limit, as ardent and passionate as Africans, who can neither read nor write and whose final argument is always the dagger.'[2] By the middle of the nineteenth century the slur was so common that, when a foreign ambassador confronted Ferdinand II about the 'African' methods he used to repress his own people, the Neapolitan king was able to throw the accusation back in his face: 'Well,' he quipped, 'Africa begins here.'[3]

The racial stereotyping of Neapolitans continued after the Risorgimento. Once Garibaldi had liberated Naples in 1860, the northern politicians and administrators who took over the city routinely called the people here 'corrupt', 'professional liars', 'unstable, lazy and ignorant'.[4] Well-meaning journalists and doctors denounced the 'African' conditions in the slums – Renato Fucini, for example, called the city 'Oriental' and compared it to the worst parts of Cairo.[5] The new governor of Naples, Luigi Farini, was famously scathing about the whole of the south: 'Italy? This is Africa. The Bedouins, compared to these vulgar louts, are the height of civil virtue!'[6]

Such images were still very much alive in the Allied imagination during the Second World War. Allied opinions about Naples were often expressed in explicitly racial terms. Those who had come here directly from North Africa could not help comparing the two experiences. 'When you go into the native quarter in Tunis and Algiers you see some terrible sights,' remembered one British officer, 'but I hadn't actually seen *starving* people before.'[7] Others agreed that the begging in southern Italy was much worse than it had been in the Middle East.[8] Even Norman Lewis called Naples an 'oriental' city.[9]

Some Allied soldiers were openly prejudiced towards the 'I-ties', 'Ginzos' and 'Dagos' they found here. 'They seemed to us a pathetic people, not very strong in character,' wrote the American combat reporter Ernie Pyle. He conceded that most American soldiers 'felt sorry' for them, and eventually 'became sort of fond of them' in a patronizing way; but there was always a hardcore who despised them and thought they should just 'go to hell'.[10] Official attitudes could be equally condescending. The high levels of crime and prostitution in Naples, for example, were ascribed not only to the economic collapse of the city, but also to the low 'moral standards of the Italian people'. Such behaviour was 'normal' in a 'primitive' place like Naples.[11]

In this atmosphere, it is perhaps not surprising that Allied servicemen felt emboldened to act in ways that they would never have considered at home. Far from the eyes of disapproving parents, in an exotic land where pleasure ruled and the people supposedly had few morals, it was easy to convince themselves that they were free to behave however they pleased. When a dose of contempt was added into the mix of emotions as well, some soldiers saw no reason to moderate their conduct at all.

The people of Naples felt this keenly. They knew that they were being treated as 'a conquered people', and sensed that the Allies despised them as 'a race inferior to themselves'.[12] When they heard the racial slurs it reopened the wounds of generations past: the people of southern Italy felt they were once again being treated as the 'Africans' of Europe.

Emotions around this subject ran particularly high in the army. Fights regularly broke out between Italian soldiers and American GIs 'because the latter are in the habit of making depreciating remarks about the Italian Army'. The French commander in Italy, General Alphonse Juin, even ordered his men to behave as 'conquerors' – an instruction that, when it became public, upset just about everyone.[13]

Italian troops knew that they were being treated with contempt. They were expected to work alongside the Allies as co-belligerents, but the vast majority of them were confined to support roles as guards, drivers and labourers. It did not escape their notice that this was exactly how most black soldiers were treated in the US Army: they were trusted to dig ditches, but not to fight on the front line. Unsurprisingly, there were few volunteers for the Italian army in 1944; and when the Allies tried to conscript them, they simply refused to turn up. As one Italian soldier explained, bitterly, this was hardly surprising. 'To see Italy's participation in the war in actual fact, it is enough to go to the Piazza della Carità in Naples and see an Italian soldier wearing a steel helmet and carrying a rifle guarding a drinking tap which is used by Allied soldiers. The only military duty of this sentry is to turn off the tap after some negro or Moroccan soldier has had a drink, and they call this Italy's participation in the war!'[14]

* * *

Neapolitans were not without their own racial prejudices. Before the war, the sight of a black or Asian face among the Neapolitan crowds had been extremely rare; now, suddenly, it was an everyday occurrence. Soldiers from every continent passed through Naples in the last two years of the war. The US Army alone contained troops of all races, including Native Americans, Japanese Americans from Hawaii, and thousands upon thousands of African Americans. The British brought whole regiments of Indian soldiers, as well as Basuto soldiers from South Africa; and the majority of French troops in southern Italy were *goumiers* and *spahis* from Morocco and Algeria. Even the Brazilians made a brief but significant appearance in the city in the summer of 1944. All of these Allied soldiers were wealthier, better fed and more powerful than the vast majority of the local population – making a mockery of the idea of Italian superiority. During the Mussolini years, when Italy had expanded its empire in Africa, many Neapolitans had grown used to the idea that they were the masters of the Mediterranean. Now they were faced with an uncomfortable truth: not only were they the 'Africans' of Europe, they had also become subordinate to actual Africans.

Neapolitans reacted to this situation in a whole variety of ways. Some people genuinely did not care about race and gladly welcomed all Allied soldiers: they opened their homes to black soldiers, sometimes fell in love with them, even married them – despite the disapproval of the US Army.[15] Some African Americans who passed through Italy in 1944 were genuinely touched by the welcome they received: 'I felt safer in Italy than I did in Alabama,' confessed one black GI in later years.[16] But there were others who were not nearly so welcoming. Some middle-class Italians, particularly those with links to the old regime, wrote with undisguised racism about the African Americans in their midst. 'The city is full of enormous negroes,' wrote the publisher Leo Longanesi in his diary towards the end of 1943, 'who walk about, slow and shambling, with their long arms hanging down and their huge hands open like bat wings. They wander around the city ... on the hunt for girls, for watches, for fountain pens and for alcohol.'[17] For such people, who had gloried in Mussolini's African conquests in the 1930s, the subordination of Italians to black soldiers seemed the ultimate humiliation.

Elena Canino, the wife of a prominent Neapolitan architect, also wrote despairingly about this 'shame'. In the immediate aftermath of the liberation she found herself stranded outside the city, begging for a lift from one of the passing Allied jeeps. When she approached an English soldier for help, he refused even to acknowledge her. Meanwhile, African American soldiers in passing vehicles enthusiastically threw her pieces of candy, which fell in the dust at her feet. She felt simultaneously rejected by those she considered her racial equals, and humiliated by the generosity of those she considered her inferiors. 'I finally understand the difference between winners and losers,' she remarked, bitterly.[18]

A few weeks later, this same diarist came across an encampment of African American soldiers in the suburb of Arenella, on the northern fringes of the city. One of the Americans, a cook, was handing out food to a crowd of hungry people gathered at the perimeter of the camp. He offered her a piece of bread filled with beans, telling her kindly that there was no shame in being hungry; but rather than see his kindness, all she could see was her own humiliation. 'I felt horror, pity and hunger. During the war the people used to say "One day we'll have our shoes cleaned by the English." Now we are reduced to begging from negroes.' The rest of the crowd did not seem to share her shame or her racist views: indeed, some of the other women were openly flirting with these 'devils' (or, as she put it, 'offering themselves to the greed of their long monkey hands'). In Elena Canino's telling, scenes like this were the ultimate proof of Italy's complete moral and physical defeat.[19]

Scoundrels

The fear of women becoming the sexual playthings of foreign soldiers has always been a motif of societies at war. Rightly or wrongly, the strength and purity of a nation has often become associated with the purity and fidelity of its women. A nation that cannot protect its women is doomed to defeat; and women who sleep with the enemy are a sign of national corruption. Such ideas have historically been used to spur people on to fight harder for the protection of their homeland;

but they have also been responsible for the deliberate use of sexual violence during wartime, particularly during the Second World War. The use of rape by the Red Army as a weapon of revenge and humiliation in 1945 is just one example of where such ideas can lead. The head-shaving of European women who had consorted with Germans during the war is another.[20]

The addition of race brings yet another dimension to this dangerous cocktail of ideas. The foreign soldier becomes all the more frightening when he speaks a different language and has different customs and different coloured skin. The humiliation of defeat is all the greater when the soldiers taking a nation's women come from a race that is supposedly 'inferior'.

All of these ideas – race, sex, fear and humiliation – came together during the spring of 1944 as the Allied armies crept slowly through the mountainous countryside north of Naples. The widespread rape of Italian women by French colonial troops is an aspect of the Italian campaign that is rarely acknowledged by the Allies or by Italians. It is made all the more shameful by the fact that the soldiers guilty of these acts were supposed to be coming as liberators.

Relations between the French and the Italians during this time were notoriously bad. The French had still not forgiven the Italians for the way that they attacked them in the summer of 1940, and occupied parts of southeast France. Fights between French and Italian troops were common enough to be documented in British intelligence reports; and even ordinary British soldiers commented that 'the French were a bit anti-Italian because of the "stab in the back"'.[21] It was not only General Juin who insisted that the Italians were a 'conquered' people: this was a common feeling throughout the French army in Italy, who, by their own admission, were 'not yet well integrated into the atmosphere of co-belligerence'.[22]

Almost as soon as the French arrived in Italy reports began to come in of some of their troops – particularly Moroccan *goumiers* – preying on the local population. In mid-February 1944 Moroccan soldiers near the town of Sessa Aurunca tied up a farmer and 'seduced' his wife, before making off with all of the family's money and supplies of flour.[23] Over the following months, French colonial troops became notorious for forcing their way into houses, stealing property, raping women and girls, and shooting any civilian who tried to stand in their way.[24] By the summer large parts of Caserta province were living in fear: 'The peasants are deserting their fields,' reads one PWB report, 'because they are afraid of the soldiers.'[25] The same thing happened in Avellino province: when French colonial troops arrived they caused such alarm that 'no civilian will go out after dark'.[26] In Brindisi, discipline broke down so badly that Italian soldiers formed their own vigilante squads to protect local women, resulting in street battles between Italians and Moroccan troops.[27]

Part of the problem was that the French military hierarchy did not appear to be taking such accusations seriously. Indiscipline among the colonial troops was rarely punished, and AMG officials reported that it was 'impossible to get any satisfaction from the French Provost Marshal', who repeatedly refused to take any action, or even to answer complaints.[28] French documents of the time show that white French officers rarely tried to control their men – partly out of loyalty to them, but also because they had their own racist assumption about colonial troops being 'dominated by rather primitive urges' that needed to be fulfilled.[29] The British also explained such behaviour away by referring to North African traditions of warfare: 'The Africans are used to comporting themselves in this way when advancing victoriously in a hostile region.'[30] The fact that Italy was not supposed to be a 'hostile region' did not seem to have registered with the soldiers themselves.

If such were the attitudes in the rear areas, things were far worse on the front lines, particularly in the remote mountain regions where the fiercest fighting took place. French colonial troops were an important part of the advance through the Aurunci Mountains between Itri and Campodimele, and were well regarded for their skills in irregular warfare. But discipline was much more difficult to maintain here, and these troops rapidly became a law unto themselves.

'They arrived like Zulus from the mountains,' said one woman who was raped by four Moroccan soldiers in turn. 'They pointed guns at our heads, making us really afraid, then they began to abuse us.'[31] Another girl told how her mother was raped in front of the whole family – she herself was only spared because her mother had thrown a

sheet over her as if she were sick. 'This was what the Allies did to us':
they were 'true beasts that had nothing human about them'.[32]

At this time the mountain communities around Campodimele and
Lenola were full of refugees who had been forcibly evacuated from the
coast by the Germans. They were then subjected to bombardment by
Allied artillery, before 'a flood of soldiers' swept over them.[33] Such
people, who were already shell-shocked, had nowhere to stay and did
not know where to hide, were easy prey for the 'devils' who came to
attack them.

'I was eleven years old,' remembered one girl, years later. 'My
mother had a little baby that she was giving milk to, and she had my
other sister under her clothes so as not to get taken. So they took me.'
Her father tried to chase them away, but they threw a bottle at him as
a warning to keep away. Then they dragged her outside into the field.
'The beatings, the blows ... they thrashed me, they did everything to
me, they violated me, they hurt me, everything ... there were five or six
of them.' Later her family came and found her in the dark. She could
no longer walk. In the weeks to come they took her to a midwife, who
was horrified by what she saw: 'My girl they have ruined you, how they
have ruined you!' she said. 'I don't know how you're alive ...'[34]

In the early 2000s, Neapolitan historian Gabriella Gribaudi collected
dozens of interviews with women who told similarly horrific stories of
gang rapes, the rape of children, the rape of men and boys, murder,
mutilation and massacre. It is impossible to know how many crimes
were committed by French colonial troops during these terrible weeks,
but in the aftermath of the war there were 209 accusations of sexual
violence in the village of Lenola alone, 63 from Campodimele, reports
of another 75 in Ceccano, and so on through the towns of Prossedi,
Pisterzo, Sezze, Priverno ... Gribaudi estimated that around 2,000
women had been raped in the province of Littoria (present-day Latina)
alone, and perhaps another 1,100 in the neighbouring province of
Frosinone. This is almost certainly an underestimate: the true numbers
could be far higher.[35]

In the aftermath of these attacks, many of the women affected found
it very difficult to rebuild their lives. Some of them would struggle in
their family relationships forever afterwards. Others would find them-

selves shunned by their communities, and especially by the men who might otherwise have become their lovers and husbands. 'They said we'd got Moroccan diseases,' explained one woman. 'Many women never married or had to be content marrying whomever they could,' said another. 'You were considered soiled, sick, they thought of you in a certain way.'[36] Nor was it only the women who were affected: men, too, had to remember the shame of being powerless to protect their wives, sisters and daughters. Close-knit communities in many parts of Campania and Lazio were stunned by a sense of communal trauma.

It was not only the bonds between Italians that were damaged by such events: the bonds between the local people and their supposed liberators were also irrevocably spoiled. 'They were scoundrels, not liberators,' claimed one woman, long after the war was over. The word she used for 'scoundrel' was, significantly, the same word that the grand tourists of the nineteenth century had always associated with the happy-go-lucky people of the Italian south – *lazzaroni*. 'They were scoundrels, the Moroccans, but the Americans were also scoundrels because they had allowed that rabble to do so many things.'[37]

Only a very few dared consider the distant possibility that generations of Italians and other Europeans might also share a tiny part of the blame. 'They did so many of those things to us,' as one woman put it, 'because the Italians in Africa had done the same.'[38] As will become clear, almost everyone at the time knew that the Italian armed forces had behaved atrociously during the conquest of Libya and other parts of Africa earlier in the century. While this can never excuse the behaviour of African troops in Italy, it might at least provide another dimension to the explanation for it. Even at the time, there was an unspoken understanding that in this new, world war the brutalities of European colonialism were finally coming home to Europe itself.

The rapes that took place in the mountain communities north of Naples only widened the racial divides between the local Italian population and the many varieties of dark-skinned troops who were taking part in the liberation of their country. The image of savage 'devils' preying on the Italian people, while wholly appropriate when describing the plight of the women in Littoria and Frosinone, inevitably spilled into the stereotyping of other black soldiers who had nothing to do with these crimes. In the coming weeks a whole series of disturbances occurred in which race was a factor, including attacks on Indian soldiers, and stones being thrown at peaceful Basuto soldiers sitting quietly in their camp.[39] American GIs also increasingly found themselves the targets of racial abuse from Italians. 'The brutalities of the Moroccans in the north are beginning to create a colour problem all over Italy, which is beginning to have its reactions on the American coloured troops,' stated one intelligence report in July 1944. 'This situation is very likely to cause real trouble in the immediate future, together with the fact that Italian men are beginning to resent seeing their women constantly in the company of Allied soldiers.'[40]

Some of this might have been avoided if the Allies had dealt with French indiscipline when it first arose. Their failure to do so would have tragic consequences later in the war – not only in other parts of Italy as the front lines advanced, but also in other parts of Europe. French colonial troops also took part in the conquest of Germany at the beginning of 1945, particularly in the southern states of Baden and Württemberg. According to Christabel Bielenberg, an English woman who lived in a village near the Black Forest, Moroccan troops 'raped up and down our valley' as soon as they arrived. Later they were replaced with other troops from the Sahara who 'came at night and surrounded every house in the village and raped every female between 12 and 80'. What happened in the mountains north of Naples, therefore, was a tragic foretaste of what was yet to come. The violent treatment of women across Europe would continue into 1945, and long after the war was supposed to be over.[41]

CHAPTER 12

A Brief History of Resentment

As the war progressed in the spring and summer of 1944, the Allied authorities in Naples were infused with an uncomfortable feeling that trouble was brewing for the future. They had arrived with such good intentions, but their hopes of a clean and efficient liberation and an orderly transition to civilian rule had degenerated into a series of unforeseen crises, botched policies and strained relations with an increasingly resentful population. There was much they could be proud of – particularly their rapid reconstruction of essential services in the city and their handling of the typhus epidemic. But their inability to feed the people, or to protect them from huge and unsustainable rises in the cost of living, had quickly undermined much of the goodwill with which the Italians had first greeted them.

The list of Allied failures in the first nine months of their occupation of Naples would have been catastrophic for any elected peacetime government. They had failed to provide homeless Neapolitans with places to live, and had indeed made the housing crisis much worse by requisitioning large numbers of buildings for their own use. They had failed to rebuild the essential industries that had been destroyed both by their own bombs and by the departing Germans, thus denying the local workforce decent, paying jobs. They had watched, powerless, as the local economy disintegrated and inflation raged out of control. As will be shown later in the book, they had also failed to bring much-needed reforms to the Italian system of government, or to give local people any meaningful say in the management of their own lives. Italians of all political persuasions were clamouring for the rebirth and renewal of all their public institutions; instead they found themselves still being managed by a combination of former Fascists and foreign soldiers with little or no experience of dealing with Italian needs and desires.

Given the demands of the war, all these failures might have been forgiven – had it not been for the behaviour of the Allied troops themselves. The British and Americans had been welcomed into Naples as saviours, but they had rapidly turned the city into their playground, and its people – particularly its women – into their playthings. They had quickly gained a reputation for arrogance and insensitivity, for public drunkenness and all kinds of other bad behaviour, and, along with the French, for violent crimes against civilians that were almost always committed with impunity.

The rest of Europe watched all this with growing trepidation. Over the coming year, the same failures would be repeated again and again not only in other parts of Italy but also in France, Belgium, Luxembourg, the Netherlands, Greece, and ultimately in Germany and Austria. Some of these failures were probably inevitable, given the desperate circumstances of the war. But many of them might have been softened if only the Allies had devoted a little more time, thought and resources to the problem of how to deal with the civilian populations under their care. It was in Naples, along with the rest of southern Italy and Sicily, that these mistakes were first made, and the template for Allied Military Government in Europe was first laid down.

In the summer of 1944, it was becoming increasingly clear that the time to come was likely to be one of increasing trouble and political unrest. I shall cover some of this future in Part III. But alongside this 'time to come' was also a 'time before'. The pre-history of the Allied arrival was a mystery to most of the men and women arriving in Naples for the first time – indeed, it remains a mystery to most non-Italian readers today. In most British and American accounts of the war in Italy, the Italians themselves are usually little more than passive bystanders in a violent drama whose main protagonists are always the Allies and the Germans.

The same was true in 1943 and 1944. When soldiers, nurses and administrators stepped off the ships in Naples harbour, they had no real idea about Naples at all beyond all the usual clichés. The first impressions of a handful of Women's Army Corps members speak volumes. 'I don't know what I expected, but I think I'm a little disappointed,' said one woman when she arrived in Naples in December 1943. Others, equally fresh off the boat, expressed surprise that Naples had lots of modern buildings, and that some of its shops sold ice cream. The streets were pretty filthy, they said, 'but they're picturesque at that'.[1]

And yet they could tell almost immediately that something was not quite right here. The massive destruction of the port spoke of some unspeakable violence that had taken place before the Allies arrived. 'The conditions under which a lot of the people live touches me deeply,' said Private Yolanda Alcuri, 'especially the little kids.' And there were hints of something dangerous and predatory just beneath the surface. 'I think I'm a little scared of the Italian men,' said Jean Bambeck, a T-5 from Ohio. 'The shops are lovely, but you can't shop because you're always stopped by American soldiers.' Naples was not what they imagined.[2]

For some of the men arriving here for the first time, the growing undercurrents of violence and resentment were much more immediate. Thomas Lister, a British driver with the Durham Light Infantry, arrived in Naples in 1944. As he and his fellow soldiers were marching from the docks with all their equipment, 'one of the young lads stepped out and spat right in my face and told me – and I had enough Italian to understand – "I hope you die!"' Before Lister had time to react, the man's friends dragged him away back into the crowd. Lister never found out what had driven this man to act in such a way; all he knew for certain was that it must have been something that had happened before he arrived.[3]

It is this 'time before' that we shall turn to next. For it is impossible to understand the dynamic between the Neapolitan people and their Allied liberators without first understanding how Neapolitans saw themselves, how they inhabited their own story, which had begun long before their liberators arrived. The same people who could spit in the face of Allied soldiers had also spat in the face of the Germans, as indeed they had spat in the faces of all of the foreign powers that had occupied the city throughout its long and troubled history.

Parthenope had never been the passive bystander that outsiders imagined her to be. When threatened, she had risen up like the beautiful monster she was and fought tooth and nail for her own survival.

PART II

Uprising

CHAPTER 13

Dreams of Revolution

Naples has never been the happy-go-lucky paradise of tourist dreams. A mere glance through its history is enough to demonstrate that this land of song and plenty has just as often been a land of revolution and turmoil. In medieval and Renaissance times, according to one German scholar, there were no fewer than fifty-four rebellions in the Kingdom of Naples – an average of at least one every ten years.[1] Even during the so-called golden age, when the Bourbon kings were in power, there were a series of full-blown revolutions: in 1799, in 1820 and again in 1848. These are not the actions of the 'happy *lazzaroni*' of Goethe's imagination. They speak of a people who are passionate and quick to anger, as wild and volatile as the volcano that looms over the Neapolitan landscape.

Perhaps the most famous revolt to have taken place in this city occurred in July 1647. The trouble began the previous year, when a new Spanish viceroy came to the city and began imposing new taxes on the people. There were already taxes on every aspect of Neapolitan life – even prostitution carried a tax under the Spanish – but until the arrival of the Duke of Arcos, Rodrigo Ponce de León, the buying and selling of fruit had traditionally been exempt. Fruit was one of the few foodstuffs that the poor could still afford. So when the duke introduced a new fruit tax the people reacted in the only way they could: they refused to pay it.

The revolt was led by a disaffected fish seller in his late twenties named Tomaso Aniello – or 'Masaniello', as he was more popularly known. Like most of the ordinary people of Naples, Masaniello had lived all his life on the margins of extreme poverty. By all accounts he was a much-loved figure among the market folk, but also notorious for his tendency to pick fights with the excise men. On 7 July 1647 he staged a demonstration in the fruit market, where two of his relatives refused to pay the tax. Things quickly escalated into a riot and, with Masaniello at their head, a mob nearly 1,000 strong rampaged through the city streets.[2]

The riot had the flavour of a spontaneous uprising, but in fact it had been a long time coming. The original brains behind the revolt was a local scholar named Giulio Genoino, who had been pressing the Spanish authorities to allow Neapolitans a greater say in their own affairs for almost thirty years. Under Genoino's tutorship, Masaniello had spent several weeks gathering together a small army of followers under the guise of organizing them for a midsummer entertainment. Genoino thought he was pulling the strings: he could not have predicted how charismatic Masaniello would be as a leader, nor how far his revolt would end up going.

Over the course of the next few days, Masaniello's army of market traders, beggars and rebellious youths ransacked the armouries and threw open the doors of the local prisons. They set fire to the tax offices and the homes of several corrupt officials and aristocrats and, according to one contemporary observer, made Naples 'burn like Troy'.[3] The Spanish viceroy, cowering in the Castel Nuovo, was forced to give in to Masaniello's demands: the hated tax on fruit was abolished, along with various other taxes. A more democratic form of local government was also agreed; and a general amnesty was granted to all who had taken part in the uprising.

Unfortunately for Masaniello, this most celebrated moment of Neapolitan history did not last long. The mob, or at least a portion of them, soon began to tire of their leader's enthusiasm. When he appeared intoxicated before a crowd at the church of the Madonna del Carmine and began declaiming his fellow citizens, he was taken away to the convent next door and murdered. While those who actually killed him were almost certainly agents of the viceroy, the people of Naples were complicit in the betrayal. They dragged his body triumphantly through the streets before abandoning it among the detritus on the beach; meanwhile his head, which had been hacked off, was paraded through the streets on a pike.

In the coming months, Masaniello's revolt would become the inspiration for a much wider revolution throughout Campania and other parts of the Italian south. A new Neapolitan republic was declared, and French forces were drawn in to help. For a while there were hopes that the Spanish could be driven from the region for good, and Masaniello's name became famous among revolutionaries across Europe. But by the following spring, the Spanish had regained control of both the city and its hinterland. They would continue to rule Naples for almost the next sixty years.

In the centuries since his death, Masaniello has become one of the most celebrated figures in Neapolitan history. He has lived on in the popular imagination as tragic cross between a folk hero and a Christian martyr – a little like Robin Hood, William Tell and San Gennaro all rolled into one.[4] He has been the subject of paintings, sculpture, music, literature and even puppet shows. At the turn of the twentieth century he was frequently the subject of spectacular theatre productions: on one occasion the cast became so enthusiastic during the revolution scenes that several of them had to be admitted to hospital.[5] He was always a favourite of the Neapolitan Socialists and Communists, who saw Masaniello as an archetype for their own struggles against a tyrannical system.[6] Even after the outbreak of the Second World War, the legendary Neapolitan actor Raffaele Viviani attempted to put on a production of the story, much to the disapproval of the Fascist authorities. In Viviani's depiction, Masaniello was 'essentially a martyr of that same people to whom he had given everything, managing in eight days to free them from Spanish taxes and bring them to a much higher standard of living, both from an economic and moral point of view'.[7]

For others, however, there were darker lessons to be learned from Masaniello's story. Writing in 1925, the liberal historian Michelangelo Schipa pointed out that, despite all of its drama and glory, in the long run the 1647 rebellion achieved none of its aims. The people were firmly put back in their place, and within a year were being exploited just as they had always been, without recourse to any kind of democracy.

The judgement of Benedetto Croce was even more damning. Masaniello's revolt, he wrote, ended like all 'proletarian movements with neither head nor tail': Masaniello himself was eradicated; the idea of greater democracy was forgotten; and the rulers of Naples were infused 'with a deep-seated fear of the citizenry and a preoccupation with the means of keeping it under control'.[8] It is not much of a leap, when reading these words, to see echoes in Croce's own time, when socialism – and indeed democracy itself – was in the process of being likewise crushed beneath the boots of tyrants.

Nevertheless, the legend of Masaniello provides a useful counterpoint to the myth of the gentle, pleasure-loving *bon viveurs* of western imagination. The various armies who passed through Naples in the 1940s might have learned something from the story: the people of Naples should never be taken for granted.

CHAPTER 14

Queen of the Mediterranean

On 24 October 1922, Benito Mussolini appeared before an audience at the San Carlo Theatre in Naples to set out what he was offering the people of Italy. Over the previous years the country had been rocked by a series of crises: a disastrous war against Austria, a post-war recession, industrial unrest, violent protests by Socialist militants, and an even more violent response by Mussolini's own followers. Now the whole country appeared to be on the brink of civil war. Mussolini was about to launch what would turn out to be a *coup d'état*, but he was here to reassure the people of Naples that they had nothing to fear – that, on the contrary, revolution and conquest was their destiny. The Fascists were on the brink of seizing power, and by doing so they would restore pride and a sense of purpose to the people as a whole.

'We have created our own myth,' he told them. 'Our myth is the greatness of the nation. To this myth, to this greatness, which we desire to translate into a comprehensive reality, we subordinate everything …' The people of Naples might share in this myth, both as a part of the Italian nation and as a proud people in their own right, if only they would bend to Mussolini's will. Under his leadership, their city would once again become not only 'the burning soul of the south of Italy' but the 'Queen of the Mediterranean'.[1]

Like all populist demagogues, Mussolini was trying to have his cake and eat it. In this famous speech, delivered just before the 'march on

Rome', he was appealing to a sense of local identity by invoking a time before the Risorgimento, when Naples had been the centre of its own kingdom, and ruler of its own destiny. But at the same time he was also invoking the spirit of the Risorgimento itself, and subordinating Naples to a larger dream of Italian glory. The 'future greatness of Naples' would come from it being both 'queen' and subject, ruler and ruled.

It was in these moments that the first seeds of the Second World War were sown. Had the people and politicians of Italy stood up to Mussolini in the days that followed, pointed out the contradictions of what he was saying, and actively opposed his revolution, some of the disasters of the next twenty years might have been avoided. But when it mattered most, Italy's leaders let the nation down: rather than resist Mussolini's march on Rome, the king, the army and the vast majority of the liberal establishment simply stood aside and watched.

The Contradictions of Violence

Fascism was founded on violence. The movement was born in the street fights against Socialists during the early 1920s; it seized power through the threat of civil war and the violent intimidation of voters; and it eradicated all competition by beating, threatening and eventually assassinating its opponents. Without violence there would never have been a Fascist regime in Italy, and its leader would have remained a minor figure in Italian history – just another newspaper editor with delusions of grandeur.

The story of Fascist violence has been told many times before, but most historians concentrate on events that took place in the north, because this is where most of the violence took place.[2] In the south, by all accounts, the people were more apathetic and the politicians more willing to sell themselves out to the Fascists: after decades of misman-agement and corruption under the Liberals, few in the south had enough faith in the political system to believe it worth fighting for.[3] Nevertheless, there was plenty of Fascist violence here as well, particu-larly in Naples and its satellite towns. Street fights were common, union leaders were regularly beaten up, Socialist marches were broken up by thugs with clubs, knives, guns and even hand grenades. On one occasion a Fascist squad even opened up on a peaceful march with a machine gun.[4]

Political violence here was every bit as commonplace as it was in the north. In fact, when the Italian Socialist Party won control of several *comuni* during the local elections of 1920, the Fascists here reacted with a speed and efficiency that their counterparts in some parts of the north could only envy. In Castellammare di Stabia, for example, Fascist gunmen manufactured a riot in January 1921, before joining the local Carabinieri in an armed siege of the town hall. In the massacre that followed at least five civilians were killed and another 100 put in hospital. The Socialists were accused of firing the first shot – and despite the fact that no conclusive proof to that effect was ever discovered, the democratically elected council was removed from office and replaced with a more 'acceptable' alternative. It had lasted just two months in office.[5]

Not long after, a similar event took place in Capua, just north of Naples – again with the connivance of the official authorities. At the end of March 1921, 200 armed Fascists broke into the town hall, beat up the councillors, took the mayor hostage and burned the local labour office to the ground. When local people demonstrated outside the town hall calling for the restoration of law and order, they were attacked on one side by the Carabinieri and on the other by the same Fascists who had caused all the trouble in the first place.[6] Similar events also took place in Torre Annunziata, another Socialist stronghold just south of Naples.[7]

It was not only in the north, therefore, where targeted political violence had a huge effect on public life. The leader of the Neapolitan Fascists, Aurelio Padovani, was just as ruthless as Roberto Farinacci or Italo Balbo were in the north.[8] Rates of violence were almost as high here as they were in Tuscany or the Po Valley.[9] If anything, the Fascist campaign of political intimidation here was more successful than it was in any other part of Italy.[10] So it was for good reason that, when Mussolini decided to launch his *coup d'état* in October 1922, it was from Naples, not Milan, that he began his 'March on Rome'.

The Fascists, like the Socialists before them, saw no problem with political violence like this. Indeed, even more than the Socialists, they gloried in the aesthetics of violence. Fascist *squadristi* dressed up in quasi-military uniforms and fetishized the weapons they carried. The Browning pistol, claimed one *squadrista*, was 'The only thing which a Fascist loves with an almost carnal love.'[11] Others idolized the *manganello* – a club or truncheon, often weighted with lead. They even created their own obscene patron saint, an image of the mother of Christ carrying her infant in one hand, and a club in the other: the 'Madonna of the Manganello'. For such people violence was not merely a means to an end, it was also an end in itself: it was the force that gave their movement meaning, and their members an identity.[12]

The legitimacy of violence was the central paradox of Fascist belief in the 1920s. Fascist leaders were fond of claiming that the law could only be served by breaking the law, and that revolution should be made a part of a state: in the words of Roberto Farinacci, their intention was 'to legalize Fascist illegality'.[13]

Following similar logic, other paradoxes ensued: it was only by submitting to Fascism that the Italian people could become strong; it was only through slavish obedience that they would find freedom; and it was only through violence that they would find peace. 'Italy wants peace, tranquillity, calm in which to work,' announced Mussolini in parliament at the beginning of 1925. 'We shall give her this tranquillity … by force if necessary.'[14]

As time wore on, the Fascist regime began to direct its violence externally as well as internally. Italy went to war repeatedly in the 1920s and 1930s. In Somalia, Mussolini's Blackshirts embarked on a campaign of horrific repression, including massacring civilians and shelling mosques.[15] At the beginning of the 1930s they turned their attention to North Africa, where they embarked on a genocidal campaign to crush dissent against Italian imperial rule. Over the course of three years they interned at least 100,000 Bedouin people in concentration camps where more than 40,000 of them died.[16] In 1935 Ethiopia was invaded, entirely unprovoked, in order to satisfy the Fascist urge for further 'greatness' in the expansion of empire: new atrocities followed, including the mass use of poison gas.[17] Then came the Spanish Civil War, in which Italian troops supported Franco's nationalist regime by conducting a terror campaign from the air. After the bombing of Barcelona in 1938, Mussolini declared himself 'delighted that the Italians should be horrifying the world by their aggressiveness for a change, instead of charming it by their skill at playing the guitar'.[18]

Once again, such violence was glorified, even celebrated, in Italian public life. 'I adore violence', declared the futurist poets, in poems that proclaimed the beauty of violent death and world-shattering explosions.[19] 'I want to cry ITALY with my chest torn open by a bomb,' wrote Piero Bellanova in a poem called 'Joy'.[20] Mussolini's own son, Vittorio, who flew bombers during Italy's brief but atrocious war against Ethiopia, wrote enthusiastically about how 'extremely entertaining' it was to drop bombs on helpless civilians and watch groups of them 'blooming open like a rose'.[21]

According to Fascist ideology, war was not a destructive force but a force for glory, honour and national renewal. It was the urge for war that drove many of Mussolini's development plans in the 1930s, not least around Naples. New industries opened up around the city, such as the brand new Alfa Romeo aero-engine factory at Pomigliano d'Arco. Huge sums of government money were ploughed into other war industries, such as the steelworks at Bagnoli, and the shipyards of Castellammare di Stabia. Like many of the big industrial cities of the north, Naples at the end of the 1930s was buzzing with new activity. But more important than this was the new sense of pride that had been engendered here by the rediscovery of Italy's martial spirit.

The people of Naples knew that their city was at the heart of Italy's new culture of conquest and imperial expansion. It was here that many of the ships were built that sailed across the sea to North Africa. This was the port from which troops embarked to Libya and Spain, and to which 20,000 Italian legionaries would return in triumph in June 1939. And it was to Naples that Mussolini brought Hitler in 1938 when he wanted to impress him with a vast naval parade of 200 ships.

Mussolini had promised the people of Naples that he would make their city into 'the Queen of the Mediterranean': now at last it seemed that this promise was coming true. As Hitler launched his attack on northern Europe, Italy prepared to reap the benefits in the south, with Naples taking its rightful place as the metropolis of the Mediterranean world. As 1940 dawned, students took to the streets of Naples with placards calling for new wars – against Tunisia, against Corsica, against France itself.[22]

Few of them stopped to wonder what the logical conclusion of this endless love for violence might be. Or what would happen once the bombs began to fall, and the bodies of Italian civilians also began to bloom like roses on the streets of Naples.

The Contradictions of Development

Naples on the eve of war was a city reborn. During the previous twenty years an astonishing transformation had taken place, with building projects appearing all over the city. In the ancient centre, the medieval religious complex of St Thomas Aquinas had been torn down and replaced with new, modern buildings made of concrete and steel. A monumental new headquarters for the Bank of Naples was built on the Via Roma, and an even bigger new post office building was constructed on Via Monteoliveto. The port had also been modernized, with a bright new maritime station for tourists and travellers arriving by sea. There were new roads, new tunnels, new tramways and railway lines, and a new funicular linking Vomero to the ancient centre below. Entire new suburbs had been built – Vasto and Arenaccia in the east of the city, and Fuorigrotta in the west, where the streets were wide and spacious and named after ancient Roman emperors. This was the soul of the new Naples, where the silver roofs of trolley buses shimmered in the sun as they carried the youth of Italy towards a bright and 'certain future'.[23]

Naples was at the centre of a much wider metamorphosis that was taking place all over the province, and in the countryside beyond. Under the Fascists, by all accounts, this whole region of Italy had been transformed from a troubled backwater into a cultural, industrial and agricultural powerhouse. The Pontine Marshes, which lay between Rome and Naples, were drained. Vast areas of uncultivated land, 'abandoned for centuries and reduced to pasture for herds of buffalo', were harnessed to the national economy for the first time in a bid to make Italy self-sufficient in food production.[24] Whole new towns were constructed – Littoria, Sabaudia, Pontinia, Aprilia – founded on the Fascist principles of progress, discipline and national pride.

South of Naples, a new road and rail network connected remote villages to the city for the first time. New industries were founded all along the bay: glassworks, chemical plants and metallurgical factories in San Giovanni a Teduccio and a new cement factory in Castellammare di Stabia.[25] New excavations of the ruins of Pompeii were authorized, and the whole of the ancient site was lit up at night for the first time by 500 searchlights. The message was simple: the glory that once was, shall be again.[26]

If all the newspapers, public speeches and propaganda of the time are to be believed, the transformation of Naples and the south was a miracle, conceived and carried out by the Fascists alone, with the unconditional support of the Neapolitan people. Mussolini had brought an end to the 'southern problem', and fostered a new sense of pride in the people of Naples and the whole of the Mezzogiorno. It seemed like an unqualified success story.

But things are never so simple. Many of the programmes that the Fascists took credit for had in fact been started by the Liberals much earlier in the century. Nor were they as planned and organized as Mussolini tried to pretend they were. Indeed, much of the development in Naples had actually been quite chaotic and piecemeal: the Fascists did not come up with any comprehensive plan for the city until 1939, by which point the approach of war had already made it redundant. As a consequence, most of the housing created was not the sort that the city desperately needed – it was unaffordable to most of the population, and was built purely to make a profit for developers wishing to cash in on the city's beautiful location.[27]

As ever, there was a vast gulf between what Mussolini promised and what he actually delivered. The pursuit of 'greatness', or at least the illusion of greatness, always outweighed what the people of Naples actually wanted or needed. A disproportionate amount of government

money went not on housing, sewers and schools, but on grandiose
buildings and vanity projects, such as the monumental new post office
– propaganda pieces built from metal and stone, whose main purpose
was to proclaim the greatness of Fascism to the world.

Meanwhile, poverty and overcrowding only became worse. In the
ten years after the Fascists seized power, almost every district in the
centre of Naples became more overcrowded, with the poorest 20 per
cent of the population living four or five to a room. Infant mortality
rates were running at 10 per cent. Unemployment soared. The gap
between rich and poor grew. The gap between Naples and the cities of
the north also grew: for all the new development that occurred in
Naples during the 1920s, three times as many new dwellings were
created in Milan and Turin, and four times as many in Rome.[28]

One could not speak of these problems because they contradicted
Mussolini's 'myth of greatness'. Instead of confronting the problems of
the Mezzogiorno, the Fascists tried to hide them. Thus, when unemployment in Naples became embarrassingly high in 1928, the
authorities simply expelled 5,000 unemployed from the city. Their
method of dealing with the infamous *bassi* of Naples – those single-
room, windowless basement dwellings where so many of the poor lived
– was similar. Various ordinances were issued in 1924, 1928, 1934 and
1936 declaring their closure: families were simply evicted and expected
to find somewhere else to live – and in the vast majority of cases no
alternative provisions were made for them. The underclasses had no
place in Mussolini's new society: in the pursuit of 'greatness', the poor
and the weak had to be swept away.[29]

What was true in Naples was also true in the rest of the rural south.
During the draining of the Pontine Marshes, the population that had
lived there for centuries was forcibly removed in the name of 'progress';
meanwhile, the tens of thousands of labourers who worked on the
redevelopment programme were interned in terrible conditions,
exploited and then dismissed without notice, many of them infected
with malaria.[30]

South of Naples the real needs of the rural poor were ignored in
favour of grandiose gestures and symbols. According to Carlo Levi, a
political dissident who was exiled to a village in Basilicata in the 1930s,

the only mark left on the village by the Fascists was a public toilet in the village square. As a symbol of progress it was magnificent – it was 'the most modern, sumptuous and monumental toilet that can be imagined' – but no one in the village wanted or needed it, and its only users were the pigs and stray dogs that occasionally wandered in to drink the stagnant water from the toilet bowls. 'What strange circumstances, what magician or fairy had borne this marvellous object through the air from the faraway North,' Levi wondered, 'and let it fall like a meteorite directly in the middle of this village square, in a land where for hundreds of miles around there was no water and no sanitary equipment of any kind?'[31]

The Fascist years were full of such contradictions, not only in Naples and the south, but across the whole of Italy.

The Mostra d'Oltremare

A perfect example of the follies and inconsistencies of Mussolini's rule was the Mostra d'Oltremare, one of the most impressive, ostentatious and badly timed projects ever conceived under the Fascists. The 'Triennial Exhibition of the Italian Overseas Territories' – to give it its full name – was a kind of Expo, or 'World's Fair', built in the west of Naples at the end of the 1930s. It was constructed with great speed and energy, but also at great expense, to celebrate Italy's growing status as a colonial power. For local people, however, it also had another, greater significance. As part of the huge regeneration project that had seen the suburb of Fuorigrotta springing out of the plain, it was also a celebration of the new Naples that Mussolini had promised them: a greater, more prosperous Naples – the Queen of the Mediterranean.

This huge, grandiose tourist destination eventually cost the princely sum of 100 million lire, a vast amount by the standards of the day.[32] It was inaugurated on the morning of 9 May 1940 by King Vittorio Emanuele III, who was hailed by *Il Mattino* as both the 'Neapolitan King' and the 'Emperor' of Fascist Italy. The streets were lined with flags, and there was a sense of excitement in the air: 'The city … seemed to be awake after many years of dreaming, resurrected it seems in this May hour which glorifies an Empire.'[33]

The exhibition itself was magnificent. There was a 'Historical' zone, which told the story of Italian imperialism from ancient Rome to the present, taking in the various recent conquests in Africa along the way. There was a 'Production' zone, which included installations demonstrating how the overseas territories could be exploited for the good of Italy. The 'Geographic' zone contained a pavilion for each of Italy's overseas territories – most of them African, although there was also a pavilion devoted to the conquest of Albania.

Africa was very much at the heart of the exhibition – but it was an Africa that was subordinate to Italy and, just as importantly, subordinate to the people of Naples. Avenues of eucalyptus and palm trees were planted to give the impression of Africa; model villages were built to show how African people lived; and African workers were brought here both to help with the building and to be part of the display. Several families were brought from Somalia, Eritrea and Ethiopia to perform for tourists: they stayed in their model villages by day, but were forced to live in military-style barracks by night, under the watchful eye of the Polizia dell'Africa Italiana. At the inauguration, Askaris in white robes and turbans were lined up to salute the Italian king.[34]

And yet there was a shadow hanging over the celebrations. Even as the inauguration was taking place, there were rumours that Mussolini was about to declare war on Britain and France. Elena Canino, who was married to the exhibition's main architect, dismissed these rumours on the grounds that the nation's leaders would surely never have embarked on such a grandiose scheme, at such vast expense, if they were planning to throw themselves into another European conflict. 'The exhibition is for tourists, but what kind of tourism could there be in a war?'[35]

It would not be long before her question was answered: on 10 June, Mussolini announced that Italy was indeed declaring war on France and Britain. The Mostra d'Oltremare was immediately closed down. The pavilions were vacated and locked up. The African families who had been brought to Naples to entertain the tourists were interned: with the Mediterranean now closed to civilian shipping, they would be stuck in Naples for the rest of the war. As for the Italian workers – the engineers and gardeners, the caterers and entertainers, the tour guides and swimming-pool attendants who had been led to believe that the exhibition would give them secure employment for the foreseeable future – they were all sent home.

The Mostra d'Oltremare would not properly open its gates again until the Americans arrived in 1943 and converted its grounds into a series of field hospitals. This gigantic white elephant, built to glorify the greatness of Italy and to symbolize the 'new life and new hopes of Naples', had lasted just a month.[36]

Resistance to Fascist Rule

One did not have to be a philosopher or a political scientist to see that there was something absurd about the pursuit of prosperity through war, or the pursuit of peace through violence. Nevertheless there were philosophers and politicians aplenty who were willing to point these things out; and some of the most prominent among them came from Naples and the south. Benedetto Croce, for example, wrote passionately of the 'doctrinal confusions and poorly spun reasoning' of Fascist intellectuals who used sophistry to justify 'deplorable violence'. Their beliefs were, he wrote in 1925,

> an incoherent and bizarre mixture of appeals to authority and demagogism, of proclaimed reverence for the law and violation of the law, of ultra-modern concepts and musty old junk, of absolutist attitudes and Bolshevik tendencies, of disbelief and courtship of the Catholic Church, of abhorrence of culture and sterile efforts towards a culture without foundations, of mystical sentimentality and cynicism.[37]

He would continue to rail against the regime in the pages of his journal, *La Critica*, right up to the start of the war and beyond.

Giovanni Amendola, the Liberal Democrat deputy for Salerno, also pointed out how empty the Fascist ideas really were. 'Fascism did not so much aim to govern Italy as to monopolize control of Italian consciences,' he wrote in *Il Mondo* in April 1923. '… It demands the *conversion* of Italians. But conversion to what? It has often been observed that Fascism didn't have enough ideas to constitute a political programme ...'[38] He was rewarded for such observations by being beaten up in the street at the end of that year by four Fascists with clubs. *Il Mondo* was forced to close down by the government less than three years later.

As the freedom of the press was gradually crushed in the mid-1920s, opponents of the regime had to find other ways to express their discontent. In Naples, where Fascism quickly took control of every part of public life, ordinary people were reduced to making everyday gestures of petty resistance: they refused to wear black shirts to school, they refused to take part in all the compulsory rallies and parades, they refused to salute Fascists in the street, or cursed them under their breath. One Neapolitan woman later recalled that when Hitler and Mussolini visited the city together in 1938 her father cursed the two dictators so loudly and continually that her mother made all the children sing at the tops of their voices in case someone outside heard him.[39]

Resistance like this was not always overtly political: it was just the natural reaction of any people who resented being told what to do by unaccountable figures of authority. Nevertheless it could get you into trouble. One boy from Fuorigrotta remembered being summoned to the local *fascio* with his father for failing to take part in one of the innumerable parades: while he was waiting outside the office door, he could hear the Fascist official inside slapping and kicking his father. The family was obliged to keep a photograph of Mussolini in their barber shop, just for show, but his father would swear or spit at it in private.[40]

With the start of the Spanish Civil War, Neapolitan resistance began to grow again, and to take on a more overtly political atmosphere. Members of 'Giustizia e Libertà' – the future Action Party – began to organize themselves; and Communists began printing anti-Fascist leaflets once again. Anyone who was caught doing such things could expect more than a beating: one Neapolitan worker, Salvatore Cacciapuoti, was sentenced to nine years and four months in prison for distributing subversive leaflets.[41] And yet, as the Second World War approached, dissent kept growing. Anti-Fascist graffiti began appearing in urinals and on the city walls; leaflets continued to be printed; activists in Torre Annunziata even burned down the local *fascio*. In Vomero, a group of students broke into an exhibition devoted to the 'Fascist revolution' and put up a sign in the window reading 'Death to Mussolini'.[42]

For those who continued to believe in the greatness of the regime, there was reason to be wary. Naples was indeed a city reborn, to a degree, but it was also a city divided. As the clouds of war began to close in, the spirit of Masaniello still lurked in the shadows.

CHAPTER 15

Descent to War

The news that Italy was now at war did not come as a complete surprise to the people of Naples. The Fascist press had already been speculating for weeks about when the declaration would be made, so, when Mussolini's voice rang out over the city on 10 June, everyone stopped to listen. Loudspeakers had been set up in town squares all around Naples to broadcast his speech. In Piazza del Plebiscito a small crowd gathered, which greeted the news – according to *Il Corriere di Napoli*, at least – with 'fervid enthusiasm'.[1] Other newspapers also reported 'enthusiastic acclamations' in Pozzuoli, bursts of 'thunderous applause' in Frattamaggiore, 'indescribable enthusiasm' in Frignano, and similar ovations, cheers and expressions of faith in many other nearby provincial towns.[2] The eagerness for war was certainly not as universal as the Fascist press liked to pretend it was – in Ponticelli, for example, disillusioned locals reacted to the news by cutting the power lines to the loudspeakers.[3] Nevertheless, there are plenty of witnesses of the time who are willing to admit that the excitement was genuine, and that they, too, found themselves carried away by the fervour of the crowds.[4] 'We were very enthusiastic about it, as if it were a good thing,' said one Neapolitan woman, years later. 'We did not know what war was, what it had in store for us ...'[5]

Within just a few days, everything in the city began to change. The first and most obvious transformation came at night, when a blackout was immediately imposed. For some people this brought an atmosphere of timeless magic to the city. 'When all of the lights in the city went out the sky appeared surprisingly full of stars,' wrote the Neapolitan journalist Aldo Stefanile, 'and ... the voice of a cricket could bring to the most insensitive hearts the echo of a distant childhood, of loving mothers, of ancient walks in the fields.'[6] But the darkness seemed symbolic in other ways, too. The bright lights along the Via Roma had always brought gaiety to the centre of the city; that gaiety was now extinguished. Around the Mostra d'Oltremare, too, 'that flood of lights, that used to announce to travelers ... the new life and new hopes of Naples, was extinguished and darkened, perhaps forever'.[7]

In the press, a series of new drives were announced in support of the war. A quest for scrap metal began almost straight away, not only in Naples itself but throughout the region.[8] Iron railings and gates were removed to be melted down and made into weapons – even memorials to the dead of the First World War were not sacred.[9] Members of the Fascist youth movement (the *Gioventù Italiana del Littorio*) went from house to house, quarter by quarter, bullying and cajoling people into handing over bed heads, bronze statuettes, belt buckles, old typewriters, bowls and washbasins and anything else that might be of use to the nation. Most of these objects were useless as scrap metal: they were simply carted away to various warehouses and caves where they sat, for years, gathering dust.

Even in these early days of the war there were already shortages of essentials like food, fuel and clothing – a result of both the worsening world situation and Mussolini's disastrous international trade policies of the late 1930s. Now long queues began to appear outside shops and stores, as people tried to stock up on food. In the coming months, an ill-prepared government would try to crack down on such panic buying by improvising a rationing system for pasta, olive oil, sugar and soap, and eventually even for bread. Draconian punishments were meted out for anyone caught dealing on the black market. Nevertheless, the queues grew longer and the prices crept higher. A new austerity began to make itself felt across the city.[10]

Safety was everyone's prime concern. Civil defence organizations – particularly the Unione Nazionale Protezione Antiaerie (the National

Anti-Aircraft Protection Union, UNPA) – suddenly gained a new importance. Ever since 1934, UNPA had been scouting out underground spaces to be converted into public air raid shelters. Many of the ancient caves underneath the city had already been linked together and fitted out with electric lighting; and the conversion of some of the tram and railway tunnels had also begun. Now UNPA officials began entering people's houses and demanding to inspect their basements as potential shelters – a practice that represented a new level of intrusion into the private lives and homes of ordinary Neapolitans.[11] And yet they complied, because they knew their lives might depend on it. There were never enough air raid shelters to go round in Naples, especially in the more crowded districts like Mercato and the Spanish Quarter. UNPA would continue searching for new 'grottoes, caverns, galleries, tunnels or any other underground spaces' right up until 1943.[12]

The city did whatever it could to protect its substantial artistic heritage. Statues and monuments were hidden away, wrapped in sandbags and boarded up. The city's various museums began packing away their most valuable objects and moving them to basements, or even to safe houses outside the city. Meanwhile, archaeologists and priests began to fret about how on earth they would protect the ancient ruins of Pompeii and Herculaneum, or the priceless frescoes and carvings of a hundred Neapolitan churches.[13] Others simply put their faith in San Gennaro, the patron saint of the city. 'Nothing can happen to Naples,' said one old woman. 'San Gennaro won't be made a fool of.'[14]

Into the Abyss

The first bombs fell in Naples on 13 June, just three days after the declaration of war. They were little more than a warning shot: they fell into the sea, and the only damage caused was to a fishing boat at Santa Lucia, overturned by the large waves they produced.[15]

A few months later, however, the bombers returned, this time in greater numbers. They claimed their first civilian victim in the early hours of 1 November – a 44-year-old worker and father of seven in the suburb of Poggioreale.[16] While his family mourned, crowds of people gathered to marvel at the damage, both here and in other parts of the city. The biggest excitement was at the Porta Capuana, the fifteenth-century stone arch at the eastern edge of the ancient centre, where an unexploded bomb was found in the middle of the road. The whole area was cordoned off, but the gathering crowd soon realized that they could get a good view of the bomb by climbing up onto the painted horses of a nearby carousel. 'From that lookout, between the mewing music and the creaking of ropes, you could see that large crack in the cobblestones, that rickety tram car lifted bodily from the rails; you could breathe trench dust, and the street urchins returned home with the proud and bold air of having seen the bomb.' The carousel owner did a roaring trade until the bomb was finally defused and carried off to the scrap metal yard.[17]

That November and December a series of British air raids targeted the port and the industrial areas around the city, and the novelty of being bombed quickly began to wear off. On the night of 14 December a cruiser was hit in the harbour, killing 26 sailors and wounding 42 more. When an apartment building in Bagnoli received a direct hit on the same night, 10 civilians were also killed and 28 wounded.[18]

Over the following two years the bombing gradually became more serious. In July 1941 the main station was hit, along with a train loaded with munitions, which exploded spectacularly. The storage facilities of the Società Italo-Americana di Petrolio (SIAP) were also hit, setting fire to 13,000 tons of gasoline. Tragically, the densely packed residential area of the Spanish Quarter was also hit on the same night, leaving at least 1,000 people homeless.[19] The following October the AGIP oil storage facilities at San Giovanni a Teduccio were also hit, creating fires that were so big that they could not be extinguished for several days.[20] A month later the city centre was hit around the cathedral, around the port and around the university, and again in the Spanish Quarter. During just five weeks in October and November 1941, the city was bombed no fewer than fourteen times.[21]

Soon the inadequacies of the air raid shelters became clear to everyone. To start with there were not enough shelters to go round, especially in the most densely populated parts of the old city such as Vicaria and Mercato. Even where the shelters were large enough, they did not always have enough entrances, or wide enough ones, to allow

large numbers of people to enter them at short notice. According to a
report by the fire brigade, the largest shelter in the city centre was
capable of holding 'thousands' of people, 'but the entrances are few
and insufficient, and the population remain under fire in the open
while waiting their turn to enter'. The report noted that at one of the
entrances at Vico d'Afflitto in the Spanish Quarter, there were dangerous crowds pressing in from every direction. 'The result is a riot in the
dark that degenerates into a furious struggle and produces an indescribable panic ...'[22]

Just how dangerous this panic could be was revealed when seven
women and two children were killed in the crush to get into this very
entrance in July 1941.[23] In December the following year, three people
were killed and another fifty or so injured in a similar crush at Vico
Purgatorio a Foria, in the north of the ancient centre; and again in
April 1943 when dozens were suffocated in the crush to get into the
shelter at Montesanto metro station.[24]

For the people of Naples, all this came as a terrible shock. It was
hard enough coping with rationing and food shortages without also
having to contend with the terror of the bombs, and sleepless nights
spent in damp, cold air raid shelters 40 metres underground. The sense
of fear only grew as time went on, especially among women with large
numbers of children to look after and keep track of.

One eyewitness described the sense of panic that took hold of the
city whenever the air raid sirens went off:

Everyone was running in indescribable confusion. All along the
via Chiaia the entrances to various shelters opened up; people
came running out of the houses just as they were, and hurried,
yelling, towards the access points for those shelters. There was a
breathless rush, shouting, a stampede, and in front of the
entrances a tremendous mass of people. Voices of mothers
calling out to their children, the cries of kids running behind
their parents, who were busy carrying the smallest ones to safety.
A tumult, a crowd, an indescribable throng. And, above it all,
the drone of the sirens and the deafening clatter of the shops
hastily rolling down their shutters.[25]

Inside the shelters, the confusion did not abate. Conditions were primitive, to say the least: many of these shelters were little better than underground caves, with nowhere for people to sit or lie down save the bare rock as it had been chiselled centuries earlier. The deep-level refuges were damp and cold, and pitch dark whenever the lights went out; while the metro stations and tram tunnels often became overcrowded and unbearably hot, especially in summer. There was often no drinking water available, and hygiene was appalling. Anything to make these spaces more comfortable had to be brought by the refugees themselves. As a consequence, it was not unusual to see families hauling mattresses, blankets, pillows, saucepans of food and even portable wood-burning stoves along with them into the shelter. Amedeo Maiuri, a local archaeologist, wrote in his diary at the time describing exactly such scenes. For several afternoons, he witnessed the daily migration to the shelters from his window in Piedigrotta. In this part of town, the main shelter was the tram tunnel that pierced the Posillipo hill parallel to the ancient Roman Crypta Neapoletana. To his eyes, there was something timeless about this daily exodus, as if it were a 'sacred pilgrimage' or 'a biblical flight from Egypt'. Even the shelter itself looked ancient, with its deep platforms carved into the rock 'like the raised floor in the cubicles of Pompeian houses'.[26]

Maiuri claimed that conditions in the shelter were not much worse than those that many Neapolitans had at home in their houses, but official reports of the time describe things rather differently, particularly in the more confined, deep-level caves beneath the ancient city. One report of 21 November 1941 described conditions so cramped that people had to spend all night on their feet. It described women and children fainting for lack of air and water, and the appalling stench of the makeshift toilets, which rendered the 'already rarified' air 'completely unbreathable'.[27]

Such circumstances might be bearable for short periods of time, but there were many who stayed down in the shelters not only for a night or two, but for weeks or even months at a time. The old, the weak and the disabled were not able to brave the crush each time an air raid siren went off, so some of them decided that it was simply safer to stay down there on a semi-permanent basis. They were joined by those who were afraid to stay on the surface, because the constant bombing had become too terrifying to face.

Given such conditions, it is perhaps not surprising that morale in the city soon plummeted. The monthly reports sent by the Provincial Police headquarters in Naples to the Ministry of the Interior over the course of the war make pretty depressing reading. In March 1941 they were already warning of low public spirits brought on by the failures of the war and 'manifestations of intolerance' caused by the shortages of basic necessities like laundry soap.[28] By the end of the year they added that 'The recent enemy aerial incursions on Naples have significantly affected the morale of the citizenry, due to the deplorable number of dead and wounded and the extent of the damage produced.'[29] As the months wore on, and the hardships increased, the reports got worse: in March 1942 the police noted for the first time that there had been a few attempts at collective protest, particularly by women.[30] By the end of that year they warned that the people were nearing breaking point. 'Overall, there are signs of tiredness everywhere and many people long for the end of the current state of affairs.'[31]

The Realities of War

Perhaps if the Fascists had achieved just a little of the greatness they so craved – the kind of triumphant success that had been promised by the Mostra d'Oltremare – then the disappointment of the people might not have been so crushing. But the glories of war were not forthcoming. Instead, the people of Naples and of Italy were confronted with a catalogue of failure and mismanagement on a grotesque scale.

In truth, the Italian people had had no idea what they were letting themselves in for when they went to war. When Mussolini had stood on his balcony at Palazzo Venezia in Rome on 10 June 1940 to announce that the 'hour appointed by destiny' had come, and that it was time for the 'young and fecund peoples' to strike a blow at the greedy 'plutocrats' of Britain and France, he had offered no explanation of how exactly they were to do this. He had merely instructed them to 'Rush to arms, and show your tenacity, your courage, your valour!'[32]

It takes more than mere courage to win a war. Mussolini was fond of boasting that he had '8 million bayonets' at his disposal, but he didn't have any tanks or aircraft that could come close to matching what the British had. Though Italy produced good-quality rifles, machine guns and artillery, there were not nearly enough of them to go round, and many units had to make do with the same weapons that they had used twenty years earlier, in the First World War. The Italian navy looked impressive in size, but had no aircraft carriers, and there were serious problems with its guns: not one shot fired by an Italian battleship actually hit its target during the war.[33] Italy lagged behind both its allies and its enemies, not only in terms of its equipment, but also in mindset. The fact that Mussolini and his generals were still thinking in terms of 'bayonets' is painfully symbolic. Italy was simply not ready for war: Mussolini knew it, and so did his generals.

The contrast with Germany was most telling. When Hitler was marching across Poland, Mussolini was lamenting the fact that his army only had ten divisions ready to fight.[34] Germany had already invaded Denmark, the Netherlands and France, and the British had evacuated all of their troops at Dunkirk, before Mussolini dared to declare war. Even then, he still shied away from actually attacking France. He waited a further ten days until Paris had fallen, and the French had already requested an armistice. Only then did he launch a disastrous, four-day war in the Alps, with virtually no preparation, against well-defended French forts. He took virtually no territory, at the cost of 4,000 casualties – almost forty times as many as his opponents.[35] Despite this, he expected Berlin to reward him by granting Italy control over Nice, Corsica, Malta and large swathes of northern and central Africa.[36] In short, Mussolini wanted to share in the spoils of war, without doing much of the fighting.

The rest of the war was merely more of the same. Italy's armed forces lurched from one disaster to another – not for lack of 'tenacity, courage and valour', but for lack of leadership, planning and equipment. In the autumn of 1940 they invaded Greece, immediately got bogged down in the mountains, and had to be rescued by the Germans six months later. The fiasco cost the lives or the health of 100,000 of Italy's 'young and fecund' soldiers. Meanwhile, in North Africa, a small but mobile British force completely outmanoeuvred their Italian counterparts, capturing 130,000 prisoners. The same thing happened in East Africa, where another 50,000 poorly led Italians were captured in Ethiopia and Somalia. Suddenly the 'greatness' of Mussolini's empire began to look decidedly shaky.

The war at sea was hardly better. In November 1940, three Italian battleships were sunk in Taranto harbour, and several other ships sunk or damaged. Four months later another three heavy cruisers and two destroyers were sunk by the British at Cape Matapan off the coast of Greece. From March 1941 onwards, the Royal Italian Navy hardly ventured out to sea again.[37]

As for the war in the air, the undeniable bravery of the Italian air force was let down by the quality of their aircraft, many of which were obsolescent, if not obsolete.[38] The dwindling Italian air force was no match for the vast fleets of British and American bombers that were now attacking Naples and other Italian cities in greater and greater numbers.

As the conflict progressed, the Italians began to rely more on the Germans. After the disastrous attempt to invade Greece, Mussolini's troops stopped embarking on adventures of their own and began following the lead of their allies instead. They followed the Germans into Yugoslavia – lands that the Fascists had always coveted; and then again with the invasion of the USSR – lands that no Italian had ever dreamed of occupying.

By the beginning of 1942, when Italians were freezing to death in their thousands on the Russian steppe, suspicions began to surface that the Italian army was no longer fighting for the glory of Italy, but for the glory of Hitler's Germany. In April that year the Neapolitan authorities organized a collection of 'Wool for the Homeland' ('*Lana per la Patria*'). Thousands of ordinary people gave up their winter coats, trousers, blankets and woollen mattresses for the sake of their brothers and sons shivering on the Russian Front.[39]

In 1943, with the war creeping ever closer to Italy itself, German troops began to arrive in the country in greater numbers. German supply ships and submarines docked in Naples with increasing regularity, and German soldiers often passed through the city on their way to fight in North Africa and Sicily. Various German garrisons were set up around the city, and it was not long before the local people began to grumble about the foreigners that were appearing in their midst. Some of it was straightforward xenophobia – many Neapolitans still hated Germans from the times when they had fought on opposite sides during the First World War. But the carelessness and arrogance of some of the German troops certainly did not help smooth relations. In the early part of the year several people were killed or injured by German military vehicles, including a 5-year-old child, run over in Piazza Principe Umberto on 6 February. Rather than apologizing for such tragedies, as any good diplomat would have known to do, the commander of the German garrison in Naples, Colonel Walter Scholl, simply told the Neapolitan prefect that such accidents were inevitable given the greater volume of traffic, and the Italians only had themselves to blame: 'the indiscipline of pedestrians in traffic,' he wrote, haughtily, 'leaves much to be desired.'[40]

As spring turned into summer an increasing number of fights and scuffles began to break out between local people and German service personnel, some of them involving firearms. In March, for example, a group of drunken German sailors stopped a tram in Via Medina, menaced the passengers and beat up the driver. In May, the Carabinieri in Torre Annunziata reported a growing number of fights between German troops and local people, as well as damage to property, all of which would culminate in a riot against the Germans later in the summer.[41]

Such events are always a possibility when foreign troops are stationed around a city, but German military commanders did little to address the diplomatic problems they caused. Complaints were routinely ignored or brushed off without concern for local sensitivities. What was worse, however, was the apparent powerlessness of the Italian authorities to deal with such matters. The Fascists, who were brutal when it came to policing their own people, seemed incapable of holding the Germans to account.

The *Caterina Costa*

In the spring of 1943 an event occurred in Naples that seemed to sum up all the failings of the Fascist regime. A fire broke out on a ship called the *Caterina Costa*, which was moored in the harbour. It was full of supplies bound for North Africa, including 900 tons of explosives, 5,000 tons of aviation fuel and various tanks and artillery pieces. Dangerous ships like this should have been moored at the outer breakwater, but for some reason it was sitting, fully loaded, in the heart of the port.[42]

According to the official report that was sent to the Minister of the Interior three days later, the fire took hold just after 2 p.m., and was probably caused by a discarded cigarette.[43] Unable to deal with the blaze while it was still small, the captain and crew simply abandoned the ship – but for those who were caught below deck, particularly at the stern, it was already too late. The shipping company later claimed that more than 100 Italian troops perished in the fire.[44]

The fire brigade was called, who recommended that the vessel be flooded immediately to prevent the explosives inside the ship from being ignited, but since it was a festival day they could not find anyone with the authority to bring this about: 28 March 1943 was the twentieth anniversary of the formation of the Italian air force, and most of the top brass were apparently too busy celebrating. The admiralty was not informed until about 3.30 p.m., but neither the Admiral Commander of the Maritime Department nor the Admiral High Commissioner for the Port could be induced to make a decision. At some point the Chief of Police requested that the ship be sunk – but to do so would have required the help of a destroyer, which was not forthcoming. And besides, there were fears that sinking the ship might spill yet more fuel into the water and allow the fire to spread. Another option was to tow the burning ship out to open water, but, again, nobody seemed willing to make such a decision. In the end, all that was done was to move the other vessels a little further away, and to evacuate the area within 500 metres of the burning ship. Nobody thought it was worth sounding the alarm.

The explosion that took place at around 5.30 p.m. was so enormous that pieces of the *Caterina Costa* were found on Capodimonte, more than 3 km inland. The ship's boilers were blown as far as Via Duomo, and huge pieces of sheet metal weighing a few tonnes ended up in the railway yard. One of the most bizarre sights the next day was that of a tank sticking out of the roof of one of the houses in Via Atri in the old city: the force of the blast had thrown it more than a mile through the air.[45] The area around the port was so badly damaged that it was equivalent to one of the worst bombing raids of the war. Windows were blown out all across the city: according to the report by the inspector of civil engineering the following day, around 50,000 buildings had been damaged, including the Carmelite church, the State Archives, the docks and warehouses and the customs office.[46] The destruction of the gas holders near the port caused an interruption in gas supplies across Naples, which particularly affected the city's bakeries. For some people this was the last straw. At one baker's shop in Chiaia a crowd of women gathered to harangue the proprietor, reportedly crying out: 'It's not enough that we're afraid, and it's not enough that we've made sacrifices, now we even have to go without bread, as if rationing weren't enough to starve our kids.'[47] According to official figures at least forty-eight people were killed and 1,100 injured; although most historians agree that the actual figures were much, much higher.[48] Aldo Stefanile, for example, claims 549 died, and more than 3,000 were wounded.[49]

Events like this simply confirmed what many were already thinking about the incompetence of the regime. Mussolini had promised to make Naples into the 'Queen of the Mediterranean' – instead he had delivered it into the hands of fools and foreigners who were incapable of protecting it from the ravages of war. According to one Neapolitan satirist, who called himself 'Masaniello', the whole idea of Italian greatness had become laughable. 'Where is the empire now?' he asked in a poem written in Neapolitan dialect, itself an act of subversion. 'Am I an emperor? Yes, only with a voice like a boss without any men!'[50]

Expressions of disillusionment and discontent, which had been largely crushed during the 1920s and 1930s, now began to resurface across the city. The resistance of intellectuals like the philosopher Benedetto Croce, who was one of the few dissenting voices to have been tolerated by the regime, began to be mirrored by students in the university – even, ironically, in the student wing of the Fascist Party itself (the Gruppi Universitari Fascisti).[51] At the end of 1942, students began printing a new, clandestine Liberal newspaper, *Libertà*, which called for an immediate and wholehearted resistance to Fascism. 'Do we want the English to destroy half of Italy, and the Germans to occupy the other half?' it asked, rather presciently.[52]

Posters and leaflets began appearing everywhere, blaming the Fascist regime for leading Italy needlessly into war, for betraying the ideals of the Risorgimento, and above all for selling out to the Germans. 'Why have we let ourselves be dragged into the terror of this war?' asked one, before going on to claim that Italy was only fighting 'for the hegemony of Hitler who, with Germany, wants to dominate the world'.[53] Another, printed in January 1943, was even more forthright. Why was it, the leaflet asked, that, having defeated Germany in the last war at the cost of 600,000 lives, Italy was now allowing the Germans to 'trample our soil as masters'? The answer was clear:

> The chameleon of Fascism, after having bled, betrayed and vilified the people, no longer feels safe. It is choking, it is afraid, badly afraid, and in order to save the filthy individuals and the miserable privileges of those who created and instituted slavery in Italy, has not hesitated to shamefully sell the nation to that war-mongering foreigner who for centuries was and will be our enemy. Enough! Italians have one and only one duty: destroy Fascism, and avenge our dead![54]

In such an atmosphere, many of the old opposition political parties felt emboldened to re-form. The old Catholic party was reborn both nationally, under the leadership of Alcide De Gasperi, and locally in Naples under the leadership of Giuseppe Spataro. Clandestine meetings were held throughout 1942 and 1943 in people's homes, in Bible study groups, and at the Catholic Youth Society in the Neapolitan parish of Santo Spirito.[55] The once-mighty Socialist Party was similarly reborn: on 1 May 1943 they printed 20,000 copies of their new manifesto, and began handing them out, more or less publicly, in Neapolitan stations, offices, factories and, above all, in air raid shelters, which were full to bursting because of the incessant aerial bombardments.[56]

The Communist Party also re-formed itself, and started producing a new newspaper, *Il Proletario*, from the beginning of 1943. According to one of the activists at the time, Gennaro Rippa, copies were handed out at factories all along the Bay of Naples, a hundred at a time; and he and his fellow Communists began to give speeches to the workers openly, almost as they had done in the rallies of the early 1920s. When they heard on Radio London that hundreds of thousands of workers had downed tools in Turin and Milan, they decided to agitate for their own strike action in the shipbuilding companies at Castellammare di Stabia – which they finally did in June 1943. 'The Fascists and industrialists were afraid,' claimed Rippa years later: 'they gave in immediately and did not dare instituting repressions or reprisals.'[57]

It was becoming clear to everyone that change was in the air.

CHAPTER 16

The Forty-Five Days

The dominoes finally began to tumble in the summer of 1943. On 10 July the Allies landed on Sicily, and began a six-week campaign to overrun the island completely. On 19 July, almost the entire strategic air force in the Mediterranean was sent against Rome: it was the first, and the largest, attack on the Italian capital, and was a deliberate attempt to pile yet more pressure on the Italian government.[1] Five days later, the Fascist Grand Council met in Rome and finally stripped Mussolini of his powers. The following day, 25 July, Mussolini was summoned to the royal palace by the king, who told him that he, too, had lost confidence in him, and was appointing Marshal Pietro Badoglio as prime minister in his place. Mussolini, shocked, left the building and was promptly arrested. That evening his 'resignation' was announced on the radio to a population that, by now, was largely glad to be rid of him.[2]

In Naples there was widespread celebration at the news that Mussolini was gone. A spontaneous party broke out in the streets as thousands of people streamed towards the centre, singing, crying and calling out to one another that peace was coming. Several Fascist head-quarters and offices were broken into, their furniture thrown into the street and ceremonially burned; and on Via Roma a group of anti-Fascist soldiers and air force men tried to break into the offices of *Il Mattino*. There were similar spontaneous demonstrations in Nola, Sorrento, Pozzuoli and many other satellite towns.[3] According to Aldo

De Jaco, people were so deluded by their joy that they began to leave lights on in their windows again, and even tore up the air raid shelter schedules. They were convinced that both the repression and the bombing were finally over. Sadly, they were wrong on both counts.[4]

The Repression Continues

Mussolini may have been ousted, and Fascism declared over, but the same hierarchy that had ruled Italy for the last twenty years was still in place. To keep them in power – and perhaps also to prevent disgruntled soldiers from finding common cause with civilians – the army was now deployed to maintain public order. Their instructions were to repress public demonstrations of any kind, using force if necessary. The results were disastrous. When crowds took to the streets in Milan, for example, machine guns were set up outside the Alfa Romeo factory to prevent the workers from joining their colleagues outside. In Bari, when a crowd gathered in Piazza Roma to demonstrate for the release of political prisoners, the army opened fire on them, killing twenty-three people and wounding a further seventy.[5] According to the historian and former partisan Giorgio Candeloro, more Italians were killed by their own army in the few weeks leading up to the armistice than were officially executed by the regime in the previous seventeen years.[6]

What was true nationally was also true locally. In Naples a few cosmetic changes were made to the hierarchy, but not nearly enough to speak of genuine transformation. On 6 August the Fascist chief magistrate for the city, Giovanni Orgera, was replaced with a royal commissioner, Giuseppe Solimena. Three days later the prefect, Marcello Vaccari, was replaced by Domenico Soprano – a man whose outlook was just as racist, nationalist and militaristic as any of his Fascist predecessors.[7] On the other hand, the editors of two of the most popular newspapers in Naples – *Il Mattino* and *Roma* – were also ousted and replaced. The new editors, Paolo Scarfoglio and Emilio Scaglione, were allowed to report much more impartial news for the first time in almost twenty years, including news taken from Allied sources.

Below the surface, other changes were also taking place. In the immediate aftermath of Mussolini's removal, representatives from all the clandestine opposition parties gathered together at the home of a lawyer called Claudio Ferri on Corso Vittorio Emanuele to form a united 'national front'. This extraordinary organization, which established a secret headquarters in Via Salvator Rosa, included Liberals, Democracy of Labour, Christian Democrats, Socialists, Communists and Action Party members all working alongside one another. It would eventually evolve into a branch of the National Liberation Committee – the political arm of the armed resistance against Fascism.[8]

As in other parts of Italy, dissent against the regime became irrepressible over the following weeks. Naples had more reason than most areas to want an immediate end to the war, especially considering the repeated heavy bombardments that the city was still suffering. In a report to the Minister of the Interior on 13 August, the new prefect described conditions in the city as a 'living tragedy'. At least 100,000 people, he claimed, were now living in underground caves and shelters, in what he described as 'a horrible, swarming human ant-hill' devoid of any proper sanitation. The destruction of their neighbourhoods was 'not dissimilar to the catastrophe of an earthquake'. Despite 'the truly prodigious resistance of this martyred people,' he concluded, 'there shakes within them a resentment and a profound indignation for being abandoned to themselves, and a deadly fatigue that might one day explode into manifestations of rebellion'.[9]

In truth, these 'manifestations of rebellion' were already making themselves felt – and, much like in other parts of Italy, were being brutally suppressed. In the suburb of Resina (now Herculaneum) a large group of women demonstrated in front of the town hall on 2 August calling for better rations. Afraid that they might break in, the prefectural commissioner requested the intervention of the army, claiming somewhat histrionically that the local police did not have enough ammunition to hold them off. Two weeks later, on 16 August, 500 steelworkers at Torre Annunziata demonstrated for the expulsion of their fellow workers who had been members of the Fascist Party. The authorities fired on them, wounding one.[10]

At the end of August, the situation degenerated further. On the 29th at least a thousand people in Portici demonstrated against the war, and against the German presence in their town. They had to be dispersed by a strong force of soldiers and Carabinieri. The following day, on the other side of Vesuvius in Ottaviano, a group of women demonstrated for the removal of German soldiers who had recently turned up in their town. The demonstration eventually fizzled out, but in the following days its ringleaders – two women named Anna Murolo and Amalia Liguori – were arrested and thrown into prison. The day after this, yet another demonstration broke out in Torre Annunziata and at Castellammare di Stabia when around 1,000 factory workers went on strike. This time the authorities used hand grenades to disperse the crowd: at least twenty people were gravely injured and dozens were arrested. In Castellammare the forces of law and order were assisted by German soldiers – a military alliance against the Italian people that was painfully symbolic.[11]

This summer of protest might have come to a head in a huge, popular demonstration in the centre of Naples had the regime not cracked down on it even before it started. Thousands of leaflets were printed inviting Neapolitans to gather in Piazza del Plebiscito on 1 September. It was supposed to be a protest about peace. 'The Italian people', claimed the flier, were growing more and more disgusted by the regime's continuing alliance with Hitler.

> The war – which for workers means hunger, and for soldiers means death, and for those who want it but don't have to wage it means great riches – the war continues. In Sicily our soldiers, tired of fighting for Hitler and our real oppressors, are surrendering en masse. In Naples submariners have mutinied, convinced that to take to the sea today is a useless suicidal gesture. In Milan our troops, aware of the identity of interests, have refused to fire on a crowd demonstrating against the war. With these revolutionary acts, the army that is the people resolutely places itself at the forefront of the people for the victory of Peace.[12]

Two soldiers who were caught handing out this leaflet were arrested and beaten until they gave away the names of those behind it – a dozen youths and a printer, who were also quickly arrested. To ensure that no demonstration took place, the Italian territorial defence commander, General Ettore Del Tetto, mounted armed guards around the city. Once again, he drew on the Germans to assist him: according to Aldo De Jaco, this was the first time that the Germans came down into the city from Capodimonte 'clattering around the streets in twenty Tiger tanks'.[13] It was a sight that did not bode well for the future.

The Bombing Continues

By this point in the war, Naples had become a target not only for the British, who bombed by night, but also for the Americans, who bombed by day. The city already had plenty of reasons to be bombed – as a major port, as an important airport, as a major manufacturing centre for weapons, chemicals, vehicles and food production – but in 1943 it suddenly became the main transport target on the Italian mainland, too. As the road and rail node closest to the beaches where the Allied landings were due to take place, the Allies considered it vitally important to destroy as much of the transport infrastructure in and around the city as possible.

In the first nine months of the year, Naples was bombed fifty-two times – far more than any other Italian city.[14] But the worst raid of all came after the fall of Mussolini, on 4 August, when the people of Naples were beginning to hope for an end to their suffering. The mission had originally been planned for Rome, as a way to continue putting pressure on the Italian government to come to the negotiating table; but because the Vatican City was located in the centre of Rome, the Allies could not afford to make any mistakes. So when the weather turned cloudy, the Rome mission was cancelled and the force diverted to Naples instead.[15]

The air raid sirens went off shortly before 1.30 that afternoon and continued for almost an hour and a half. This was exactly the time when shops and offices were closing for the afternoon, when the streets and stations were at their most full. The official target for the bombers were the dockyards, but according to the American mission report 'Several strings of bombs were seen to hit short of the target'. Actually the bombs ended up being scattered across the whole of the city, from Posillipo and Mergellina in the west to the area around the main railway station in the east. In terms of precision, it was not the USAAF's finest hour.[16]

The devastation caused by this raid was worse than anything that had gone before. Major buildings were destroyed in Via Toledo, Corso Umberto I, Via Mezzocannone, Via Chiaia, Via Vergini in the Rione Sanità, and all over the most densely populated parts of the city. Several of the big hotels around Santa Lucia were destroyed, as was a wing of the Pilgrims' Hospital near Montesanto. Alongside scores of residential buildings, several historically important buildings were damaged or, in some cases, completely destroyed. The Palazzo Doria d'Angri, from whose balcony Garibaldi had announced the creation of the Kingdom of Italy on 7 September 1860, received a direct hit, which destroyed parts of the roof and six of the eight statues that adorned the top of its façade. The Royal Palace was hit repeatedly, as were the fourteenth-century monasteries of San Domenico and Santa Chiara. The church of Santa Chiara, in particular – one of the most ancient and important buildings in Naples – was completely gutted. The San Carlo Theatre received a direct hit, and the vaulted iron and glass dome of the nineteenth-century arcade that stands opposite it, the Galleria Umberto I, was comprehensively smashed.[17]

When the people came out of their air raid shelters towards three o'clock that afternoon, they found some of the most beloved parts of their city utterly transformed. 'As you stop and linger in the streets of the city, the spectacle of ruin and devastation shows the full martyrdom to which Naples has been subjected,' lamented the newspaper *Roma* in the following days. 'A macabre scene of gutted buildings exposes an immense mess of beams, walls and ceilings, wrecked floors and furniture – all the rubble of things which used to pulsate with the normal rhythm of life before that life was violently suppressed. Every area of the city has these corners of ruins and death …'[18]

More people died in Naples on this day than on any other day of the bombing war. According to official figures published in *Corriere della*

Sera two days later, 210 were killed and 464 wounded, although the numbers registered in the individual *comune* seem to show a much higher figure of at least 342 victims. Witnesses who saw the carts loaded with bodies coming into the cemeteries in the following days swear that there were probably many more than that. The historian Aldo Stefanile, who gathered data on all of the 'one hundred bombings of Naples' in the 1960s, estimated that probably more than 500 were killed in this single raid.[19]

As the long, hot summer of 1943 wore on the bombs kept coming – partly as a way for the Allies to put pressure on the Italians to come to the negotiating table, and partly as a way to soften up southern Italy for the invasion that everyone now knew was coming. The airports at Capodichino and Pomigliano d'Arco were hit several more times. On the night of 23–24 August, the British bombed the coastal strip west of Naples, killing at least 150 people in Fuorigrotta, Pozzuoli and especially in the industrial town of Bagnoli, which was heavily damaged.[20]

Destruction was piled upon destruction – so much so that the city as a whole was conferred the title of 'Grande Mutilata' by the National Association of War Wounded (Associazione Nazionale Mutilati e Invalidi di Guerra), its highest honour. The newspapers began to describe it as a 'skeleton' with shattered 'nerve centres and vital arteries' – a 'martyr' to the rain of bombs.[21]

In a perverse twist of fate, even the ancient ruins of Pompeii were hit that summer. On the same night that Bagnoli was struck, another raid targeted the ILVA steelworks in Torre Annunziata at the foot of Vesuvius, but some of the bombs missed their mark and fell instead on this ancient archaeological site. The museum received a direct hit, which destroyed both the building and many of the artefacts inside. The temple of Venus was damaged, as was the temple of Jupiter, the house of Triptolemus and many other parts of the site. The chief architect for the region, a distraught Amedeo Maiuri, described the scene in his notebook:

[T]he whole area around the Porta Marina was reduced to a pile of rubble, and the Pompeii Museum beside the gate received a direct hit, destroying both the building and the objects inside.

The inconceivable had happened: the blind horror of the war of men was destroying what the earth's most terrible cataclysm had not destroyed. At dawn, when the painful clear-up operation began, the full extent of the disaster became visible. Of the long vaulted gallery, created at the time of Fiorelli between the old walls of the *horrea* of the city, only the unsteady walls of the ground floor remained standing: the rest was rubble and glass. And amongst the rubble emerged the shattered artefacts of the displays; and the remains of the dead of two millennia ago lay upside down, twisted, mutilated, just like the victims of this latest catastrophe ...[22]

*

By the time the Armistice was announced on 8 September 1943, Naples itself seemed like a modern echo of ancient Pompeii. Large areas of the city and its environs had been reduced to rubble. Countless thousands of people had been killed, buried beneath the buildings as they collapsed under the ferocious Allied bombardment. The official death toll for the bomber war was around 3,000, but, by compiling detailed lists from each of the *comuni* in and around Naples, Gabriella Gribaudi has reached a more realistic figure of at least double that for 1943 alone. Stefanile suggested a number as high as 20,000 for the bombing war as a whole, but this is almost certainly an exaggeration. The true number will probably never be known.

Perhaps worse than the number of deaths was the manner in which they occurred. The collapse of buildings with all their inhabitants inside; the sudden, inescapable violence that destroyed whole blocks of this most ancient of cities; the suffocation of those who were crushed in the panic to escape; and, perhaps worst of all, the darkness and squalor of the shelters themselves, deep in the bowels of the city, some of which received direct hits.

The Armistice was therefore greeted with universal relief. The continued pressure of all the bombing, along with considerable pressure from the Italian people themselves, who had been demonstrating and striking for peace in many cities all over Italy, including Naples – it had all finally paid off: after weeks of vacillating, the Italian government had finally agreed to surrender to the Allies. The news was first announced on the BBC, but later confirmed by Italian radio that evening.

Aldo De Jaco, at the time a young architecture student who would later become one of Naples' most celebrated journalists, recorded the sense of joy that filled the streets when the news finally came:

We had just emerged from an air alarm; now in the war-ravaged streets, among the burnt out skeletons of buildings, among the ruins that in many cases had buried and killed entire families, the joy of the Neapolitans began to overflow; we greeted each other, celebrating the end of the nightmare together: we were finally at peace, there was no doubt, the massacre of the bombings was over ...[23]

It was the second time that Naples had celebrated a so-called 'end of the war' in just a few weeks. But, as before, the celebrations – including a procession through the streets from Via Foria to Piazza Carità – were painfully premature. Because a new nightmare was about to begin. Only this time the terror would not come from the skies, but from the guns of Italy's former allies, the Germans.

CHAPTER 17

The Germans Seize Control

H ad the new prime minister Badoglio and his generals been the men of action they professed themselves to be, they might have prevented at least some of the tragedy that was about to occur. But when they found themselves caught between the Germans on one side and the Allies on the other, these supposedly dynamic military men simply froze. The brutal decisiveness they had shown when waging near-genocidal campaigns in Africa during the 1930s was singularly lacking when it came to defending their own people.

By now it should have been clear to Badoglio and his government that there were really only two options open to them. On the one hand they could side with Germany, continue repressing their own people and mount a robust defence of their heartlands in a long, grinding war of attrition. The Allied bombing would continue; the hunger would worsen; but the nebulous Fascist values of honour and glory might somehow be salvaged. On the other hand they could side with the Allies, eject the Germans from their midst before they became too numerous, and put an end to a war they should never have embarked on in the first place. Paralysed by indecision, Badoglio and his government did neither. A third option, to proclaim themselves a neutral country, was not really open to them because neither the Germans nor the Allies would allow it – but in any case they did not really pursue this line either. They simply prevaricated, tried fruitlessly to play one side off against the other, and alienated just about everyone – the

Germans, the Allies, the Italian people, and even many of their own supporters.

In the forty-five days between Mussolini's fall and the announcement of the Armistice, Badoglio's government tried desperately to reassure the Germans that their allegiances had not changed, and that they were still committed to defending Italy shoulder-to-shoulder with the Wehrmacht. On 15 August, for example, German and Italian generals even held a conference in Bologna to plan their mutual defence.[1] But at exactly the same time a variety of other generals were also sent to neutral Spain and Portugal to negotiate a separate peace deal with the Allies. Neither of these two courses of action were conducted decisively or wholeheartedly – indeed the Armistice negotiations with the Allies were fairly shambolic.[2] It was obvious that they were playing for time, even though time was the one thing not on offer.

The Germans were no fools: they knew that Italy was an unreliable ally. They had also been keeping a close eye on Italian morale. On the day before Mussolini was ousted, the German military attaché in Rome described the general atmosphere of exhaustion and apathy here. 'The population,' he wrote, 'no longer believes in even the slightest chance of victory, and also rejects any attempt to influence it through the press, radio, etc. It puts its hopes in the future generosity of the enemy and until then bears everything with resignation.'[3]

With this in mind, the Germans drew up a plan about what to do in case Italy were to seek a separate peace. They named it, somewhat ominously, Operation Alaric – after the Gothic ruler who had sacked Rome in the fifth century. Even before the fall of Mussolini they had already begun to move troops into the Italian mainland, ostensibly to help defend Italy, but also to shore up their own position here.[4] After Mussolini's arrest, however, they began using their status as Italy's allies as an excuse to move eight more divisions through the Alpine passes and into the country. They did not ask permission to do this, and the Italians, afraid of provoking even greater German distrust, simply let them. By the time the Allies landed at Salerno on 8 September, Italy was already effectively an occupied country.[5]

As soon as Badoglio made his historic announcement on the radio, the Wehrmacht put its plan – now renamed Operation Axis – into action. Across the country, German troops occupied government buildings, radio stations, airfields and other key strategic points. Italian barracks and garrisons suddenly found themselves besieged, their commanding officers offered a stark choice: surrender or die. Rome was surrounded, its centres of power seized. In the south, retreating German troops began a scorched-earth policy, requisitioning everything of value that could be taken with them and destroying whatever had to be left behind. The entire operation was carried out with speed, efficiency and great brutality. According to Albert Kesselring, the commander of German troops in the south, it was a 'blessing' to be able to drop the polite façade with regard to his former Italian allies. Now that their 'treachery' had been exposed, 'I no longer had to pull my punches'.[6]

While the Germans had been preparing all of this, Badoglio and the rest of the Italian hierarchy had made no meaningful preparations whatsoever. They knew that their own Military Intelligence Service leaked like a sieve, and were terrified that the Germans might discover what they were up to. Thus, when they made some half-hearted plans to defend themselves against a possible German attack they did not even dare use the words 'German attack' for fear of provoking a reaction.[7] For the same reason they kept their Armistice negotiations with the Allies secret from just about everyone, even after they had signed the document. The first that most Italian commanders heard about it was when Badoglio announced it on the radio on 8 September. While such secrecy was undoubtedly necessary, it did not give anyone any time to prepare for what was about to hit them.

Meanwhile, those at the very top, who did know what was going on, repeatedly failed to act in the country's best interests. Mario Roatta, Chief of Staff of the Army, turned down the opportunity to withdraw his troops to safety in the south of the country – an opportunity that the Germans themselves suggested – because he did not want to 'let our game become known'.[8] Vittorio Ambrosio, the Chief of Defence Staff, not only allowed German troops to continue flooding into the north of the country throughout August, but actively invited them in – presumably for the same misguided reason. But perhaps the worst failure of such men was their inability to prepare even a rudimentary defence of their capital city. It was certainly this that most astonished the Allies. On the eve of their invasion, General Maxwell Taylor flew to Rome in secret to liaise with the Italians, but, rather than discovering a frenzy of activity, he arrived to find the Italian leadership quite literally asleep – Badoglio had to be woken up to meet the astonished American in his pyjamas. Taylor had come to offer the Italians an airborne division to help with the defence of Rome, but when he saw how utterly disorganized they were he hastily cancelled the operation.[9]

If any of these men had been even half so energetic in their defence of Italy as they were afterwards in covering up their failures, things might have been very different. Perhaps with clear leadership, the Italian troops might at least have been able to put up a fight: they might have saved Rome; they might have secured vital ports like Naples and Ostia; they might have cut off the German lines of retreat from southern Italy; they might even have been able to conduct their own fighting retreat to join up with the Allied forces landing at Salerno.

But clear leadership was the one thing that was lacking. Badoglio's radio announcement of the Armistice was a perfect example of how uncertain the Italian position had become: although he stated clearly that all hostilities between Italy and the Allies must stop, he said nothing about what the new relationship with Germany should be. Other orders issued by the military supreme command were equally vague and contradictory.[10] When confused officers tried to contact Rome for clarification, they received no reply, because Badoglio, the king, the government and a large part of the senior military staff had all abandoned their posts. They were fleeing to Pescara as fast as they could. From there they would be shipped to the heel of Italy – as far away from the fighting as possible – where they, unlike most of their countrymen, would be safe from harm.

What happened next has been a source of national shame ever since. The collapse of the Italian armed forces in the following days began at the top, and cascaded down through the ranks like a waterfall. Senior officers throughout Italy and the overseas territories abandoned their posts and fled. In some cases they first took the care to instruct their men to do likewise, but in other cases they slipped away without even bothering to tell their men, let alone leaving them any kind of orders or guidance. The bitterness this created is one of the great legacies of 8 September and its aftermath: the feeling that Italian soldiers were abandoned by their officers features strongly in their memories of the war. Those officers who did stay at their posts did not generally put up much of a fight. When the Germans approached them with an ultimatum they usually capitulated – either because they preferred to throw in their lot with the devil they knew, or because they understood what would happen to them if they dared to resist. When the garrison on the Greek island of Cephalonia chose to defend themselves, for example, the Germans reacted with extreme brutality: after an eight-day battle ended in Italian defeat, thousands of Italian prisoners were massacred in reprisal.[11]

With the leadership collapsing before their eyes, it was often left to junior or middle-ranking officers to make the decision whether to stand up to the Germans or not. Some of them resisted bravely – but without any proper central direction, their resistance was scattered and uncoordinated, and almost universally ended in capitulation. In Tuscany, for example, local officers disobeyed orders from above to surrender the port town of Piombino to the German navy. In the pitched battle that ensued, they sank several German ships, but were eventually forced by their own divisional commander to give up the town.[12]

Many Italian soldiers recognized which way the wind was blowing and decided to escape while they could: some of them took their weapons with them and headed for the hills; but most simply took off their uniforms and went home. It is difficult to blame them for this; after all, if they were not supposed to resist the Allies nor the Germans, what was the point of the armed forces any more? They were disillusioned by war, and unwilling to make any further sacrifices for a leadership that had repeatedly let them down. When the advancing Allied troops came across these soldiers, trudging home in groups of three or four, they could not help but feel some sympathy for them. 'They reminded me of the descriptions I have read of the return of defeated Confederate soldiers to their homes at the close of the Civil War,' wrote General Fred Walker, one of the commanders who landed at Salerno.[13]

Those who stayed loyally in their barracks, awaiting orders that never came, usually regretted it. When the Germans confronted them they had little choice but to surrender: without any guidance from above they did not know what else to do. In some cases the Germans let them hand over their weapons and go home; but vast numbers were disarmed and interned, and eventually sent back to the Reich, where they would spend the rest of the war working as forced labour. At least 650,000 Italian soldiers were captured in this way – some estimates go up to 850,000. Most of them never fired a shot before being taken away.[14]

All of these eventualities occurred in the towns and villages around Naples. In Capua, where, according to one town official, the abandoned soldiers were 'materially and morally destroyed', the garrison simply surrendered.[15] In Nola, by contrast, the men of the Italian 48th Artillery Regiment initially resisted, despite receiving no orders from any of their senior officers. When a stand-off ensued, their rather weak-willed colonel tried to appease the Germans by ordering his men to stand down. As a reward, the Germans entered their barracks and arrested everyone: the colonel and nine other officers were then lined up and shot.[16]

Isolated attempts at resistance took place in many other places in the region, particularly in Castellammare di Stabia, where civilians also took to the streets.[17] But it was in Naples where the greatest defiance took place; and it was here that the most famous, and most brutal, reprisals were carried out. From a German point of view the city and its port were simply too valuable to be allowed to fall into Allied hands intact. It was here, therefore, that the full consequences of Operation Axis would be felt.

CHAPTER 18

The Terror Begins

R uling and holding the city of Naples has always been difficult. During its long history it has been invaded repeatedly, and suffered dozens of internal uprisings, some of them quite prolonged and violent. Outsiders, whether Italian or from the ruling dynasties of other countries, have generally confined themselves to controlling the major entrances and exits to the city. The city itself, with its warren of narrow alleys and close-knit communities, has always been virtually impermeable to police control, let alone military control.

In medieval and Renaissance times the rulers of Naples relied on troops based in four huge castles, situated in strategic parts of the city. The Castel dell'Ovo and the Castel Nuovo stand on either side of the headland, guarding the bay in both directions, and overlooking the city's all-important port. By the city's eastern gate is the Castel Capuano, built in the twelfth century by William the Bad, one of the early Norman kings of Naples. Later, when the Angevin kings moved residence to their 'new castle' in the fourteenth century, the Castel Capuano housed the law courts and the common prison. To the west, on top of the hill, is the last of the four: the Castel Sant'Elmo looms over the entire city, a brutal symbol of power and control.

At the beginning of the sixteenth century, after a brief but bloody war between the French and the Spanish, Naples came directly under the control of the Spanish crown. For the next 200 years the city would be ruled by a succession of viceroys, whose main job was to extract as much tax out of the city as they could. In order to consolidate Spanish control here, Don Pedro Alvarez de Toledo, who served as viceroy between 1532 and 1553, built a brand new street running north from the Viceroy's Palace and the Castel Nuovo: its main purpose was to make it easier for him to transport his troops down into the city from the Castel Sant'Elmo up on the hill. To this day it still bears his name – Via Toledo* – and it is still the city's main north–south axis. In later years this street would become the city's centre of glamour, but its military significance was not lost on successive generations of invaders and liberators, who also used it as their main thoroughfare for transporting their troops in and out of the city.

Between Via Toledo and the Castel Sant'Elmo, on the slopes of the hill, the Spanish viceroy also built a new suburb to house his troops: the area is still known today as the Spanish Quarter. This new quarter was supposed to be a symbol of Spanish dominance over the city, but it quickly became a symbol of Neapolitan lawlessness. When large numbers of traders, workers, craftsmen, beggars and prostitutes moved in alongside the barracks this area became just as overcrowded as the rest of the city, and even more notorious: it would remain the centre of prostitution for the next 400 years. The bodies of Spanish soldiers were frequently found at the end of one of the quarter's narrow *vicoli*, stabbed in the back during the night for some perceived slight. (A similar fate occasionally befell Allied soldiers in 1944 who ventured into these streets in search of wine and women, despite the signs declaring the whole area 'Off limits'.)

Over the centuries, various rulers have added further layers of control. Customs offices were built in the port and beside the market district in order to extract taxes from everything that was bought, sold or traded here – by force if necessary. By the Second World War, the most important of these was the Caserma Zanzur, not far from the Castel Nuovo, which served as the headquarters of the Guardia di Finanza (the finance and customs police). Large military barracks were constructed on the headland and around the perimeter of the city – buildings that, after the

---

* At the time of the Second World War this road was officially known as the Via Roma. It had been renamed a few years after Italian unification, in honour of the new national capital. It reverted to its original name in 1980.

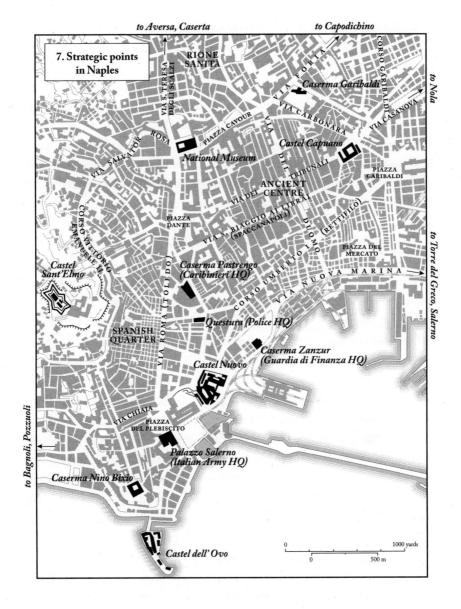

7. Strategic points
in Naples

RIONE
SANITÀ

to Nola

VIA S. TERESA
DEGLI SCALZI

VIA FORIA

CORSO GARIBALDI

Caserma Garibaldi

VIA CARBONARA

VIA SALVATOR ROSA

CORSO VITTORIO EMANUELE II

PIAZZA CAVOUR

National Museum

VIA DEL TRIBUNALI

VIA CASANOVA

Castel Capuano

VIA DEL

ANCIENT
CENTRE

PIAZZA
GARIBALDI

Castel
Sant'Elmo

PIAZZA
DANTE

VIA S. BIAGGIO AI LIBRAI
(SPACCANAPOLI)

DUOMO

CORSO UMBERTO I (RETTIFILO)

PIAZZA DEL
MERCATO

Caserma Pastrengo
(Caribinieri HQ)

VIA ROMA (TOLEDO)

Questura (Police HQ)

VIA NUOVA MARINA

SPANISH
QUARTER

Caserma Zanzur
(Guardia di Finanza HQ)

Castel Nuovo

VIA CHIAIA

PIAZZA
DEL PLEBISCITO

to Bagnoli, Pozzuoli

Palazzo Salerno
(Italian Army HQ)

Caserma Nino Bixio

to Torre del Greco, Salerno

Castel dell' Ovo

0   1000 yards

0   500 m

Risorgimento, would house Italy's national military police force, the Carabinieri. Among the most significant barracks were those on Piazza del Plebiscito at the base of the headland, which functioned as the regional headquarters of the Royal Army; and the Caserma Garibaldi on Via Foria, to the north of the old city, which during the war served as the centre of a whole complex of military buildings. All of these various barracks and fortresses were, of course, supplemented by other, more local centres of police and military power, dotted throughout the city in all directions. By the time of the Second World War there were more than 50 military barracks in and around Naples, 37 Carabinieri stations and 60 other various police and militia stations.[1]

Each of these places would play a prominent role in the events of September 1943. In order to control the city, one had to control these strongpoints, which guarded the port, the headland and the tunnel linking the city centre to Chiaia on the other side of the headland. Crucially, they also guarded the main roads in and out of the city.

Had the Italians seized the initiative on 8 and 9 September after the announcement of the Armistice, they might have been able to hold on to Naples. The territorial defence force under General Ettore Del Tetto had at least than 7,000 men based here.[2] There were also tens of thousands more Italian troops in the wider area under the command of General Riccardo Pentimalli, not to mention the thousands of armed policemen, Carabinieri, coast guards, customs officers, sailors and airmen who were also stationed in and around the city. With the Italian people behind them – many of whom would show themselves more than willing to take up arms for their city in the coming weeks – all of these forces might have been able to put up a robust defence of Naples, if only they had been better led.

The same is true for the wider region. The routes into Naples from the north were controlled by an arc of strategically important towns – Aversa, Afragola, Acerra, Nola – all of which would feature tragically during the German takeover and gradual withdrawal over the coming month. Some of these towns, such as Nola, were well garrisoned with troops, as was Caserta further north, on the road towards Rome.

The approaches from the west – from Pozzuoli, Bagnoli and Posillipo – were dominated by a series of tunnels through the headlands. Whoever controlled the tunnels also controlled the major routes into town. And yet no real effort was made to secure and control these or any other key points after the Armistice.

The approaches from the southeast were even more important: this was the direction from which the Allies would be coming. After landing at Salerno, the British and American forces would have to fight their way across the Sorrento Peninsula via Nocera, Angri and Pompeii. When they finally reached the Bay of Naples, they would have to fight their way along the coast road from Castellammare di Stabia and Torre Annunziata through Torre del Greco and into the west of Naples. An alternative, longer route ran around the back of the volcano, via Ottaviano or Sarno. With some forethought and a proper plan, perhaps one of these routes might have been secured.

Given the strength of the German forces already stationed in Campania it is unlikely that the Italians would have been able to hold on to all of these areas. But at the very least they might have held up the flow of German reinforcements to the beachhead where the Allies were struggling to establish themselves. We will never know, for no comprehensive plan was drawn up, and neither was there any serious attempt by the senior leadership to improvise a defence against the German takeover. In the coming months both Del Tetto and Pentimalli would be tried for treason and cowardice, and for wilfully failing Naples in its hour of need.

Instead it was left to a few junior officers to improvise a defence in whatever way they could – often, as we shall see, with tragic results.

The Subjugation of Naples

As with the proclamation of Mussolini's downfall, the first instinct of many Neapolitans on hearing news of the Armistice was to celebrate. Marshal Badoglio's announcement was broadcast at 8.30 p.m. on 8 September, and immediately afterwards people began taking to the streets convinced that, this time, the war really *was* over. A spontaneous procession formed, stretching all the way from Via Foria, north of the ancient city walls, round to Piazza Carità, as tens of thousands of rejoicing people headed into the city centre. The following morning, too, large crowds gathered in Piazza del Plebiscito and in all the major thoroughfares, full of joy, but also anxious about what might happen next.[3] 'ARMISTICE!' wrote one Neapolitan woman in her diary in capital letters, before adding, more cautiously, 'but every now and then alarms and some shooting ...'[4]

They were right to be worried. On the day after the Armistice was announced, Wehrmacht forces in and around Naples began to execute Operation Axis. At first the Germans trod carefully, mindful of the fact that they were still relatively weak: until 11 September, when they would be reinforced with a dozen units of the Göring Panzer Division, there was still only a single German battalion in the city, and a few hundred supply troops. Consequently they concentrated their initial efforts on requisitioning food supplies and motor vehicles, and disarming only those soldiers that they encountered on the streets. Such efforts were met with understandable indignation right from the outset, and various skirmishes broke out, particularly with soldiers and police officers attempting to protect Neapolitan property.[5]

The first organized resistance occurred that evening in the area to the north of the railway station and ancient centre. This was a critical part of the city, because it controlled the entrances to Naples from the direction of the airport at Capodichino and beyond, where there were large concentrations of German troops. When a detachment of German soldiers set up position in Piazza Principe Umberto, a unit of 'Arditi' – the ardently Fascist Italian shock troops – was sent to cause a deliberate incident with them. According to Alfonso Ciavarella, their commanding officer, this was done specifically 'for the purpose of testing the mood of the people and probing the possibilities of their reaction'. A brief firefight ensued, before the Germans retreated to a building in a side street to the north of the square. Eventually they were surrounded, forced to surrender and taken prisoner. In Ciavarella's account, however, the episode was not followed up because the local population did not rise up to help: in his opinion the time was not yet ripe for a more general uprising against the Germans.[6]

Meanwhile, just a kilometre away, similar events were taking place around the all-important Garibaldi barracks on Via Foria, where a firefight had broken out between German soldiers and a mixture of Italian civilians and soldiers. By chance, the commander of the German 57th Artillery Regiment, Major Fritz Marold, who had spent the afternoon reconnoitring the city, found himself caught up in the middle of this skirmish. He and his driver took cover in a building where they were eventually rescued – and arrested – by two Carabinieri officers. Over the next two days the fighting around the Garibaldi barracks would develop into a full-scale battle, involving dozens of casualties on both sides. The Germans alone counted at least fifty dead and wounded.[7]

The Carabinieri officers who had arrested Major Marold took him straight to the Garibaldi barracks to be held. The Italian army command was informed that they had captured an officer – but instead of being delighted, they seemed flustered. After several years of fighting alongside the Germans as allies, and twenty years of deliberately repressing the kind of general uprising among the people that now seemed imminent, senior army staff seemed bewildered by the rapidly unfolding situation. Following a series of talks at the highest level, the commander of the Naples defence force, General Del Tetto, finally stepped in and instructed the soldiers at the Caserma Garibaldi to release Major Marold along with his driver and his vehicle.[8] It was the first in a whole series of misunderstandings and betrayals between the lower ranks of the army, whose first instinct was to fight, and the higher ranks, whose first instinct was to collaborate.

At dawn on 10 September, the fighting on the streets began again, and gradually spread across the whole city. By now, news of German attempts to requisition Italian stores and vehicles had got out, adding to the many resentments that local people already had towards the Germans. So, too, had the news of the Allied landings down the coast at Salerno. Enthused with hopes of a rapid Allied advance north to Naples, people all over the city began to resist in earnest.

In the suburb of Chiaia, for example, which lies on the western side of the headland, a series of incidents occurred around Piazza Torretta when German forces tried to requisition supplies of food from the stores and warehouses around the Odeon cinema. Gunfights developed both in the stores themselves, where a 12-year-old boy was killed, and in the streets, where German soldiers tried to seize two trucks loaded with sacks of flour. Once again it was a mixture of civilians and military men who took several German prisoners, but after the intervention of the Italian liaison officer, Colonel De Stefano, they were instructed to release them all, along with their weapons.[9]

Similar events occurred at the opposite end of the city, in the north-eastern suburb of Arenaccia. The Germans had set up a roadblock in Piazza Ottocalli where they were stopping and requisitioning any vehicles that passed through. When one truck driver tried to burst through the roadblock the Germans fired on him, causing him to crash into a wall. At that point a dozen civilians appeared with guns and drove the Germans away.

What happened next is one of the many mythical events of the uprising. According to Aldo De Jaco, the Italian insurgents took the body of one of their neighbours who had been killed, strapped him to the bonnet of their car and drove through the city crying out for the people to join the uprising with the words 'Look what the German assassins have done!'[10] This scene would later be immortalized in Nanni Loy's 1962 film dramatization, *Le Quattro Giornate di Napoli*. It seems like the kind of action that one of the ancient Greek heroes might have carried out during the Siege of Troy – but, as one or two Neapolitan chroniclers of this era have pointed out, it does not seem like the kind of thing that might be done by God-fearing Neapolitans, whose traditional veneration of the dead is also legendary.[11] Historian Giuseppe Aragno identified the same story arising in 1914 when a Socialist worker was shot by police during a violent demonstration, and speculated that it might have been resurrected as a part of public memory in 1943.[12] We will probably never know for sure.

Meanwhile, a major nucleus of resistance was forming in the south of the city. By the afternoon of 10 September, fighting had broken out all along the shore from the port to the headland at Santa Lucia, and in the streets just north of Piazza del Plebiscito. This whole area was particularly important to the defence of Naples because it housed all the major institutions: the local government buildings, the Royal Palace, the university and the local headquarters for the army, the navy, the Carabinieri, the police and the Guardia di Finanza. By this point the Germans were growing bolder, and were attempting to break into several of these institutions. The Carabinieri headquarters at Caserma

Pastrengo, for example, came under attack from veteran German para-troopers, and the Royal Palace was temporarily seized by a group of ten German soldiers, before another force of Carabinieri officers managed to capture them.[13] In one particularly dramatic episode a group of Italian Public Security agents engaged a large group of German soldiers who had been trying to break into the Prefecture building. Surprising them from the rear, they managed to capture twenty Germans at once, including an officer. Like the other prisoners who were taken that day, they were marched off to the regional army headquarters on Piazza del Plebiscito. But all Italian efforts came to nothing when the head of the Carabinieri, General Emilio Radice, personally admonished his men for daring to arrest these Germans. Not only did he order them to give the Germans back their weapons and set them free, but he also apologized for his men's behaviour.[14] Despite all evidence to the contrary, Radice still seemed to be under the impression that the Germans remained Italy's allies.

Taken on their own, each of these episodes might be considered isolated skirmishes; but taken together, they amounted to so something much, much bigger. What had begun with a few discrete actions around the port area, the Garibaldi barracks and the Porta Capuana was quickly becoming a full-blown battle. The German command post was surrounded by hundreds of Italian soldiers and armed civilians. Roadblocks were thrown up all over the city, manned by soldiers, some of them with heavy weapons like grenade launchers. In the words of the local German commander, these were 'intolerable conditions for the German forces in Naples'. Reinforcements were immediately called in.[15]

That the Italians did not press home their advantage and drive the Germans out once and for all was entirely down to the inertia of their leaders. With proper leadership, they might have been able to coordinate all this disparate action into a single, combined operation. For example, the Italians had plenty of artillery, which, because of the surprise nature of the Armistice announcement, was still pointing at the sea or the sky, towards a threat that no longer existed. This could have been redeployed to guard the entrances to the city against German reinforcements that would inevitably be on their way. But rather than reorganizing such defences, the generals did nothing. During his trial for collaboration the following year, General Del Tetto claimed that he had only ever had the good of Naples at heart: 'if we had moved, they would have destroyed everything.'[16] In reality all he was doing was handing over control of the city to a foreign army who, once there was no one left to oppose them, would destroy everything anyway.

On Saturday 11 September the tide finally began to turn in the Germans' favour when reinforcements from the Göring Panzer Division began to arrive in the city. The newly freed Major Marold gave the Italians fighting around the Garibaldi barracks an ultimatum: if they did not disarm and evacuate the barracks by 4 p.m., 'all the German batteries would open fire on Naples'.[17] True to form, General Del Tetto immediately caved in and ordered his men to surrender: he himself then put on civilian clothes and ran away to hide in a convent.[18] To their credit, many of the men in the Garibaldi barracks and the surrounding buildings did not listen to him: fighting continued here for at least the next two or three days. According to official records, forty-one Italians would be killed in fighting here between 12 and 14 September, twice as many as in the previous three days.[19] Nevertheless, by the 17th the whole area had been pacified.

In the south of the city, too, the newly reinforced Germans quickly took control. On Sunday the 12th they stormed the Castel dell'Ovo, the ancient fort that stood on the island of Megaride right beside the headland. The twenty or so men of the Italian 21st 'Centro di Avvistamento' (Look-out Post), who had already held the Germans off for three days, desperately tried to spike their big guns, or tip them into the sea, before they were overwhelmed. They were eventually taken prisoner and marched away to the Admiralty building, where eight of them were put up against the wall and shot. Afterwards, according to an Italian military chaplain who witnessed the massacre, the German officer made a little speech explaining that he had shot the Italians in reprisal for the deaths of his men, who had died in combat – an act that contradicted all the laws of war. According to Aldo De Jaco, the bodies remained there for three days before they were transported to the cemetery by local people.[20]

On the same day the Germans also overwhelmed the Pastrengo barracks, the headquarters of the Carabinieri in Naples, which had likewise held out against repeated attacks before finally succumbing.

In the port area, the Zanzur barracks of the Guardia di Finanza was also stormed. The men inside were marched off to Piazza Giovanni Bovio, where another drama was also unfolding. In the meantime, tanks continued firing on the buildings all around this area to drive the point home: the Germans were now in charge.

Atrocities Around the University

It was not enough for the Germans merely to neutralize the army and the various branches of the Italian police and public security forces: resistance to their takeover of Naples had been much more widespread than that. In order to subdue the people more generally, the commander of the German garrison, Colonel Walter Scholl, prepared an event that would terrorize the city into submission.

He began by surrounding the university district, which was known as a centre of dissent against the old Fascist regime. An armoured column drove along the Corso Umberto I, past the university's main entrance and up into the ancient city along Via Mezzocannone. Machine-gun posts were set up behind the university in Piazza San Domenico Maggiore and Piazzetta Nilo. On Corso Umberto itself, guards were mounted at the entrances to all the side streets, and two tanks were positioned with their gun barrels pointing into the university district. Meanwhile, bands of German soldiers went from house to house, beating on doors and instructing everyone to leave their homes and make their way down to the Rettifilo – the popular name for Corso Umberto I – to gather in Piazza Giovanni Bovio.[21]

The University of Naples is one of the oldest such institutions in the world. It was founded in 1224 by the Holy Roman Emperor Frederick II, and it forms the cultural heart of Naples, and indeed the whole of the Italian south. On Sunday 12 September it was still closed for the summer vacation, but the Germans insisted on blowing in the doors with explosives and firearms in order to search for resistance fighters inside, claiming that they had seen shots fired from some of the upper windows and balconies.

This was certainly the excuse that was given to Marussia Bakunin, a professor of chemistry at the university, when German soldiers burst into her apartment on the first floor of the university building, over-looking Via Mezzocannone. She and her family were among the very few people on campus at the time. They were given just a few minutes to grab some things while the Germans searched their home. Finding nothing to incriminate them, the German soldiers nevertheless doused the whole apartment with gasoline and set fire to it.[22]

Meanwhile, another group of German soldiers had arrested the university caretaker, Mariano Petino, and forced him to accompany them through the Zoological Institute. 'All of the doors had been broken in with firearms,' he later explained; 'the shooting was hell-ish.'[23] He watched helplessly as the place was searched and then comprehensively looted: radio equipment, recording machines, type-writers, calculators, microscopes – anything of value was removed and loaded into lorries waiting outside. While this was going on, Petino's apartment was also set on fire: his family had to take refuge in their basement shelter in order to escape the flames.[24]

Several other parts of the university were also set alight that day, including the main building, for no better reason than to send a strong message to the people of Naples about who was now in charge. In one of the worst acts of cultural vandalism of the entire war in Italy, German soldiers broke into the library of the Royal Society, shooting the two guards who tried to prevent them. They doused the book-shelves with gasoline and set them on fire; and to make doubly sure of the destruction they then threw hand grenades into the flames. Some 200,000 volumes and documents were destroyed, many of them irre-placeable. According to the university rector, Adolfo Omodeo, the fire lasted for four days before finally burning itself out.[25]

While all this was going on, the people who lived around the univer-sity, and south of the Rettifilo in the port area, were being rounded up and herded towards Piazza Bovio. Before long the crowd numbered in the thousands, filling the piazza and stretching along the Rettifilo as far as the now-burning university building. They were being assembled to witness a series of events that would become grimly iconic of the fate of the city during its brief German occupation.

The spectacle began with an explosion inside the Exchange building, the Borsa, which opened out onto Piazza Bovio. The crowd started in alarm, but since every avenue of escape was blocked by German soldiers they had no choice but to stay where they were. The order for silence was then barked out at them, as four men were led up onto the steps outside the Borsa – two *finanzieri* and two sailors – alleged to have been found with firearms on them. A firing squad lined up in front of them and shot them before the crowd.

This was only the opening act. According to Mariano Petino, at one point the tanks on the far side of the piazza opened fire on the Borsa, for no obvious reason other than to increase the terror of the crowd. 'I don't know how to describe what happened,' he later wrote, before adding,

> many were wounded by falling masonry and pieces of glass, all
> mostly wounded in the head because, given how crowded it was,
> only their heads were exposed; and if this barbaric treatment
> were not enough dozens of machine guns were aimed at the
> crowd, so much so that we were all fully convinced that we were
> about to be machine-gunned without even knowing the reason
> for such treatment.[26]

Directing these proceedings was the commander of the German garrison, Colonel Scholl himself, seated on top of an armoured car surrounded by his staff.

Among the crowd that day was an electrician named Enrico Ferrante, who had got caught up in the German round-up while transporting a cartful of his tools and materials across town: he had been trying to keep them safe from all the looting that was taking place across Naples at this time, but was now stuck in the midst of this turmoil with no way of securing them. An acquaintance he met in the crowd, who was president of the Railwaymen's Club – a Fascist official – handed him a badge – a Fascist emblem symbolizing the German–Italian–Japanese Axis. He told him to pin it on his lapel and go and speak to the German commander: if the Germans believed he was a Fascist collaborator they might let him take his tools and go.

Ferrante tried to approach Colonel Scholl, but was told by an Italian interpreter to be patient. At this point, a unit of German soldiers was arriving in the piazza with a large group of Italian prisoners. Ferrante recognized them as customs and excise officers: they were, in fact, the men of the Guardia di Finanza who had just been captured during the storming of the Caserma Zanzur earlier in the afternoon. It quickly became obvious that they had been brought here to suffer the same fate as the other groups who had resisted the German onslaught.

Since Ferrante was now standing among the group of Germans and Fascists, he decided to bluff his way to try to save these men. According to Ferrante's own account, he pointed indignantly at the men and, 'in the firm voice of one who is accustomed to command', shouted, 'These men are my team, employed by me; they are the only ones who have stayed faithful to me, and now you're taking them away from me.' His borrowed Fascist badge appeared to win him the credibility he needed to be allowed access to the prisoners. After a little negotiation, both with the Germans and with the leader of the customs officers, who seemed determined to martyr himself and his men, Ferrante succeeded in getting them all set free.[27]

In the meantime, the Germans were preparing the next act. A young Italian sailor was driven up into the square, under armed guard, and presented to Colonel Scholl with the claim that he had been caught in possession of a hand grenade. Without hesitation, the colonel ordered his execution. The sailor, 'a big, handsome lad, tall and robust', was paraded around the square before being led out along the Rettifilo to the steps of the burning university building. The crowd was driven out after him, almost like a procession behind a martyred saint.[28]

According to those who were in the crowd that day, an armoured car was lined up opposite the university with a cine camera mounted on top of it – suggesting that what was about to happen had all been pre-planned. Via an Italian interpreter, the crowd was instructed to kneel in the street. The charge against the young man was then announced – that he had been caught throwing bombs at the Germans – and he was led up the steps of the university building, crying out his innocence all the while. For a moment he stood before the burning doorway, glancing inside as if tempted to run into the blaze, before three German soldiers stepped forward, took aim and fired. One of them then mounted the steps to administer the *coup de grâce*. As a final insult, the crowd was now instructed to applaud – presumably for the benefit of the cine camera that was filming the whole event. It was not enough that they be terrorized and humiliated, they were also obliged to pretend that they were grateful for it.[29]

It is impossible to be certain of the exact details of what happened on that terrible afternoon. No evidence of any German film has ever been found; and according to Carlo Gentile, the pre-eminent scholar on German atrocities in Italy, it is extremely unlikely that German film crews were active in the area at this time.[30] It is possible that eyewitnesses of the time were mixing up different memories together; on the other hand, the most important testimony was recorded in 1944, when these events were still fresh in people's minds. Trauma affects different people in different ways: sometimes it clouds their judgement, and sometimes it etches events upon their memory with unrivalled clarity.

What is certain, however, is what happened next. The crowd was kept kneeling for more than two and a half hours that evening, before finally being told to stand up. Towards eight o'clock they were separated into two groups: women, children and the old were allowed to go home, while all the men were marched off towards the railway station. That night they were force-marched to Teverola, 15 km north of Naples, where they were finally released for lack of any means of transporting them further. But even now this tragic saga was not quite over. Forty or so men were held back, including fourteen Carabinieri officers who had defended the central telephone exchange the day before. These fourteen were forced to dig their own graves before being lined up and shot, along with two civilians. The remaining men were told to bury them, and then go home.[31]

Throughout these few days the Germans showed not only a clarity of purpose that was distinctly lacking in their Italian counterparts, but also a ruthless disregard for the laws of war. Prisoners were routinely shot for the 'crime' of defending themselves and their property, or in reprisal for German deaths in combat. This ruthlessness began at the top, and was transmitted throughout the ranks. At one point, staff officers at the XIV Armoured Corps headquarters instructed the commander of one of its regiments to act in 'the most brutal and ruthless way' to crush Italian resistance, claiming that any action was justified, no matter how violent, 'even if it means setting the whole of Naples on fire'. German officers were instructed specifically to shoot Italian officers like bandits, and to show 'No mercy for the civilian population'.[32] The response from Italian commanders was not only cowardly but misguided: General Del Tetto agreed to impose counter-measures on the Italian population, including joint German–Italian patrols, so as to restore order. Such men were so accustomed to repressing their own population that they were incapable of seeing that the real danger was now coming from elsewhere.[33]

The terror worked, at least in the immediate short term. Over the next few days all resistance fizzled out, and by 17 September 1943 'no further shooting against the Germans have been reported'.[34] All the major barracks and police stations were occupied and stripped of their weaponry. The people became subdued. And for a while the occupiers were allowed to go about their looting and requisitioning without hindrance.

But that was not the only way in which these events proved a turning point. Years later, Enrico Ferrante described how he had been affected by the events he had witnessed:

[T]he foreign occupier gave the population of Naples a show of terror to render them incapable of reacting. That day of blood, 12 September 1943, had the opposite effect: I became a partisan, and the Neapolitan resistance, which culminated in the historic 'Four Days', was the spark that … showed the other peoples of Italy, harassed by the Nazi-Fascist dominance, the way of the partisan in every Italian region …[35]

Plenty of others felt exactly the same way. Thousands of soldiers and policemen disbanded over the following days, but many of them kept their weapons, despite an order printed in the newspapers and on posters throughout the city instructing people to hand in all weapons to the Germans on pain of execution.[36] Many of these soldiers and policemen would reappear in two weeks' time as impromptu leaders of the resistance.

Others began looting whatever arms the Germans left behind. According to Giuseppe Sanges, a veteran of the First World War and a member of the anti-Fascist group 'Italia Libera', these actions began as soon as the Armistice was announced. But after 12 September they only increased:

> From then on we started our hunt for weapons, rifles, machine guns, hand grenades, which we found above all in the city barracks, abandoned by our leaderless soldiers after the precipitous flight of most of their superior officers. All of these weapons were collected and hidden in the houses of various fighting comrades.[37]

The looting and hiding of arms would become an important feature of the next two weeks, involving everyone from shopkeepers and street vendors in Vomero to hospital staff and patients in the ancient centre, and even Naples' ubiquitous street kids – the infamous *scugnizzi*, who would become such an iconic part of the liberation of the city in the days to come.[38]

Even the Germans themselves sensed that, while things might be quiet for the moment, the battle was not yet over. In his report of the events of the first half of September, the commanding officer of the German 57th Artillery Regiment warned of future clashes with local people. 'The mentality of the population is base and evil, and the influence of Communism strong,' he wrote. 'Due to the inadequacy of food supplies, there is also the risk of hunger riots, which are capable of unleashing the revolutionary elements of the city on everyone and everything.'[39]

He was right to be worried, as anyone who knew the history of Naples could have told him.

CHAPTER 19

Countdown to Revolution

As Operation Axis was put into effect the Wehrmacht began to strip the city of everything it could take. All military materiel and supplies were immediately requisitioned and taken northwards. The Germans did not limit themselves to military depots: they also comprehensively looted shops, stores and warehouses, taking not only weapons and ammunition but also vehicles, spare parts, fuel, shoe leather, clothing, radio sets, photographic equipment – in short, anything that might be of use to the war effort. The tobacco factories in the port area and the industrial zone north of the station were also completely emptied: thousands of boxes of cigarettes were loaded onto lorries and driven away. The Germans also shamelessly stole anything of financial value, including artworks, clocks and watches, and the entire collection of silverware belonging to the Italian navy. It made no difference if these items were originally intended for military or civilian use: they took it all.[1]

One soldier, who witnessed the looting of the military camp where he worked, attests to the comprehensive nature of the looting. 'In the following days the looting continued …' he stated after the war. 'The aeronautics warehouse, the barracks, civilian radio and electricity warehouses, shoemakers, watchmakers, fabric shops. Banks: they entered, they broke in, stole, and left, new bank notes flying from their vehicles. They entered the houses, they took whatever they liked best: food, clothing, utensils, furnishings, safes, pianos.'[2]

Worse than any of this was the comprehensive looting of food stores. Every area of the city had its own 'Provvida', a warehouse of foodstuffs for distribution to local shops, bakeries and food producers. One of the largest was the warehouse at Albergo dei Poveri, near Piazza Carlo III in the northeast of the city. On 13 September the Germans broke into this store and packed up huge quantities of flour, pasta, cheese, oil and wine onto lorries. The local population, which had already suffered three years of increasing rationing and deprivation, were forced to look on as the last of their food supplies were carted away. Anyone who tried to snatch a loaf of bread or a flask of wine for themselves – and there are plenty of eyewitness accounts of this – was shot on sight. One such eyewitness, for example, named Giuseppe Iaccarino, tells how he watched an old man grab a loaf of bread from the back of the German truck. Unfortunately the driver saw him do it: he told a nearby German officer, who immediately took the old man aside and shot him in the back of the head. This was the moment when Iaccarino, who had never considered himself a political man, swore to take up arms against the Germans as soon as possible.[3]

It must be said that the local population were not entirely innocent of the looting frenzy that took place across Naples that September. In her 2005 study of the war, Gabriella Gribaudi describes the way that local people broke into factories and food stores all over Naples, often competing with the Germans over who could empty them first. Some eyewitnesses describe wild scenes of warehouse floors flowing with wine and oil from broken bottles and containers, and children filling their shirts with rice because the sacks were too heavy for them to carry.[4] Unlike the Germans, however, local people were not doing this for military or ideological reasons, but simply for survival. 'I and other boys used to go and steal,' claimed Ernesto Minino, who was a teenager at the time, but 'my sentiments were not bad, like those of a thief, but those of a boy who needed to live.' According to Minino, the conflict over food was one of the main sparks behind the insurrection against the Germans: once deprived of the last scraps of food that were keeping them alive, Neapolitans had little left to lose.[5]

The Germans were aware of the terrible deprivation that already existed in Naples, but were only concerned with the military necessity of denying as much as possible to the Allies when they arrived. However, they were also aware of the dangers of leaving the local population completely without food. To avoid the threat of 'hunger riots', German commanders began to arrange the urgent transport of food supplies from the north. Even in the supposedly efficient German army, the right hand did not always know what the left was doing.[6]

The Evacuation of the Coast

Soon worse was to come. On 22 September, the puppet government in Rome issued orders to evacuate the west coast of Italy between Naples in the south and Livorno in the north, to a depth of 5 km. This was a simple military measure to ensure that the coast could be better protected against any future Allied landings (such as those at Anzio, which would take place the following summer); but it was also a good excuse to round up whole populations and conscript the men as manual labour for the building of new fortifications against the Allied advance.[7]

Such a comprehensive evacuation of the coast was not possible in a city the size of Naples at such short notice, so here a compromise was struck: the evacuation would only be carried out in the certain key suburbs of the city, and only to a depth of 300 metres from the shoreline. The prefect, Domenico Soprano, issued an order to this effect on 23 September – first to the people of Mergellina and Posillipo, and subsequently to all the other coastal communities along the bay (but not in Chiaia or the ancient city centre). They were given until 8 p.m. the following day to take whatever they could carry and leave their homes: any unauthorized Italian found in the 'military security zone' after that time would be shot.[8]

Around 35,000 families were affected, or 200,000 people in total. Within hours of the order being issued a vast stream of humanity was seen tramping inland carrying bags of food and valuables, mattresses precariously balanced on their heads.[9]

Filippo Caracciolo, an aristocratic anti-Fascist who would later make a career in politics, recorded the sight of this desperate river of humanity in his diary, 'with their tired faces, absent eyes, bent over beneath the weight of boxes of suitcases'. Many women were in tears.

I see one of them leaning against a wall as if she would never be able to pull herself away from it again. She is holding a child who is too heavy for her, a child whose legs dangle like dead things. A wheelchair passes by, pushed by two men accompanied by a young woman. It creaks, bumping on the pavement and inflicting cruel jolts on an old paralytic woman, who sits there rigidly, so white and pale in the face that you would say she were dead, were it not for the extraordinary vitality of her hands, bent to support and protect a cage full of little birds that rests in her lap.[10]

Many of these people had nowhere to go: indeed, some of them were already camping like refugees in Caracciolo's garden. Those who had no family or friends to put them up would have to make do with makeshift accommodation in schools or metro stations. The remainder would head to the city's caves and air raid shelters, most of which were already overcrowded with people made homeless by the Allied bombing campaign.

'Mud and ashes'

While this was taking place, the Germans had already begun enacting the second part of their plan: the complete destruction of anything of military worth that could not be taken with them. Teams of sappers armed with explosives and incendiaries entered the massive industrial complexes east of Naples and began to systematically destroy all the factories and machinery they found. For three years the Allied air forces had been targeting these areas, but the damage they had done was nothing compared to what the Germans were able to achieve. Soon, plumes of smoke were rising not only from Vesuvius, but also from the Cotoniere Meridionali textile factory just north of Salerno, the Alfa Romeo plant in Pomigliano, the Cellulosa-Cloro-Soda chemical plant, the IMAM aircraft factory, the glassworks, the docks, the shipwrights, and many other smaller factories along the bay.[11]

After they had begun destroying factories to the south and east of Naples, they set about doing the same in the west. The Armstrong engineering works at Pozzuoli, the Silurificio shipyards at Baia and the Ansaldo weapons factory were all destroyed in mid-September. The huge ILVA steelworks at Bagnoli were systematically destroyed over a period of days: the cranes and water towers on the first day, the blast furnaces and the locomotive workshops on the second day, followed by the steel mills, the laminators, and all the other workshops.[12]

Alongside the industrial and military infrastructure, they also attacked the civil infrastructure. The harbour was mined, and ships and boats were booby-trapped and sunk. The railway junctions and marshalling yards were sabotaged, along with petrol stations, electric power stations, gas supplies and aqueducts. Many of the larger public buildings had bombs set off inside them, including the Prefecture building, and all of the major hotels along the seafront of Santa Lucia were set alight.[13]

The destruction was so comprehensive that even some of the Germans themselves were appalled. 'Entire parts of the city are turned into piles of rubble,' wrote one staff officer in his diary. 'What is this people being punished for – for patiently enduring the tyranny that led them to war, or for betraying their unloved ally?'[14]

In the old city, Carolina Nobile Fiori described the destruction in her diary. 'Unending fires can be seen throughout the industrial area. The detonation of the mines for this destruction sound like thunder.'[15]

From the Posillipo hill, the scene was even more apocalyptic. 'Naples is a constellation of fires,' wrote Filippo Caracciolo on the night of 23 September. 'The Castel dell'Ovo stands out, illuminated by the flames like a gigantic stage set for a film about Nero.'[16]

The cultural damage done by the Germans before they departed was immeasurable. One of the biggest explosions along this stretch of coast took place just west of Pozzuoli in one of the ancient Roman tunnels linking Naples to the Gulf of Gaeta. The Grotta di Cocceio was one of the great feats of ancient Roman engineering: like the Crypta Napoletana, it had been built in 36 BCE, in this case to move troops and supplies between Cumae and the military port in Lake Avernus. For Amedeo Maiuri, the archaeologist in charge of Campania's antiquities, this tunnel in particular had a kind of epic grandeur, partly because it had been built in the volcanic landscape that had inspired the poet Virgil when describing Aeneas's journey to the underworld. 'Whoever travelled through it just once, passing from the mirrors of Cuma to the dark waters of Lake Averno, could not forget the play of the light filtering through the oblique windows and the light wells that flared down so that in some places, cutting through the walls, they gave the tunnel the depth of a cathedral vault.'[17]

Unfortunately, since the end of 1941 the Grotta di Cocceio had been used as an underground munitions store for the Italian navy. Before the Germans abandoned this part of the coast, they blew the store up, destroying the tunnel along with it. The explosion was so enormous that local people feared a new volcano was erupting on the eastern shore of Lake Averno. When Amedeo Maiuri heard the news, he thought it painfully symbolic:

> Virgil, having Aeneas accompanied by the Sybil in the realm of
> the afterlife, had poetically imagined the gates of Avernus to be
> the scene for deadly war, the thorn beds of the Eumenides
> and the madness of Discordia. And we had made the sad visions
> of the Poet into a reality: we had mined even the road that led
> Aeneas to Elysium.[18]

Manhunts

While they were taking everything of worth, and destroying whatever was left, the Wehrmacht finally embarked on the last part of their plan: to round up as many men as possible and take them away to serve as forced labour. This had been an integral part of Operation Axis from the beginning, but until now the Germans had simply not had enough guards, trucks or facilities to carry it out. (This explains why, for example, after making the effort to march hundreds of men out of Naples in the aftermath of the Piazza Bovio atrocities, they had eventually just let them all go.) By the end of September, however, they had set up a holding camp at Sparanise north of the Volturno river, and had already begun to fill it with young Italian men seized from the towns and villages around Naples. According to German army documents, between 20 and 27 September some 18,000 young men were rounded up and transported northwards to be used as forced labour. These documents did not mince words about what the fate of these men would be: they are routinely referred to as *Sklaven* ('slaves'), and the round-ups as a 'Sklavenjagd' (a 'slave hunt').[19]

At first, the Germans hoped that they might be able to convince people to show up for work duty of their own accord. They ordered Prefect Domenico Soprano to issue a decree on Wednesday 22 September instructing all men born between 1910 and 1925 to report for 'obligatory work service' over the next few days.[20] But by the end of that Saturday only 150 men had reported for duty, rather than the 30,000 that had been expected. As a consequence, the German commander, Colonel Scholl, issued a second decree on 26 September, this time in his own name: 'Starting tomorrow, by means of military patrols, I will put a stop to this shirking. Those who fail to present themselves are in contravention of published orders, and will be shot by the patrols without hesitation.'[21]

The announcement produced an immediate scramble among men aged between 18 and 33 all over the city. Those who had not already hidden themselves away in the farms and caves around Naples now headed for their gardens, cellars, churches, convents – anywhere to hide from the German patrols. They locked themselves in cupboards, or hid in holes beneath the floor. They gathered in back rooms, and had their wives pull wardrobes across the doorways to hide them. Some disguised themselves as women. One group of women in the suburb of Materdei even went so far as to brick their husbands and sons up behind a wall in the cellar and pile onions in front of it to make it look as if the wall had always been there.[22]

On Monday 27 September German patrols began conducting house-to-house searches throughout the older quarters of the city. Despite their best efforts to hide away, thousands of men were caught: on that day alone around 2,000 men were captured and loaded onto trucks in Piazza Dante, to be taken away to captivity. Many of these men were not within the prescribed age range, but were often much older, and in some cases also younger than the decree specified.[23]

Alfredo Parente, who would later become the director of the

National Association of Italian Partisans (ANPI) in Naples, described
the tragedy as it unfolded:

> From the windows of the balcony on Piazza Dante I witnessed
> the parade of a thousand men, poorly dressed, some still in
> pyjamas because they were pulled out of bed at dawn and
> roughly torn from their families. The sad procession was also
> escorted by Fascists in black shirts – and this was the most
> shameful thing: Italians leading Italians to the sacrifice. It was
> pouring with rain and those poor men were completely
> drenched. Some old women trudged along the edge of that sad
> parade, trying to shelter their dear sons with umbrellas.[24]

For the Germans, such an operation was far from easy. Not only did
they have to contend with the rain, but they were obstructed every step
of the way. Children announced their arrival with shouts of 'The
Germans are coming!', giving their fathers and brothers time to scramble out of windows and escape across the rooftops. Women barred the
doors, pleaded with the Germans, wept, and generally made a nuisance
of themselves. Sometimes they even threatened violence: in the Spanish
Quarter a mob of angry women managed to intimidate the German
patrol so effectively that they actually let their prisoners go.[25] Even after
their menfolk had been taken away, women continued to pester the
Germans, sometimes so persistently that one or two even managed to
get their husbands or sons back. Rosa Fusaro remembers going to
Piazza Dante with her mother to see if they could reclaim her brother
Antonio after he had been marched away. Her mother harried a succession of officers, claiming that Antonio was far too young to be taken
off to war, until she finally found one who was sympathetic. 'My
mother didn't give up and went to another captain, and he replied: "if
you can get him back home then do it, because all of these boys that
you see are never coming home again." In the meantime, despite other
Germans standing in her way, my mother managed to get my brother
and bring him home.'[26]

In some respects the German round-ups in Naples could be considered a success: in total they managed to gather around 8,000 forced

labourers, some of whom would be used to build fortifications further north, and the remainder carted off to work camps in Germany.[27] But in the immediate short term they proved disastrous, because they provided the final spark for the insurrection that was about to engulf the city.

This, at least, was the conclusion that Filippo Caracciolo came to when he ventured through the Spanish Quarter as the insurrection was in full swing. Every woman he spoke to told him the same thing: 'that this show of popular anger was fuelled above all by resentment for the manhunt carried out by the Occupation Authorities.'[28]

Those who took part in the insurrection in other parts of the city appear to agree with him. 'The principal motive out of which the people of Naples rebelled against the Germans,' claimed Antonio Amoretti, one of the partisans in Rione Sanità, 'was that the Germans were rounding up their youths and deporting them; it was an instinct for defence and was a spontaneous movement of the people.'[29] Another fighter, Giuseppe Iaccarino, put it more bluntly. 'Those people were looking for me, they wanted to make me a slave. I said, if they want me, they'll have to take me dead! Horizontally!'[30]

In the turbulent days leading up to 27 September the people of Naples had already been pushed to their limit. They had been defeated and humiliated, deprived of food and driven from their homes. They had watched their workplaces and cultural institutions being blown up and burned to the ground. But it was the forced enslavement of the city's young men that proved to be the last straw.

CHAPTER 20

The Four Days
of Naples

Many suburbs of Naples lay claim to being the first to rebel against the Germans. The first sparks were probably lit in Pagliarone, on the Vomero hill, where 200 disbanded soldiers left the farm where they had been hiding and took to the streets: today a stone plaque at the site announces exactly this. But in fact there were lots of sparks in lots of different suburbs, which combined to set the entire city alight. 'The city was transformed, in a short time, into an immense battlefield,' wrote one partisan leader in his memoirs, adding that this was not just a matter of a few ex-soldiers, but 'thanks to massive popular participation' throughout the city.[1] 'At dawn on 28 September, the streets of Naples were flowing with armed citizens of all ages,' wrote another resistance leader. 'The very air they breathed that morning was revolutionary.'[2]

The 'Four Days' would be a very different kind of uprising from the one that had happened earlier in the month. That fight had taken place in the city's fortresses, barracks and police stations: strongholds that, by themselves, had not been capable of resisting the concentrated German assault. This time the resistance would take place in the streets.

From a German point of view this was a much trickier prospect. It was one thing to concentrate all your firepower on a handful of key buildings to subdue a small core of soldiers and policemen; another thing altogether to take on a whole city, where every street was a potential battlefield, and every citizen a potential fighter. Neapolitans, who knew their home city far better than any German soldier could, were free to concentrate and disperse again wherever they wanted to. For two weeks the Germans had considered themselves masters of the streets. Now they were not safe anywhere.

And yet, there were similarities between the earlier resistance and the revolt that was about to start. Strategically speaking, the principles were just the same: both sides needed to control the major routes in and out of the city. The Porta Capuana and the nearby Piazza Nazionale were still chokepoints that guarded all of the routes westwards out of the city. The Via Foria was still the key road heading out towards the airport at Capodichino and all routes north and northeast. The single most important road junction remained the one that lay near the northwest corner of the ancient city, beside the National Archaeological Museum. This was where the Via Foria converged with the city's main north–south axis (Via Roma/Toledo); and also to the Via Salvator Rosa, the winding road that led up to Vomero and the high ground that overlooked both the coastline and the Neapolitan plain. Whoever controlled these key points effectively controlled the city.

Since each area of Naples has its own unique character, it is probably best to treat each of them in turn. The various communities suffered and exalted in different ways over this extraordinary few days, and the different street patterns forced each group to use different methods of fighting. There is a vast gulf between events in the city centre and the experience of those who dared to take up arms around the periphery.

And yet, taken altogether, the struggle in and around Naples at the end of September 1943 would show all the characteristics that would become familiar to other Italians in the months to come. Clandestine attacks, full-pitched battles, betrayal, infighting, civil war, atrocity and eventual triumph – all the aspects of the better-known struggle that took place in the north of the country over most of the next two years would first occur here, condensed into just a few intense days.

War in the Ancient Centre

The hub of resistance activity in the historic centre was the hospital that sat at the top of the small hill at the northernmost edge of the ancient city – the depressingly named Ospedale degli Incurabili (Hospital of the Incurables). Earlier in the war a handful of political prisoners had been transferred here from the island of Ventotene. They were half dead when they arrived, because of the harsh conditions they had been kept in on their island prison, but with a little food and some good care from the hospital staff they were soon returned to health. Among them was a 32-year-old Socialist named Federico Zvab, a veteran of the Spanish Civil War, who was brought here because he was badly in need of an appendectomy. During the many months he spent at the hospital, he recruited dozens of doctors, nurses, patients and their families to his cause. According to Zvab, by the time Mussolini was deposed in July 1943 he and his fellow activists could count on 600 supporters, 300 of whom were already armed. Their ranks were swelled still further after the Germans seized control of Naples, and scores of soldiers took refuge in the hospital to avoid being taken prisoner.[3]

Over time, Zvab and his fellow activists amassed an arsenal, which they hid in various dark corners around the hospital. Guns were smuggled in by sympathetic soldiers and policemen, or stolen from the army and police barracks that had been abandoned after the German takeover. Hundreds of hand grenades also found their way into the hospital. At one point Zvab was brought three belt-fed machine guns, along with thousands of rounds of ammunition. Unsure what to do with them, he hid them in the hospital mortuary to keep them safe from prying eyes.[4]

Zvab's group called itself the 'Partisans of Revolutionary Action' (*Partigiani d'azione rivoluzionaria*). They had always planned to rise up against the Fascists and the Germans at some point, but after the events of Monday 27 September all agreed that the time for waiting was over. That evening their executive committee met in an abandoned room on the top floor of the hospital and unanimously elected Zvab its military and political head. Orders were issued to all the various cells around the city 'to immediately attack the nazifascists everywhere'.[5] At the same time other leaders were appointed to take detachments of men out to key points around the perimeter of the old city – to Piazza Cavour, Porta Capuana, Piazza Dante, and even into other suburbs further afield. A poster was designed, printed and circulated the following morning, calling for the people of Naples to rise up and free themselves from 'the bloody tyranny of a miserable regime', and 'avenge those who have been barbarously killed'.[6]

In the early hours of Tuesday morning, the revolutionaries gathered all the 200 or so soldiers hiding in the hospital, found clothes for them in the hospital cloakroom and set about collecting and checking their concealed weapons. 'In the early afternoon of the same day,' wrote Zvab years later, 'we went out en masse and with all our weapons we crossed the various wards of the hospital. It is no exaggeration to say that no medical centre was ever the scene of such a spectacle.'[7]

Outside, the ancient city was already a hive of activity. Since the night before, improvised groups of partisans, ex-servicemen and ordinary civilians had been hastily constructing barricades all along Via Duomo, Piazza Cavour and at other key points around the ancient centre. Rubble, sandbags, chunks of masonry and even heavy pieces of furniture were piled up, blocking the entrances to the warren of alleys that lay beyond. The old town was being converted into a fortress.

Zvab initially set up his headquarters in an apartment belonging to the mother of two fellow partisans in Vico Cinquesanti, but as the insurrection grew they moved into the municipal office building at Piazza San Gaetano, at the very heart of the ancient city. It was the logical place to locate his command centre: the piazza sat on Via Tribunali, one of the two ancient Greek thoroughfares that cut across the heart of the historic centre, and the convent that stood here had a spacious courtyard that would serve as a barracks and first aid post when the time came.

Unfortunately, if Zvab's group knew this, so did the Germans, who immediately targeted the area where the partisans were setting up their HQ. At around 4.30 p.m., two German tanks and an armoured car approached Via Duomo from the direction of the port, at speed, and turned into Via Tribunali. They easily rolled over the barricade at

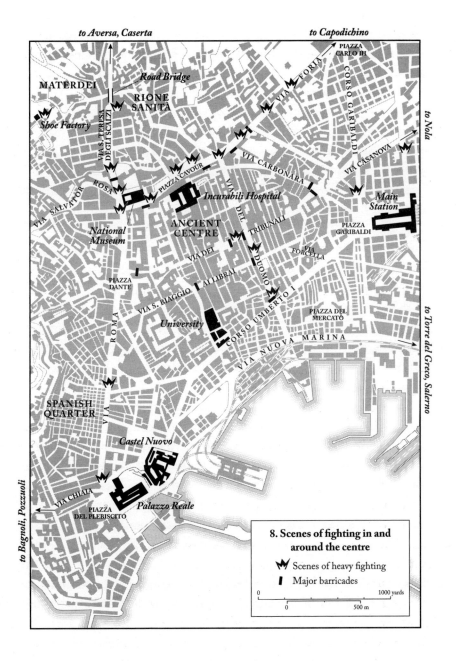

to Aversa, Caserta   to Capodichino

PIAZZA
CARLO III

MATERDEI

RIONE
SANITÀ

Road Bridge

VIA FORIA

CORSO GARIBALDI

Shoe Factory

VIA S. TERESA DEGLI SCALZI

VIA CARBONARA

VIA CASANOVA

to Nola

ROSA

PIAZZA CAVOUR

Incurabili Hospital

Main
Station

VIA SALVATOR

VIA DEL TRIBUNALI

PIAZZA
GARIBALDI

National
Museum

ANCIENT
CENTRE

VIA DEI

VIA FORCELLA

VIA DUOMO

PIAZZA
DANTE

VIA S. BIAGGIO

AI LIBRAI

CORSO UMBERTO I

University

PIAZZA DEL
MERCATO

VIA ROMA

VIA NUOVA MARINA

to Torre del Greco, Salerno

SPANISH
QUARTER

VIA

Castel Nuovo

to Bagnoli, Pozzuoli

VIA CHIAIA

PIAZZA
DEL PLEBISCITO

Palazzo Reale

8. Scenes of fighting in and around the centre

W Scenes of heavy fighting

❚ Major barricades

0   1000 yards

0   500 m

the mouth of the ancient street, which was not yet completed, and headed down towards a second barricade that had been set up to protect Piazza San Gaetano. This is where, despite their massive fire-power, the German tanks were finally halted. Via Tribunali is the widest street in this part of the old city, but it is still far too narrow for tanks to manoeuvre effectively. Hemmed in by thick walls made of volcanic stone, the vehicles were forced to approach in single file under a rain of hand grenades and small arms fire coming not only from the barricade in front of them but also from the windows above them and from the tiny, impenetrable alleyways on either side. Before long, they gave up the fight and reversed back down the way they had come.[8]

The next day they tried again. By this time the Neapolitans had built up much more effective barricades not only along the entrances to the ancient city in Via Duomo, but also at the mouth of Piazza Nicola Amore, where the Via Duomo itself joined the wide main thoroughfare of Corso Umberto I. After a short fight, the German armoured column crossed over the barricade and headed up Via Duomo at speed.

The partisans had set up one of their heavy machine guns here, but, since they did not have anyone properly trained to fire it, it ended up being not very effective. What *was* effective was the rifle fire coming from the houses all along the Via Duomo; and the hand grenades thrown by the defenders of the barricades that now blocked off all the entrances to the ancient centre. As two German tanks approached the mouth of Via San Biagio dei Librai, dozens of partisans and civilians began enthusiastically throwing hand grenades. The Germans stopped and tried to engage them, but within a few minutes both German tanks had been disabled. After picking up a couple of the soldiers who had alighted from their vehicles to fight, the armoured car turned and fled. Shortly afterwards an ambulance also came hurtling down Via Duomo, firing on either side as it went. But this, too, was stopped and put out of action, and its two occupants killed.

From this skirmish alone – and there were many others – the Germans lost twenty men, nine of whom were either dead or mortally wounded. The remainder were either taken prisoner or escorted up to the hospital for treatment. The Neapolitan defenders also had several wounded, though thankfully none of them too seriously.

Once the dust had cleared, they made a gap in one of their barricades and dragged the two tanks and the ambulance down Via Tribunali to their command headquarters – partly to deny them to the enemy, partly to bolster their own defences, but also, one suspects, as trophies. Inside the vehicles they discovered twenty sacks of looted flour and two barrels of olive oil, a true bounty for a people who had gone hungry for several weeks.

From that day onwards, the Germans dared not venture down Via Duomo again, let alone into the maze of alleyways that spread away on either side of it. Until the arrival of the Allies on 1 October, the ancient centre was entirely free of Germans, like a liberated island right in the heart of Naples.

Piazza Cavour and Via Foria

For centuries, Naples existed only within its city walls. One of the main reasons why the historic centre is so cramped and overcrowded is that the Spanish viceroys, who were perpetually worried about security, banned any building outside the walls for fear that it might compromise the city's defences. It was not until after the Spanish had been ousted at the beginning of the eighteenth century that Naples finally began to expand. Just north of the city walls, in the greenery of the Rione Sanità (the 'health district'), a whole new suburb began to spring up, as elegant new palazzi were constructed for noble and wealthy bourgeois families. In the following years, however, poorer Neapolitan families inevitably followed, and it was not long before this area was almost as impoverished and overcrowded as the slums they had all been hoping to leave behind. A similar process took place with all the other new suburbs that were built north and west of the city: Montecalvario, Avvocata, Materdei, Stella.

Between the city walls and the new suburbs, like a cordon stretching along the northern fringe of the old city, was a broad thoroughfare some 40 or 50 metres wide, and about 400 metres long. In the nineteenth century this broad strip of ground was given the name Piazza

Cavour, after the politician who had masterminded the unification of Italy. At one end of the piazza, opposite the northwest corner of the old city, a huge building dominates the area: it was originally built by the Spanish in 1585 as a cavalry barracks, but since the end of the nineteenth century it has been the National Archaeological Museum. At the other end of the piazza, at the northeastern corner of the old city, is the beginning of the Via Foria, one of the few main roads that leads out of Naples.

For the Germans, who were in the process of evacuating Naples – and for the Neapolitans, who were trying to trap them – this was one of the most important strategic points in the city. It was the Wehrmacht's main escape route from the heart of the city out to Capodichino, from where they could link up to the national routes to Benevento, Avellino, Caserta and Rome. 'It is easy to imagine what strategic importance this route had for the Germans,' wrote Mario Orbitello, a lawyer and one of the resistance leaders in this part of the city, before adding, bitterly, that this importance 'can be demonstrated by the large number of Neapolitans who fell in that area'.[9]

On 28 September, as the insurrection was first starting to take hold, a group of German soldiers tried to force their way into the National Archaeological Museum. Had they succeeded, they would have been able to dominate not only the whole of Piazza Cavour, but also the road that led westwards up to the heights of Vomero, as well as the city centre's main north–south axis. They fired several shots at the locks of the museum's robust entrance gate, but were not able to get in: all they really managed to do was to damage one of the neoclassical statues in the museum vestibule. Eventually they were forced to give up and retreat up the hill towards Capodimonte.

After the Germans had gone, the partisans also tried to occupy the museum. Unlike the Germans, however, they approached the museum director and asked his permission. He refused, despite considerable pressure, because he didn't want to turn this cultural treasure house into a target for German artillery. Eventually the partisans also gave up, but only after the director had promised not to allow anyone else to use the building for military purposes. The museum would remain unoccupied by either side throughout the uprising.

The museum director kept a record of all these encounters, as well as the frantic activity that was suddenly happening in the streets outside. '[A]ll the openings around the Museum are occupied and manned by the partisans,' he wrote in his notebook. Italian machine guns were set up on the other side of the street, riflemen appeared at the windows and balconies opposite, and a partisan 'Defence Command' was set up in the building next door, which overlooked the museum's northern courtyard. It was not long before 'intense shooting from the windows begins and the launching of bombs against every vehicle and traveler who is in any way suspicious or doesn't know the password. Boys and *scugnizzi* slip quickly from door to door carrying ammunition and news.'[10]

Down on Piazza Cavour, events were moving quickly. On the city wall side, Federico Zvab's 'Partisans of Revolutionary Action' had blocked off all the entrances to the historic centre with barricades, which were now being manned by a coalition of partisans, ex-soldiers and ordinary civilians. On the northern side of the piazza the same thing had happened to all the entrances leading into the Rione Sanità. Here a variety of other groups had taken responsibility for the uprising. In Via Miracoli, for example, the chief of the local fire brigade, Lieutenant Giacomelli, was busy arming 200 men with the rifles he had kept hidden for the last few weeks in one of the city's wells. Another group was led by Mario Orbitello and his like-minded friend Vittore Occhiuzzi. Still other groups, each of them independent from the last, set up positions on the roof of the Cinema Partenopeo, on the steps of the Botanical Gardens, and at many other points along the Via Foria.[11]

One of the first skirmishes to take place in the battle for this thoroughfare came at around twelve noon, when Vittore Occhiuzzi's group stopped a German army truck that was entering Via Foria at speed. As the truck skidded to a halt, Occhiuzzi approached it with his pistol raised and demanded that the three soldiers inside surrender. As they were getting out of the truck one of the soldiers reached for his gun: in the ensuing flurry of gunfire Occhiuzzi was lightly grazed by a German bullet, but two of the Germans were killed. The third was taken prisoner and led off to the fire station, which before long would become a makeshift prisoner-of-war camp.[12]

As the day drew on, dozens of similar skirmishes took place between Germans and Neapolitans along this stretch of road, with casualties on both sides. Salvatore Cacciapuoti, a Communist worker who took part in the fighting further along the road, gives a taste of the chaos and confusion:

> I am at the corner of an alley in Via Foria, on the right-hand side coming from Piazza Carlo III, a little further up from the Garibaldi barracks on the other side of the road not far away. The bullets of the machine guns placed in front of the barracks reach our group and beyond. German vehicles pass quickly, firing left and right. Groups positioned at the corners of the alleys shoot back. From the corners of our alley we fire against the machine guns of the barracks and the German vehicles. Bullets whistle over my head. I don't see anything and I don't understand but I keep shooting … I look to the ground: there's one of our comrades. I think he's in shock, or shielding himself belly to the ground. I tell him to get up. The shooting begins, so we shake him. Our comrade has died without having had time to utter a single cry. He has been struck by a blast from a machine gun. I didn't have the time or the strength to look at his face, I was seized by a sense of nausea. The others in the group told me that he was our poor and good comrade Pianto.[13]

At one point in the afternoon the fighting intensified still further with the arrival of two light tanks in Piazza Cavour. One of the first places they attacked was a bar on the piazza run by Vincenzo Pinto, a 47-year-old republican well known for his anti-Fascist views. Throughout the 1930s, Pinto's bar had been a meeting place for anti-Fascists: now it was a natural focal point for the uprising. According to Pinto, the tanks arrived around 3 p.m., and there was little they could do to resist them:

> Unfortunately, the shots of rifles and muskets, the explosions of hand grenades were not much use against their armor, against their tracks: they approached the bar, took a frontal position there and violently opened fire. The huge damage caused to the

room is still visible today. After they had blown through the walls with their projectiles, I, my son Italo and signorina Rosa Maraniello were injured. Our reaction was prompt, fierce and vigorous: we scrambled out of the bar on all fours with hand grenades and bottles of petrol, and counterattacked. Targeted from everywhere, especially by the *caribinieri reali* from the top of their barracks in front of the bar, who were firing precise and lethal shots, the two tanks were forced to abandon the ground, with wounded on board.[14]

It is difficult to know whether these tanks really were chased away, or whether they were simply moving on to another part of the city – but, either way, it was obvious that they were not able to subdue resistance here.

Things might have been different if more tanks and armoured cars had arrived in the Via Foria that afternoon. The German commander, Colonel Scholl, had actually ordered an armoured column to come down from Capodichino and quell the nascent uprising, but as they made their way towards the city they were brought to a sudden and unexpected halt. To their utter surprise, they found themselves being fired upon by an Italian anti-aircraft battery, hidden in the woods above them at Moiariello, less than 2 kilometres away. Unbeknownst to them, the men of 318 Battery had hidden their artillery pieces at the time of the Armistice: now, led by Lieutenant Edoardo Droetto, sixty former soldiers and civilians had unearthed these guns for use in the uprising. When they saw the German armoured column snaking their way down from Capodichino into the city they opened fire. According to Aldo De Jaco, eight tanks were hit, and several of them completely destroyed. Faced with the threat of annihilation, the column was forced to turn back.

Unfortunately for Droetto and his followers, their *coup de main* could not be repeated. Once they had given their position away they were soon surrounded and overcome by the Germans. But there is no doubt that, without their intervention, the carnage and destruction around Via Foria and Piazza Cavour would have been far, far worse. As it was, the whole area remained in the hands of the partisans, who made this road virtually impassable for German soldiers trying to escape the city.[15]

Materdei and the Central Route North

The second main route out of the city is the central north–south axis that runs virtually in a straight line all the way from the Royal Palace near the port up to the wooded hills of Capodimonte. This road has several different names along its course. The southernmost stretch has always been known as the Via Toledo (even though its official name after the Risorgimento and for much of the 20th century was Via Roma). North of Piazza Dante it becomes Via Enrico Pessina. And beyond the National Archaeological Museum and its junction with Piazza Cavour it changes its name again to Via S. Teresa degli Scalzi.

In the eighteenth century, the northernmost stretch of this road would have been something of a road to nowhere: not far north of the museum the terrain dips suddenly into the valley of the Rione Sanità, before rising steeply again on the other side, making any journey northwards cumbersome and impractical. It was only at the beginning of the nineteenth century, when the city was briefly part of Napoleon's empire, that a bridge was finally built across this valley. It was Napoleon's brother who started the project in 1807, and his brother-in-law Joachim Murat who finished it three years later. The building of the Ponte della Sanità was hugely controversial at the time. On the one hand it involved the partial destruction of a monastic complex in the valley below to make way for the bridge's huge brick arches; on the other it created a clear route out of the city to Capodimonte for the first time. It also created another opportunity: an aqueduct was chanelled beneath the bridge, bringing fresh water down from the hills to the northern quarters of the city.[16]

All of this was desperately important in the autumn of 1943. The German plan was to continue rounding up men in the overcrowded suburbs that lay on either side of this main road, and to continue looting goods and equipment, before channelling them all northwards across the bridge and out of the city. Once they had completed their extraction they would blow up the Ponte della Sanità behind them, destroying both the road bridge and the aqueduct. For good measure, they would also blow up the water reservoirs at Capodimonte, thus depriving the Allies – and the city itself – of a vital water source.

On the morning of 28 September, the first part of this German plan seemed to be going well. The day began, just as the previous one had, with the continued round-up of Neapolitan men in Piazza Dante, who were marched northwards to captivity through the rain. There were some early signs of resistance along the route: barricades had appeared at some of the mouths to the alleyways, for example, and early in the afternoon the partisans set up a heavy machine gun on the high ground to one side of the road near the Archaeological Museum. But there was not much that the people here could do at this point: the Germans were simply too numerous and too well armed to be effectively resisted until later on that afternoon.

Once they ventured off the main road, however, it was a different story. To the northwest of the museum lies the suburb of Materdei, a maze of narrow alleys that lead off the main road at Via S. Teresa degli Scalzi. Some of these alleys rise towards Vomero further west, others descend steeply northwards into the Rione Sanità in the valley below. It was here, in one of these alleys, that another different type of conflict was sparked.

In Via delle Trone there was a shoe factory that produced boots for the Italian army. On the morning of the 28th a dozen or so German soldiers turned up here with a lorry and began looting the factory of all its shoe leather. At the same time, sappers began laying mines and canisters of liquid incendiary around the building. The factory was deserted at the time, because most of the male shoemakers were in hiding to avoid being taken away – but people who lived in the same street immediately ran off to find them and warn them of what was happening.

When they returned they brought dozens of partisans and shoemakers with them, armed with guns stolen from a navy barracks nearby. They surrounded the building and decided to deliver the Germans an ultimatum: leave the factory intact, and the lorry full of shoe leather behind, and their lives would be spared. The only problem was how to deliver this ultimatum, since any man who entered the factory was likely either to be taken prisoner or shot. It was at this point that one of the female shoe workers volunteered, arguing that as a woman she was less likely to be killed. Unarmed, she stepped through the factory gates, and into the history books.

Maddalena Cerasuolo, Lena or Lenuccia to her friends, has become a legendary figure in Naples. The daughter of a decorated war hero who had been in and out of prison for repeated acts of defiance against the Fascists, resistance seemed to be in her blood. In the coming months she would join the British Special Operations Executive (SOE) and parachute behind enemy lines to work as a spy – but for now she was still just an ordinary factory worker along with all the others.[17]

Her gamble paid off: she was able to enter the factory, deliver the ultimatum and return unharmed. Unfortunately, however, the soldiers inside did not trust the Neapolitans to honour the deal and came out firing. A ferocious battle ensued, which lasted several hours. Unable to reach their vehicle, the Germans fled to another building and spent the afternoon besieged there. At one point seven or eight Neapolitans made a charge for the door, but were beaten back with intense gunfire: during the course of the afternoon two of them were killed and several injured. Lenuccia Cerasuolo took part in this from start to finish, distributing hand grenades among the men, and firing a gun of her own. The Germans finally escaped towards evening – but they were forced to leave behind the truck loaded with leather. The factory that they had taken such care to mine remained intact.

Back on the main road, meanwhile, another battle had broken out. A group of local people had caught sight of some German sappers mining the bridge over the Rione Sanità, and had gathered at the southern end of the bridge to open fire on them. Before long there were dozens of local people here, including Lenuccia and her father Carlo. The Germans, exposed on the open road, had nowhere to take cover except behind their lorry. Their attackers, by contrast, had the luxury of being able to hide behind the low walls at the entrance to the bridge, and also behind a large stone memorial dedicated to the dead of the First World War. The stand-off here lasted over half an hour, during which time Lenuccia's father was hit in the leg. While he was carried off home for treatment, Lenuccia herself continued fighting.

The battle came to an abrupt end when a couple of partisans ran down into the valley below and back up to the other side of the bridge. When the Germans discovered they were being fired on from both sides, they scrambled back into their truck and sped off towards Capodimonte. Once they had gone, the mines were removed from the bridge. Over the following few days, despite various attempts to retake the bridge, the Germans were never able to replace these mines: both the road and the aqueduct that ran beneath it were saved.[18] At the same time, a completely different group of Neapolitans in Capodimonte attacked the German forces that were attempting to mine the reservoir that fed this aqueduct. Taken completely by surprise, the Germans were forced to surrender, and these vital links in Naples' water supply were saved.[19]

That evening, at around six, a rainstorm broke out, drenching the city. For a few hours, German armoured cars continued to race through the dark, wet streets. Along Via Toledo there were various clashes between German forces and armed youths shooting from the mouths of the alleys leading up into the Spanish Quarter. One woman who ventured out onto her balcony opposite *Il Mattino*'s offices was caught by a burst of machine-gun fire.[20] At the southernmost end of Via Toledo, in Piazza Trieste e Trento, a series of skirmishes occurred with casualties on both sides. Two young boys, one 17 years old and the other just 13, were killed while throwing hand grenades at German vehicles. They were both posthumously awarded Italy's highest award for valour, the Gold Medal.[21]

Over the course of the next two days, the fighting along this route in and out of the city only intensified. On the morning of 29 September, Neapolitan partisans led by Alfredo Parente turned a tram car on its side just north of the Archaeological Museum and piled up masonry around it to form a massive barricade across the road. When a German armoured column drove down from Capodimonte it came under attack from partisans manning this barricade. Unfortunately the upturned tram car did not completely block the road, and the German tanks were able to get around it.

Several Neapolitans were killed here, and dozens wounded. Among the dead was another legendary figure of the 'Four Days' – a third, even younger child gunned down while throwing a bomb at the tanks. Like the two boys killed the evening before, 12-year-old Gennaro Capuozzo was also posthumously awarded the Gold Medal for valour. According to his medal citation, he faced the tanks 'with indomitable courage', throwing hand grenades at them 'until the explosion of a shell blew him up at his post along with the machine-gunner who was at his side'.[22]

Although the stand at this barricade was much more organized than the fighting that had occurred the day before, it was still a community affair, even a family affair. Once again Lenuccia Cerasuolo was in the thick of the action, and she especially would have felt the loss of the young boy at the barricade: Gennaro Capuozzo was her cousin.[23]

Despite their heroic efforts, the partisans were never quite able to close off this road to German traffic. On the 29th, the tanks made it all the way into the centre of the city. But once they got to the foot of Via Roma, where there was yet another barricade, they could do little more than turn back and return the way they had come. There was certainly no question of them being able to subdue the uprising, which, by now, had spread to every corner of Naples.

From this point on, all plans for the Germans to continue their looting and destruction of the city had to be abandoned. The best they could manage was to extract the bulk of their troops from the city alive.

Vomero

Events in the suburb of Vomero during this tumultuous time were different all over again. People here were very probably the first to take up arms against the Germans, although it is difficult to say for sure. They were served by several outstanding, proactive leaders, whose aggression and ambition was rewarded with some spectacular success in the days to come. Several of the most important chroniclers of the 'Four Days' also fought in Vomero, meaning that the events that took place here would become much more famous than those in other parts of the city. Much of the myth-making that has built up around the Neapolitan uprising started in Vomero.

To begin with, however, it is important to note that the terrain here was very different from other parts of Naples already described. Vomero is a much newer part of the city than Sanità, Materdei, or most of the other suburbs around the historic centre. Built on the hill directly to the west of the ancient city, it was originally conceived as a suburb for the wealthy middle classes, away from the poverty and cramped conditions of the streets below.

Running around the neck of the hill, with views over the old city on one side and the coastal strip of Chiaia on the other, is the long main road that links the west of the city to the centre: the Corso Vittorio Emanuele. In September 1943 this is where the German commander had his headquarters, in the Hotel Parker. Above this, where the hill levels out a little into more gently undulating ground, the tree-lined streets are laid out in orderly grids and geometric patterns. Most of the elegant, spacious apartment blocks here were built in the late nineteenth and early twentieth centuries, with large windows and balconies overlooking the streets below.

Rising above them all, at the very top of the hill, stands the Castel Sant'Elmo. The ancient fortress was largely deserted by this point, but there were concentrations of German troops at various other points around Vomero, particularly in a park overlooking the coast called the Villa Floridiana, and in a sports stadium towards the west of the suburb, the Stadio del Littorio.

However, the Germans were not the only ones to have large concentrations of fighters here. On the western fringe of the suburb, in Via Belvedere, some 200 or so resisters were hiding together in the grounds of the Pagliarone farm. They were an eclectic group that included disbanded soldiers, local youths trying to evade the German round-ups and even a handful of escaped Allied prisoners of war. Out of this group emerged one or two natural leaders, who organized the looting and distribution of weapons and urged the others to take their fate into their own hands by confronting the Germans head-on. Among them were a street vendor named Vincenzo Sacco, another activist called Ugo Tripitelli and a former criminal, Vincenzo Stimolo, who was posing as a retired artillery captain. This last character is easily the most famous of the bunch. Despite his shady past, Enzo Stimolo ended up

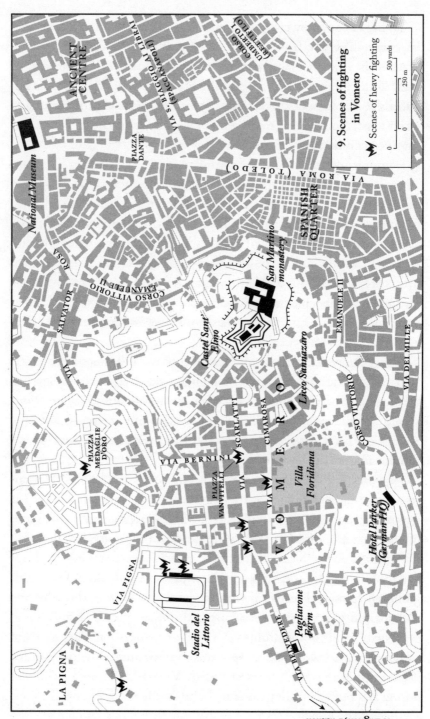

ANCIENT CENTRE

National Museum

PIAZZA DANTE

VIA S. BIAGGIO AI LIBRAI (SPACCANAPOLI)

CORSO UMBERTO I (RETTIFILO)

SPANISH QUARTER

VIA ROMA (TOLEDO)

CORSO VITTORIO EMANUELE II

SALVATOR ROSA

Castel Sant' Elmo

San Martino monastery

EMANUELE II

VIA DEL MILLE

CORSO VITTORIO

Liceo Sannazaro

VIA SCARLATTI

VIA CIMAROSA

VIA BERNINI

PIAZZA MEDAGLIE D'ORO

PIAZZA VANVITELLI

VILLA FLORIDIANA

V O M E R O

Villa Floridiana

Hotel Parker (German HQ)

VIA PIGNA

LA PIGNA

Stadio del Littorio

VIA BELVEDERE

Pagliarone Farm

to Bagnoli, Pozzuoli

9. Scenes of fighting in Vomero

⚡ Scenes of heavy fighting

0   250 m   500 m
0   500 yards

being one of the most resourceful and courageous of all the leaders in the Naples uprising. Like Maddelena Cerasuolo, he would go on to fight for the Allied secret services behind enemy lines for the rest of the war.[24]

On the evening of 27 September, Stimolo led an expedition to the other side of Vomero to gather weapons that had been deposited in the Castel Sant'Elmo by the Carabinieri in the previous days. It was a dangerous thing to do. The Germans had imposed a strict curfew, and a dozen men crossing the suburb together after dark were bound to attract attention. As cover, one of them put on a Carabiniere uniform. The ruse seems to have worked, because when they returned a few hours later they brought with them a cart loaded with rifles, two machine guns and 5,000 rounds of ammunition.[25]

It was probably impossible to hide so many men in the Pagliarone farm without someone noticing the clandestine comings and goings. At around eleven o'clock that night, a man in German uniform came sniffing around the entrance yard to the farm. The two guards on duty that night, Vincenzo Sacco and Eduardo Salvatore, immediately grabbed him and tied him to a tree.[26] This intruder turned out not to be a German at all, but an Italian volunteer in the German army named Galdi, who, according to Salvatore at least, had spent the previous days threatening the local population with wholesale bombardment if they did not submit to the German will.[27] The men of Pagliarone decided to make an example of him. The following morning they gathered their weapons and left the farm en masse with the unfortunate Galdi walking before them carrying an Italian flag, and being made to shout various slogans such as 'Viva l'Italia!' and 'I am a traitor'.[28]

Around midday, this procession encountered a pair of German soldiers on a motorbike. Tripitelli, who was a little ahead of the others, immediately threw a grenade at them, causing the death of at least one of the pair. But in the confusion that followed, the traitor Galdi ran away and returned immediately to warn the Germans about what was happening in the streets of Vomero. Allowing him to escape turned out to be a costly mistake. Shortly afterwards three truckloads of German soldiers left their barracks in the nearby sports stadium and headed down to Via Belvedere to suppress the growing uprising. They did not come across Enzo Stimolo and his group of fighters, who by now had moved on, but they did encounter one of the machine guns that had been set up there. A short battle commenced, which ended with the two men manning the machine gun running for their lives. All they had really achieved was to enrage the Germans, who kicked over their machine gun, threw their Italian flag to the ground and started stamping on it.[29]

Furious, the Germans spent the next hour or so terrorizing the area. They fired at the windows of the houses, and killed several people on the streets who tried to run away from them, including a 15-year-old girl.[30] They then rounded up forty-seven hostages among the local civilians and took them back to their barracks at the Stadio del Littorio. This did not bode well. Earlier in the month the Germans had already announced that they would execute ten Italians for every German soldier killed. Even if these hostages were not killed, the best they could probably hope for was to be sent northwards along with the thousands of others who had already been rounded up, and forced to work for the German war machine.

By now, fighting had broken out all over Vomero. Enzo Stimolo and his group had moved on to Via Cimarosa, at the southern brim of the hill, to set fire to the Fascist headquarters there. Ugo Tripitelli had taken another group of men towards Piazza Vanvitelli, where others were already fighting groups of Germans and their Fascist sympathizers, who had barricaded themselves inside some of the houses. Another group of partisans had formed in this area under the leadership of Edoardo Pansini and Antonio Tarsia in Curia, who, over the course of the following twenty-four hours, would set up a command and control centre for the uprising based in a local school, the Liceo Sannazaro.[31] Further north, in Piazza Medaglie d'Oro, another battle was taking place against a German command post guarding the route out of the city towards Arenella.[32] The sound of guns, and occasional explosions, could be heard everywhere.

As in other parts of Naples, the fighting was brought to an end that evening when the heavens opened and Germans and Neapolitans alike retired indoors to escape the rain. But the following morning hostilities were resumed. Major confrontations took place once again around Piazza Medaglie d'Oro to the north and Piazza Vanvitelli to the south. On one occasion some German trucks descended into Piazza Vanvitelli from the direction of the Castel Sant'Elmo, only to be greeted with a rain of fire from the windows above them. A group of German soldiers abandoned one of the trucks and tried to fight their way down Via Scarlatti: the battle lasted a couple of hours before they finally made it back to their vehicle and raced away again.

According to eyewitnesses, Enzo Stimolo was in the thick of the action, as were many other groups, all of them supporting one another.[33] But the main event of the day was the siege of the German garrison in the Stadio del Littorio, where the forty-seven hostages were being held – and, once again, Enzo Stimolo found himself at the very heart of events. Indeed, the way this particular drama unfolded would eventually make his name famous throughout the city.

The siege had actually been begun by yet another natural leader, an artillery lieutenant named Giovanni Abbate who happened to live in the large apartment building opposite the main entrance of the stadium. Abbate had seen the Germans bringing in the hostages the day before, and decided to try to do something to save them. He gathered a dozen men with rifles and deployed them around the stadium perimeter. Outside the front of the stadium, in a construction site, he set up a machine gun and trained it on the building where most of the Germans were concentrated. Knowing how thin on the ground his men were, and how poorly armed compared to his much more numerous opponents, he tried to bluff the Germans into surrendering. Calling out to them across the street, he declared that they were surrounded, and demanded their immediate and unconditional capitulation. The German officer in charge, a highly experienced major named Hugo Saggau, responded by sending up a flare calling for reinforcements.

Stimolo arrived on the scene at around 5 p.m. He brought many more men with him and, since he claimed he was a captain, Abbate relinquished command to him without any fuss. After further fighting, the Germans waved a white flag and asked to talk to the partisans. Abbate immediately warned Stimolo with more or less the following words: 'Captain, don't listen to this man, who in bad faith has already signalled calling for reinforcements.'[34]

What ensued was a game of cat and mouse. Major Saggau was obviously playing for time, hoping for reinforcements to relieve him so that he and his men could leave the city, taking their hostages with them. On the other hand he could not wait too long because he knew the Allies would soon be in the city, and did not want to fall into their hands. In the meantime his men had run out of water – since the Germans had already cut the water mains to this part of the city – and it would not be long before thirst began to take its toll.

Stimolo, on the other hand, had time on his side – but he was desperately trying to conceal his shortage of men and ammunition. In the previous hour he had continued Abbate's policy of firing regularly from all around the stadium to give the impression that his men were much more numerous and well equipped than they actually were. He also had the hostages to think about: his main priority was to secure their release without any of them coming to harm.

According to those involved, Stimolo's first parley with Saggau did not go well. They met out in the street, under a white flag, and communicated through an interpreter – an Italian collaborator named Ezio Berti, who later wrote a highly self-serving and slightly fictionalized account of the encounter.[35] Each side appears simply to have told the other to back down. Since neither side was willing to do so, they each returned to their men, and fighting resumed as before.

While this was taking place, Giovanni Abbate decided to leave the scene. It was obvious that Stimolo had the situation more or less under control, and he had heard that the Germans were mining a bridge leading out of the suburb towards the northwest in Via Pigna. Abbate and a handful of men headed out to find them – unsuccessfully, as it turned out. Instead, they found themselves running into a column of German armoured cars, along with a tank, coming up the curving road out of the wooded valley below. These were the reinforcements that Major Saggau had summoned with his flare to relieve him and his men at the Littorio stadium.

Abbate and his men had no choice but to take cover in the nearest building, the last house on the road. According to the affidavit signed by one of them just a week later, the battle that took place here was a desperate affair. 'Following the lieutenant, we hid in the doorway,' claimed Mario Sepe:

> The German [at the head of the column] threw a hand grenade at the door and the explosion was so loud that he was stunned. The lieutenant told us: 'Let's do it boys,' and so it was that he was the first to run up the stairs of Palazzo Del Gaudio (to be precise, Via Pigna no. 130). In the dark stairs the lieutenant shouted like a madman: 'Pintore! Pintore! Here is the reserve machine-gun ribbon', but Pintore did not answer because he had already gone to take up his position with the machine gun. I, Sardu and Buonfiglio followed Lieutenant Abbate to the top floor onto the open roof terrace and all four of us began firing with rifles. The lieutenant had us load his rifle while he fired his pistol. When the German armoured cars arrived below us, the Lieutenant began throwing hand grenades; he threw four or five and then said to us – while the Germans who had seen us angrily fired volleys of machine guns at us – the Lieutenant shouted to us: 'Give me the grenades; I'm throwing the grenades.' I gave the Lieutenant three more bombs that the lieutenant threw standing on the terrace. We patriots dropped a further two bombs. At one point the Lieutenant fell to the ground. I asked him if he was hurt and after a while he assured me he wasn't. When the Lieutenant heard that we had no more ammunition he told us: 'So, boys, let's not waste any more time. I'm responsible for your lives; I'll take you to safety', and after more than half an hour, while the cannon thundered against the building, the lieutenant took us three patriots back to Captain Stimolo. It was almost 10 in the evening.[36]

Abbate and his men were not the only ones to engage this German column: several locals also joined in the fight, as well as a group of escaped British prisoners of war who attacked the column with hand grenades from behind.[37] But according to eyewitnesses, as well as the official letter recommending Abbate for a medal, it was Abbate's group that caused the most serious losses among the Germans, and cost them an armoured car, a civilian car, a motorbike and two heavy machine guns. More importantly, through their combined efforts, German reinforcements were prevented from reaching the sports stadium, where Major Saggau was still under siege.[38]

Meanwhile, back at the stadium, the cat and mouse game between Saggau and Stimolo was continuing. Waving a white flag, the German had once again requested a conference with his opposite number. This time he said he was ready to hand over the forty-seven hostages, in return for being allowed to leave the stadium with his men unharmed. However, there was a catch. Saggau claimed that he didn't have the authority to make such a decision on his own, and needed first to travel to the main headquarters to get permission from Colonel Scholl. This was probably a ruse to go and gather reinforcements, but Stimolo decided to call his bluff. If the major needed to go to his headquarters, then Stimolo would go with him.

So a ceasefire was called between the two groups of fighters while Stimolo, Saggau, the interpreter and one or two others climbed into one of the German trucks and headed off towards the German head-quarters on Corso Vittorio Emanuele. Their journey was not quite as straightforward as they thought it would be. The German driver, who was not as familiar with Naples as a local driver would have been, ended up taking the long way round, crossing the whole of Vomero to reach Corso Vittorio Emanuele at its northern end – a much longer route than simply heading south. By this time the streets were full of men with guns, who were more than willing to take shots at any German truck. Along the way they were stopped by an angry mob who wanted to lynch the German major; they had to be talked down by Stimolo. The group tried changing to a less conspicuous civilian vehicle, but when they reached Piazza Mazzini they were stopped at a roadblock by some adrenalin-fuelled partisans from CIS Park. This was a part of town where Stimolo was completely unknown, and there was no reason to suppose he was not a Fascist collaborator trying to rescue a high-ranking German. For a while it looked as though they would all be shot, but Stimolo managed to convince the partisans to take them prisoner instead. Back at the partisans' headquarters he argued urgently with the local commander until he agreed to let one of them take the all-important message through to Colonel Scholl. This job fell to the interpreter, Ezio Berti. Stimolo and Saggau were held hostage and were told that if the interpreter did not return within twenty minutes they would both be shot.

There are several different and conflicting accounts of exactly what happened that night, but the general gist of them all is the same: fortunately for everyone concerned, the message was delivered, and consent was given for Saggau to release his prisoners.[39] Later on, Saggau and Stimolo were summoned to the Hotel Parker to meet Scholl in person and negotiate the deal in full (while, somewhat surreally, an orderly served them tea). The Germans agreed to free all the hostages, unharmed – but in return Stimolo agreed to allow the Germans to withdraw their troops from Vomero without any further attacks on them.

After the war this remarkable achievement was triumphantly portrayed as a full-blown German surrender, but in reality it was a simple truce. By this point all the Germans really wanted to do was to withdraw in good order, so the deal suited Scholl as much as the Neapolitans. Nevertheless, the sight of German troops being escorted out of Vomero the next morning by armed Italian partisans left an indelible impression on the local population. It was a demonstration of what they had collectively achieved. Naples had not been destroyed, and had not been subdued. Its own people had risen up to take back control.

In the next twenty-four hours fighting continued between the Neapolitans and small groups of retreating Germans, particularly on the northwestern fringes of Vomero, in Pigna. The Germans also continued to bombard Naples with artillery until they finally left on 1 October. But, thanks to Stimolo, the rest of the suburb was entirely free of Germans. For a brief moment, before the arrival of the Allies, the people of Vomero were at last the masters of their own destiny.

Fascist Snipers

All of the above offers a flavour of the fighting that took place in Naples during the Four Days. There are several localities that have barely been mentioned, simply for the sake of avoiding repetition. Vasto, for example, just north of the central station, saw considerable violence quite similar to that which was taking place in parts of Vomero, particularly around Porta Capuana and Piazza Nazionale.[40] The northeastern suburbs of the city, Arenaccia and San Carlo, also suffered terribly: like Via Toledo they were invaded by tanks, and like Vomero they also saw dozens of civilians held hostage.[41] The people of Montecalvario and the Spanish Quarter, with their tall houses and narrow streets, guarded their areas exactly as those in the ancient centre did; and Chiaia saw fighting that was very similar to what was going on in the streets of Vomero up above.[42] The partisans of CIS Park in Avvocata, where Enzo Stimolo and his German counterpart were temporarily detained, also played a pivotal role in guarding the vital road junctions around the Archaeological Museum. In the middle of the Four Days, this area also hosted a meeting of leaders from different areas of Naples with a view to setting up an overall command structure, and the beginnings of a unified local government.[43]

In popular memory, the whole of Naples rose up together as one to fight against the Germans. 'It was a wholesale rebellion,' claims Antonio Amoretti, who took part in the fighting in the Rione Sanità, 'the whole city rebelled against the Germans, even those who didn't actively participate expressed their solidarity.'[44] Antonio Tarsia in Curia, one of the main protagonists of the Four Days and one of its first chroniclers, agrees: '[The battle] was fought everywhere, in Vomero as in Piazza Garibaldi, in Piazza Trieste e Trento as in Capodimonte and in the suburbs of Ponticelli as in Piscinola a Barra as in Soccavo.'[45] In his 1956 book, probably still the most famous and widely read narrative of the uprising, Aldo De Jaco stressed this sense of unity among the people of the city:

It is often impossible and unjust to differentiate between the youth, the ex-soldier, the worker, the intellectual in the front line and the man or woman who offered them a weapon, stood on lookout to signal danger and watched to see where the sharp noise of Fascist gunfire was coming from – which was very often aimed precisely at them; it is impossible and unfair to differentiate between the fighters and the men or boys who ran back and forth carrying bullets from the distant barracks or makeshift weapons stores, and the women who collected the wounded, carried them home or pushed them on carts through the deserted streets to the nearest hospital, and those who reassembled the bodies of the dead disfigured by the discharge of machine guns … the fundamental characteristic of the 'Four Days' armed rebellion was the active anti-fascist solidarity of the broadest popular masses who supported, helped, made possible the struggle of the fighting avant-garde.[46]

It was for this reason that, the following year, the city as a whole was awarded Italy's highest award for military valour, the Gold Medal.

While all the above statements are true, they are not the only truth: the full picture is somewhat darker and more complicated. Every part of Naples did indeed rise up to some extent, but some communities were much more enthusiastic in their resistance than others. As Neapolitan historian Gabriella Gribaudi has pointed out, old parts of the city with long-established communities fought much harder than any of the newest suburbs, such as those around Fuorigrotta; and working-class artisans, shopkeepers and manual workers fought much harder than upper-middle-class professionals such as teachers and lawyers, who barely feature at all in the lists of the dead and wounded.[47] Neither was anti-Fascism the primary motive for many. Indeed, as many recent studies have pointed out, plenty of Fascists also took part in the fight against the Germans, most of whom remained ardent Fascists even after the war.[48]

More shocking, however, is that some Neapolitans actively chose to side with the Germans against their own people. The same protagonists who sing the praises of Neapolitan unity also acknowledge that they often came under attack from people who should, rightly, have taken up arms alongside them. These included not only the usual suspects – volunteers who had signed up to fight for the Wehrmacht, far-right members of the security forces, old Fascist hierarchs and *squadristi* – but also ordinary members of the public. In Via Duomo, for example, partisans manning the barricades repeatedly found themselves under attack from a Fascist sniper who shot at them from the windows of no. 70. When they eventually stormed the building they found a massive stash of grenades and ammunition, but no sniper: he had escaped across the roof terraces. The apartment turned out to belong to a local primary school teacher called Fiorillo, who was arrested several days later.[49]

The presence of Fascist snipers was one of the most difficult problems for the Neapolitan insurgents to defend themselves against. Since these people were local, they knew the streets better than the Germans: they knew how to attack their neighbours and how to escape, and in the end often melted back into the city centre without ever being caught or brought to justice. 'They were the most dangerous and fanatical,' claimed Giuseppe Sanges, a partisan who took part in the uprising in Avvocata; 'as is the custom with cowards, they fired from the houses at partisans and passers-by and then disappeared again in order to get themselves out of any open struggle.'[50] According to Antonio Amoretti, despite the massive firepower of the Wehrmacht, 'the deaths during the Four Days were more down to the Fascists, collaborators with the Germans, than to the Germans themselves'.[51] Federico Zvab agrees: 'How many casualties were caused by those bold Fascist cowards nobody knows or will ever know precisely. The undeniable truth is that the Fascist snipers made Neapolitan mothers shed more tears than the Germans did, despite their undeniable ferocity.'[52]

Dozens of buildings became notorious as snipers' nests during those four days, particularly the apartments along Via Duomo in the old city, those along Via Scarlatti in Vomero, and those overlooking Via Salvator Rosa in Avvocata. One Fascist sniper barricaded himself in a church opposite the Caserma Garibaldi on Via Foria and fired on his fellow Italians with a machine gun from the cupola.[53] Other snipers began firing on the barricades beside the Archaeological Museum, giving the Neapolitan partisans the impression (wrongly, as it turned out) that the firing was coming from the museum itself.[54] In Montecalvario, a group of Fascist *squadristi* terrorized locals by firing at them from an abandoned military headquarters called Caserma Paisiello. After a three-day siege, the partisans eventually stormed the building, only to find it empty: the militiamen had once again made their escape across the rooftops, and the partisans were too exhausted to pursue them.[55]

One of the most important snipers' nests was in the 'Torre degli Arditi' at Porta Capuana. This was the headquarters of the Arditi, who were notorious supporters of the Fascist regime. Ironically, many of the Arditi themselves had decided to fight *against* the Germans: the snipers who had occupied their HQ and the building adjacent were a different group of Fascists, who had barricaded themselves inside the building along with some Wehrmacht sappers. During the course of those four days they killed a number of people around the building, most of whom were unarmed civilians who had only ventured onto the streets in search of water. According to the leader of the Neapolitan Arditi, Alfonso Ciavarella, the building changed hands a couple of times, and was only finally neutralized after a frontal assault and two hours of 'very bitter' fighting.[56]

Usually Neapolitan partisans had to attack such strongholds by storming through the front door and making their way upstairs. Often they found that, by the time they had done so, the snipers had escaped across the roof terraces to safety. But in the old city, Federico Zvab's men tried an alternative method. His fighters entered the building opposite and fired on the Fascists from the windows there. But this was really only a distraction: while the partisans in the building opposite were making as much noise as possible, a second group climbed onto the roof above the snipers' nest and began removing roof tiles. When they dropped down into the building a vicious firefight ensued. One Fascist was killed and another wounded, but according to Zvab several others escaped, probably by hiding with sympathetic families in other apartments in the same building.[57]

What these eyewitnesses are describing was not the story so beloved of Neapolitan popular memory – a straightforward story of the city's liberation from the Germans. It was in fact a civil war, and it was conducted with that special hatred that can only be found between neighbours. The fighters of the Four Days nurtured a visceral resentment for the German collaborators in their midst, and routinely called them 'traitors', 'cowards', 'vipers' and other such names.

Zvab claimed that when such people were caught they were always treated fairly as prisoners of war, or simply released: 'Vendettas found no home in our breasts!'[58] But even if this was true, to a degree, among Zvab's men, it was certainly not the case elsewhere.

In Avvocata, under the partisan leaders Eugenio Mancini and Alfonso Baldaro, special squads were set up to purge former Fascists from among the partisans themselves, to seek out former Fascists among the local population and to neutralize any remaining snipers and German spies.[59] One of those to be summarily executed was a *squadrista* named Porro, who was accused of being found with 'a radio transmitter and documents, from which his sharing of intelligence with the enemy appeared irrefutable'. His possession of a radio transmitter was especially damning at this late stage in the conflict. After the Germans had withdrawn from Naples they continued to bombard it with artillery from beyond Capodimonte: the idea that local spies might be directing their fire by radio was clearly intolerable. According to Giulio Schettini, one of the other partisan leaders in the area, this particular traitor was executed in Piazzetta Capecelatro and his body left 'on a pile of rubbish'.[60]

Another Fascist, named Tommasone, was accused of sniping from the rooftops opposite the Archaeological Museum and killing several people who were manning the barricades below. He evaded capture at that point, but appeared later in Materdei, where he once again terrorized the people from the roof terraces: among his victims was 'a two-year old girl'. During an exchange of fire on the roof terraces above Via Salvator Rosa he also shot and killed a fellow Fascist, Marcello Martone, who unlike Tommasone had thrown in his lot with the partisans – Fascist killing Fascist in an exchange that showed just how many layers this 'civil war' had already developed. When he was eventually caught, there was no question of keeping Tommasone captive for later trial: he was simply taken down to Piazza Mazzini and shot.[61]

There are plenty of other examples of Fascist fighters who were either executed, or who committed suicide in order to evade capture. But among the most shocking is the story told to Gabriella Gribaudi by Franco Vassetti, a resident of Materdei who was a child during the Four Days. Vassetti remembers the misery of rationing, and the outrage of his parents when, earlier in the war, a local Fascist official skipped the bread queue at the local bakery and commandeered all the bread – presumably for his own family and friends. In the wake of the Four Days, this same official was shot and his body dumped in the street. 'And they put him like that,' said Vassetti, gesturing to his interviewer, 'with his arms hanging out and dead, like that, and everyone who passed spat in his face. Me too, I spat in his face.'[62]

As we shall see in the next chapter, there are echoes here of events in Ponticelli, on the outskirts of Naples, where one of the most notorious acts of vengeance against the Fascist regime took place. There are parallels, too, with the final liberation, at the end of April 1945, when similar treatment would be meted out to the body of Mussolini himself. From now on, the war in Italy would not simply be a war of national liberation against the Germans. It would also be civil war waged with all the bitterness and hatred that had built up over twenty years of Fascist corruption and repression.

CHAPTER 21

Parting Shots

From a German point of view September 1943 was an extremely stressful time. When the Italians announced their armistice with the Allies, it was viewed as a betrayal at every level of command from Hitler downwards: after years of working and fighting together side by side, the Italians had become Germany's enemy almost overnight. This might explain, though never excuse, some of the ferocity that German troops directed at Italian soldiers and civilians alike, and the deliberate humiliations that were routinely meted out to them.

There was certainly a degree of fear involved, too. It was one thing to fight conventional battles against an easily identifiable, uniformed enemy who were approaching from a distance; but it was another thing altogether to be facing an unknown, hidden enemy that was all around you at all times, and could fire at you from any window or doorway.

The ferocity and determination of some of the Italian attacks also took the Germans by surprise. German soldiers had grown used to regarding their Italian counterparts as cowardly and inept: the previous years had been marked by one Italian failure after another in Greece, in Yugoslavia and in North Africa. But there had been nothing cowardly or inept about the defence of Naples during the insurrection. When German prisoners of war were interrogated by the Americans in the autumn of 1943, their interviewers reported a marked change of attitude among them. 'They discovered that the Italians knew how to fight with bravery when in the service of a cause they could believe in,' stated one report. '… German soldiers are ever more convinced that tremendous difficulties are waiting for them in the north of the country.'[1]

The events in Naples at the end of September had left German troops full of adrenalin, perpetually nervous about real or imagined threats that surrounded them, and eager for revenge. When coupled with official orders to loot, destroy and enslave local populations – orders that required great brutality and encouraged indiscipline – it is perhaps not surprising that the units in and around Naples began to engage in what the Germans euphemistically called 'excesses', but which Italians have come to regard as a killing spree. The people who lived in the densely packed streets of the city centre were spared the worst of these atrocities. But out on the periphery, where German units could move more freely, and where smaller populations lived in communities that were more difficult to defend, things were very different.

The Ponticelli Atrocities

It was not only the central suburbs of Naples that resisted the Germans during the Four Days. Ponticelli was a working-class suburb on the northeastern edge of the city, partly industrial but also partly rural. As a centre of Socialist and Communist activity there had been regular scuffles here between locals and the Fascist leadership ever since the 1920s. When Mussolini was deposed on 25 July 1943 the community celebrated by burning down the local Fascist headquarters and singing songs until the small hours. The suburb already had a reputation as a troublesome place.[2]

Here, as in other parts of Naples, the Germans seized control in mid-September and quickly began requisitioning all the food stores and livestock. And, as in other parts of Naples, when they turned to rounding up young men and taking them away, the local people began to resist. Indeed, Ponticelli is one of many places in Naples that claim to have started the uprising: there appear to have been one or two incidents between armed locals and German soldiers as early as 27 September.[3] More organized attacks on the Germans took place the following day. But the real trouble did not begin until the 29th, when two armoured cars and a patrol were sent to pacify the area. At first the local insurgents resisted enthusiastically: by now many of them were armed with rifles looted from the barracks and air raid batteries abandoned earlier in the month. Most of the fighting centred around Via Principe di Napoli, where a Sardinian officer named Francesco Casu had set up a rudimentary partisan command centre in a school; but another flashpoint also developed in Via Ottaviano, a road that led out of the built-up area towards the neighbouring village of Cercola. This road was lined with houses on either side, but behind and beyond them were fields where the local factory workers also grew food and kept livestock.[4]

The insurgents were no match for the better trained and better armed Germans, and several would-be heroes were killed in their doorways or on their balconies.[5] Realizing that they were outgunned, most of the Italians withdrew into their houses, or hid in the nearby fields. In anger, the Germans pursued them and killed whatever fighters they found. At the end of the war, one of the local mothers described what happened to her 13-year-old son:

> On 29 September, during the bloody battles against the
> invaders, a group of Germans went to a shelter in via Ottaviano
> and seized six people, including my son, Enrico Grieco, and
> shot them against a wall in front of the shelter. Since my son
> had not yet expired, one of the Germans detached his head from
> his torso with a bayonet. My son belonged to a group of patriots
> in the area and had taken part in several fights.[6]

Until this point, actions such as this were just part of the ordinary violence that occurs in any war, and which, indeed, had already happened in other parts of Naples. The killing of prisoners and the mutilation of their bodies is unequivocally an atrocity, but during the white-hot fury of combat it is at least comprehensible. What makes the events in Ponticelli really stand out is what happened next.

Not content with killing those who had been firing at them, the Germans marched along Via Ottaviano and began systematically searching the houses on either side. They pulled out any man they found inside, fighter or not, and shot him. Before long, bodies were lining the street and scattered at the edges of the fields. Most of them were killed with a single shot to the back of the head, but some had their throats cut – 'As one does with pigs', as one indignant eyewitness later put it.[7] It was a systematic, cold-blooded massacre.

After the Germans withdrew, it was left to the locals to clean up the mess, a task that was enormously distressing to all concerned. Witnesses spoke of the gutters being filled with blood, of the bodies being piled up in one place so that their wives and mothers could come and claim them. One woman remembered trying desperately to reassemble the pieces of her dead neighbour's head so that his wife would not have to find him in pieces when she came home.[8]

That evening a wave of mourning swept down Via Ottaviano. 'Everything was a lament, a cry … From the beginning of the street all the way to Cenzi dell'arco,' remembered one resident. 'Everyone wept because everyone had relatives who had been killed.'[9] In all, thirty men and boys had been murdered. At least twenty-five more would be killed the following day at the local glassworks, by the same German units, who did not finally withdraw from the area until 1 October.[10]

It was perhaps only natural that the people of this close-knit community should demand some kind of revenge. Their opportunity came the next day, when the secretary of the local *fascio*, Federico Travaglini, was captured in nearby Barra and dragged back to Ponticelli to face justice. Travaglini had not been involved in the massacre, but he had probably collaborated with the Germans during their earlier round-ups of men and livestock, and in the absence of the actual perpetrators he would have to do. A mob gathered in Piazza Margherita and began to tear into him, kicking and beating him mercilessly. One person poured a can of petrol over him and threatened to set him on fire.

Seeing what was happening, the Carabinieri intervened and bundled Travaglini into the police station in an attempt to save his life; but when the police station itself came under attack from the mob, they appeared to think again. According to some accounts the crowd actually broke into the station and hauled Travaglini out; other accounts claim that the Carabinieri, fearing for their own safety, opened the doors of their own accord and gave him up to the mob. Either way, Travaglini did not last long. Once outside he tried to take refuge in the pharmacy across the road – the pharmacist, who was also a Fascist, was a close friend – but he was shot in the doorway and died almost instantly. In a final act of vengeance, one of the local men stabbed his body three times, and held up the bloody knife triumphantly for all the crowd to see.

When an inquest was held into these events by the Court of Assize in Naples three years later, the judge proclaimed Travaglini entirely innocent of the atrocities that had engulfed this tragic neighbourhood the day before: the Fascist secretary had been a scapegoat, pure and simple. But the judge had no mind to punish anyone for his lynching. After everything that the community had already suffered, it was probably better just to draw a line under it all.[11]

Massacre at Acerra

The countryside around Naples suffered terribly during the last three weeks of September 1943. As the Wehrmacht prepared to retreat north-wards they stripped the Terra di Lavoro of everything of worth, and destroyed whatever they could not take with them. For a region that was already notoriously poor, the most devastating blow was the system-atic requisitioning of all food stores and livestock. When farmers were shot while trying to stop the soldiers from stealing their pigs or chickens it was often because they reasoned that they had little to lose: without these vital sources of winter food, they were as good as dead anyway.

Of the many attempts at resistance that took place all across this region, perhaps the most tragic was that at Acerra, an agricultural town about 10 km northwest of Naples. Acerra was on the main route of retreat for the Germans as they pulled back from Salerno towards the Volturno river. As such it was picked out for special treatment by German troops wishing to deny the town and its facilities to the advancing Allies.

According to Aldo De Jaco, the destruction of the town centre began at the very end of September when one or two of the major public buildings were burned down – the tax offices, for example, and various other offices run by the municipality.[12] But the real damage began on the morning of 1 October when troops of sappers arrived in the town in force. In the historic centre they went methodically from house to house, breaking down doors, chasing the inhabitants out onto the street, grabbing anything they could find of worth and then setting fire to the buildings. They concentrated on the largest, wealthiest houses, presumably calculating that these would contain the richest pickings, and would be the most useful as billets for the Allies when they arrived. But there was undoubtedly something vindictive about such destruction. From a military point of view, it certainly inconvenienced the Allies; but it also sent a stark message to the Italian people about the price of 'betrayal'.

While this was going on, any young men who were discovered were marched to Piazza San Pietro in the town centre and forced to sit there under armed guard. Among them was the parish priest, Tommaso Carfora, who had been hounded out of church along with his congregation in the middle of his Friday morning service. Before long 200 men were gathered here, ready for deportation. The bishop of Acerra, Nicola Capasso, tried to intervene on their behalf, but he, too, was arrested and held captive for several hours until the afternoon, when all 200 were marched out of the town towards Caivano. Eventually these men would be taken north to work as slave labour in the construction of the German defences along the Gustav Line.[13]

Any attempts to negotiate with the German troops were unsuccessful. In one particularly ugly episode, a wealthy homeowner named Ignazio Laudando attempted to woo the Germans with charm. He invited a group of sappers into his home and offered them lunch, which they reportedly accepted quite happily. But after eating their fill, they got up and started pouring flammable liquid all over the house anyway. When Laudando argued with them, berating them for treating 'friends' in such a way, they shot both him and his 13-year-old nephew Salvatore, and left their bodies to be consumed by the flames. The maid who had served the Germans lunch was also shot as she tried to escape the burning building.[14]

By nightfall, some fifty or so buildings had been torched, and an unknown number of people killed within them. Nobody yet knew the fate of the 200 who had been marched away, but they feared the worst, and various groups of citizens resolved to defend themselves in case the Germans returned. It is unclear how many people were involved in this improvised resistance, but there were certainly already some groups of partisans in the area, one of which was led by a local man named Ferdinando Goglia (today there is a street named after him in Acerra). Like many other towns around Naples, Acerra had a long tradition of Communist activity, and one local Communist, a mechanic named Enrico Pirolo, was instrumental in encouraging the local community into action. Barricades were thrown up round the town centre using tractors, carts and other agricultural equipment. Guards were placed on some of the roofs, armed with weapons gathered by Goglia earlier in the month, and taken from the local Carabinieri barracks. So when the Germans returned the following morning, the locals thought they were ready to resist them.

The day began when a German truck approached the town from the north, and ran up against one of the barricades. Two German soldiers climbed down from the vehicle to investigate, and the town's defenders opened fire on them, wounding one. The soldiers managed to clamber back into their truck, and sped off back the way they had come.

When they returned, early that afternoon, they came in force. Three tanks attacked the barricades, easily blasting through them. Alongside the tanks, under the command of the 23-year-old Second Lieutenant Gerhard Tschierschwitz, were a few dozen Panzergrenadiers, who combed the streets of the ancient centre, killing virtually everyone they came across. Once the streets were free of both barricades and partisans, they began entering the houses one by one, dragging out any men they found and shooting them on the street. Sometimes they threw grenades into the houses and the stables for good measure, killing whoever or whatever happened to be inside. There was little discrimination in terms of age or sex: of the 88 people they killed were 13 women and 12 children under 15 years old.[15]

Amid the carnage that day are several stories of individual cruelty that have lived on in popular memory ever since: an old man whose legs were blown off by a grenade, and who was then dragged into a burning building to die in the flames; two young boys who were shot even as their father tried to shield them with his body; a 3-year-old boy bayoneted as he clung to his mother's skirt. Some of these stories are difficult to verify, but they convey something of the horror that took place that afternoon and evening.[16]

Perhaps the most damning indictment of the Wehrmacht's actions that day appears in its own account of the action. The war diary of the Hermann Göring Division described the massacre in brief but chilling terms, its author not even bothering to spell the town's name correctly:

2 October 1943 … Rearguard Tschierschwitz reaches the Accera bridge in the evening. Clashes with Italian bandits in Accera. The locality is completely destroyed, the inhabitants annihilated.[17]

The following morning, the people of Acerra walked out into their town in shock. One woman described looking frantically for her 14-year-old son at dawn, in streets that were still 'littered with corpses and dead animals'. She finally found him lying dead beside the fountain in Piazza San Pietro.[18] Those who could stomach it set about collecting the dead. Others gathered up the 'hundreds' of dead animals that had been blown up in stables and stalls around this agricultural town. They were piled up in a heap just outside the town and burned.

And yet still the tragedy was not quite over. The day after the massacre was a Sunday, so the sacristan went to the bell tower to call the community together for a service to honour the dead. But as a parting gift, the Germans had mined the building: no sooner had he begun to ring the bells than the whole tower blew up, collapsing on the unfortunate sacristan and killing him instantly. He was the last victim of the Germans in Acerra.

Other Atrocities

As the German army retreated northwards, increasing violence and misery accompanied them. Not all of this was inflicted by the Germans themselves: the Allies relentlessly bombarded all those towns and areas where German soldiers congregated, with disastrous consequences for Italian civilians. But by 1943 the bombing of Italian towns and cities had become a 'normal' part of the war – devastating, terrifying, but also random and impersonal, like an act of nature. It is much easier to hate an enemy when you have seen his face as he deliberately targets your home, your loved ones and your community.

North of Naples the atrocities continued in town after town. In Giugliano thirteen people were machine-gunned in Piazza Annunziata, in reprisal for the death of a single German soldier.[19] The following day four priests were shot in nearby Mugnano di Napoli because they had not left the area as instructed by the Germans.[20] Twenty-three were shot in Orta d'Atella on 30 September in reprisal for the capture of two German soldiers, despite the fact that the soldiers had been quickly released again for fear of exactly such a reprisal.[21] Two days later a further eight were shot in Afragola, on the main route northwards between Naples and Caserta.[22]

Further north still, yet another tragedy was unfolding in the town of Bellona, on the other side of the Volturno river. On the evening of 6 October a group of German soldiers tried to rape a local girl, but one of them was killed when the girl's brother and uncle stepped in to defend her. The following morning, the Germans rounded up all the local men, and shot fifty-four of them. The families of these men believed they were simply being conscripted as forced labourers, but instead they were taken to a nearby tuff quarry and killed. The Germans then blew up the quarry to cover the bodies.[23]

Countless atrocities occurred along the Volturno river, which was the new line of defence once the Germans had retreated from Naples. Capua, which lies on the river itself, suffered particularly harshly, both under the relentless tactical bombing by the Allies and the equally relentless depredations of the Germans who occupied the city. The Germans ordered a complete evacuation of the area to a depth of 5 km from the new front line, and punished anyone who appeared to be defying that order. Men were rounded up and taken off to work; women and children were left to find shelter wherever they could. No consideration was made for those who were too old or infirm to be able to leave town, or even to leave the buildings that were being mined by the Germans. On 4 October, for example, a paralysed woman in her seventies was shot in her bed because she was unable to leave her house when told to by two German soldiers. In the north of the city a 77-year-old man who was too ill to move from an air raid shelter was simply shot where he lay. Another disabled man, Luigi Polito, was killed in his shop because he was unable to leave when told.[24]

In Caiazzo, just north of the Volturno and a little further inland, two families who had been hiding in a remote farmhouse were massacred in their entirety for no discernible reason. According to some sources, they were killed because they made the mistake of cheering some soldiers who were passing through on the assumption – wrong as it turned out – that they were the advancing Allies. Other sources claim that a junior German officer, Second Lieutenant Wolfgang Lehnigk-Emden, thought he had seen someone flashing signals from the house. Whatever the case, Lehnigk-Emden's men killed everyone in the house by throwing a hand grenade through the door, before entering to dispatch the survivors with pistols and bayonets. When the Allies finally did arrive a few days later they discovered several children among the dead, some of whom had been stabbed through the heart and the head. One 3-year-old girl had had her right leg torn from her body.[25]

This was one of the rare cases when the officer in charge of the massacre was caught by the Allies fairly quickly, and partially confessed to his crimes. He was never brought to justice, however. After the war he was accidentally released by the Allies; and when proof of his crimes was sent from Germany to Italy it was locked away in the Palazzo Cesi-Gaddi war crimes archive – the so-called 'cupboard of shame' – and forgotten. When he was finally put on trial in 1993 the case was thrown out because the statute of limitations had expired.[26]

And so the list goes on: 25 massacred in Sparanise in reprisal for a single shot fired at the Germans; in Mondragone, on the coast, another

17 shot in a quarry that was blown up to cover the bodies; in Teano, 7 killed on 25 October, followed by another 7 a few days later.[27]

As the historian Carlo Gentile has pointed out, there was a pattern to all this violence. After their experience in Naples and some of the surrounding towns, German soldiers were often acting out of fear of a more general insurrection by partisans. Their savage reprisals, which were carried out in response to any kind of resistance whatsoever, sometimes provoked the very reaction they feared, since some people in the local populations clearly began to believe that they had little to lose by fighting. The violence was particularly bad in and around the combat zones, where tensions were already high. And there were certain units that were more notorious than others. The three divisions of the XIV Panzerkorps – the Hermann Göring Division, the 3rd Panzergrenadier Division and the 15th Panzergrenadier Division – were worse than any of the German units fighting in Puglia and other parts of Italy. And those units that had a particularly macho 'war culture', such as the Hermann Göring Division, were the worst of the worst.[28]

Between the end of September and November 1943, more than 1,600 civilians were murdered in Campania. The provinces that suffered worst were those of Naples and Caserta, where 826 and 745 people respectively were killed. There were many other deaths in these places that were more directly linked to the fighting – people who were killed during combat operations, or in Allied bombing raids. But in these two provinces, half of all civilian deaths were not caused directly by the war: they were cold-blooded executions by German soldiers.[29]

This was a pattern that would be reproduced in other parts of Italy as the war slowly moved northwards over the following eighteen months. In British and American narratives of the conflict, this period is portrayed as a conventional war between two heavily armed and mechanized opponents. But for the Italians who were caught in the middle, it had already become a war of scarce resources, of clandestine resistance, and of terror.

CHAPTER 22

The Price of Myth

The uprising that took place in Naples between 28 September and 1 October 1943 was one of the most remarkable events of the Second World War in Italy. With virtually no time to prepare, the people of Naples rose up against a savagely brutal occupier that had better training, better equipment and vastly superior firepower. 'Despite all the troops and tanks deployed, we are no longer able to handle the situation,' wrote one German soldier in his war diary. Within days, he and his comrades had been forced to flee the city.[1]

This was the first major uprising against the German occupation of Italy; indeed, apart from the various ghetto uprisings by Jews in occupied Poland, it was the first such uprising in the whole of mainland Europe. Entire communities were involved, with women and children playing a major part alongside men of all ages, classes and occupations. Together they prevented the Germans from completing their apocalyptic plan for the city. They damaged or captured dozens of German vehicles, and killed, wounded or captured at least fifty German soldiers, and possibly many more – it is impossible to say with any accuracy, since many of the lists of German losses have since disappeared.[2] At the same time, they ousted a Fascist power structure that had controlled and exploited them for more than twenty years. All this came at a fantastic cost: more than 600 people in Naples are known to have been killed by German soldiers and their Fascist collaborators during these few terrifying days.[3]

Had such events occurred in Milan or Turin, they would have been celebrated not only locally but also nationally and internationally. And yet the Four Days of Naples rarely warrants more than a quick mention in most histories of the Italian resistance. British and American military histories of the war often do not mention it at all, giving the impression that it was the Allies who liberated Naples, rather than the Neapolitans themselves. German histories of the war acknowledge the atrocities that took place here, and the inconvenience that was caused by the insurrection, but the emphasis is usually on the bigger picture: the Wehrmacht achieved most of its immediate aims in the Campania area, and managed to withdraw in good order. Only in Naples itself has the insurrection won the near-mythical status it rightly deserves. Each year local organizations hold emotional commemorations, the local press interview veterans and plaques and monuments are regularly raised around the locations where the fighting took place.

Unfortunately, however, the very myths that so many Neapolitans hold dear are partly responsible for the lack of recognition that the Four Days has achieved elsewhere. These have combined with other, older stereotypes about Naples and Neapolitans to undermine the importance of what took place here. It is only through confronting these myths and stereotypes that these events can be restored to their rightful place in Italian and European wartime memory. Over the last twenty years this process has at least begun in Italy; but historians in other countries, particularly in Britain and America, have yet to catch up.

Days of Chaos and Personal Myth-Making

In the days immediately after the uprising, everybody was a hero. Those who had given the partisans little more than moral support suddenly remembered themselves with a gun in their hands. Those who had merely watched the fighting from behind closed windows managed to convince themselves that they had actually been down on the barricades. Such things are natural after any period of intense, violent combat, and are not always wholly cynical: they are reconstructed memories born of adrenalin, personal pride and a desperate desire to have been a part of the momentous events one has lived through. Nevertheless, it was galling for genuine fighters to hear the hollow boasts of those who appeared only to have taken up arms after the fighting was all over.

Given time, such exaggerations and enhancements generally iron themselves out. Those who genuinely took part in events know who they are, and know who their leaders were – and theirs are the stories that usually make their way to the front of the queue. Journalists, historians and government officials compile reports, interview protagonists and cross-check stories, weeding out the most dubious and fantastic claims along the way. Mistakes are sometimes made, naturally, but at the end of the process an acceptable, canonical version of events is constructed.

These processes happened in Naples – first through the gathering of eyewitness reports by journalists,[4] then through official inquiries by the police and by government commissions,[5] and finally by the efforts of early historians[6] – but unfortunately there were one or two factors here that partially undermined the results.

The first was the terrible state that Naples found itself in immediately after the uprising. Over the course of the previous month the city had been thrown into utter chaos. The armed forces, the police force, local government institutions and many of the other traditional structures of civil society had been deliberately torn down, leaving the city in the hands of improvised militias without the resources, the experience or the inclination to make detailed and accurate reports. Those pre-existing Fascist bureaucracies that survived, or were reinstated, had a built-in incentive to play down the heroism and sacrifice of the political dissidents that they had spent the previous twenty years trying to suppress. And the Allies that took over in October 1943 lacked any local knowledge at all. They had not been present during the uprising, and in any case had their own agenda. In such circumstances, the precise details of exactly what happened, and who was present, inevitably got lost.

A perfect example of how the events in Naples that autumn have been undervalued over the years can be seen in the statistics of the victims. In 1945, the Carabinieri in Naples recorded an official death toll of just 120 people in the entire city during the Four Days.[7] A few years later an official commission was set up, chaired by the resistance leader Antonio Tarsia in Curia, to ascertain exactly who had or had not actively supported the uprising. According to this commission, a total of 337 people had been killed during both the Four Days and the battle to prevent the German takeover earlier that September.[8] This remained the most accepted figure for the next fifty years. It was not until the beginning of the present century that a research team from the University of Naples conducted a proper investigation, cross-checking names on local records with those of the city administration and Tarsia's commission. Their conclusion was that at least 663 people had been killed – nearly twice the number estimated by Tarsia's commission, and more than five times the original Carabinieri estimate.[9] Far from exaggerating the number of victims, which is what usually happens in the immediate aftermath of such tragic events,[10] official bodies had consistently *underestimated* the sacrifices made by the people of Naples.

From the very beginning, therefore, there was always a gap between the exaggerated claims of individuals and the overly cautious official assessments of the uprising – and into this gap crept uncertainty.

The post-war Commission for the Recognition of Partisan Qualification should have been an institution that reduced this uncertainty. Its whole purpose was to establish the facts about who had been a 'patriot', who deserved the status of active 'partisan fighter' and who had either died or been disabled in the name of the struggle for liberation. This was a noble idea, and did indeed lay strong foundations for later historical research into the resistance all across Italy. The problem lay in the fact that any Italian who was recognized by this commission automatically became eligible for financial compensation. Thus, once again, individuals had a vested interest in exaggerating their participation in the resistance still further, and the authorities had a vested interest in limiting the number of people they recognized. The gap between personal memory and official recognition only widened.

In northern Italy this was not as much of a problem as it was in the south. In Milan or Bologna, the resistance had had eighteen months to establish itself, and there was more often clear evidence about who had been a 'partisan fighter' and who had not. But in Campania, where the resistance had arisen and dispersed again in just a single month of extraordinary violence, it was much more difficult to ascertain who had genuinely taken part and who was merely spinning a story in order to claim some government cash. For this reason dozens of partisans in Naples never even put their name forward to the commission, because they didn't want to give anyone the impression that they were only in it for the money. Others resented the commission for political reasons, and refused to put themselves forward for scrutiny by an organ of the central government that they felt had never really represented them.

At the centre of controversy in Campania was the president of the commission himself, Antonio Tarsia in Curia. He had been chosen for this role because of his credentials as a partisan leader in the suburb of Vomero, but there were many who doubted that he was the hero he proclaimed himself to be. According to Edoardo Pansini, another partisan leader in exactly the same suburb, Tarsia's greatest contribution to the resistance was typing up a few leaflets that the majority of genuine fighters never even saw: 'Professor Tarsia thinks of himself as the leader of the Neapolitan resistance and from time to time ... he proclaims this fact on the radio, perhaps to convince himself of it.' In Pansini's eyes, such a man did not deserve his inflated reputation, and had no right to judge the eligibility of others to call themselves 'patriots'. Pansini himself never sought official recognition from this body.[11]

Other people who had fought bravely in Vomero were even more bitter about Tarsia and his commission – and with good reason. Giovanni Abbate, the leader who had originally besieged the Vomero sports stadium, and then had fought off the German column that came to relieve it, was recommended for a Silver Medal, but turned down by the commission, who implied that he had greatly exaggerated his role. Although Abbate was eventually recognized for his actions, his name was permanently tarnished, and he had to endure people calling him a 'false partisan' for the next thirty years. Eventually he became so angry that he published a 700-page book of letters and documents in an attempt to clear his name, and to demonstrate to the rest of Naples the shoddy treatment he had received. According to Abbate the commission's refusal to recognize him was probably a result of his politics (he was an ardent monarchist, unlike the republicans who were judging him). But he also blamed Tarsia personally, 'who usurped my qualification as a commander of the partisan brigade in Vomero out of insatiable thirst for glory, despite never having fired a single shot from a gun'.[12]

There is little doubt that Tarsia did exaggerate his role in the Four Days, and increasingly so over the years. For example, when he first told the story of Enzo Stimolo's dramatic siege of Vomero sports stadium in 1943, he made no pretence of having been involved in those events himself. In 1950, however, he claimed that he and Stimolo had planned the siege together; and four years later he went so far as to suggest that the whole thing had been his idea, and that he himself had given precise orders to Stimolo on how to handle the siege tactically. There are plenty of other examples.[13]

The purpose here is not to demolish Tarsia's reputation – even Pansini conceded that Tarsia was a brave and committed anti-Fascist who had stepped forward when it counted – but merely to point out that memory is mutable and fallible, and so are government commissions. When there is no solid, documentary evidence to back up verbal accounts, mistakes are inevitably made – even by organizations whose job is to iron out those mistakes. Along the way, the true passage of events becomes blurred.

This has consequences, and not only for individuals like Giovanni Abbate. The very public squabbling that took place between different partisan leaders and different political factions within the various partisan organizations inevitably tarnished their reputation. More depressingly still, it opened the door for former Fascists and their sympathizers to deny that the uprising had ever been as heroic or as widespread as its exponents claimed it was. Such views have even found their way into the historiography, in the form of a book by the right-wing historian Enzo Erra entitled *Napoli 1943: Le Quattro Giornate che non ci furono* ('Naples 1943: The Four Days that Didn't Happen').[14]

The Myth of the 'spontaneous revolt'

One of the aspects of the Four Days that Neapolitans are most proud of is its spontaneity. In popular memory, the people of Naples did not need to be called to arms: they rose up to defend their city without being asked, bravely, selflessly, and as one. In the words of Mario Orbitello, one of the leaders of the revolt around the Archaeological Museum, 'There was no central organization, everything was spontaneous, natural, inevitable. There was no action by parties; no political party existed in Naples at the end of September, and even when it did it was forced to live in the shadows, and so was unable to prepare an insurrection, which required open, courageous and immediate action.'[15]

Even those who had themselves been involved in political action long before September 1943 still seemed happy to proclaim the unplanned nature of the uprising. According to Antonio Tarsia in Curia, impulsive action is what Neapolitans have always been good at:

> The 'four days' should be considered a spontaneous, irresistible explosion, the holy rebellion of a people unwilling to tolerate the foreign yoke. It is part of the historical cycle of Neapolitan revolutions that goes all the way from Masaniello's revolt in 1647, through the revolutions of 1799 and 1821, to that of 5 May 1848, and marks the beginning of the partisan war of liberation in Italy, which was also a war of redemption for our country.[16]

There is something beautifully satisfying about the idea that uprisings in Naples might be cyclical events, like the explosions of Vesuvius, which occur whenever this hot-headed population builds up enough internal pressure. It appeals to all the popular clichés, embraced almost as much by Neapolitans themselves as by foreigners, that they are a spontaneous and passionate people – or, alternatively, an unpredictable and violent one.

This is not history, but mythology. Anyone who has studied Masaniello's revolt in 1647 will know that it was not nearly as spontaneous as it is remembered to be – some of the main protagonists had been campaigning for democratic reform for years before the revolt, if not decades.[17] Neither were the other uprisings mentioned by Tarsia in 1799, 1821 and 1848, each of which was carefully planned and politically motivated. There are undeniably echoes here but, as Tarsia himself made clear, there was one major difference that set the 1943 uprising apart: unlike all those that had gone before, this one was, for once, successful. Far from being a mere flash in the pan, it removed the Germans from the city for good, and signified a major shift in the entire political landscape not only in Naples but throughout the rest of the country, too.

It would be foolish to pretend that the Four Days did not rely on the spontaneous involvement of thousands of people, many of whom had never before imagined themselves taking part in any uprising – the speed of events that September required exactly such spontaneity. The word 'spontaneous' is repeated so often in eyewitness reports it is no wonder that early historians of the resistance like Roberto Battaglia refused to consider it a proper insurrection at all, describing it instead as 'a phenomenon of nature', without direction or logic, as furious and destructive as a wildfire.[18]

But spontaneity is only one side of the coin. Just because large parts of the population were acting on impulse, that does not mean that other parts were not acting in a much more organized way, inspired by years of political resistance. Federico Zvab, for example, had already spent several months in 1943 building networks of contacts within Naples, and a cache of arms in his hospital. Eugenio Mancini, who led a group of partisans in Materdei just west of the museum, had not only spent twenty years resisting Fascism, but worked feverishly throughout the Four Days to establish links between different groups of fighters so that they might coordinate their actions.[19] Such people became natural leaders of the uprising, and it is precisely because they were already known to be actively critical of the regime that people who rose up 'spontaneously' at the end of September naturally gravitated towards them.

There are hundreds of other examples. Indeed, by comparing lists of recognized fighters with lists of political dissidents of the time, historian Giuseppe Aragno has compiled a list of more than 350 such people, who not only had a history of resistance to Fascism but were also acting out of recognizable political motives, and often according to a pre-determined plan.[20] These included Anarchists, Socialists, Communists, Liberals and Nationalists, and many who considered themselves apolitical, but decided to act purely out of a sense of moral repugnance against the corruption and violence of the regime. That such people had not yet organized themselves into formal political parties is hardly surprising: in September 1943, political parties were only beginning to resurface after twenty years of repression, and they were just as organized in Naples as they were in any other part of the country at this time.[21]

Italy's chroniclers of the resistance have often used the idea of the 'spontaneous uprising' to relegate the events in Naples to a lesser tier, as if they are not nearly as impressive or important as the events that took place later in the north. It is not entirely clear why such spontaneity should be any less inspiring than a resistance that took longer to achieve its aims. But in any case, the whole reasoning behind this belittling of the Four Days is flawed; because, like many of the uprisings of earlier centuries, the Neapolitan revolt of September 1943 was not nearly as 'spontaneous' as it seemed.

The Myth of the *Scugnizzi*

In November 1943, a series of photographs of the uprising in Naples were published in *Life* magazine, under the name of Alessandro Aurisicchio De Val. Among them were several pictures of boys carrying weapons: these were Naples' notorious *scugnizzi* – street urchins famed for getting into mischief. They seem impossibly young to be holding their rifles. According to the captions of the photos, the oldest is just 15. One photo shows a 9-year-old holding a pistol and dressed in a looted army coat that is so big for him that the sleeves have to be rolled up several times.[22]

Images of children are familiar in the communal memory of the Four Days uprising. In the post-war years, only four fighters were awarded the Gold Medal for military valour, and two of them were children: 12-year-old Gennaro Capuozzo, who died while trying to throw a hand grenade at a tank on the main road near the museum; and 13-year-old Filippo Illuminato, who was killed near the southern end of Via Toledo while similarly attacking a German armoured car. (The other two were not much older: Mario Menichini and Pasquale Formisano were both only 17 years old, and died while performing similar heroics.)[23]

Scugnizzi also feature heavily in Nanni Loy's famous 1962 film dramatization of the uprising. There are numerous scenes that feature boys from a home for juvenile delinquents, who break out of the correctional facility to take part in the fight against the Germans (events that are very loosely based on a real-life juvenile prison on Salita Pontecorvo[24]). The film itself is dedicated to Gennaro Capuozzo, and his death is depicted in one of its most moving scenes.

A typical account of the *scugnizzi* was given by the Italian film star Sophia Loren, who grew up in Pozzuoli and Naples, and witnessed the insurrection as a little girl. In her account these 'ragged little boys from the slums' were exclusively responsible for the uprising. 'What these little boys did I witnessed with my own eyes, but even so, I find it difficult to believe that what I remember actually happened.' She described boys 'ranging from five to ten years of age' swarming over German tanks with petrol bombs, running at them with bales of burning hay, attacking soldiers with pairs of scissors or nail-spiked boards, or dropping paving stones on them from the rooftops:

> For four days these incredible boys were a continual, deadly harassment. Day and night I watched them running, dodging, scurrying in and out of alleys and over walls and rooftops, ever attacking, achieving with their courage and brazen tactics what the Italian men, who were now in work camps or in hiding, had failed even to attempt.[25]

It is easy to see why politicians and filmmakers alike might want to emphasize the role of children during the uprising: it gives a very real sense of the David vs Goliath nature of much of the fighting, and makes the success of the Neapolitans even more impressive. However, it also has the effect of infantilizing and discrediting a movement that was actually much more grown up, and much more organized, than it is often given credit for. As several historians have pointed out, there were good reasons why groups of all kinds after the war should want to minimize the events of the uprising in this way.[26] Former Fascists and their political heirs were delighted to be able to portray the insurgents as little more than juvenile delinquents playing with guns. The Communist Party was sometimes willing to go along with this myth, because it drew a veil over its own failure to lead and direct this particular 'revolution'. The CLN, which had been hopelessly timid during the Four Days, was glad to minimize the role of other, more active resisters. The Christian Democrats, who dominated the postwar political landscape for decades, were equally glad to pretend that the uprising had been a non-political, child-like affair – particularly since so many of the uprising's heroes and leaders had come from the political Left.

Meanwhile, the readers of *Life* magazine, who knew no different, were happy to have their own myths confirmed by these photographs. They did not know that De Val, the photographer, had been obliged to sell his roll of film to the Americans so that he could afford to eat. Nor did they know that he was a militant Communist, who had presumably taken the photographs with a very different narrative in mind.[27] Rather than becoming symbols of a unified Neapolitan underclass rising up in revolution, De Val's photographs became part of an American story, allowing American wives and parents to imagine their GIs as strong, professional soldiers in contrast to the skinny, barefoot children who, until very recently, had been fighting for the other side.

Without wishing to take any glory away from the *scugnizzi* of Naples – they did indeed fight bravely during the Four Days – the statistics do not justify them taking centre stage in the way that they did for decades after the war. Of the 4,400 or so people who were officially recognized as combatants in Campania in September 1943, only 390 were children under 16 years old – or about 8.9 per cent of the total.[28] While it is true that the *scugnizzi* did fight on the barricades – indeed, twenty-nine of them fell in combat – for the most part they were not firing guns or throwing hand grenades, but doing other tasks to which they were better suited. They brought food and ammunition to the front line. They carried messages, and news of where the Germans were advancing from, or where the Fascist snipers were hiding. They were rarely alone, as they appeared in most of the photos, but alongside their families and communities. Gennaro Capuozzo, for example, was at the barricades near the museum along with his cousin, Maddalena Cerasuolo, who in turn had fought alongside her father the day before. The famous photos of armed children are therefore quite misleading: they were just a small part of a much wider uprising involving people of all ages, classes, occupations, and of both sexes.

In the aftermath of the war, those who wished to propagate a narrative of community, agency and political action during the Naples uprising often found themselves frustrated. The artist Edoardo Pansini, who had led the fight in Vomero, campaigned for years to have a memorial built, but was repeatedly turned down both by the local administration and by central government. When a monument was finally built in 1969, it was dedicated not to the men and women of all ages who fought and died, but specifically to the *scugnizzi*. A whole generation had passed, but the uprising that defined the city's communal heroism during the war was still being downplayed, minimized, infantilized.

The myth of the *scugnizzi* was very convenient for the Allies. It fulfilled the same function as the myth of the 'happy *lazzaroni*' in Bourbon times and the myth of the 'Africans of Italy' after the Risorgimento – it made the people of Naples seem inferior. According to this myth, such people needed to be governed by those who knew better: the children may have liberated themselves, but what they really needed was for the grown-ups to arrive and look after them.

In the immediate aftermath of the Four Days the people of Naples, adults and children alike, were indeed grateful for the structure and guidance that the arrival of the Allies gave them. But as time went on, and the bumbling performance of Allied Military Government got worse, their appreciation inevitably waned. It was not long before they began calling for a greater say in their own affairs. Their fight for some kind of recognition, and some kind of justice, is what we shall turn to next.

In May 1940 the king came to the city to inaugurate the Mostra d'Oltremare, pictured here: a vast, expensive 'World's Fair' showcasing Italy's empire overseas. It was closed down just a month later when Italy declared war.

During the early years of the war, relations between Neapolitans and Germans were good. They only deteriorated in 1943 when the war started to go badly.

Naples was the most heavily bombed city in Italy. These bombs were dropped during the biggest raid of all, which took place on 4 August 1943. Dozens of buildings in the historic centre were destroyed, and hundreds killed. (NARA)

The ruins of the fourteenth-century church of Santa Chiara. Dozens of other cultural treasures were damaged by the Allied bombing raids, including the Royal Palace, the San Carlo Theatre and the Galleria Umberto I. (NARA)

People made homeless by bombing raids were forced to take up residence in air raid shelters; or, as pictured here, to sleep out in the open.

The Four Days of Naples was one of the first popular uprisings against the Germans in all of Europe. Barricades were erected all over the city, such as this one just north of the National Museum. (ICSR)

The indomitable Maddalena Cerasuolo, who fought alongside her father during the Four Days. (ICSR)

Only four fighters were awarded the *Medaglia d'Oro* for their heroism during the uprising, and all were under 18. This iconic photo depicts the pathos of an uneven battle against the mighty Wehrmacht, but has also been used to infantilize the uprising. (ICSR)

The two faces of victory. *Above*: Neapolitan fighters celebrate after the Germans have been forced out of the city. (IWM) *Below*: Robert Capa's famous photograph of Neapolitan mothers grieving for their dead sons. (Magnum)

As if the war and its attendant crises were not enough, in March 1944 Vesuvius erupted. Whole villages on the slopes of the mountain were consumed, and a blanket of volcanic ash ruined crops for miles around. (NARA)

A makeshift warehouse in a Naples church. The Allies shipped millions of tons of food and other goods through the city, but much of it ended up on the black market.

It was rumoured that one could buy anything on the Neapolitan black market, even a Liberty ship. In reality most of what was for sale was more mundane: food, clothing and everyday essentials. This girl is selling cigarette butts.

In March 1944 frustration with Allied military rule began to boil over. Here, thousands of Neapolitans fill the Galleria Umberto to demand a return to democracy. In the following months such demonstrations would frequently degenerate into violence. (NARA)

Two giants of the anti-Fascist movement: Count Carlo Sforza (left) refused to work with Badoglio and the king in 1944 because of their links to Fascism. Benedetto Croce (right) was more willing to compromise.

The head of the Allied Control Commission, General Noel Mason-MacFarlane, ran southern Italy for the benefit of the Allies. When he finally allowed the Italians to appoint their own prime minister in June 1944, Churchill had him sacked. (IWM)

In the meantime, however, it did not take long for the Allies to forget the role that the Neapolitans had played in their own liberation. Some of the very first newspaper reports in Britain referred to the Allied arrival in Naples solely in terms of a 'conquest'.[29] By January 1944, some of the troops themselves were beginning to claim that they had 'taken' Naples, rather than walking into the city unopposed.[30] By the end of the war, the Allies were routinely remembering the way that they had 'slugged their way into Naples', despite the fact that the vast majority of their actual 'slugging' had taken place a long way outside the city itself.[31]

The true fighting in Naples, which had been conducted exclusively by Neapolitans, was gradually forgotten in favour of yet another self-serving Allied myth.

PART III

Compromises and Betrayals

CHAPTER 23

Vesuvius

On 18 March 1944, Vesuvius erupted. In nearby Pompeii, the chief archaeologist saw it as he reached over to close his window: 'a great strip of purple fire furrowed the mountain from top to bottom.'[1] There had been no roar, no tremor, just the silent emission of molten rock, spilling over the rim of the crater at a rate of half a million cubic metres per hour.[2]

So began yet another catastrophe that was to befall the people of Naples and its hinterland. In the next few days Vesuvius would erupt again and again, sending vast rivers of lava down the mountainside. The pyroclastic flow did not travel fast – it moved less than 300 metres each hour – but it was vast and unstoppable, burning and engulfing everything in its path. At its greatest extent it swelled to a wall of molten rock more than 12 metres (40 feet) high, advancing on a front almost a kilometre wide. Whenever it reached the edge of a cliff, as it did on the morning of 20 March, the lava 'literally swept over it like an enormous cataract of fire'.[3]

This vast molten river flowed in three directions. To the south and southwest two streams headed towards Torre del Greco, a major town on the bay, which had already been buried in a similar eruption in 150 years earlier. To the northwest the lava flowed towards the villages of San Sebastiano, Massa di Somma and Cercola, where some 20,000 people had their homes and farms.

While the first two streams, mercifully, stopped short of Torre del Greco, the people of San Sebastiano were not so lucky. As the wall of fire crept inexorably towards them they scrambled to save whatever they could from their homes. Bedding, furniture and personal posses-sions were piled onto wagons and hand carts and dragged down the mountain. Some of the villagers prayed fervently for their deliverance – a statue of San Gennaro was even paraded before the lava flow in the hope that the saint might intercede – but all to no avail. In the early hours of 21 March the whole village was slowly engulfed, making 2,150 people homeless.

The Allies did whatever they could to help. The civil affairs officer for Naples province, Colonel James L. Kincaid, hastily put together an emergency evacuation plan. Volunteers from nearby hospitals and airfields joined the entire headquarters staff of the provincial Allied Military Government to evacuate the population and rescue as many of their belongings as possible. Two hundred trucks were made availa-ble as transport; soup kitchens were set up by the American Red Cross in nearby Cercola; and the local cinema in San Giorgio was comman-deered as an emergency homeless shelter. And all the while the lava kept on coming, like a 'large, glowing coke fire that towered over the buildings'.[4] It swallowed up a second village, Massa di Somma, and headed towards the fringes of Cercola.

By day, the whole mountainside was obscured by smoke, but by night the lava 'looked like a mighty, slowly-advancing orange dragon' snaking down the mountainside, and reflecting 'fiery symbols' like 'serpents' across the waters of the bay.[5] The deep red glow could be seen lighting up the sky over 100 miles (170 km) away at Anzio.[6] American Red Cross workers wondered if the 'Pagan Gods of Fire and Epidemics were showering their wrath down upon Man below'.[7]

Unfortunately, the lava flows were only the opening act. On the evening of 21 March the top of the crater suddenly exploded: 'Ashes and smoke erupted in one continuous roar, and a gigantic cumulus of rolling, expanding smoke cloud rose above the volcano to a height of twenty thousand feet.'[8] Over the next twenty-four hours the eruptions continued more or less without pause. 'The shaking of the ground gave one a terrifying feeling that at any moment one might be swallowed up,' remembered one British aid worker.[9] From a nearby airfield, the sight was terrifying and awe-inspiring in equal measure. 'That lava, and the smoke!' exclaimed one American aircraft mechanic. 'You could see flames going up through it ... And at night you could see little flashes of lightning up in the cloud.'[10] According to a British officer, the sky 'was the deepest of blood reds, and pulsating everywhere with lightning reflections'.[11] Eighteen months later, eyewitnesses would say similar things about the mushroom cloud over Hiroshima.[12]

With each new explosion, thousands of tons of volcanic matter were blasted into the air. Soon pieces of rock began falling from the heavens all over the region. Most of it was dust or small pebbles, but as the technicians at the nearby Pompeii airfield made clear, 'Some of it was rocks the size of your head ... These big old rocks came down and went right through the planes.'[13] This infernal hail 'shredded' the canvas tents where the technicians were bivouacked, forcing them to take cover in a farmhouse – but eventually the sheer weight of all the dust and stones piling up on the farmhouse roof caused it to cave in. Much like San Sebastiano on the other side of the volcano, the Pompeii airfield eventually had to be evacuated. Those without helmets had to protect their heads with pots and pans as they hurried to get away.[14]

For the archaeologists at Pompeii, the sound of the lapillus falling on the rooftops had terrifying echoes of the eruption that destroyed the ancient town in 79 CE. 'From the terrace of the Aquila farmhouse, in the middle of the excavations, it sounded like the deep roar of an immense cascade of water advancing or receding,' remembered Amedeo Maiuri.[15] After the rain of stone came a more insidious rain of ash, 'like a big snow storm', which covered everything in a blanket of grey, 'giving the ruins the most desolate appearance I have ever seen'. At the airfield it got into the engines and equipment of all the grounded planes, rendering dozens of them completely irreparable.[16]

The wind carried much of this ash and dust southwards over the Sorrento Peninsula and towards the island of Capri. According to the Allied situation report of 23 March, the entire area between Pompeii and Salerno was covered in a layer six inches deep, and 'In some places drifts as high as 14 feet have been formed.'[17] For several days, the road and rail network south of Naples became virtually impassable. The dust cloud also caused problems much further afield. Pilots flying to Naples from Palermo encountered a cloud of black smoke so thick, and so deep, that after flying in pitch darkness for forty minutes they were obliged to change course.[18] Ash and mud fell from the sky as far away as Bari, more than 200 km away on the opposite side of Italy.[19]

The 1944 eruption was the worst to hit Campania for seventy-one years, causing tens of millions of dollars' worth of damage across the region. The lava flow had consumed three-quarters of San Sebastiano, where only the top of the church bell tower, poking forlornly out of the smoking rock, bore testimony to the community that had recently lived here. Half of Massa di Somma had also been engulfed, as well as some houses on the outskirts of Cercola. Of the 20,000 people evacuated, at least 2,700 people were now permanently homeless. Even those who still had a roof over their heads would continue to need aid: dozens of square kilometres of their gardens, vineyards, orchards and farms had been destroyed.

The rain of ash and stone, while less dramatic than the lava, had been much more insidious: of the thirty or so people killed, the vast majority had died under falling rocks, or when the roofs of their houses had collapsed under the weight of all the volcanic dust and debris. To the south of the volcano, hundreds of square kilometres of farmland had been covered in a poisonous layer of volcanic ash and mud. In a region that was already hovering on the edge of starvation, this was just the latest in a whole series of devastating blows.[20]

On the face of it, the eruption of Vesuvius has nothing to do with the Second World War: it would have taken place regardless of the conflict in this part of Italy. But the response to the eruption was symbolic of some of the problems that were beginning to grow between the Allies and the local population, and shone a light on the difference in attitudes between them.

From an Allied point of view, the eruption was only a temporary crisis, but one that required immediate and urgent intervention. Some of those who rushed to the scene did so out of a sense of duty, others out of a sense of adventure, but all of them came away with a sense of wonder at the sheer power of this natural phenomenon. Norman Lewis later wrote that it was 'the most majestic and terrible sight I have ever seen'; other accounts routinely called it 'fantastic', 'exciting', or 'a sight

I'll never forget'.[21] Ken Roth, one of the aircraft technicians at the nearby Pompeii airfield, claimed that it was 'the highlight of the whole trip, even the war'.[22] One British hospital worker confessed that he had only volunteered to help with the evacuation because it 'seemed like a good idea to see this unique event at close hand'. He mistakenly thought that the whole operation 'was going to be a picnic'.[23] Even the Allied press, initially at least, treated it with a certain amount of levity. Before its reporters discovered how badly the communities on the slopes of the volcano were suffering, the *Stars and Stripes* went with a particularly flippant headline: 'Mt Vesuvius Lets Loose Loudest Belch in 15 Years'.[24]

For the Italians, by contrast, this was no mere adventure: from the very beginning it was a tragedy that enveloped entire communities. In San Sebastiano women wept openly on the street, and children 'stared unbelievingly at the destruction of the only homes they had ever known'.[25] If they invoked the Virgin Mary or San Gennaro it was because they felt powerless: no matter how much help the Allies provided them, they knew that only divine intervention could save them from this slowly unfolding disaster. Amedeo Maiuri's diary entries are perhaps representative of the Italian point of view: he drew parallels with the many previous eruptions that had taken place since ancient times, but also painted a vivid picture of the 'sad' and 'desolate' present-day 'disaster'. He particularly lamented the damage done to the local farms and orchards now buried beneath mounds of ash: 'all the budding crops destroyed!', and all the trees now 'leafless, stripped and bent over as if by a blast of grapeshot'. There was no question of this being merely a story to tell the folks back home. It was a long-term catastrophe with consequences for his entire community.

As with the volcano, so with the war. For many Allied soldiers, sailors and airmen – particularly for Americans and Canadians – the war was an immensely important interlude in their lives, but an interlude nevertheless. When it was all over they would go home, secure in the knowledge that they had done the right thing, with a kitbag full of exciting, terrible and occasionally traumatic stories to tell their friends and families. But for the Italians there was much more at stake. It was not only their lives that were on the line, but also their homes, their communities, their whole way of life: the very ground on which they lived was being torn up by violent forces beyond their control. They did not have the luxury of regarding the war only as a series of short-term battles that needed to be fought and won before moving on to the next one. Each of these battles had much wider, long-term implications that the average Allied soldier – for all his good intentions – had absolutely no notion of.

Kincaid's emergency operation to evacuate local people from the rage of the volcano was like all of the emergency operations carried out during this time – fast, efficient, well-resourced and deeply appreciated by the communities affected. But once the immediate danger was over the operation came to an end, and the Italians were left more or less to fend for themselves. In the short term, the Allied response had been exemplary; the long term was something for other people to worry about.

As we shall see in the remainder of this book, this conflict between the short-term necessities of the moment and the long-term interests of the Italian people was perhaps the most important feature of the Allied occupation of Naples, and Italy, between 1943 and 1945. It is no coincidence that critics of the Allied government characterized its repeated inability to come up with long-term solutions as 'a slow and steady rain of ash' that smothered the entire region (see Chapter 6).[26] The errors of AMG would pave the way for the political, moral and economic stagnation that would trouble Naples for much of the rest of the century.

CHAPTER 24

The *Epurazione*

W hen the Allies first entered Naples at the beginning of October 1943, Fascists were still firing from the rooftops and partisans were still chasing them down in order to enact their revenge. It was essential that Allied troops brought this to an end as soon as possible: they could not afford to allow any kind of civil war to develop behind their front lines. One of the first proclamations issued by the Allies was for all civilians to hand in their weapons and cease fighting immediately. Failure to do so was punishable by death.[1]

At first, some of the partisans were under the impression that this did not apply to them. Many of them were still technically in the Italian armed forces, and felt obliged to hold on to their weapons; others who had taken up arms against the Germans regarded themselves as allies of the British and Americans. Eugenio Mancini, for example, who had been one of the leaders of the Four Days in central Naples, apparently had pretensions of setting up his own armed Communist police force to help keep law and order before the Allies insisted on all police powers being retained by the local Carabinieri.[2] Edoardo Pansini, one of the main partisan leaders in the suburb of Vomero, had to be reined in repeatedly for attacking local Fascists and their property.[3] For reasons that no one has ever been able to explain properly, Federico Zvab, leader of the resistance in the ancient centre, spent the first few weeks of the liberation locked in a cell in Poggioreale prison.[4]

While Allied soldiers busied themselves with breaking up 'the mass lynching actions of some of the local citizens',[5] Allied administrators set about dealing with the multiple crises left by the retreating Germans. This required them to keep in place as many local officials as possible, whether or not they had been committed Fascists. Indeed, the very first proclamation they issued on entering the city required all local officials to stay at their posts and carry on their duties as normal.[6] From an Allied point of view, it simply made no sense to start a purge of the police force until law and order had been re-established. Similarly, they were extremely reluctant to start arresting financial experts and business leaders when the entire local economy was on its knees.

Whatever the rights and wrongs of these policies, they did not create a good first impression. To many Neapolitans it seemed as though the heroes of the Four Days were being repressed, while Fascist leaders and businessmen were being protected. Justice, democracy and the will of the people – the very things that the Allies claimed they were fighting for – seemed very far down their list of priorities.

Maintaining the status quo might have seemed necessary from a military point of view, but it had serious repercussions for the local people. By failing to prosecute obvious traitors with any kind of urgency, by keeping all the main political and economic structures in place, and by turning a blind eye to forms of corruption that were still fresh in everyone's minds, the Allies were implying that they approved of these things. At the very least they seemed willing to tolerate the intolerable. As we shall see in the following pages, the Allied point of view was rather more complicated than that. Nevertheless, the failure to get to grips with these problems quickly, or to understand the strong emotions they aroused in the breasts of the Italian people, would have profound effects not only on Naples and the south, but on the whole of Italy.

The Protection of *Prominenti*

The Allies might have made a better first impression, particularly among the more volatile parts of Neapolitan society, if they had begun their rule by making a handful of high-profile arrests. They were certainly not short of candidates. There were several high-ranking Fascists in the city, such as Domenico Tilena and Nicola Sansanelli, who had both been provincial leaders of the party – Sansanelli had even been on the Grand Council of Fascism. There were public officials who had collaborated with the Germans during the destruction of the city, such as Domenico Soprano and Giuseppe Solimena. There were the generals who had done likewise – Ettore Del Tetto and Riccardo Pentimalli. And there were the millionaire businessmen who had profited from the war, from corruption, and by actively courting the Germans – people like shipping magnate Achille Lauro and the telecommunications boss Count Ugo Pellegrini.

Most of these men were not arrested until public pressure to do something about them had been building for almost a year. In most cases the Allies actively supported such individuals, despite the huge weight of public opinion against them.[7] The only ones to be arrested promptly were the two generals, who were captured a week or so after the liberation and tried the following year. Achille Lauro was also taken into custody relatively early, in November 1943. Tellingly, however, he was not arrested for his personal links with Mussolini or his spectacular corruption, but for smuggling goods to and from Japan.[8]

To see how blind the Allies were to local sensibilities one need only look at the way they treated Domenico Soprano when they first arrived. The prefect was widely hated in Naples because of the way that he had collaborated with the Germans in the forced evacuation of the coast and the rounding up of forced labour. Evidence of his collaboration was not exactly hard to find: his signature had appeared on the orders published in the city's Fascist newspaper, *Roma*.[9] Despite this, the Allies did not arrest him. In fact, they did not even remove him from his job: instead he was allowed to take time out 'for health reasons', while his equally despised deputy took over his duties. Soprano was not officially replaced until the following month, and was not charged with

German collaboration until June 1944. (To the disgust of just about everyone in Naples, he would eventually be acquitted of all charges and freed.)[10]

As with the prefect, so, too, with the rest of Neapolitan public life. In the first six weeks of Allied rule, only a handful of people were arrested; and only a few dozen public employees were dismissed for being 'ardent Fascists', without any further punishment. All the police chiefs were kept on, including the head of the state police Giovanni Lauricella, who had been responsible for the violent repression of political dissent both before and after the fall of Mussolini.[11] The law courts were also largely left alone. The president of the Court of Appeals was removed from office early on, but within a couple of weeks US Counter Intelligence Corps had already given a 'clean bill of health to all other members of the local judiciary'. The consequences of such leniency were profound: it meant that those who had been in charge of law and order during Fascist times would continue to be in charge of it under the Allies.[12]

The story was similar in the provinces beyond the city limits. In the whole of Naples province only 385 officials had been removed from public positions by the end of the year. In Benevento province the number was only seventy-seven, and in Avellino province it was only sixty-nine. After twenty years of Fascism, in a region made up of hundreds of separate communities, with a population of several million people, it was not much of an *epurazione*, a purge.[13]

Allied Failings

There are many reasons behind the failure of the Allies to cleanse the Augean stables, and not all of them are completely straightforward. But high on the list was Allied indecision. On the face of it AMG had the clearest of goals: 'the total elimination of Fascism from Italian life and the removal of Fascists from positions of economic influence and power and from all levels of government.'[14] But the practicalities of government made such a comprehensive purge impossible. In the words of one AMG official, 'to remove everyone possessed of a Fascist membership card would be equivalent to removing every office bearer and functionary from civil or military office'. Such zeal would lead to the whole country being 'practically paralyzed'.[15] The problem was therefore where to draw the line – an issue that the Allies did not properly get to grips with until it was far too late.

It was months before any proper guidance was issued to Allied officials about how to discover who had been a Fascist, or to ascertain exactly how 'Fascist' they had been. The first standardized questionnaires for public employees, the *schede personali*, were not issued until the beginning of December, almost five months after the invasion of Sicily. The first instructions about which categories deserved automatic dismissal did not come until the end of the year; and detailed orders about procedures, appeals processes and so on were not finalized until the summer of 1944. These were issues that should have been considered before the invasion. Instead, Allied officials had to wait almost a full year.[16]

From indecision flowed incompetence. In the first instance, the screening of local officials was carried out by officers of the US Counter Intelligence Corp and the British Field Security Service, but neither of these bodies had either the manpower or the local expertise needed to carry out such a massive task: as a consequence the process 'was necessarily slipshod and based on hearsay rather than facts'.[17] In Naples and Campania a separate Intelligence Division was set up by AMG in order to carry out more detailed investigations of their own civilian employees, but it had a staff of only seven. By their own admission, they were 'young and inexperienced' and lacked any intelligence qualifications.[18]

In such an atmosphere, former Fascists were able not only to hold on to office, but also to wheedle their way into new positions of power under Allied supervision. The Economics and Civilian Supply Division of AMG in particular became notorious for employing prominent Neapolitans as advisers, many of whom were later revealed to have been involved in various corruption scandals.[19] Once they had made themselves useful, they proved extremely difficult to remove. Allied officials were reluctant to go through the process of finding replacements for people they had come to know and like, and were disturbingly willing to overlook past indiscretions for the sake of expediency.

One example that speaks volumes is the case of Giuseppe Frignani, the director of the Bank of Naples. Frignani was described in intelligence documents as one of the 'most dangerous' Fascists in the city. In the violent days of the early 1920s he had been the head of a squad of Blackshirts in Ravenna, and was on first-name terms with the entire Fascist hierarchy, including Mussolini. He was also a founder member of the Italo-German Friendship League, and during the short German occupation of Naples in September 1943 was reputed to have misappropriated bank funds in order to pay a huge bribe to the Wehrmacht in return for their agreement not to blow up his bank building.[20]

Despite Frignani's murky past, the Allied Military Government almost immediately appointed him as an adviser to the Finance Division. As Allied officials got to know him, they started doing him favours. For example, when his villa in Resina, near the ancient site of Herculaneum, was requisitioned by the Allies, the head of the city's AMG, Colonel Knight, personally intervened to get it returned to him.[21]

Frignani was finally arrested and interned on 22 November 1943 by Fifth Army intelligence officers, but a whole list of Allied figures immediately rallied to his defence, including Knight and AMG's Chief Finance Officer, who insisted that 'the best interests of AMG would be served by allowing him to remain in office'.[22] In the following weeks the Vatican also came to his defence. The Cardinal Secretary of State, a personal friend of Frignani's, claimed somewhat implausibly that he had 'always been a public spirited Neapolitan citizen whose Fascism was nothing but a reluctant and necessary concession to the political exigencies of the Italian situation'. As a consequence of such interventions a succession of telegrams passed between London, Algiers and Naples, clamouring for his immediate release.[23]

To all intents and purposes, the dismissal of Frignani from office should have been an open and shut case. He was a former *squadrista*, he took part in the March on Rome, he had been decorated for his services to Fascism, and he was a *gerarcho* – i.e. a man who owed his position in power predominantly to his Fascist Party contacts. These were all four of the categories that, according to AMG's own guidelines, merited immediate dismissal from his job – and yet AMG did everything they could to ignore them. It is to the credit of Fifth Army intelligence officers that they held firm despite this considerable pressure, and kept Frignani interned pending trial.

Frignani was just the tip of the iceberg. Neapolitan historian Paolo De Marco has highlighted numerous other figures, each with a similarly dubious past, who acted as advisers to the Allies throughout the early days of the liberation – from the head of the Cirio food consortium, Paolo Signorini, who was interned around the same time as Frignani, to the shipping agent Carlo De Luca, who was eventually arrested for fraud. The whole system was rife with corruption.[24]

Reasons for Allied Failings

It is easy to blame the Allies for their failures to deal with this situation, but there were good practical reasons why they were reluctant to pursue the *epurazione* with any vigour. The Frignani affair was a case in point. Just because Frignani was the product of a violent and corrupt system, it did not necessarily follow that he himself was violent or corrupt. Frignani was eventually cleared of all corruption charges; and by all accounts he was supremely competent at his job. By removing him from office at a time when Naples was in the midst of a financial crisis, all the Allies seemed to have achieved was to make their own lives more difficult.

There were also good philosophical reasons for proceeding with caution. The immediate dismissal and arrest of all characters like Frignani might have sent a clear message to the people of Italy about what sort of a political system was acceptable and what was not; it might have signified a new beginning for Italy after years of dictatorship; and it might have given satisfaction to all those who had suffered under its heel. But from a moral point of view, arresting people for their political beliefs would have been dangerously close to the way that the Fascists themselves had behaved during the previous twenty years.

The Allies were at pains to show the Italian people that there were better ways of running society than through policing people's political beliefs. At the beginning of November, for example, they had to discipline one of the Italian police chiefs for arresting fifty former Fascists purely on political grounds. 'The questore explained that under the fascist regime he arrested anti-fascists as a political source of danger to the State. Since the arrival of the Allies he considered it his duty to arrest fascists as a political source of danger to the Allied cause.' Allied officials had to explain to him that in a democratic society people were free to hold whatever political opinions they wished – even ones that the Allies themselves disagreed with. They instructed him to release the prisoners immediately.[25]

If the Allies had pursued a more comprehensive purge than they had, it would have opened up all kinds of new problems that they were equally unprepared to deal with. The most important of these was who would be appointed in place of all the people they dismissed. Where would they find thousands of competent, experienced Italians who were free from any taint of Fascism? If they only appointed people they approved of, didn't they open themselves up to accusations of political meddling; and if they ruled directly themselves, couldn't they be accused of their own kind of military dictatorship? Indeed, who were they to decide these things at all? Shouldn't it be up to the Italians to choose who governed them? Wherever possible, the Allies preferred to leave it up to the Badoglio government to take the lead over the prosecution of former Fascists.

All of which led to the biggest problem of them all, and the one which the Allies had never prepared themselves to address: how could they pursue a policy locally that was not also being pursued nationally? Any purge worth its name must surely begin with the head of state. King Vittorio Emanuele III was one of the most compromised men in the whole of Italy: not only was he the one who had appointed Mussolini in the first place, but he had turned down several opportunities to sack him, even after the violent nature of Fascism was beyond doubt. He had supported and endorsed twenty years of Fascist crimes, and had only finally done the right thing when the Allies were already knocking on the door.

His prime minister was hardly less tainted. Pietro Badoglio was a war criminal who had committed acts of genocide in Africa, and had actively supported the declaration of war against Britain and France in

1940. He was also a coward who, along with the king, had abandoned Rome to the Germans without even attempting to organize any proper defence.

Were these really the right people to entrust with reforming the Italian administration? The vast majority of Italians certainly did not think so. In the words of the main trade union body, the Confederazione Generale del Lavoro, 'the first *epurazione* that is necessary must be carried out in Salerno [the seat of central government]; and until it is complete, the Italian people will be justified in their suspicion that Fascism is not over'.[26]

And yet, for better or worse, this was the government that the Allies had committed themselves to upholding.

Italian Failings

Rather than admit that the king and Badoglio were part of the problem, the Allies set about trying to convince themselves that they were part of the solution. Allied officers repeatedly reminded themselves that, even before they had arrived in mainland Italy, the Badoglio government had already carried out a purge of sorts. In the six weeks after the fall of Mussolini it had replaced most of the prefects in the south of Italy, and at least some of the mayors of the larger towns and cities. Naples was a good example: the prefect had been removed, as had at least seventeen mayors (*podestà*) in various *comuni* around the city's outskirts and in its main satellite towns. The same was true in the other nearby provinces: fifteen mayors had been replaced in Benevento province, and a further two in Avellino province. The Allies recorded these numbers alongside their own, as if they and the Badoglio government were singing from the same hymn sheet. Thus the *epurazione* was presented as a single process: begun under Badoglio, supported and continued under the Allies.[27]

However, there were fundamental problems with Badoglio's so-called purge, just as there were with the Allied purge that followed. To begin with, it was lacking in quantity: a handful of dismissals barely scratched the surface of a Fascist system that had grown up over the course of twenty years. It was also lacking in quality: most of the new appointments made by Badoglio were not much better than the men they were replacing. As had been demonstrated during the German occupation, Domenico Soprano turned out to be as bad as the Fascist prefect he replaced, Michele Vaccari. Likewise, Giovanni Lauricella had been a like-for-like replacement for the previous police chief, Riccardo Pastore.[28]

From a political point of view, this lack of credibility would become a huge problem in the months to come. It was not only that Badoglio's replacements were tainted by years of collaboration with Fascism, but also that they were all cut from the same political cloth. All came from the political Right, and often from the far Right. This handed the moral high ground to the parties of the Left – a position that they would exploit mercilessly, but somewhat powerlessly, for the rest of the war, and even long after the war was over.

After the invasion of mainland Italy had taken place, the Allies took control of the administration of Naples and the surrounding area, promising to hand it back to the Italian government once the fighting had moved further north. In the meantime, the Allies would keep a keen eye on how Badoglio and his cabinet governed the rest of the south.

Determined to convince the Allies that they were taking the purge process seriously, Badoglio's government began drawing up anti-Fascist legislation. By the end of the year, they had produced the first properly detailed description of how the *epurazione* should be conducted: Royal Decree Law 29/B on the 'defascistization' of public life. This law, passed on 28 December 1943, described exactly which former Fascists were considered unfit for duty, and how they should be removed.[29]

But over the next six months little action followed. Badoglio did not get round to appointing a High Commissioner for the National Epurazione until the end of February 1944. Even then he made sure that the High Commissioner's remit was so narrow that he would be all but ineffectual.[30] Other changes were equally slow to come about. It was not until the end of May that the Fascist seizure of power was made retroactively criminal; and it was not until the end of July that a final, comprehensive system was created for conducting a proper purge.[31] By this point Rome had been liberated, and Badoglio himself had at last stepped down as prime minister. He had succeeded in delaying the purge for a full year.

What came next was hardly better. A few high-profile cases were tried in Rome with satisfying results – at the end of 1944, for example, Ettore Del Tetto and Riccardo Pentimalli, the generals who had abandoned Naples to the Germans, were each sentenced to twenty years' imprisonment.[32] But others were less successful. When the Fascist hierarch Ugo Pellegrini and the hated prefect Domenico Soprano were both acquitted, there was widespread outrage in the city.[33]

The less high-profile cases were even more disappointing. Countless notorious Fascists continued to walk free simply because the process of gathering evidence was so slow: rather than being carried out by hundreds of policemen, it was carried out by a small number of overworked magistrates who simply did not have the time or resources to do a thorough job. Some of those magistrates were themselves tainted with links to Fascism, and predisposed to be lenient. Evidence often went missing or mysteriously disappeared – in Avellino, saboteurs broke into the office of the provincial Epurazione Commission and stole documents relating to local Fascists. Even when arrest warrants were issued, police sometimes arrived to find that the accused had been tipped off.[34]

In Naples, an Italian Epurazione Commissioner was not appointed until November 1944. At the beginning of 1945, he told Allied intelligence staff that, although 2,000 people had been sacked at the beginning of the Allied occupation, almost all of the state employees 'had since been re-entered on the payroll'. He also pointed out that there had never been any purge of the police force, and several high-ranking officers from OVRA, Mussolini's equivalent of the Gestapo, were still working for the Allies. Fourteen months after the Allies had first arrived, the longed-for purge had still barely progressed at all.[35]

Consequences

The agonizingly slow pace at which the purge process took place was to have profound effects on the future of Italy. In the south it crushed all dreams of a political rebirth. The period between the Allied landings and the liberation of Rome was an extraordinary time for the people of the south: for the first time in their history the national government was located here, and they had the opportunity, at last, to set the political agenda. The people of Naples had already shown what they were capable of during the Four Days. Had this been followed up with a comprehensive purge and widespread political reform, they might have blazed a trail for the rest of Italy to follow. Instead they had been forced simply to stand and wait. There are all kinds of reasons why this happened, some of which will be covered in the next chapter, but the disillusionment it caused was tragic. The purge, or what passed for it, did not take place until after Rome was liberated. The centres of power moved north. And the south found itself once again marginalized.

The failure of the purge in the early days of the liberation also had profound effects in the north. In areas that were still behind the German lines, where atrocity piled on atrocity over the next eighteen months, Italian partisans watched what was happening in the south and slowly began to understand that if they wanted any kind of justice there was no point in waiting for it to come from the courts. As the north was liberated in the spring of 1945, partisans everywhere took the law into their own hands. Mussolini would not be handed to the Allies or put on trial – he would be executed and hung up by his feet at a petrol station for all the world to see. Thousands of his followers would meet a similar fate in the months that followed. Summary executions of Fascists and their collaborators were common at the very end of the war and during its aftermath: estimates range from between 12,000 and 20,000 people executed, predominantly in the north. Had the partisans had any faith in the Italian justice system at all, some of this post-war political violence might have been avoided.[36]

Inevitably, such differences between the way the purge was conducted in the south and the way that it was conducted in the north would only deepen the divide that lay between them, and increase negative stereotypes about the south. After the war, politicians and historians would often speak of the 'wind from the north' as a force for radical change and reform; while the 'wind from the south' was characterized as a force that brought conservatism and corruption into the heart of politics.

There were some good reasons for this reputation – but the failure of the purge should not be counted among them. The people of the south had always had the potential to be just as radical as their brothers and sisters in Milan and Turin; it was the Allies who frustrated them, along with an Italian government led by a despised king and his equally discredited prime minister.

CHAPTER 25

A New National Politics

I f the fall of Mussolini opened the door to Italy's political renaissance, it was the liberation of Naples and the south that finally threw that door wide open. With the arrival of the Allies, all the old political parties were suddenly reborn. They were joined by brand new parties of every conceivable persuasion from monarchists to republicans, from radical socialists to free-market libertarians, from internationalists to nationalists to regional separatists. According to one Italian eyewitness of the time there was even, briefly, a Party of the Beefsteak, which 'promised that if they got into power, everybody would get a beefsteak a day per citizen'. Even in times of hardship Neapolitans retained their sense of humour.[1]

Unlike in occupied Rome and the north, where all political activity still had to take place in secret, in liberated Naples people debated openly in the streets, at the university and even in the newspapers. Various groups declared their manifestos in *Risorgimento*, the only newspaper allowed in the city during the early days of the liberation because of restrictions on paper. But as time went on ten or twelve new newspapers were granted licences, each one catering to a different political point of view: *Il Popolo* (Christian Democrat), *La Voce* (Communist and Socialist), *L'Azione* (the organ of the Action Party), *Il Giornale* (Liberal), *Il Lavoro* (Labour Democrat), *Il Giorno* (Liberal Democrat), *Bandiera Rossa* (Revolutionary Socialist), *La Repubblica* (Republican), *Il Cimento* (Italian Patriotic Movement) and so on. At the same time, trade unions also re-formed. In November 1943, they gathered together to re-establish the Confederazione Generale del Lavoro (the General Confederation of Labour, CGL). In the coming months this body would become the focal point for increasingly heated clashes between Italian workers and the Allied and Italian authorities all across the south.

This explosion of political activity was not welcomed by the king's government, whose first instinct was always to repress any activity that challenged its own authority.[2] Meanwhile in areas controlled by AMG, the British and Americans were also extremely nervous about allowing too much freedom too quickly. In battle zones all political activity was banned. Even in Naples all public meetings were also forbidden unless the organizers first obtained a licence for them. For example, when unauthorized political meetings took place among students at the university the rector, Adolfo Omodeo, was 'severely reprimanded' by AMG officers.[3] When a rash of strikes broke out across the region in May and June, the Allies reacted by making all work stoppages illegal. More draconian still was their proclamation on vital war industries, such as telecommunications: anyone causing stoppages in these industries would face the death penalty.[4] The Allies always insisted that they had pledged themselves 'to a gradual democratic re-education of the Italian people' – but at the same time they reserved the right to repress any groups that incited 'public disturbances'. It was not always clear where they drew the line.[5]

Such was the primeval soup out of which Italian post-war politics would eventually evolve. There were so many different groups, with so many conflicting interests, that it is difficult today always to understand which groups were important and which were mere bystanders. For the sake of clarity, therefore, perhaps it is worth starting with a snapshot of the basic political landscape as it was when the Allies first entered Naples at the beginning of October 1943. Everything that came later developed from this moment.

Naples in the Immediate Aftermath of the Liberation

When the Allies first arrived in Naples, they brought with them various political dissidents who had spent the last fifteen years or so in exile. Foremost among them were the activists of the Mazzini Society, an Italo-American association established by dissidents who had fled Mussolini's Italy in the 1920s. The founders and leaders of this society were men like Alberto Tarchiani, the former editor of *Corriere della Sera*, and Carlo Sforza, who had been the country's foreign minister before Mussolini seized power. By the time Naples was liberated, Count Sforza in particular had become something of a celebrity in Italian expatriate circles.

Sforza and his colleagues had spent many years trying unsuccessfully to set up a kind of government-in-exile for the Italians – similar in a way to what Charles de Gaulle had done for the Free French. Unlike de Gaulle, however, Sforza did not enjoy the support of the Allies. The Americans, who at this point still thought that the future of Italian politics was none of their business, refused to back him; and the British actively opposed him because of his anti-monarchist views. And unlike de Gaulle, Sforza had no army to back him, and no wellspring of support among the Italian resistance, which was itself only just finding its feet. In fact, almost the only things Sforza had going for him were his experience, his popularity and his prestige, none of which were quite enough to propel him into a position of power in the absence of free and fair elections.

Badoglio and the king understood how well respected Sforza was, especially among the Americans, and hoped to use him to give their own regime greater credibility. Shortly after Naples was liberated they offered him a place in their government as foreign minister: he already had experience in this post, and his good relations with the Americans would undoubtedly be an asset. But Sforza recognized a poisoned chalice when he saw one. He knew that a compromise with Badoglio's government at this early stage would destroy his reputation as a man of principle; and he strongly suspected that any real reform of Italian politics would be impossible while the king remained head of state. So he refused to be a part of Badoglio's government unless Vittorio

Emanuele first abdicated. Unsurprisingly, that was a concession that the king was simply not prepared to make.[6]

The second important political group in these very early days was a brand new organization called the Fronte Nazionale della Liberazione (National Liberation Front). This group, which did not last very long, was set up on Capri a few days before the Allies entered Naples. Among its founders were the returned exiles Alberto Tarchiani and Alberto Cianca, the Italian general Giuseppe Pavone, the philosopher and historian Benedetto Croce, and Croce's son-in-law Raimondo Craveri.

Of this group, Croce was easily the most famous. He had been a senator since 1910 and had once even been Italy's education minister. After Mussolini had seized power, Croce had written the 1925 'Manifesto of the Anti-Fascist Intellectuals', which was signed by some of the most famous figures in the country. He was virtually the only intellectual inside Italy who managed to remain openly critical of the regime throughout the 1930s and 1940s without being arrested. The Allies considered him so important that even while the battle was still raging on the beaches of Salerno they sent a Special Operations Executive unit by motor launch to rescue him from his Sorrento home and carry him to safety on Capri.[7]

The main idea championed by Croce's group was the creation of an Italian force to fight alongside the Allies for the liberation of their country. It was to be called the Gruppi Italiani Combattenti, and was to be made up of Italian volunteer soldiers, fighting under an Italian flag with Pavone as their general. The idea was initially greeted with enthusiasm by General Donovan, the head of the American Office of Strategic Services (OSS). But when the Italian king got wind of it he opposed it so vehemently that the newly formed groups were soon disbanded.[8] Croce watched this happen with great bitterness. He strongly suspected that the king, who feared any group being formed that was not explicitly monarchist, was to blame. But he also suspected British policy, 'which wants Italy as a battlefield', but didn't want a strong Italian army that might one day grow to become a future rival in Europe.[9]

Southern Italian forces would eventually fight alongside the Allies for the liberation of their country, but not as equal partners with the

Allies, and certainly not as a volunteer army led by an anti-monarchist like General Pavone.[10] For the most part, the Allies only allowed them to contribute as drivers and labourers – only about 60,000 men were ever allowed to become proper combat troops. Thus, while the people of the north were winning plaudits for their resistance to the Nazis, those of the south were excluded from joining in with the liberation of their own country.[11]

The final political force in Naples during this time was the newly formed Comitato di Liberazione Nazionale (Committee of National Liberation, CLN). This was by far the most important anti-Fascist movement in Italy. First formed in Rome in the days after Mussolini had been ousted, it had branches not only in the liberated areas like Naples, but also in cities like Rome and Milan that were now under German occupation. In the north, the CLN would eventually grow into a powerful government-in-waiting, with its own resistance armed forces, ready to seize power in each area as it was liberated. But in the autumn of 1943 the CLN was still in its infancy, and did not wield nearly the same influence that it would do as the war progressed.

The CLN consisted of a broad coalition of the six biggest opposition parties: from the political Left there were the Communists, the Socialists and the Centre-Left Action Party; and from the Right there were the Liberals, the socially conservative Democracy of Labour party, and the Christian Democrats. Despite their many and profound ideological differences, these six parties had agreed to collaborate with one another for the sake of the common goals that mattered to all of them: the expulsion of the Germans from Italy, and purging the nation of Fascism.

At a national level, the CLN would quickly become the only credible alternative to Badoglio's government: with its broad appeal, and hundreds of thousands of potential followers, it offered the only real possibility of a government of national unity. At a local level, however, it did not yet have quite that authority. It was still a very young organization, formed only a matter of weeks before the Allies arrived. The Neapolitan CLN also had its own particular problems: during the Four Days its members had been 'timid and uncertain', choosing to wait quietly in the background rather than rising up with the rest of the city to seize the day.[12] As a consequence, the people of Naples did not take them particularly seriously at first. The Allies did not take them seriously either: one Allied report dismissed them as 'simply so much hot air'. In a city where the British and Americans had the final world on almost every matter, that was a real problem.[13]

Nevertheless, most Italians who were at all politically inclined ended up supporting the CLN in one way or another. Many of the returned exiles, such as Sforza and Tarchiani, aligned themselves formally or informally with the Action Party. Benedetto Croce resumed his old association with the Liberals. The renascent trade unions restored their old connections to the Socialist and Communist parties. The Church stood firmly behind the Christian Democrats. Even former Fascists saw which way the wind was blowing, and rushed to redeem themselves by joining one or other of the six CLN parties (see Chapter 24). Everyone could see that the political future of Italy lay with the CLN.

But not yet. In the winter of 1943–4 the CLN did not yet have the reputation, the experience or the support that it needed to oust Badoglio or the king from power, let alone to lead the country in a new war against Germany. Even now, the Allies refused to give them any formal support, adopting instead a policy of politely accepting their suggestions 'while refraining from actively encouraging more frequent relations'.[14] As time dragged on, it became increasingly clear that if the democratic parties wanted to wrest control from the hands of the tainted men who had led it to disaster in the first place, they would have to do so the hard way.

The Growth of the Comitato di Liberazione Nazionale

The CLN were a constant thorn in the side of both the Badoglio government and the various Allied authorities that oversaw them. Less than three weeks after the liberation they issued a proclamation in *Risorgimento* calling for an immediate purge, and the formation of a new government 'as soon as possible'.[15] On 29 November they issued another statement declaring no confidence in the Badoglio government and demanding the abdication of the king. 'Only a democratic government,' they declared, could 'restore faith to the people and purge the civil and military administrations from the accomplices and co-perpetrators of Fascism'.[16]

As the Allied purge struggled to get under way in Campania, and as the Italian government's purge failed to materialize in any of the regions further to the south, the CLN's uncompromising position on this gained popularity everywhere, but especially in the industrial towns around the Bay of Naples. Demonstrations and riots took place all over the region against Fascist officials who were supposedly still lurking in local councils. In Torre Annunziata, for example, a crowd of about 2,000 people broke into the town hall at the end of the year demanding the removal of various council employees. Five weeks later they tried again, this time armed with sticks, and had to be dispersed by the local Carabinieri. Similar events occurred in several towns around Salerno, Benevento and Avellino.[17] It must be stressed that none of these clashes were endorsed by the CLN, but it was clear that the sympathies of the people involved were with the CLN, and particularly with the parties of the Left.

The first real clashes between the CLN and the Allies occurred towards the end of November 1943 when AMG banned them from organizing any kind of political activity close to the front lines. This was a fairly reasonable order – the last thing the Allied armies needed was any political disturbance just behind the battle zone – so the CLN graciously agreed to limit their activity to the city of Naples itself for the moment.

A few weeks later, however, the Allies placed further restrictions on the CLN by banning them from holding their national congress in the city itself. Again, the reason given was that 'political activity of such a scope could not be allowed in an area such as Naples under military government and so close to the front'.[18]

This time the CLN were not so happy to fall into line. A group of CLN members, now with Benedetto Croce at their head, came to AMG headquarters to demand how on earth a meeting of just fifty delegates from around the country might constitute a threat to military security. They strongly suspected the ban to have been requested by Badoglio, and accused the Allies of unwittingly playing into the hands of neo-Fascists. In the following days they drafted a letter to Roosevelt,

Churchill and Stalin demanding that the Allies stand by their recent promises to restore freedom of speech and of association to the Italian people. Eventually the Allies agreed to allow them to reorganize their conference in Bari, much further away from the fighting, early in the new year.[19]

It is worth stressing at this point that, despite the passions involved, disputes like this were always carried out in an atmosphere of mutual respect. Indeed, at a personal level, Allied officers and Italian politicians seem to have got on very well together. In the memoirs of people like Croce, Sforza and Filippo Caracciolo, Allied officers are almost always characterized as kind, patient and reasonable people. Likewise, AMG documents are often quite warm in their descriptions of the CLN: even the report on the meeting above stresses that it took place 'in rather a friendly atmosphere'. But this seemingly cosy arrangement concealed differences of outlook that were so irreconcilable that any chance of true friendship was virtually impossible. The Allies plainly regarded the CLN as an irritation that needed to be tolerated but not necessarily listened to. Meanwhile, the CLN were under no illusion that good relations with the Allied officers in Naples would make any difference to their cause. They knew that the true levers of power lay in London and Washington, and that the only way to force these faraway places to listen was to make a constant nuisance of themselves.

It was not long before the two sides clashed again, and this time relations were strained almost to breaking point. On 22 February, Winston Churchill made a speech in which he pledged support for Badoglio and Vittorio Emanuele III. He insisted that the current military and monarchical regime was easier to trust than the CLN, which was still something of an unknown quantity: 'When you have to hold a hot coffee pot,' he quipped, 'it is better not to break the handle off until you are sure that you will get another equally convenient and serviceable.'[20]

The CLN was incensed as much by his flippant tone as by his characterization of them as somehow less legitimate than Badoglio's government. They also deeply resented Churchill's implication that the Italian people were too hot to handle without a military regime to keep them under control. They immediately sent a telegram of complaint: the Italian people, they stated, would show themselves worthy 'as soon as Italians, too, are allowed that liberty which it is the aim of the war to bring about'.[21]

Meanwhile, the three left-wing parties – the Communists, the Socialists and the Action Party – went one step further and decided to call a strike in protest. Pamphlets were printed calling for the whole city to join in. 'By paralysing … the economic and administrative life of the city,' it read, 'the Neapolitans will tell Churchill what our country wants.'[22]

This was a really serious matter: striking in any area controlled by AMG was technically a 'war crime', punishable by imprisonment.[23] The head of the Allied Control Commission, Noel Mason-MacFarlane, summoned the leaders of the CLN to his office and warned them to call the strike off or suffer the consequences. They refused.[24]

The stand-off between the Allies and the CLN marked the beginning of a major political crisis in Naples. It is important to note that the strikers did not want to disrupt the war effort, merely to draw attention to the lack of any kind of democracy or justice in their everyday lives. To demonstrate that their strike was only supposed to be symbolic, they declared that it would only last ten minutes, and that all the workers taking part should work an extra fifteen minutes at the end of their shifts to make up for any time lost. But as far as the Allies were concerned, even this would set a dangerous precedent. 'We can only deal with this situation by being tough,' MacFarlane warned AFHQ on 2 March, two days before the strike was due to take place. 'The leaders of the 3 parties of the Left cannot be permitted to flout our authority in this way.'[25]

In the following days Carabinieri officers visited shops along the Via Roma and informed the owners that anyone who lowered their shutters during the strike would have their licences taken away. Italian Pubblica Sicurezza agents raided a print shop and confiscated 7,000 copies of the strikers' manifesto. Orders were issued to arrest the leaders of the Communist, Socialist and Action parties, all of whom immediately moved out of their offices in order to escape such arrest. There was a zealousness about some of the police actions in the run-up to the protest that spoke of older rivalries, particularly against the

Communists. According to one British intelligence officer, some of the Carabinieri 'were very happy to wait for that strike so that they could shoot at them'. It was all beginning to look horribly familiar.[26]

In the end it was the strikers who blinked first. The workers were already hungry and demoralized and their main union body, the CGL, was not prepared to put its workers' lives at risk for the sake of a strike – not even a ten-minute one.[27] So at the last minute they called the strike off. Instead they agreed to a much milder protest – a public demonstration, to take place on their day off. Mason-MacFarlane wisely decided to let the demonstration go ahead, on the grounds that it would release some of the built-up frustrations of the last two weeks. It took place in the Galleria Umberto on Sunday 12 March, attended by thousands, thankfully without serious incident.

For the CLN, this was a seminal moment in the life of their movement. On the one hand it showed that they were a growing force in Italian politics that had to be taken seriously. But on the other it demonstrated their greatest weaknesses. Despite their passion and vehemence, they had been unable to stand up to the Allies. Furthermore, the affair had exposed the serious divisions that existed within the CLN. Only three of the parties had agreed to support this strike, while the Liberals, the Christian Democrats and Democratic Labour had been firmly against it. The Christian Democrats had denounced not only the strike but also the demonstration that was held instead, claiming that any action of this sort undermined 'the interests of the Nation'. Democratic Labour was even more critical, and released a statement alongside various other, smaller political parties in support of the King.[28] For all their attempts at unity, the CLN was deeply split over how to oppose the Badoglio government, and how far that opposition should actually go. These differences were not minor: they were absolutely fundamental, and would also have serious consequences for the whole future of Neapolitan, and Italian, politics.

The Formation of a New Government

In the late winter and early spring of 1944 a series of events occurred in Naples that changed the political landscape entirely.

The first was the wholesale transfer of Badoglio's government from Brindisi to Salerno in early February. At the same time the king also moved to Ravello on the Amalfi coast. In the early days of the liberation it had been easy to dismiss Italian politicians as distant and irrelevant; now, suddenly, they were right on Naples' doorstep. For the first time regular contact could be established between the Italian government, the Allied Military Government, the ACC and the parties of the opposition, who were now all within easy driving distance of each other.

The second event was more specific for the Communist Party, but ended up having profound consequences for all of the parties in the CLN. At the end of March the Communist leader, Palmiro Togliatti, returned from exile in Moscow. He brought with him instructions for a radical change in policy: the Communists would no longer demand the abdication of the king, but would press instead for the creation of a government of national unity. The logic was quite simple: as far as Moscow was concerned, the only thing that mattered was the war against the Germans, and this would best be achieved if the Italians could stop squabbling and work together – even if that meant collaborating with the king.[29]

The news of this volte-face came as a shock to just about everyone. 'This decision marks a sudden and the most complete reversal of policy imaginable,' remarked the correspondent from *The Times*. 'Walls in towns and villages all over southern Italy are scrawled with such phrases as "Down with the King" and "Away with the Fascist King". Now all these bold words are to be quickly swallowed and the Communists are to kiss hands.' The correspondent predicted that the Communist faithful would probably fall quickly into line, but that the other parties in the CLN would be thrown into disarray.[30]

The next surprise came less than a week later. For months now the king had been under intense pressure from all sides to abdicate, but had so far stubbornly held his ground. At the beginning of April, however, the Neapolitan senator Enrico De Nicola finally managed to convince him to step down. He promised to do so only after Rome was liberated, and only in favour of his son, Prince Umberto, who would rule as regent in his place. Nevertheless it was a remarkable concession from a man who had proven himself exceptionally intransigent and thick-skinned. The question over whether the monarchy as an institution should continue to exist or not, which could only be decided by plebiscite, would be postponed until after the war.

The Allies watched these developments with a great deal of relief. Until this point the CLN had always refused to cooperate with the Italian government precisely because it contained tainted figures like the king. Now that he had agreed to step down, the chance of creating a government of national unity began to look very real. A government that included the new political parties would make the administration of liberated Italy much less of a headache for everyone. They began to apply pressure on both sides, but particularly on Badoglio, to make a deal.

In April, therefore, Badoglio approached the CLN with a proposal. He invited the six opposition parties to form a new government with him, and offered each of them at least one ministry and one undersecretariat in his new cabinet. Badoglio himself would remain prime minister and minister of foreign affairs, and various other military figures would retain control of the army, the navy and the air force. The king would remain head of state, but as soon as Rome was liberated he promised to abdicate.

The proposal put the CLN into complete disarray. On 18 April, their executive council met to discuss Badoglio's proposal, and tensions between them almost immediately boiled over. The Liberals, Christian Democrats and Democratic Labour all announced that they were happy to accept the deal; and after Togliatti's volte-face the Communists were similarly on board. But after months of calling for Badoglio's removal, the Socialists and the Action Party were extremely reluctant to serve in any government that still had Badoglio as prime minister. 'How can you still support such a man?' asked one of the Action Party leaders, Vincenzo Calace. 'Have you already forgotten his shameful flight from Rome and his overwhelming responsibility for the abandonment of Italy to the Germans? Don't you know that our comrades in occupied Italy have sentenced Badoglio to be shot?'[31]

The arguments continued over the next two days, but eventually both the Socialists and the Action Party had little choice but to fall into line. It was obvious that the other parties were likely to go ahead with or without them, and neither party was strong enough to stand in opposition alone. Reluctantly, they swallowed their principles and signed up to the deal. The new government was sworn in by the king, at his villa in Ravello, on 24 April.

The Consequences of Political Weakness

The creation of the new government in Salerno was a momentous event in Italy's political history: it was the first real step back towards democracy after twenty years of Fascist and military rule. But it came at a terrible cost. The CLNs in Rome and the north had never wanted their colleagues in Naples to make any kind of deal with Badoglio. Some of them had even sent urgent messages southwards instructing the Neapolitans not to compromise under any circumstances.[32] And yet the southerners had gone ahead regardless. They had made what many northerners regarded as a pact with the devil.

In the following weeks, the Neapolitans' choice to collaborate was at least partially vindicated. For the first time, decisions started to be made a little more democratically. A new purge process was finally begun, and a High Commission for National *Epurazione* was constituted. Six weeks later, when Rome was liberated, the king abdicated just as he had promised, and his place was taken by his son, Prince Umberto. Badoglio also stepped down as prime minister, to make way for another new government, this time without him. In the end, almost everything the Neapolitan CLN had campaigned for was granted them.

And yet the sense of betrayal still lingered. Benedetto Croce later described the atmosphere that he and the other southern politicians encountered when they flew to Rome to meet up with their newly liberated colleagues. '[W]e were received coldly and with diffidence and a kind of silent rebuke, as though we had travelled away from the

straight road of which they alone possessed the key and knew the direction.'[33] Northerners never fully forgave the southerners for their failure
to maintain their ideological purity. In fairness, some southerners
found it equally difficult to forgive themselves, calling their collaboration with Badoglio 'the first surrender of anti-fascism'.[34]

In hindsight, they were probably angry with the wrong people. It
had been the Allies, after all, who had insisted on keeping the old
regime in place until Rome was liberated. And it had been the Allies,
particularly the British, who had given their unwavering support to a
monarchy that was almost universally despised by the Italian people. If
the Neapolitan CLN had finally come to terms with Badoglio it was
only because they were bowing to political reality: they had no choice
but to play the hand that the Allies had dealt them.

The full extent of Allied responsibility for these events was rarely
acknowledged at the time, least of all by the Allies themselves. Allied
officers often asserted that they took no interest in Italian politics, and
only ever intervened if there was a threat to social stability. But in
reality they meddled in political decisions at every level of society.

At a local level, Allied policies had political implications from the
very start. Their ban on large meetings might have been made for military reasons, but it inevitably also had political consequences: it actively
prevented the newly reborn political parties from organizing and gathering support. Their ban on legitimate strike action among workers
and shopkeepers was also perhaps understandable, but inevitably
favoured the political Right over the Left. In fact, whether by accident
or by design, their policy almost *always* favoured the Right, and often
the far Right: almost by definition, their desire to maintain the status
quo was a Fascist-friendly policy.

There were also plenty of moments when they intervened directly in
political processes that should have had nothing to do with them.
Towards the end of 1944, for example, the Allies vetoed the nomina-
tion of a new Communist mayor for Naples. When a Socialist
alternative was put forward, they vetoed this choice, too. In the end
they simply installed a Liberal mayor that they found more acceptable.
If this was not direct meddling in political affairs, it would be difficult
to know what was.[35]

They did the same thing at a national level. In June 1944, when the British head of the ACC, Noel Mason-MacFarlane, allowed the Italians to appoint Ivanoe Bonomi as their new prime minister, Churchill had Mason-MacFarlane sacked. Churchill had wanted to keep Marshal Badoglio in charge, despite the fact that he had lost the confidence of just about everyone else in Italian politics at the time. The following November, when Bonomi resigned over yet another political crisis, the British stepped in once again. They vetoed the appointment of Carlo Sforza as the next prime minister because Churchill did not want such an outspoken anti-monarchist in charge.[36]

Such meddling in European affairs would become commonplace in the years to come, especially with the rise of Communism and the advent of the Cold War. But it was in Italy, and particularly in Naples and Salerno, where it all began.

CHAPTER 26

Political Corruption

O ne of the consequences of British and American meddling in the political system was that it undermined faith in the very democracy that the Allies claimed to be promoting. And when there is no faith in democracy, people are more likely just to shrug their shoulders at corruption. This took place all over Italy, but it was particularly bad in the south.

There are many reasons why political corruption ended up being so much worse in the south than the north, but chief among them must be the unique history of politics in this part of the country. The Allies were not the first outsiders to take over Naples: the people here had been used to feeling ignored and marginalized since long before Fascist times.

The *Clientela* System

Politics in the south of Italy have never been the same as in the rest of the country, let alone in other parts of Europe and America. Back in the 1860s, after the unification of Italy, the leaders of the new nation had tried to bring political and social reforms to an old, monarchical system that was itself already fantastically corrupt. They swept away the old royal court; they disbanded the Neapolitan army, or subsumed it into the new state; they secularized schools and severely curtailed the power of the Church.[1] But while they were quite zealous in dismantling

Neapolitan institutions, they were not particularly good at replacing them with new ones. Benedetto Croce, who was born during this time, was scathing about the way the new Italian authorities neglected their responsibilities towards the south: 'Practically speaking,' he wrote, 'they abandoned the southern provinces to their fate.' Poverty and crime went unchecked. Corruption flourished. And a new political system was allowed to develop that was every bit as immoral and unjust as the autocracy that had just been deposed.[2]

The politics of Italy as a whole was fairly chaotic after the Risorgimento, but Naples and the south developed their own particular problems. The perversion of politics during these years was described in great detail by some of the very men who were involved in it. The ruling party of the day – the liberal *Sinistra* party, or 'Historical Left' as it is now known – regularly gave huge sums of central government money to the south, ostensibly to deal with the terrible poverty there. But behind closed doors they promised not to look too closely at how that money was spent. In return, southern politicians offered their unwavering support for the government line, regardless of whether that line was beneficial to the south or not. To ensure that they stayed in power, southern politicians used this government money to dispense favours and contracts to a network of personal friends and supporters, who in turn bribed or bullied the *clientele* in their own districts into providing the votes that kept those politicians in place. It was a system that was rotten from top to bottom, and which provided the reformist liberals of the *Sinistra* movement with an unassailable majority in parliament for the best part of forty years.[3]

At the turn of the century, things had become so bad that the prime minister himself, Giovanni Giolitti, felt obliged to declare in parliament that 'half the communes of Italy are in the hands of the *camorra*'. An inquiry was called, and when its leader came to Naples in 1901 he confirmed that, sadly, Giolitti had not been exaggerating: 'nearly all the communes of the Province of Naples and nearly all the charitable institutions are in the hands of groups of delinquents'. Needless to say, neither man acknowledged the role that central government, and particularly Giolitti's own political movement, had played in allowing this situation to develop in the first place.[4]

The first real opportunity to overturn this system came after the First World War. The conflict had left the entire country in a state of economic crisis, and waves of social unrest swept the nation. In Naples and its surrounding towns, riots and strikes broke out, much as they did in Turin and Milan. Increasing numbers of workers began to identify with the Socialist Party, which, because of its ideology, was excluded from any involvement in the old, *clientela* networks.

Those old networks were under severe strain. Since government coffers were empty, the ruling parties were no longer able to dispense favours the way they had in the past and, for the first time, activists with a more radical agenda began to make inroads into the political life of the south. In the local elections of 1920, several major industrial towns around Naples elected Socialist councils, including Capua, Torre Annunziata and Castellammare di Stabia.

This was when the old, corrupt system showed itself for what it really was. Unable to bribe their way back into power, the traditional elites in the south simply seized it, often through the use of naked violence.

What happened in Castellammare di Stabia was a prime example: the Socialist council here lasted just a couple of months before a combination of Fascist thugs, the police and the Liberal establishment engineered a kind of local *coup d'état*. It began with a protest march, organized by the Liberal Democrats, against some of the reforms that the Socialist council was carrying out. When the demonstration reached the town hall it degenerated into a street battle and several people were killed, including a police officer. It has never been entirely clear who started the violence; but in any case, the Carabinieri immediately took the side of the reactionary demonstrators and began firing on the Socialists in the town hall. After a day-long siege, they finally entered the town hall and arrested 150 people, including sixteen Socialist councillors. The following day the democratically elected council was disbanded and replaced with a commission appointed by the regional prefect. All the Socialist policies agreed over the previous weeks were repealed. And Liberal power was restored.[5]

The Socialist councils in Capua and Torre Annunziata lasted a little longer, but eventually suffered a similar fate.[6] Much has been written about Fascist violence against the Socialists during this era, but it was the Liberal establishment that allowed this violence to happen, and that profited from it in the short term. In the south, that meant re-establishing the corrupt *clientela* system that kept them in power.

Socialism was not the only radical force that grew up in the turbulent days of the early 1920s. The other was, of course, that of Fascism. On the face of it, the early Fascists in Naples opposed the *clientela* system as much as the Socialists did. The leader of the Neapolitan Fascists, Aurelio Padovani, styled himself as a radical activist who wanted to overthrow the Liberal system and introduce real change for the benefit of everyone. 'The salvation of the South,' he told an interviewer from the newspaper *Mezzogiorno* in November 1922, 'depends principally on the elimination of the old *clientela* system.' He wasn't interested in signing up career politicians, and playing 'the game of the usual self-serving parties'. He, too, wanted to purge Naples of its corruption and start afresh.[7]

Regardless of whether or not Padovani truly believed this – and there are plenty of examples that show that his actions did not match his words[8] – rhetoric like this gained him a fanatical following in Naples. The thirst for change here was insatiable. But the national leaders of the Fascist Party had other ideas. During the March on Rome, Mussolini deliberately and ostentatiously courted the king, much to the annoyance of anti-monarchists like Padovani. He did the same thing with career politicians: in 1923 Mussolini promoted a formal merger with the Nationalist Association; and in 1924 he invited various other parties to join him on a 'National List' to make sure that he won an overall majority in the elections. Several prominent Liberals duly obliged, including two former prime ministers and the Liberal deputy for Naples, Enrico De Nicola.[9] Rather than sweeping away the old southern elites, Mussolini sought to make use of them – just as the Liberals had done before him.

At a local level, the coercion was slightly more direct. In the towns and cities around Naples, street fights broke out once again as the Fascists sought to bully the population into supporting them. Fascist violence, which the Liberals had turned a blind eye to when it suited them in places like Castellammare di Stabia, was now coming back to haunt them.

The town of Nocera, just north of Salerno, stands as an example of what happened all over the region. In 1923 there were virtually no Fascists in Nocera until lorryloads of *squadristi* were sent from Naples to make a show of force. They drove through the town firing weapons, before destroying the Socialist club and occupying the Democratic Union club. Taking the hint, several of the town's councillors resigned from their political parties and joined the Fascists instead. Within a week, according to one contemporary observer, the town went from having hardly any Fascists at all to a situation where there were 'only about fifty of its responsible citizens who say they are not Fascists (and I am not even sure of that)'.[10]

Far from destroying the old, corrupt *clientela* system of Naples and the south, therefore, the Fascists merely adopted it and put it to their own uses. There was no revolution. There was not even much of a transfer of power: on the whole, the same people who had governed under the Liberals continued to govern under the Fascists – they simply changed their affiliation and carried on as before. This applied not only to the deputies and councillors, but also to the thousands of local officials who had always arranged elections to suit themselves and keep their paymasters in power.

The reason why all of this was relevant in 1943 and 1944 was that it coloured the ideas of all the different political parties who were now emerging in Naples in the aftermath of the liberation. For the Liberals, the Christian Democrats and Democracy of Labour it was enough merely to sweep away the Fascists and return to the way things had been before Mussolini. They saw the last twenty years as a terrible aberration in the normal course of democracy – but they saw nothing particularly wrong with the system that had existed before then. The old *clientela* system had at least given the nation some kind of national stability. This was what they believed Italy now needed once again.

The parties of the Left, by contrast, wanted much more radical change. For them, Fascism was not the real problem: it was only a symptom of much deeper corruption that had existed long before the

1920s. This was a problem throughout the country, but especially in the south, where the liberal elites had been kept in power for decades by the corrupt *clientela* system. Now was their opportunity to finish the job that they had started in the aftermath of the last war: to sweep away this whole system and bring about a true social revolution.

The history also had a bearing on how the different parties viewed the purge. The politicians of the centre and Centre-Right were much more inclined to be lenient towards those who had compromised themselves during the Fascist years – perhaps not surprisingly, considering the way they themselves had behaved during the 'Liberal sell-out' of the 1920s. There were plenty of figures in and around the Naples CLN in 1943 who were compromised in one way or another. Enrico De Nicola was a perfect example: when he had been deputy for Naples in 1922 he had actively welcomed Mussolini to the city before the March on Rome. Later, during the 1924 elections, he had stood beside Mussolini on his 'National List', and he had been made a senator by the Fascists in 1929. It was a pretty compromised curriculum vitae for the politician who would one day become president of Italy.[11] Even Benedetto Croce was not quite as pure as he at first seemed. Despite his famed resistance to Fascism, he had initially supported them when they first seized power, and had only repented of this support after the murder of his fellow parliamentarian Giacomo Matteotti in 1924. Such people, who had been tolerant of Fascism in its early days, were more likely to be forgiving of those who had continued to compromise themselves through the rest of the 1920s and 1930s.[12]

In stark contrast, the parties of the Left and Centre-Left wanted a much more unforgiving purge. This was particularly the case among the Socialists and the Communists who, unlike the Liberals, had never even been offered the opportunity to sell out. There was certainly an element of revenge in their zeal, but there was also a matter of principle at stake. The idealists in these parties believed that a thorough, root-and-branch purge of the whole system would not only destroy Fascism for good, but also bring an end to the political corruption that had plagued the south ever since the Risorgimento.

At least, that's what they said. What they did in practice, especially at a local level, was something altogether different.

The Purge Falters

Most historians concentrate on the national politics of this era, and unsurprisingly so. Italy's national politics was exciting, volatile and desperately important: this was the time when the post-war nation was being formed. But local politics during this period could be just as volatile, and just as formative.

According to one of the most trusted British intelligence sources, the true politics of liberated Italy was not to be found in Salerno or Naples, but in the regions and provinces that were farthest away from the national government and the prying eyes of the Allied Control Commission. 'It is in these districts that the real political meetings are being held. It is here also that certain military and naval officers are intriguing, and that public propaganda is violent, active and full of recriminations, while leaders of all colours are trying to attract a following.' The purpose of all this agitation had nothing to do with the construction of a new Italy, and everything to do with preparations for the election that would one day take place after the war was over. 'It is this campaign which will decide the fate of Italy, which will determine the extent and manner of its reconstruction and help to formulate upon its Foreign and Internal policy.'[13]

To win locally, one needed support. Only the parties that signed up the most supporters, and won control of all the local institutions, would have a chance of winning any post-war election. As a consequence, a cynical battle for followers began all over the south as the different parties competed to sign up as many members as they possibly could.

Leading the way in this battle for followers were the Communists, who were rapidly expanding all across the south, just as they were in the north. Over the next two years Togliatti would build his party into the biggest Communist Party in western Europe, with over two million members. In fierce competition with them were the Christian Democrats, who had the power of the Church behind them. Priests all over the south often instructed their congregations to join the party, and preached just as actively against the Communists. In one Naples church, the priest was accused of refusing to give absolution to those who came to confess unless they first promised to join the Christian Democrats, and pay 20 lire for a membership card.[14]

Others found ways of winning support that were just as suspect. Unlike the representatives of the other main parties, the Liberal Democrat Raffaele De Caro had joined Badoglio's government shortly after the Allies had arrived. He had used his brief tenure as the minister for public works to try to recreate the old *clientela* system all around his hometown of Benevento: he appointed his own followers as local mayors, government inspectors and in all kinds of other positions of local power. According to his rivals in both the Action Party and the Communist Party, these followers had then coerced ordinary citizens into joining the Liberal Democrats by threatening to deny them ration cards if they refused. In some *comuni*, farmers were denied access to pesticides unless they, too, signed up. As a consequence the Liberals and Liberal Democrats had almost unrivalled control over this part of Campania.[15]

In reaction to such naked power grabs, the other political parties began signing up as many followers as they could, regardless of their political background. What happened in the small border towns between Benevento province and Avellino province is a perfect example. Here, the Communist Party in particular launched an unseemly scramble to sign up as many ex-Fascists as possible. At San Martino Valle Caudina, they appointed an ex-Fascist political secretary; at Altavilla Irpina, they appointed an ex-Commander of the Fascist Youth Movement; and at Tufara, a former lieutenant in the Fascist Militia.[16] According to one Communist leader, the order not to look too closely into the new members' political or even criminal background came right from the top, in a circular signed by Togliatti himself.[17]

It was not only the Communists who behaved like this. At Cervinara, the leaders of all the local political parties were former Fascists. The leader of the Liberal Party was the former secretary of the local *fascio*; the leader of the Christian Democrats was a former Fascist *podestà*; the head of the Republican Party was one of the original *squadristi* who had joined the Fascists in 1919; and the Communist Party secretary was not only the former head of the Fascist workers' syndicate, but had been decorated for taking part in the March on Rome. Even the local police chief was another former *squadrista*. Seemingly the only person who wasn't a former Fascist was the mayor himself, Orazio Moscatiello, who, according to British intelligence, was simply 'too weak to control the situation'.[18]

For an idea of the calibre of person who was now signing up to the new political parties, the mayor of Rotondi in Avellino province stands as a good example. Baron Carlo De Bellis was a 32-year-old lawyer who claimed he was a 'fervent anti-Fascist' who had previously been imprisoned for his political beliefs. When the Allies first arrived here in 1944, he styled himself as the local leader of the Liberal Party. On the grounds that he had 'the support of all social political classes', he was duly appointed mayor.[19]

However, it did not take long for the Allies to change their opinion of him. Later in the year, new reports showed that he had been lying through his teeth. Not only had he never been a political prisoner – in fact he had been convicted in the 1930s for fraud – but he had also been a Fascist for at least the last eight years, during which time he had headed the local Fascist Youth movement. Through his Fascist Party connections he had managed to get his sentence for fraud cancelled; but other favours he asked for were denied, even by the Fascists, 'because everybody considered him a thief'.[20]

When the Liberal Party discovered all this, they expelled him from the party – so he set himself up instead as the local leader of the Christian Democrats. When they, too, expelled him, he switched to the Labour Democrats. It was obvious that he had not entered politics out of any particular convictions, but simply as a way to whitewash his name – and perhaps also to enrich himself. By the autumn of 1944 he was not only in charge of the *comune*, but had hired his mistress as a government employee, and had filled the local food surveillance squad with various friends – 'common delinquents' who went about sequestering food, and then sharing it out among themselves and with the mayor. According to British intelligence officers, 'The people are exasperated and have frequently applied to the Allied authorities' to do something about him. But by now the province had been returned to Italian control and there was nothing the Allies could do.[21] Meanwhile, the Italians were reluctant to remove him because the only viable alternative in Rotondi was the Communist Party. Their leader, it turned out, was also a former Fascist.[22]

The political corruption that grew up in the south in the aftermath of the liberation would have profound consequences for the future of the region, and for Italy as a whole. In the short term it fostered an atmosphere of wholesale disillusionment with the Allies, with the Italian authorities, even with the concept of democracy itself. By the middle of 1944, few people believed that either national or local politics had changed for the better, and levels of political engagement remained abysmally low – especially compared to levels in the north.[23] Many people in the south refused to believe that the politics of the region had changed at all: around Benevento, for example, local farmers appeared to believe that Fascism had been restored.[24] It was not much of an endorsement of the new era of politics that was supposed to have been born in 1944.

In Naples, many people coped with their disillusionment in the same way they always had: they simply turned away from the rhetoric and ideals of their leaders – the worthless 'hot air', as AMG officials characterized it – and concentrated instead on looking after themselves and their families. They did not engage in politics. They did not engage with the idea of rebuilding Italy. Many people did not even bother abiding by the normal rules that might allow the city to function healthily: since many of these rules were being imposed by outsiders, they did not feel they had any real stake in them. As we'll see next, crimes of all kinds ballooned in the city during these years, and the foundations were laid for the resurgence of Mafia activity after the war was over.

In the long term, therefore, the consequences of political corruption would be deeply disturbing. A vicious spiral evolved, whereby corruption led to disillusionment, and disillusionment allowed corruption to flourish even further. Even before the end of the war, the old *clientela* system had re-established itself. After the war, this system would allow populists like Achille Lauro and Nicola Sansanelli – who had been imprisoned for corruption and links to Fascism – to take a stranglehold on Neapolitan politics throughout the 1950s.[25]

Even worse, the old links between politics and organized crime would be allowed to re-establish themselves. Clientelism, once the force that kept the Italian Liberals in power, would soon become the domain of Christian Democrats. After the war, the clientelistic relations between the Italian government and organized crime flourished – with money flowing in both directions – until the Tangentopoli scandal brought the whole system crashing down in the 1990s.

It is possible that a tiny part of this might have been avoided if only the transition from Fascism to democracy had been handled a little better in 1943 and 1944. The inability to get to grips with the purge, and to bring much-needed reforms to the south of Italy, were perhaps the greatest failures of the Allies and the newborn Italian government in the aftermath of the liberation. The people of Naples and the Mezzogiorno would pay the price of these failures for the rest of the twentieth century.

CHAPTER 27

Organized Crime

In the last year of the war the people of Naples and its surrounding provinces lived in a state close to lawlessness. After twenty years of Fascist corruption, few people had much respect for the law any more. Allied military police did not know how to keep control in a country they did not properly understand; and the local police were overwhelmed, demoralized and tainted by their connections to the old regime. As a consequence, as one AMG official reported, there was a 'complete disregard for all forms of authority including the police'.[1]

It is difficult to convey just how chaotic the security situation was in southern Italy at this time, and how compromised the ordinary running of society was because of the war. The crime wave that swept Naples in 1944 and 1945 was unlike anything the city had experienced in the previous sixty or seventy years. Its root cause was the conditions in which people were forced to live. With inflation running rife, and the black market governing every area of life, it was virtually impossible for people to feed their families without indulging in theft, prostitution or illegal trading of one sort or another. Even the police, who were barely paid enough to survive, had little choice but to trade on the black market along with everyone else.

In the suburbs and small towns around Naples things were just as bad, if not worse. Groups of criminals posing as Allied military policemen began forcing their way into people's homes and 'requisitioning' money and valuables. Occasionally they were joined by Allied deserters, whose appearance and foreign accents gave their groups an air of authenticity.[2] In the countryside larger groups began to form, who preyed on travellers, stole from Allied stores and even occasionally held up Allied trains.[3] At times, Campania seemed as lawless as any Hollywood depiction of the American Wild West. According to intelligence reports from the spring of 1944, Naples province alone had 'several dozen armed bands' roaming the countryside in groups of between five and twenty, including some that were organized and led by deserters from the Allied armies. Over time they gathered the support of a whole network of forgers, receivers, black market specialists and corrupt officials, and became well enough armed to be able to fight 'pitched battles with machine-guns and hand-grenades' against police.[4]

To gain an insight into how chaotic the situation was, one needs only consider what happened in the town of Pietravairano, just north of Caserta, after the Allied armies had swept past on their way to Cassino. In mid-November 1943, a deserter named Walter Driscoll from the US 7th Infantry arrived in the town: along with four other deserters, he managed to convince the townspeople that he was the new representative of Allied Military Government. He set himself up in office in the town hall. He released prisoners, issued passes and removed restrictions on the grinding of grain. He also requisitioned weapons from the local Carabinieri barracks. It was not until he struck one of the Carabinieri officers that anyone suspected that he might not be a bona fide AMG official after all. It is not quite clear what his ultimate plan was, and whether his motivations were political, criminal, or merely an inflated sense of his own grandeur – but in any case, he managed to govern the *comune* for more than a month before he was finally caught by the Allies and court-martialled for desertion.[5]

Naples and its surrounding provinces were a land of opportunity for men like Driscoll, and for all manner of other thieves, fraudsters, gangsters, corrupt politicians and devious business owners looking to make a profit out of the sudden absence of enforceable rules and regulations. The vast majority of these people were just opportunists, who would return to their normal lives as order was gradually restored.

But there were a few who would use this boom time of criminality as a springboard for crime on a much larger scale that would continue and flourish in Naples long after the war was over.

The Internal Black Market

Throughout the last twenty months of the war, the most ubiquitous, and most profitable, form of crime was the illegal trade of rationed goods on the black market. It is difficult to condemn people for taking part in this illegal activity: even the Allies themselves acknowledged that black market trade was probably the only feasible way of getting enough food into the city to feed the population.[6] Nevertheless, there were differences between those who entered the black market out of necessity and those who sought to exploit it for massive personal gain.

In the early days of the liberation, when the port was not fully working and the relationship between the Allies and the Italians was still quite tentative, it was not yet possible to acquire many supplies from Allied stores. The vast majority of illicit food, therefore, was brought into the city from Italian sources. This was not an easy process. Desperate parents would head out of the city on foot or by bicycle to see if they could bring back small amounts of food from the nearby farms. Initially they bartered and traded for enough food to feed their families, plus a little extra to sell; but as food became scarcer, and prices higher, they began to buy as much as they could to stock up against an uncertain future.

The further one travelled from Naples, the cheaper prices were, and it was not long before caravans of desperate people were trekking to the other side of the country, or to the deep south of Italy, to find food they could afford. Allied officers in the province of Avellino, 50 kilometres east of Naples, saw a huge traffic of illegal goods passing along its roads. 'Contraband is practiced on a wide scale,' reported its Public Safety officer, 'from the truck load of 40 or 50 quintals of grain down to the cyclist from Naples who buys a few kilos for his own use.'[7] Many of those passing through were coming from as far away as Bari or Foggia on the opposite side of the country, a journey that could take two or three weeks on foot.[8]

When the Allies finally opened up a limited train service for civilians in December 1943, some of these epic journeys became much quicker. Getting a train ticket was not an easy matter: since places on the trains were so limited, one needed a very good reason – and an official travel permit – to travel on them. But almost everyone ignored these restrictions. By January Allied officers were already reporting that the trains were packed with travellers who had none of the necessary documents. Many of these people were on trips to other parts of the country to find and buy food. 'They were hanging on the steps of the carriages and out of the windows,' read one report about a train arriving in Battipaglia late at night. 'Allied soldiers on duty at the station were compelled to use firearms in order to clear the passage and intimidate the crowd.' In all the darkness and confusion, several people were injured and had to be rushed to the hospital in Salerno.[9]

Train tickets very quickly became a black market item in their own right. Reports regularly came in of railway clerks selling tickets illicitly, of touts buying up tickets and then selling them on at a profit, or of people bribing train drivers to stop the train just outside Naples so that clandestine passengers could climb on board without either permits or tickets.[10] As a consequence, the trains were usually crammed so tightly that it was impossible for anyone to check who was there legitimately. 'Passengers who have obtained tickets in the regular manner cannot get seats or even climb through the windows,' wrote one Allied intelligence officer. 'Boys travel on the buffers and soldiers and others climb on the footplates.'[11]

Such conditions were ripe for tragedy. People inevitably fell from the trains, or were crushed beneath the wheels when they tried to board them while they were moving. At the beginning of March 1944 hundreds of people suffocated on a train that got stuck in a tunnel near Balvano. It was so overloaded with passengers and their belongings that it could not make it up the slope: smoke from the struggling locomotive filled the tunnel, and more than 600 people died of carbon monoxide poisoning.[12]

Those who could get some kind of official access to trains – railway employees, for example, or postal workers – had a much easier time of it. In February 1944, postal inspectors discovered that large quantities of illicit olive oil were being smuggled from Bari to Naples hidden in mail sacks. Some of this oil was destined for the families of the postal workers themselves, but a large amount had been paid for by a local businessman, who regularly sent men posing as postal workers to travel on the train illegally. There was a considerable amount of money to be made if you were willing to risk defrauding the official systems.[13]

For those who had access to motor transport, there were even greater opportunities, and minimal risks. As one Italian mayor complained to AMG, the small-time traders on the black market were being prosecuted far more than those who transported illegal food in larger quantities: 'It was always easier to be arrested if you were walking with a bag on your shoulder than if you were travelling in a well-laden truck.'[14]

As with the trains, there were all kinds of regulations around private motor transport during these years. It was not enough simply to own a vehicle: one also needed a permit to transport goods, paperwork explaining exactly what the goods were and where they were destined for, and a plentiful supply of petrol. But once again, all these restrictions were routinely ignored or brushed aside by black marketeers in search of vast profits. Petrol was stolen or bought from illegal sources.[15] Travel permits were acquired by false pretences, by bribing the officials who issued them, or simply stolen from AMG offices.[16] Vehicles were stolen, or rented from their owners for 'excessive charges'.[17]

Alternatively, black market operators would approach Allied drivers and offer them huge bribes for the use of their trucks for an evening or two. In July 1944, one British corporal was offered 30,000 lire (the equivalent of £75 sterling) to travel to Bari and back for a group of black marketeers. On this occasion he informed the authorities, and a sting operation was launched, but AMG officials were rattled by the brazenness of the black market dealers. 'Their rather pathetic faith in the British Army and their frank and open methods in fixing up this particular deal, lead one to think that this form of bribery must be very common ...'[18]

The incredible scale of this illegal traffic was too great to imagine, let alone measure. An inkling of its size was revealed that spring, when a squad of policemen at a single roadblock seized 24 tons of illegal grain in just four days. AMG officials sensed that this was just a tiny drop in the black market ocean: 'Unfortunately lack of personnel does not permit of the necessary number of roadblocks to really make any great inroad on this traffic.'[19]

For anyone who took part in this trade, the rewards could also be huge. In September and October 1944, bank employees reported a new phenomenon in the city of Naples: individuals from the poorest neighbourhoods had begun appearing at banks with vast amounts of cash. One bank manager described a woman who had appeared at his bank and presented him with a box filled with 1,000 lire notes 'thrown in anyhow'. After he had counted out a million lire for her (the equivalent of $10,000) he asked if he had counted enough – she looked in the box to see what was left, and told him he should probably take a bit more. She clearly had no idea how much money was in there. Such people, reported British intelligence, 'are so absolutely ignorant that they refer to their money not in quantity but in weight'. Rather than claiming they had a million lire, they would simply say that they had 2 kilos of 1,000 lire notes, 'since apparently one kilo is the approximate weight of half a million lire'.[20]

If such fortunes were being earned by those at the very bottom of the black market, those higher up the chain were making unimaginable sums of money. As historian Paolo De Marco has pointed out, the real winners on the black market were not the smallholders who made personal deals with desperate families who came to barter their wristwatches or jewellery, but the large landowners and agricultural consortia who had access to fleets of vehicles. Similarly, it was not the women selling cigarettes or bags of flour from their *bassi* in the backstreets of Naples who were making the real money, but the wholesalers, transporters and investors who were behind the large-scale marketing of clandestine goods.[21]

A series of scandals at the beginning of 1944 showed how deeply the black market had penetrated the normal running of business in and around the city. In January, AMG received a complaint from the Provincial Association of Artisans in the name of 5,455 shoemakers who had suddenly found themselves without shoe leather because the big tanneries had sold all their supplies on the black market. A few months later, the directors of the biggest textile company in the south were arrested for diverting large quantities of their products to the black market. Even the electricity company was accused of dealing in clandestine food products to the tune of millions of lire. The black market was big business. And big business was right at the heart of it.[22]

Theft from Allied Stores

In the winter of 1943, after the port was repaired and shipments of Allied goods began to pour into the city, the people of Naples began to realize that there might be easier ways of obtaining illicit goods than by travelling to the other side of the country. The Allies clearly had huge supplies of everything they needed. They simply had to work out how to get their hands on it.

One of the most persistent stereotypes about Naples is that it is a city full of thieves – a stereotype that in 1944 many Neapolitans them-selves were willing to admit to. 'We've been picking foreigners' pockets in wholesale lots for centuries,' one Italian craftsman told Bill Mauldin that spring. The people in other parts of Italy were just the same, he went on: the only difference was that they were less willing to admit it. 'We are open, honest crooks here.'[23]

By all accounts, the everyday pilfering that took place in the city occurred on a scale that few Allied soldiers had ever encountered before. 'It was a place where anything goes,' remembered one British artillery officer. 'You had to watch your kit, watch your cars, never park your jeep outside any office because when you came out the tyres and wheels were gone. They were the quickest people at getting wheels off cars! You never put anything down.'[24]

Probably the most common crime was theft from Allied personnel. Having one's watch stolen or pocket picked was almost a rite of passage for soldiers on leave, and those who had been drinking were particularly easy targets. In June 1944 the Provost Marshal warned GIs to carry their wallets in their shirt pockets rather than on their hips: an average of five soldiers a day had their pockets picked in Via Roma alone.[25]

Sometimes this type of theft could be more serious. 'One time one of our GIs was going into Naples, and maybe a half hour later he comes back stark naked,' remembered one of the mechanics in an

American auto maintenance company. 'They'd just rolled him, beat him up and took everything he had.'[26] According to the testimonies of other Allied servicemen, this was a fairly regular occurrence.[27]

The theft of vehicles, or more often just their wheels, was also very common. 'Cars with or without merchandise are often stolen,' reads one Allied report from October 1944. 'Sometimes jeeps are jacked up at night on wooden blocks and their tyres and wheels removed.' The Allies also had to tighten up on the issuance of petrol to civilian cars in their employ because 'much of the petrol is syphoned out for sale on the Black Market.'[28] One group of British mechanics became so fed up with their wheels going missing that they took their guns to the nearest block of flats and went from apartment to apartment demanding their equipment back. 'We never found the wheels, but we found gallons and gallons of petrol in cans.'[29]

Another favourite crime was to jump onto the back of Allied supply trucks as they drove through the city and help oneself to the goods. According to Norman Lewis, this was something that gangs of *scugnizzi* were particularly notorious for.[30] Bert Scrivens, a British technical storeman, concurs. 'The kids in Naples were thieves to the last of them,' he said. 'One could never drive a lorry in Naples without having somebody in the back of it to prevent the kids coming over the tail board ... and throwing out half the goods you were carrying.'[31]

Sometimes the theft from these trucks was more organized. Everyone knew that the trucks driving up the Via Roma were full of sacks of flour en route from the port to the Allied supply depots. Since Via Roma was probably the busiest street in the city, traffic was often slow, giving people the perfect opportunity to jump onto the back of them. 'I have seen men on Via Roma step in front of the supply trucks to force the driver to slam on his brakes,' claimed one American infantry-man. 'As the truck jerked to a stop, twenty or thirty men would swarm up onto the bed and throw bags of flour to friends.' According to this witness, this was not just a one-off: 'This happened many times.'[32]

Theft like this could be a dangerous business, particularly when the Allies began posting guards on the back of all their trucks. According to Norman Lewis, some of these guards would slice down with their bayonets onto the hands of anyone grabbing hold of the tailboard: this led to a spate of children being admitted to hospital with severed fingers.[33] Other witnesses saw boys being shot dead as they climbed onto the back of supply trucks; and in March 1944 the Italian police chief reported an incident where a passing pedestrian was accidentally shot in the thigh by a bullet meant for one of these thieves.[34]

By this time, theft throughout the city had reached epidemic proportions. Norman Lewis again: 'Nothing has been too large or too small – from telegraph poles to phials of penicillin – to escape the Neapolitan kleptomania.' Reports came in of cars, buses and even rail-way locomotives being stolen and dismantled. Roman cameos were stolen from museums, statues stolen from public squares, musical instruments from the San Carlo Theatre.[35] 'Nothing was sacred,' remembered Paul Brown years later. 'Manhole covers disappeared. Telephone wire was stolen and sometimes the telephone poles too.'[36]

One particularly ambitious man was caught trying to steal 3 tons of Allied sugar: he was rewarded with a five-year sentence. Another man caught cutting Allied telephone wires in order to harvest the copper got twenty years (he was lucky not to be executed, since cutting phone lines was technically an act of sabotage). Almost everybody seemed to be involved in some kind of theft or another. In one hospital in Salerno, six doctors and a priest were arrested for their part in stealing large quantities of clothing sent by the British and American Red Cross for their patients.[37]

Some of the thefts carried out in 1944 were so audacious that they beggared belief. In Castellammare di Stabia thieves scaled the 30-foot walls of the castle and stole the wheels of all the cars inside the headquarters of the Field Security Headquarters.[38] In Naples itself, others broke into army encampments and walked away with entire canvas tents and all their contents.[39] They entered storerooms in and around the port by climbing in through the sewers and appearing unexpectedly, like the *monaciello*, from manhole covers among the stacks of supplies.[40] Nowhere was sacred. In the main Naples courthouse was a room where stolen money and valuables were stored as evidence. It contained items worth around 20 million lire: but in October 1944 someone broke into this room and stole it all over again.[41]

There is one final category of theft that must be mentioned: the falsifying of ration cards was so widespread, and conducted on such a massive scale, that in the spring of 1944 the Allies were obliged to tear up the whole system and begin again.

The problem started with people claiming for relatives who had died, moved away, or been interned by either the Allies or the Germans during different phases of the war. There was no malice in this: as we have seen, the people were starving, and saw no reason to forgo an extra ration for their families if the authorities did not know that one of them was missing. But it was not long before people began forging ration cards in the Naples print shops and trading them on the black market.[42] The worst offenders were some of the region's bakers, who became notorious for claiming flour rations for far more people than they were actually serving. One baker in Salerno province, for example, was caught claiming 6,799 extra flour rations each day: in the space of just a month he managed to accumulate 5 million lire by trading this extra flour illicitly.[43] In another instance, a baker was claiming flour for 7,700 customers, when he actually only had 200: when he was caught, he offered the inspector a bribe of 100,000 lire – the equivalent of US $1,000.[44] Nor was it only bakers who were defrauding the authorities in this way. In February 1944, the director of a new Italian military hospital was found to be claiming food allocations for 100 patients, but 'Since the hospital will not be ready for another couple of weeks, and there are no patients there, it is believed that the food finds its way to the black market.'[45]

Investigations by Allied Control Commission officers estimated that there were as many as 135,000 counterfeit ration cards in Naples alone, and tens of thousands of official cards registered to people who did not exist. Tens of thousands more had been stolen from the local administrative offices. After the new registration was completed that spring, the official number of rations dropped from around 1.1 million to just 800,000: more than 300,000 false or fraudulent ration cards had been withdrawn from the system.[46]

Theft by Allied Servicemen

It is easy to stereotype the Neapolitans for their theft, but the Allied troops were just as bad – and, unlike the people of Naples, did not even have the excuse of hunger and poverty. The vast majority of Allied produce that ended up on the black market was not stolen by Neapolitans at all, but by Allied servicemen and staff.

As with civilian pilfering, it started off on a small scale. Soldiers would happily sell their cigarette rations to Italians, or exchange them for goods and services, particularly if they did not themselves smoke. Cigarettes were so plentiful in the US Army that nobody noticed if the occasional carton went missing. Some servicemen also sold their soap rations: 'You could make a fortune selling soap and tobacco,' remembers one British sailor. 'But it was small scale stuff.'[47] Others went as far as selling their clothes or their bed linen, safe in the knowledge that it could be replaced from official stores. 'I'd sell my clothes every time they moved me,' said one GI. 'Next morning I'd say I lost my clothes in transit, and they gave me some more.'[48]

The Americans in particular had so many supplies flooding into Naples at this time that nobody seemed to care if one or two items went missing. Stanley Gladstone, the British Army photographer who had been one of the first to enter Naples in October 1944, was astonished by how easy it was to get equipment from the American quartermasters.

If we wanted to draw some food from a British quartermaster he wanted to know who we were, when we'd drawn it last, how many days we were entitled to, and so on. If you went to the Americans and said, 'Can we have some food, we're going off for a couple of days,' they said, 'Sure, buddy!' and, 'Take a case' and 'Have another one!' You were loaded up with enough food for a fortnight and nobody kept a count of it.

At the time Gladstone was exasperated with British red tape, and thought this was 'a marvellous way of getting on with the job without too much nonsense'. But it was obviously a system that could easily be abused by anyone wanting to make a fast buck.[49]

Once people realized that there was good money to be made from selling Allied food and supplies, a few sharp operators began to pursue trading opportunities on a larger scale. According to Italian police reports, by November 1943 there was already 'a vast traffic in American cigarettes' in the warehouse district just north of the main station. GIs regularly came here and sold their cigarettes to an American deserter, who then sold them on by the truckload to his Italian contacts.[50]

Clothing was another item that could be sold on in bulk. According to anecdotal evidence, one or two of the American storeroom officers in the Naples military hospitals realized that they could sell large numbers of brand new uniforms on the black market. Their method was simple: every time they discharged a soldier from hospital, they claimed that he was issued with new clothing. In fact those soldiers were being issued with their *old* clothing, complete with bullet holes: the storeroom officers were keeping the new issue for themselves.[51]

One British seaman working on the supply convoys to Naples soon realized that, if he could sell his own issue of naval soap for a large profit, he could do the same for all his shipmates – and indeed those on other ships. Back in Belfast he bought up all the laundry soap he could find, and on his next trip to Naples took it surreptitiously ashore in a motor launch that was so overloaded that 'the water was coming over the gunnels'. By cutting in several of his shipmates, one of the officers and the lookout at the local Royal Marines station, he was able to make £200 for himself, and a similar amount for each of the others, from just one trip.[52]

Scams like this quickly developed into a highly organized market in clandestine goods. Its centre was at the eastern edge of the old part of Naples, in Via Forcella – an area that would remain notorious for its gangsters long after the war was over. In September 1944, British intelligence documents described exactly how the trade worked:

> In the street Forcella near the Via Duomo there is a permanent centre of exchange for Black Market goods. Even during the hours of daylight Allied soldiers, both white and coloured, can be seen arriving in this street with large packets of Allied food and clothing under their arms. These are quickly sold to local dealers who, in their turn, get rid of the merchandise almost immediately by passing it to their regular clients who are standing nearby. These latter, in their turn, distribute it to other centres of the Black Market, for instance, at Il Cavone, La Sanità, Borgo Loreto and the district of S. Antonio Abate.

The report goes on to observe, with typical understatement, that 'It is the cause of some surprise that the Allied police, who are ready enough to arrest anybody whom they find smoking English or American cigarettes, have taken no steps to suppress the Black Market in this locality.'[53]

Before long it was not just packets of Allied supplies going missing, but whole truckloads. The security systems around the Naples port were so lax that it was not difficult for Allied troops to steal huge amounts of food and other goods and just drive them away. Truck drivers quickly learned which entrances to the port were least well guarded, and which were those where the MPs never bothered to check documents. By the spring of 1944 'lorry loads of goods' were routinely being sold at railway crossings, 'and the police apparently do not interfere with these clandestine sales as they make between 20,000 and 30,000 lire out of them' in bribes.[54]

By now it was clear to everyone that the majority of black market activity did not stem from individual Italians bringing home a few litres of olive oil from Puglia, or from individual soldiers selling their kit at railway stations. The sheer volume of Allied goods appearing on the market spoke of a much bigger problem, involving whole networks of soldiers and civilians working together. And it all came from the same source: the port.

'The biggest cargo port in the world'

By the spring of 1944, Naples had become the world's biggest cargo port, outstripping the port of New York in the volume of supplies that passed across its wharfs.[55] On any given day the harbour would be filled not only with warships, but also with dozens of freighters, tankers, refrigerator ships, coasters, LSTs, LCTs, and all kinds of small craft passing continually back and forth across the water. Some of these ships were taking on troops and supplies for the fighting at Anzio further up the coast, and later for mounting the invasion of southern France; but the vast majority were here unloading supplies from the USA. On the shore, hundreds of vehicles came and went – mostly 6x6 army trucks, but also petrol tankers, water tankers, bulldozers, ambulances and jeeps – and also hundreds of American mules on their way to the front lines in the mountains. Vast quantities of materiel accumulated on the docksides at all times, waiting to be transported away. 'That port of Naples was quite a sight during its busiest times,' remembered one port worker years later. 'I sometimes thought, "My God! Is there anything left in America?"'[56]

In the early days of the liberation, the main priority of the Allies was to rebuild the port and get it up to capacity as quickly as possible. Supplies of all kinds were urgently needed everywhere. With so many men engaged in combat duties and reconstruction work, there were simply not enough personnel both to unload the ships and to guard the cargo once it was on the dockside. Allied planners had to create unloading systems and timetables from scratch and, inevitably, short cuts were taken. In short, pilfering was easy. As an UNRRA report into the workings of the port put it, 'The urgency of unloading ships in the shortest possible time in a badly damaged and congested port made some losses almost impossible to avoid in the early days.'[57]

Within a month of the port first opening, certain Allied officers were already beginning to express serious concerns about the amount of cargo that was going missing between the docks and the warehouses onshore. Most of them drew attention to the way hungry Italians routinely jumped on the back of trucks to steal tins of food or sacks of flour, but some also drew attention to the larger-scale pilfering that was being conducted by the Allied troops themselves. One report by a former port security officer in Scotland stated clearly that 'the policing of ports and docks here is in sore need of drastic reorganisation and tightening up'. His advice was simple: 'Check each individual truck when leaving the starting point and [again when] unloading, and compare the sheets.' There were huge discrepancies between what Allied drivers left the docks with, and what they actually delivered to the warehouses.[58]

By the end of November 1943, theft from the port became so bad that Fifth Army HQ sent a special investigator to look into the problem. The following January, AMG also conducted their own investigation, which turned up similar results: cargos were not being catalogued properly as they were unloaded from the ships; trucks were being sent from port to warehouse without guards, without number counts or tonnage checks; nobody knew how much was going missing, because nobody had bothered to keep a check of what was there in the first place. By March, according to yet another report, these problems still had not been fixed: 'Drivers apparently leave the port without their loads being properly tallied and in some astounding way it is apparently possible for a complete load to be disposed of without the knowledge of the consignees.'[59]

In an effort to curb pilfering, a special court was set up within the port itself, run by the Judge Advocate of the Port Command. By the beginning of 1944 it was already hearing around 1,000 cases each month. And yet still the losses kept mounting, leading to an acrimonious blame game between the various officials involved. The port authorities blamed the courts for not meteing out sufficient punishments to act as a deterrent. In reply, Allied lawyers blamed the port authorities for security so lax that it only invited theft. Petty pilfering was not the main problem, they pointed out, and punishments would be much greater if only they could try some of the bigger culprits. 'The fact is that they can't even catch them, much less punish' them.[60]

One lawyer was particularly damning in his assessment of conditions in the port, where little had changed after nearly nine months of operations. 'Normal unloading regulations are consistently disregarded,' he reported:

> Trucks are loaded direct from the cargo nets with no check of
> quantity loaded. Trucks have been loaded from dumps with no
> quantities indicated on the manifest. Trucks were not sent out
> in guarded convoy. Until recently trucks were not guarded at
> all. Apparently the only thoughts in the minds of the port
> authorities were to keep the docks cleared of supplies and even
> the most common-sense precautions known to business were
> disregarded. As a result Allied soldiers driving the trucks quickly
> discovered their opportunities and stole and sold supplies by the
> truckload. The heavy losses of supplies from the Port are not
> due to pilfering but to wholesale thievery with the connivance of
> Allied soldiers.[61]

Allied intelligence reports of the time concurred. Allied truck drivers were all familiar with the exits and entries to the port 'where least control is exercised' and 'where the MPs never examine documents'. As a consequence, 'The sale of lorry loads of goods' was continuing in various points all over Naples.[62]

Anybody who was stationed in Naples during 1944 could see for themselves how big the problem was. 'The waste was incredible,' remembered one port worker. 'Half the stuff was pilfered and ended up on the black market before it got to its intended destination'.[63] Norman Lewis claimed that a third of all Allied imports ended up being stolen and sold illegally on the black market.[64] He was exaggerating, but only by a little: according to official estimates at the beginning of 1944, as much as 30 per cent of Allied supplies was going missing.[65] At a time when troops on the front line were frequently reporting a scarcity of equipment and supplies, such statistics represent a staggering and unforgivable loss.[66]

The Mafia

The sheer scale of losses from Allied stores, and the highly organized way in which the thefts took place, inevitably drew speculation that a much bigger criminal organization was at work. Accusations against various Allied officials began to accumulate, alleging that they were in league with the Mob. Some of these accusations were based on mere rumour and speculation; but others had much stronger foundations.

As far as Allied Control Commission were concerned, there was no trace of large-scale organized crime in Naples during their time in charge. In March 1944, the regional Public Safety Office reported that there was 'no evidence of any criminal societies such as the "mafia" or "camorra" being in existence'; and the following month they reiterated that there was 'no evidence of criminal societies' in and around the city.[67] In the summer they again stated that, regarding the Mafia, 'there is no trace of this organisation anywhere in the Region'.[68]

In a sense, these reports were correct: it really depends upon how one wants to define this type of organized crime. The small groups of criminals who exploited the black market during the war were certainly nothing like the Camorra that had once controlled large parts of Naples during the nineteenth century. At the time of the Risorgimento, the entire police force in the ancient centre had been in the hands of the Camorra: it was only through a vicious and sustained crackdown that the new Italian state was able to wrest control of the city back from them three years later. In the 1880s and 1890s the organization had become so powerful that it was able to act almost like a parallel state in and around Naples. It extracted 'taxes' in the form of protection money, and dispensed 'justice' according to its own rules. Indeed, it was sometimes difficult to tell where the Italian state ended and the

Camorra began. Compared to a criminal fraternity on this scale, the groups of petty thieves and small-time crooks who popped up during the Allied occupation were pretty insignificant.[69]

If the Camorra was but a shadow of its past and future selves, then so, too, was the Mafia, especially compared to the situation that was unfolding in wartime Sicily. When the Allies had first arrived in Sicily in the summer of 1943, they had deliberately enlisted the Mafia's help. The notorious New York crime boss Lucky Luciano had provided them with a list of contacts who could supply intelligence, engage in acts of sabotage and help to maintain law and order behind the lines. With an astonishing disregard for the long-term consequences of their actions, the Allies installed known gangsters as the mayors of various towns and villages, and allowed them to take control of local law and order and the distribution of Allied rations and supplies. Documents written by US diplomats at the time clearly show that they knew exactly who the Mafia leaders were, and had no qualms about putting them in positions of power.[70] This process did not happen when the Allies finally landed on the Italian mainland. The Sicilian Mafia did not have nearly such a strong presence in and around Naples at this time, and the Allies were much less aware of who was who in the Neapolitan underworld. Almost a year after their arrival on the mainland they were still claiming, quite truthfully, that they had received 'no reports of mafia activity' in the city of Naples.[71]

Just because the Allies had no knowledge of any organized crime networks at this time, that does not mean that they did not exist. At the very time when these reports were being made, one of the most important Mafia bosses was living in Nola, just a few miles northeast of Naples. Vito Genovese, the head of one of the 'five families' in New York, had fled to Italy before the war to escape a murder charge. He seems to have bought his way into the Fascist hierarchy by bribing party members, eventually becoming close friends with Mussolini's son-in-law, Count Ciano. According to local legend he financed the building of a new Fascist party headquarters in Nola – although nobody has ever been able to definitively prove this.[72]

When the Allies arrived in Nola at the end of September 1943, Genovese immediately switched sides and offered his services to the new Allied civil affairs officer, an American major by the name of E. N. Holmgreen. Major Holmgreen was so impressed with Genovese's services as an adviser and interpreter that he wrote him an enthusiastic letter of recommendation 'in an effort to express my appreciation for the unselfish services of this man'. According to Holmgreen, Genovese 'would accept no pay; paid his own expenses; worked day and night and rendered most valuable assistance to the Allied Military Government'.[73]

It is a mark of the naivety and incompetence of AMG that such a man was given access to the heart of AMG, where he could make contacts, bribe officials and help himself to Allied supplies. Major Holmgreen can be forgiven for not being familiar with Genovese's history with the police on the other side of the Atlantic, but just a tiny amount of research would have revealed his involvement with the Fascists, which alone should have disqualified him from being employed by AMG. But as we have seen, Allied civil affairs officers like Holmgreen were understaffed, overworked and entirely ignorant of the intricacies of local affairs. Worse, they were completely uninterested in the long-term effects of such decisions: according to their instructions the only thing that mattered was the short-term goal of establishing law and order locally so that the Allied armies could keep moving forwards.

The true motives behind Vito Genovese's apparent generosity were not discovered until the summer of 1944 when a particularly tenacious American policeman, Sergeant Orange C. Dickey, discovered that Genovese had established a whole network of corrupt officials, deserters and local hoodlums to supply the black market in and around Naples. Genovese's men had been stealing army trucks from the Naples docks, filling them with stolen supplies and then driving them to a vineyard outside Nola where local vehicles would be waiting to pick up the goods. The trucks were then burned to destroy the evidence.

Dickey arrested Genovese on 27 August 1944 when the Mafia boss came to Nola's town hall to renew his official travel permit. Despite months of bureaucratic, incompetent and possibly suspicious foot-dragging by the military authorities, Genovese was eventually shipped back to America to stand trial for the original pre-war murder.

(He was acquitted in 1946 after the main witness against him died in mysterious circumstances.) He was never tried for his black market activities in Italy.

In the years since then there has been much speculation about how Genovese was allowed to gain access to so many Allied supplies, about who was helping him and how far up the chain of command the corruption went. Norman Lewis claimed in his memoirs that the head of the Allied Military Government himself, Charles Poletti, had appointed Genovese as his personal adviser in some kind of dodgy deal with the Mafia.[74] Others claim that Poletti was heavily involved in the Mafia during his time in Sicily, that Genovese acted as his personal interpreter there, and that Poletti received personal gifts and bribes from him, including a car. This corrupt relationship is supposed to have continued after Poletti moved to Naples at the beginning of 1944.[75]

While there is a great deal of circumstantial evidence that the Allies actively colluded with the Mafia in Sicily, there is no such evidence when it comes to Naples. The stories about Poletti's personal relationship with Genovese are clearly untrue: Poletti did not even come to the Italian mainland until March 1944, long after Genovese's official involvement with AMG was over. Indeed, there is no evidence that the two men ever even met. For obvious reasons, the history of the Mafia is filled with such rumour and speculation; it should not be surprising when some of it turns out to be complete nonsense.

Nevertheless, it was clear that there was a great deal of clandestine activity taking place beneath the surface of Neapolitan society, and that some of it was highly organized. In January 1944, for example, a schooner chartered by AMG to transport foodstuffs from Naples to Reggio Calabria disappeared: it was eventually found sailing through restricted waters and seized by the Allied Navy. 'The circumstances are highly suspicious,' claimed the official report, but nobody ever seems to have discovered what was really going on.[76] Six months later, British intelligence reported that Italian schooners laden with contraband were travelling regularly from the small port of Scario, south of Salerno, to Sicily and other destinations.[77] Again, nothing much seems to have come of these reports. The fact that complex smuggling operations like this could take place during the height of wartime implies that those taking part were not only highly organized, but also had deep pockets, and possibly also friends in high places. These were the beginnings of an international trade in contraband that would be controlled and directed by the Sicilian Mafia after the war, and that would make Naples one of the main centres of Mediterranean smuggling for the rest of the century.[78]

The Allies had no way of knowing this in 1944. But even the lowliest GI could see that the Allied occupation was having some catastrophic effects on southern Italy, particularly in terms of law and order, and that the society that would emerge from the war would be very different from the one that had existed here before the Allies arrived. The massive disruption caused by the violence, the desperation of the people, the huge wealth that was flowing through the port, the sloppy security of the Allied armies, the failure to tackle political corruption and, above all, the boundless naivety of the Allied Military Government – all these factors provided the perfect seedbed in which criminal gangs could grow.

After the war a whole variety of Camorra groups would operate in and around Naples: the Giuliano family in Forcella, the Simonetti family in Nola, the Maisto family in Giugliano, the Moccia family of Afragola, and so on. The Mafia, too, would establish a major presence here: after being exiled from the USA, Lucky Luciano would take up residence in Naples, which he ran as his own criminal fiefdom throughout the 1950s.[79]

It was the Second World War that first created the opportunity to establish these criminal fraternities. The people of Naples, and indeed of Italy more generally, would continue to suffer the consequences long after the Allies had packed up and gone home.

CHAPTER 28

The Last Crisis
of the War

As 1944 advanced, the Allied armies moved slowly but inexorably northwards along the Italian peninsula. In June, after the landings at Anzio and the devastating bombardment of Cassino, Allied troops flooded north to take Rome. By August they had reached Florence on the western side of the country, and in September they liberated Rimini on the east coast. The fighting was brutal and desperate all the way. Bogged down once again in a stalemate along the Gothic Line, they did not break through until April 1945, when the American Fifth Army finally sliced through the German position and into the wide-open spaces of the Po Valley.

Meanwhile, the Italian resistance had grown in strength, and were fighting an increasingly violent civil war behind the German lines. In the last week of April 1945 they declared a general uprising across the north, and rapidly liberated Bologna, Milan and Turin. At the end of the month, partisans captured Mussolini as he was trying to flee the country. The following day they executed him and displayed his body in Piazzale Loreto in Milan.

By this point the German defences had all but collapsed across the whole of Europe. Bowing to the inevitable, the German commander in Italy, General Heinrich von Vietinghoff, finally came to the negotiating table. On 29 April he signed the instrument of surrender in the Royal Palace that had been built for the kings of Naples in Caserta during the golden age of their reign. The war in Italy formally came to an end on 2 May 1945.

Refugees

All of this involved a vast amount of destruction from both sides. Allied air forces continued to attack Italian cities with vast fleets of bombers right up until the last months of the war; and the Luftwaffe responded by bombarding Allied positions, including the port of Naples. The war on the ground was even more devastating, as tanks and artillery reduced small towns and villages to rubble across the country.

The trauma that such destruction caused among Italian civilians was immeasurable. John Miles was an aid worker in Italy throughout 1944 and 1945, and witnessed first hand some of the devastation that took place north of Naples around Cassino. Miles's job was to travel between the various refugee camps that had sprung up around Naples, and reunite family members who had become separated from one another in all the chaos and confusion. 'During that first year in Italy sorrow and tragedy, generally speaking, were the orders of the day,' he remembered years later.

> As I toured the Cassino area looking for stray people, masses of rubble and devastation all around brought home the terrible price that must be paid when a land is ravaged by warfare. On one occasion a woman held out her dead baby as if to say, 'This is what your bombs have done!'

Tragic stories began to circulate about children who had been found huddling in caves with the bodies of their dead parents, or women who had become so malnourished that they could no longer produce milk for their babies. By the time they arrived in the refugee camps, most of them were in a terrible state. 'They had suffered so much that all had a faraway look on their sunken faces and could hardly speak. Their tattered clothes were in rags. Some even arrived naked.'[1]

The refugees were gathered together in camps north of Naples, but, when these began to overflow, whole communities were transported en masse further south and across the sea to Sicily. According to Miles, few people wanted to make long journeys far away from their devastated homes and communities: they preferred instead to remain reasonably close by, so that they could return and rebuild their lives once the armies had moved on. In the meantime, many people settled in Naples, at least temporarily. A house for refugees and displaced persons was set up in Piazzetta Forcella, in the heart of the black market district – but when demand ballooned early in 1944, accommodation had to be found for at least another 2,000 people in other parts of the city.[2] Many refugees chose instead to lodge with distant friends or family, or to set up makeshift homes amid the rubble alongside those who had been bombed out of their homes. Soon refugees were spread out all over the city.

They were joined by all kinds of refugees from all over the country: economic migrants from the villages of the south, Yugoslavs freed from Italian prisoner-of-war camps, Italian soldiers who had escaped being rounded up by the Germans, and so on. At the end of the war there was another influx of Italian forced labourers returning from captivity in Germany, and Fascists fleeing persecution by vengeful partisans in the north of the country. Eventually prisoners of war who had been interned by the Allies years before would also return from Russia, Britain and the USA.

Among those returning were around 200 survivors from Naples' tiny pre-war Jewish population. Amid all the horror and atrocity of the war, their story represents a small but significant ray of light. Before the war, according to Mussolini's 1938 race laws, all foreign Jews were supposed to have been deported. Several dozen were sent to internment camps around the country, and from there to Germany, but others simply went into hiding with friends and relatives. Then, in 1942, all Italian Jews between the ages of 18 and 55 had to be registered for forced labour. They were rounded up and sent to the villages of Tora and Piccilli, about 75 km north of Naples, where they were simply abandoned in a field with nowhere to live. Eventually, the people who lived in the nearby houses and farms took pity on them. The local aristocrat in particular, Baroness Falco, defied all laws against fraternizing with Jews, and was instrumental in finding them places to stay.

Local Communists were equally welcoming: one of the Communist leaders, Simeone Farinaro, took in two families. Over the following year friendships formed between the Jews and the local population. Even the Fascist *podestà* was repeatedly reprimanded by the regional prefect for being too lenient towards them. As the war swept over the region, the Germans occupied he area – but no one in these two villages let slip that 200 Jews were living in their midst. Eventually the Germans moved on, the Allies arrived and the Jewish refugees were free to return to their families and communities in Naples.[3]

According to UNRRA documents, the official number of refugees passing through Naples in the spring of 1944 reached a peak of around 7,000 every week, but there were many more arriving in the city unofficially.[4] All these refugees and migrants descending upon Naples in the last months of the war put a huge pressure on the city. The housing crisis had still not been addressed, and thousands continued to live in caves and air raid shelters long after the war was over. The pressure on rationing was also substantial – with thousands of extra mouths to feed in the city, greater amounts of aid were required, particularly after July 1944, when the Allies substantially increased the rations they provided in a belated attempt to mitigate the food crisis.

But perhaps the most difficult issue caused by all these extra people was the strain on the market for jobs. This was already a problem in 1944, but it really came to a head in 1945 when Italian forced labourers and prisoners of war began to return to the country: around 1.5 million people in total, and 100,000 in Naples alone.[5] This was the last great crisis of the war, and one which the Allies never even began to address.

Failures in Economic Reconstruction

The massive destruction caused to the city in the summer and autumn of 1943 left a terrible legacy in Naples. Between May and October that year, hundreds of factories and other places of work were completely destroyed. Unemployment in the city rose fivefold: according to the Labour Division of AMG, when the Allies arrived there were 110,000 unemployed in Naples alone. The figures were similarly high all over the region.[6]

In the months that followed, some of these stricken industries tried to rebuild themselves, but without Allied help they struggled to get very far. The glass industry, for example, which had once employed thousands of people in Naples and Salerno, now only employed around 400.[7] The destruction of its factories, the requisitioning of buildings by the Allies and the sudden lack of fuel or raw materials had made any hope of a return to mass production seem all but impossible. Similarly the glove industry, which in peacetime had supported 20,000 manufacturing jobs in and around Naples, and thousands more in related industries, was now at 'a complete standstill'. The lack of leather, or indeed any of the other raw materials needed for tanning and dying, had driven thousands of artisans to look for work elsewhere.[8]

The Allies not only failed to do anything to reverse this situation, they actively made things worse. Factories that might have been repaired and put back into action were requisitioned by Allied units looking for billets, storage space or workshops for repairing their own vehicles and equipment. The MCM textiles factory, for example, was requisitioned by the British as a motor repair shop. British soldiers moved all the looms and spinning machines to make way, but the careless manner in which they piled them on top of one another wrecked their delicate machinery beyond repair. As a consequence, the production of textiles in this factory was made impossible even after the British finally moved on. Not only had several thousand textile workers been put out of a job, but the people of Naples were rendered even more reliant on the massive black market trade in stolen Allied clothing.[9]

The short-sightedness of some of the Allied requisitioning was sometimes thoughtless in the extreme. For example, one of the reasons why laundry soap was in such short supply in Naples was that its manufacture required caustic soda, and the chemical plant that produced this essential ingredient was out of action. On investigation, it turned out that damage caused by the Germans had mostly been patched up, but after the Allies came they had requisitioned and cannibalized the plant's motor generators. Without power, the plant could not work. Thus, a city that was in the midst of a typhus epidemic found itself without soap, and valuable shipping space had to be set aside for importing soap from the other side of the Atlantic.[10]

Similar stories abounded. When the US Army requisitioned the warehouses of the Montecatini chemical plant in Bagnoli, the whole factory had to be cordoned off for security purposes. As a consequence, hundreds of local people lost their jobs; but more importantly the region was denied an important producer of fertilizers and insecticides at a time when all southern Italy was in the midst of a food crisis.[11]

A year after the Allies arrived, the industrial situation in Naples was worse than ever. According to an Allied report in October 1944, the cotton industry 'is practically stopped', the chemical industry 'has suffered considerably' and the cement works in Bagnoli and Salerno were 'not working for civilian requirements'. Of the sixteen food canning plants in the region, thirteen were still idle. Similarly, despite the food crisis, many of the flour mills were not working because there was still not enough grain to be milled. The only industries that might have recovered more quickly were some elements of the metallurgical and mechanical industries, but the recovery had been prevented by yet more factory requisitions and by a lack of raw materials.[12]

There were plenty of Allied figures who objected strongly to such short-sightedness. At the beginning of 1944 the US Foreign Economic Administration (FEA) sent a survey mission to Naples, headed by the future governor of Illinois, Adlai Stevenson. Its purpose was to survey the damage done to the Italian economy by the war, with a view to understanding what the future economy of Europe might look like once the war had been won. Stevenson was unashamedly critical of the Allies' lack of vision when it came to economic reconstruction. He knew that Allied commanders had insisted that no reconstruction could be carried out unless it contributed directly to the war effort, but pointed out that such a policy would end up costing the Allies far more than it saved them. Without a functioning local economy, valuable Allied shipping space would continue to be filled with civilian aid rather than military supplies. A disgruntled, unemployed populace would require much more policing, and the Allies would be forced to waste valuable resources on maintaining law and order in rear areas. Worst of all, they were storing up problems for the long-term future. It was in America's interest to lay the foundations of an enduring peace, not only in Italy but in Europe more generally. Years before the

Marshall Plan was even imagined, Stevenson was already advocating American investment in rebuilding the entire European economy. 'A total war is not won by winning battles alone. The peace must also be won.'[13]

Stevenson was not the only one who argued these points. Many in AMG, particularly in the Labour Division, also put forward ideas for 'an industrial revival', but they were almost always ignored. The Naples Labour Division, in particular, complained that 'Many aspects of these problems have been presented to the competent Allied offices, but up to date, nothing has been done.'[14] Italian sources also raised the same concerns. Why were the Allies wasting shipping space transporting sugar to Naples when there was a perfectly good sugar refinery lying idle in Caserta? Why was the Eternit cement factory occupied by Allied troops, its workers all laid off and its machinery 'piled up in a disorderly manner' when Naples was in such dire need of the roofing materials it produced?[15]

The haphazard military occupation of essential Neapolitan factories continued for the whole of the rest of the war, and even after the war was over. As late as August 1945, the Neapolitan prefect was complaining to the Allies that, if they would only derequisition the factories they still occupied, jobs could be created for 27,000 workers. Their reply was that 'there would be no derequisitioning until 1946 and then only gradually'. The economic reconstruction of Naples would simply have to wait.[16]

Labour Unrest

In fairness to the Allies, what they failed to provide in long-term industrial jobs they made up for by providing short-term employment for the Allied cause – and often at more than market rates of pay. As outlined in Chapter 9, the Neapolitan economy underwent a wholesale reorientation during the war: shoemakers and steelworkers who had once contributed to Italian industry quickly became labourers and car mechanics in the struggle to win the war. But such a reorientation came at a cost. Skilled workers left their industries, sometimes for good, and concentrations of artisans dispersed and moved away. Whole industries crumbled even further into disrepair. No matter how well paid people were when working for the Allies, their jobs were only ever temporary. What would happen once the war was won and the Allies went home?

Shortly after the war ended, Naples had a taste of what was to come. In the summer of 1945, thousands of German prisoners of war were brought to Naples to work as prison labour in the port. With so many unpaid Germans working for the Allies, local labour was no longer needed. By the end of the summer, according to the Communist newspaper *Il Voce*, 10,000 Italian port workers had already been laid off, and a further ten or eleven thousand were facing imminent unemployment.[17]

The reaction was not long in coming. In September, thousands of indignant workers began calling for action from both the Allies and the Italian government. Hundreds demonstrated outside the Prefecture building and in the centre of town, bearing banners reading 'Out with the Germans' and 'Let's repeat the Four Days'. Groups of 'delinquent youths' routinely whistled and jeered at Allied supply trucks being driven by German POWs, and on one occasion a truck was seized and taken, along with its terrified drivers, to an Allied military police post.[18]

Things came to a head when the Italian prime minister, Ferruccio Parri, visited the city on 21 September to meet with various workers' groups at the labour office in Via Constantinopoli. As he arrived there were already crowds of disgruntled workers demonstrating outside. They were joined by hundreds of unemployed military veterans, recently returned from captivity. As Parri entered the building, some of the demonstrators began shouting 'Death to Parri' and one spat at him. When he emerged again ninety minutes later, demonstrators attacked his car and that of the prefect, smashing the back windows with bottles. After the cars had sped away to safety, various pockets of protesters headed off to Piazza Dante, where they smashed windows and looted shops, before finally being dispersed by police.[19]

This event was just one of a series of demonstrations, strikes and industrial disputes that happened all across Campania in the immediate aftermath of the Second World War. The Communist and Socialist parties in particular, flushed with the successes of their partisans in the north of the country, began agitating for all kinds of reforms in the south. The same month that Parri was almost lynched in Naples, intelligence reports started coming through that the Socialists had sent crates of arms to the city. The Carabinieri began warning of the possibility of a 'Red September'.[20]

In order to calm things down, the Allies announced that they were repatriating all German POW labour from the port, and reinstating Italian workers instead. But everyone knew that the Allies could not guarantee Italian jobs for long. They would be handing over administration of the port back to the Italians at the end of the year. They had already begun withdrawing their troops and administrative staff from the city, and laying off the staff they had employed for the past two years. The real problems were yet to come.[21]

The aftermath of these events pointed the way to many of the future problems that would plague Italy for decades to come. Firstly they showed the growing boldness of the left-wing parties – as well as the growing fear of what they might be capable of. In the coming years, Communist activity would only increase, and the various authorities of the state would start intervening against them more and more proactively. There would be violent clashes between the Carabinieri and peasants campaigning for land reform; and repeated tensions between trade unionists and employers. At a national level there would be a security crackdown on Communists more generally, and a concerted effort by America to prevent the Communists winning too many seats in the post-war Italian general elections. These were the first expressions of a much larger battle between global capitalism and global Communism, which would eventually solidify as the Cold War.[22]

Alongside this Communist resurgence came a second, more surprising political revival. According to American intelligence documents, the demonstrators who tried to lynch Parri in September 1945 were almost certainly not stirred up by Communists, but, rather, by right-wing elements in the crowd. These elements had their own reasons to dislike Parri, who had been an enemy of Fascism from the very beginning. As 1945 drew to a close, neo-Fascist groups began marching through the streets of Naples quite brazenly, often in uniform, often in military formation, and sometimes even carrying banners with Fascist slogans on them. They were careful not to antagonize the police or Allied soldiers directly. Instead they were 'more concerned with battling Communism' and felt completely justified 'in taking the law in their own hands when it suits their purposes'.[23]

Fascists and neo-Fascists would play a prominent part in Naples in the following years. In the 1940s they agitated for the monarchist cause. In the 1950s they put down strikes and fought pitched battles against trade unionists. Fascist posturing, which should have been brought to an end by a comprehensive purge and a period of concerted soul-searching, was allowed to continue with impunity, even to the point where it posed a significant threat to law and order. On a national level, the violent rivalry between extremists at both ends of the political spectrum would eventually culminate in the terrorist *anni di piombo* (the 'years of lead') of the 1970s and 1980s.

North and South

The failure to begin a proper programme of reconstruction in Naples was disastrous for the city, and everyone knew it. After the end of the war, the Allies directed much of the blame, somewhat unfairly, at the local and national governments. In August 1945, for example, the Allied Commissioner for Naples urged the Neapolitan authorities to begin a massive public works programme to take care of the 125,000 Allied employees who would soon be losing their jobs. In the meantime, the American intelligence chief in Naples also criticized the Italian national government for dragging their feet. 'Although several Ministers and Under-Secretaries from Rome have recently visited Naples in order to study the reconstruction problem, reconstruction is not yet underway and the program is still in the planning stage.'[24]

There were many faults with both the Neapolitan and the Italian administrations of the time, but criticism like this from the Allies was a bit unfair. Local government in Naples did not have anything like enough resources to employ 125,000 extra people, and the Allies knew it. Neither did the national government yet have the capacity to begin a comprehensive programme of reconstruction for the south. In 1945,

Italian national policy was still being directed by the ACC, and the Italian economy was still entirely at the mercy of aid shipments from the USA. Politicians like Ivanoe Bonomi and Ferruccio Parri were obliged to focus their gaze wherever the Allies directed it – and, as the war came to an end in 1945, all eyes were pointing north.

It was in the summer of 1945 that the huge differences between the experience of the Second World War in the north and in the south first became glaringly apparent. While the cities of the south had been liberated quickly, those in the north had been obliged to endure a further twenty months of German and Fascist rule. The kind of atrocities that had taken place in Campania during and after the Four Days had also taken place in the regions of the north, only on a much larger scale. Crucially, and tragically, many of these atrocities had been carried out not by Germans but by Italians: while the south had been able to maintain an uneasy peace between its people and its institutions, the north had been torn apart by a brutal civil war in which the Mussolini government of Salò had mercilessly persecuted its own people in the service of a foreign power. Leading the resistance against them were the parties of the Left – the Communists, the Socialists and the Action Party – who had massive support throughout the region, but particularly among the working classes in the big cities. (The Centre-Right parties, while very active in the political resistance, did less of the actual fighting.)

The collapse of the German army, along with its Fascist puppets at Salò, represented a massive victory not only for the Allies but also for the Italian partisans. Unlike the vast majority of the south, much of the north succeeded in liberating itself before the Allied armies arrived. Now, flushed with success, the partisans and their supporters in the mass parties of the Left were demanding the fruits of victory: the right to rewrite the constitution, to conduct their own purge, and to bring about massive social and economic changes. Workers set up factory committees to help oversee the reconstruction of industry – but also to drive out particularly hated managers, and force factory owners to share the profits of their businesses a bit more equitably. Partisans set up their own courts to try those they regarded as Fascist collaborators. From an Allied point of view it all looked a little bit like revolution.

Given their fear of Communism, and their determination to restore law and order at all costs, it is not surprising that the Allies concentrated all their efforts after the war on bringing the north under some sort of control. To do so they not only sent combat troops into Lombardy and Piedmont, but also began directing large amounts of aid there. This included shipments not only of food and clothing, but also of vital fuel and raw materials. For example, when 91,000 tons of cotton arrived in Italy in the summer of 1945, none of it was allocated to the textile industry in the south: the entire shipment was sent north to support factories there instead. As the Naples newspapers pointed out, the workers of the MCM textile factory had been crying out for such raw materials for almost two years – now almost 3,000 Neapolitan jobs had been put at risk.[25]

There were sound economic reasons why valuable raw materials were sent to northern Italy rather than kept in the south to help kick-start the long-awaited industrial recovery. Industry in the north was in much better shape than in the south: in contrast to the wholesale destruction of Neapolitan factories, only 10 to 15 per cent of northern industrial capacity had been destroyed. Piedmont, Lombardy and the Veneto were simply in a better position to lead the economic rebirth that Italy so desperately needed.[26] But in truth the main reasons why the Allies wanted to support the north were political. The last thing the Allies wanted was a vast mass of unemployed workers causing trouble on the streets of Milan. Naples, which had already been brought under control, could wait.

If Parri's government had been a little stronger it might perhaps have been able to intervene on the south's behalf – but it, too, had good reason to prioritize the needs of the north. The parties of the Left were eager to support both their comrades in the CLNAI, and the mass movement of workers that represented their best chance of achieving power in any forthcoming national election. Meanwhile, the parties of the Right, like the Allies, were willing to do anything to prevent an escalation of Communist and Socialist agitation. Personal reasons undoubtedly also played a part. As the former Minister for Industry, Commerce and Employment pointed out, bitterly, three-quarters of Parri's cabinet and all the main leaders were northerners. Why should they send resources south when their hearts and minds all belonged to the north?[27]

For a while in the summer of 1945 the Neapolitan newspapers were filled with angst and indignation. 'The people of the South must know that they are playing for their destiny for at least the next fifty years,' said an editorial in *Il Giorno*.[28] Few were hopeful about how this game would play out. The eternal story of the south, said some, was about to repeat itself: 'to pay, so that the money will be spent elsewhere; to sacrifice itself, so that its sacrifices will go to the benefit of others.'[29] Others looked back to the era of Giovanni Giolitti, the Liberal prime minister who had presided over decades of southern neglect: 'all the political parties, disoriented by tumultuous events ... are inclined to forget the South.'[30]

As minds turned towards the coming election in 1946, as well as a referendum on whether or not to retain the monarchy, a combination of conservatives, monarchists and former Fascists exploited these divisions mercilessly. If the north was controlled by parties of the Left, they seemed to say, then the south could only make its voice heard by turning to the Right.[31] They resurrected memories of the days when Mussolini had proclaimed Naples the 'Queen of the Mediterranean'. Under the Fascists, they claimed, there had at least been law and order; unlike the squalor that had arrived with the Allies, and the revolution being fomented by Communists and Socialists. A new political party was set up – Il Fronte dell'Uomo Qualunque (the 'Common Man's Front') – which opposed any kind of purge, any kind of reform, any kind of meddling from central government, and indeed any kind of engagement with politics in general. In a matter of months, Left-leaning Naples became a hotbed of populist resentment.

The north–south divide was made plain for all to see in the general election held on 2 June 1946: while the north voted predominantly for the parties of the Left, the south voted overwhelmingly for the Christian Democrats and the parties of the Right. The results of the referendum, held the same day, were even more stark. While the north voted overwhelmingly to abolish the monarchy, the south voted overwhelmingly to retain it. There was a painful symmetry to the numbers – almost two-thirds of the electorate in each case. Naples recorded one

of the very highest votes in favour of retaining the monarchy, with
almost 80 per cent voting to retain the king.[32] When the results finally
came in a week later, and Neapolitans discovered that the rest of Italy
had voted to form a republic, they felt ignored all over again. There
were riots on the streets. Seven died, and more than sixty people were
seriously injured.[33]

These events, too, created a legacy. In the years to come, the north
came to see itself as a region of heroes and revolutionaries who not only
defeated Fascism, but ushered in a new era free from the old, sclerotic
institutions of the past. At the same time, they saw the south as a
region of backward-looking reactionaries. Memories of Naples as
a revolutionary city, which had resisted Fascism just as strongly as the
cities of the north, quickly began to fade.

Legacy

When the Allied jeeps first rolled into Naples in October 1943 there were great hopes for a radical transformation of Neapolitan fortunes. The city had been subjected to a month of atrocities by the Germans, three years of continual bombing by the Allies, twenty years of repression by the Fascists and eight decades of political and economic neglect by the Italian state. But the glorious uprising by the Neapolitan people, and the triumphant arrival of the liberating armies, had at least created the opportunity for change.

During the next nine months the city became the de facto capital of free Italy. The Italian central government established its headquarters at Salerno, just south of Naples; and the Allied Fifth Army established its headquarters at Caserta, just north of Naples. But the combined Allied Military Government and Allied Control Commission made its headquarters in Naples itself, and it was from here that all of the major decisions about the future of Italy were made. At the same time, the port of Naples also became the economic hub not only of the Allied effort but of the whole of southern Italy. The city had at last become what Mussolini had always promised it would be – the 'Queen of the Mediterranean'.

In the early days of the Allied occupation the people of Naples were hugely impressed with the energy and efficiency with which the Allies faced the various emergencies in their city. When they saw the speed with which the Allies had repaired the aqueducts, re-established the electricity supply and patched up the docks; when they saw how efficiently they had dealt with the typhus epidemic and the volcanic eruption; and when they saw the great riches that were pouring into the port every day, they dared to believe that anything was possible. If the same energy and focus could be directed at repairing the city's political and economic institutions, its army and its police force, its schools, hospitals, factories and farms, then Naples would not only rise from the ashes but might also play a fundamental role in the liberation and restoration of the whole of Italy.

But as the months passed, and the dreamed-of rebirth of the city failed to materialize, disappointment inevitably set in. What the people here failed to appreciate was that the Allies had a completely different set of priorities. They had no intention of repairing bomb damage to housing, of rebuilding schools or repairing farms and factories damaged in the conflict. Nor were they prepared to allow the people of southern Italy to repair such things for themselves. All resources had to be directed at one thing only – the prosecution of the war. Despite the vast riches passing through the port every day, Allied resources were not unlimited. There would be no attempt at economic reconstruction.

The longed-for reform of Italian institutions turned out to be an even bigger disappointment. While a purge of sorts was carried out when the Allies first arrived, only the most obviously corrupt Fascist officials were removed from office. The central government itself was never purged. The king, despite being almost universally despised by the Italian people, was untouchable. Badoglio was likewise kept in place for a full nine months after the Allies first arrived on the mainland. At a local level things were hardly any better: mayors stayed in place, as did police chiefs and all the main functionaries of local government. As Giorgio Amendola put it in 1946, 'There are areas of southern Italy where everything seems to have remained as it was before under Fascism; the political and state apparatus has not changed, and power remains in the hands of the same families.'[1] It had always been the explicit policy of the Allies to maintain the current hierarchies wherever possible. Thus a corrupt, unpopular and undemocratic system had been deliberately kept in place, and the possibility for meaningful political reform in the south was smothered at birth.

The disappointments kept coming. During the Allied occupation, inflation soared, official rations often never materialized and the black market boomed. After two years of disastrous economic mismanagement, resentments inevitably began to bubble over. Rumours began to circulate that the Allies were deliberately keeping the people in a state of poverty in order to better dominate them.[2] Guido Dorso, one of the greatest champions of the 'southern problem', wrote bitterly at the end of the war about how the Allies risked being remembered not as liberators and saviours, but 'as ruthless enemies who consciously frustrated the last hopes of rebirth in the country'.[3]

At the heart of such resentments lay a fundamental misunderstanding between the Allies and the people of Naples. Neapolitans failed to see that the Allies did not have the resources, the manpower or the political will to solve all their problems. They were busy fighting a war across three continents and oceans: the concerns of the Neapolitan people were merely details in a much larger picture.

But what the Allies failed to appreciate was that such details mattered. Naples was not merely a supply hub for Allied needs, or a place of entertainment for drunken Allied servicemen on leave. It was also a vibrant and close-knit community with its own needs and aspirations. The economic and political frustrations of a whole society cannot simply be ignored. The hunger of hundreds of thousands of people cannot be blithely brushed aside. The treatment of Naples and its people would have repercussions that would last for decades, and spread far beyond the confines of the city.

Lessons for the Allies

In the summer of 1944, another big change came. After the breakthrough at Cassino the Allied armies surged north; and Naples, once the centre of all their operations, was reduced to a mere backwater, far behind the battlefront. Rome was reinstated as the capital of free Italy and the Italian government moved back to its traditional seat of power. The Allied Control Commission followed, and simplified its name to the Allied Commission. The Allies maintained a substantial military headquarters in the Royal Palace at Caserta, just north of Naples – but after the liberation of Livorno in Tuscany, Naples itself became just another supply port.

Italy itself also became something of a backwater that summer. On 6 June, the Allies landed on the Normandy beaches and began their push to liberate France, Belgium and the Netherlands. Ten weeks later, a second Allied force landed on the south coast of France near Marseilles. The whole focus of the war had moved away from Italy and the Mediterranean towards France and northern Europe. Naples and its continuing problems inevitably slipped down the list of Allied priorities.

Nevertheless, over the coming months the legacy of the Allies' time in southern Italy would make itself felt. From a purely military point of view, the Allies had learned some important lessons from the Italian campaign. Their landings in Normandy and southern France would be more concentrated, better concealed and better planned than any of their previous landings in Italy. They would not allow themselves to get bogged down so easily as they had done on the Italian mainland: as soon as an opportunity to break through German lines presented itself, they would seize it. As a consequence, while the battle for Italy dragged on, France was liberated in just three months: Caen was taken at the end of July, Paris in August and Lille at the beginning of September.

As the armed forces fought their way through Belgium, the Netherlands and into Germany itself, the Allied administrators who followed also brought with them some of the lessons they had learned in Italy. To begin with, they were much better prepared than they ever had been in Italy. For example, in all the newly liberated territories, DDT powder became a standard part of the Allied toolkit: refugees and displaced persons were routinely dusted as a precautionary measure, as were the inmates of work camps, POW camps and concentration camps. The methods of typhus control pioneered in Naples were used throughout liberated Europe, and as a consequence the continent-wide pandemic feared by some Allied planners never came to pass.[4]

The Allied Military Governments that established themselves in France, Belgium and the Netherlands were also much better resourced than the AMG in Italy had been. Rations here were far more generous from the outset – the standard daily bread ration envisaged for France at the end of 1944, for example, was 350 grammes, and that for Greece was 400 grammes. This was more than three times the amount originally granted to the people of Naples a year earlier.[5] In the Netherlands, the Allies acted far more quickly and decisively than they had done in Italy. During the infamous 'Hunger Winter' of early 1945, which claimed at least 16,000 lives, the Allies emptied emergency stockpiles of food in Britain and shipped hundreds of thousands of tons of food across the Channel as a matter of extreme urgency.[6] The rush to bring relief to the Netherlands was a vast improvement on the complacent attitudes of 1943, when it was assumed that the people of Naples would be able to feed themselves without much Allied help at all.

Political issues were also taken much more seriously in northern than in southern Europe. Unlike in Naples and southern Italy, Fascists and German collaborators in other parts of Europe were routinely removed from the police forces and the civil service, the press, schools and universities and even from the business world. Trials and tribunals took place all over France, Belgium, the Netherlands, Denmark and Norway. The results, naturally, were fairly mixed – but they were always much more satisfactory than the feeble efforts made in Naples in 1944. Importantly, the purge trials that took place in northern Europe were generally overseen by judges who were not themselves tainted by years of collaboration with Fascism – a state of affairs that was simply not possible in Italy. As a consequence other parts of Europe emerged from the war with a much greater faith in the justice system than Italy did.[7]

The purge in Germany was pursued even more rigorously. In stark contrast to the laissez-faire attitude in southern Italy, the Allied authorities in Germany pursued former members of the Nazi Party with zeal. Personal questionnaires were issued to all public employees, just as they had been in Italy, only much more promptly. The results were also examined more carefully, and transgressors were much more likely to be held to account – at least in the short to medium term. Those who had committed serious crimes were tried in Allied courts all over the country, most famously at Nuremberg. The process that was entirely lacking in Italy – no Italian was ever brought to justice for their war crimes in Libya, Somalia, Ethiopia or the Balkans – was pursued with

true vigour, especially by the Americans. In the American Zone of
Germany alone, 3.5 million people were identified as potential criminals, more than 169,000 cases were tried and over 100,000 imprisoned.
The corresponding processes in Italy saw only fractions of these
numbers.[8]

Inevitably, however, there were also lessons that the Allies failed to
learn in 1944, either because it was inconvenient to do so or because
they represented problems that were essentially unsolvable. Prostitution
and the exploitation of women followed the Allies around Europe like
a dark but unacknowledged shadow. So too did looting, theft, drunken
behaviour, the black market and crippling levels of inflation. The
Allied authorities never truly got a grip on their men's behaviour, or
managed to control their pilfering, profiteering and black market trading with local people. Nor did they ever properly try to curb their
spending. In Germany, prices on the black market doubled and tripled
as quickly as they had done in Naples: in the autumn of 1945, the price
of a carton of American cigarettes in Berlin had risen to as much as
$165.[9]

Other mistakes and misjudgements were repeated over and over
again. The same lack of investment, lack of reconstruction and lack of
raw materials took place all over Europe, with the same results: social
unrest was universal after the war, and the entire continent languished
in economic crisis for at least the next three years. It was not until
Communist agitation threatened to embroil Europe in revolution that
the US Congress finally decided it would better serve American interests to invest in the reconstruction of Europe than to let it languish in
squalor and turmoil. The Marshall Plan came just in time to save the
western half of the continent from falling prey to the same totalitarian
forces that were already re-enslaving the East. The lesson of Naples,
which Adlai Stevenson had tried in vain to make heard in 1944, had
finally been understood: rebuilding the European economy was the
only way to lay 'the foundations of enduring peace'.[10]

Lessons for Italy

While the Allies were moving on from Naples, the Italians also turned their attention away from the city during 1944. Once Rome was liberated, all eyes automatically turned northwards towards the capital. The newspapers began to fill with stories of new, Roman tragedies – the terror of the German occupation, the massacre of civilians in the Fosse Ardeatine, the arrest and deportation of Rome's Jews. There were new political hurdles to leap – the creation of a new Italian government, for example, and the thorny issue of what to do about the monarchy. Many of the same phenomena that had overwhelmed Naples also began to make themselves felt in Rome – soaring inflation, growing hunger, the proliferation of prostitution. Even the black market reoriented itself away from Naples and towards Rome. And as the battlefields moved northwards there were new heroes, new tragedies, new refugees. Naples was old news.

By the end of the war, the focus of the nation had turned to the big cities of the north: Genoa and Turin, Verona and Milan, Trento and Trieste. As I laid out in the last chapter, precious resources were diverted northwards in order to keep the rebellious workers there occupied. After nearly two years of struggle against their German and Fascist oppressors, the people of the north needed to be shown that their sacrifices had been worthwhile. Those of Naples and the south, as we have seen, felt left behind.

And yet, the problems of the south were never entirely forgotten. During their time in Naples and its surrounding towns and villages, a whole generation of politicians and activists had seen the poverty here with their own eyes. In the late 1940s and 1950s, after the Italian government had been released from the constraints placed upon them by the Allied Commission, a genuine effort was made to address the age-old 'southern problem' once and for all. Agrarian reforms were announced by the agriculture minister, Fausto Gullo, to help southern peasants to avoid undue exploitation from landlords. A new agency was set up to stimulate economic growth and investment in the region, the 'Cassa per il Mezzogiorno', which would distribute billions of lire to various development projects across the south. Innovative new housing projects began to spring up all over the region, directed by another central government agency, INA-Casa. A massive road-building programme finally brought about what Mussolini had always promised but failed to deliver, a comprehensive network that linked the towns and villages of the south to each other and to the rest of Italy for the very first time. The harbour was cleared of shipwrecks. The docks and quays were properly repaired, as were the plants and factories. The hotels around the point at Santa Lucia were rebuilt. Villas and apartments across the city were repaired.

There were many admirable projects in the post-war years, which brought something of a revival to the south – but there were also many abject failures. For example, the agricultural reform programme, despite its good intentions, had very mixed results. The combined opposition of the Liberals, the Christian Democrats, rural landlords and the Mafia meant that any group of tenant farmers asking for their rights often found they were fighting a losing battle. In some cases that battle was quite literal: rural protests often ended in violence and bloodshed, with the peasantry always coming off worst.[11]

The industrial revival of the south was equally patchy. After the Allies finally departed, derequisitioned factories returned to production and big companies like Cirio and Alfa Romeo expanded their operations around Naples. Artisan glovemakers and shoemakers returned to their traditional occupations, as did the shipbuilders of Castellammare di Stabia and the steelworkers of Bagnoli. But the economic revival here was never so great as it was in the north, which continued to receive the lion's share of investment, both public and private. Many of the projects funded by the Cassa per il Mezzogiorno were built in out-of-the-way places, rising like cathedrals in the desert, and never quite managed to link up into integrated systems of industry. Many new factories were full of machinery, provided few long-term jobs and were run by northern companies that took their profits with them. Naples did not do too badly by the standards of the south, but compared to other parts of Italy did not really experience the economic miracle of the 1950s and 1960s.[12]

The building boom that took place in Naples after the war was also a mixed blessing, to say the least. For every carefully planned INA-Casa development, hundreds of cheap, shoddy buildings were constructed, covering all the most picturesque parts of the city in concrete. Planning restrictions and building regulations were routinely ignored, with tragic consequences when dozens of these buildings collapsed in land-slides during the 1960s and in the 1980 earthquake.[13]

It was not the central Italian government that was predominantly responsible for such failures, but the politicians and other elites of the south itself. Political corruption was rife in and around Naples in the aftermath of the war. Neapolitan politics in the 1950s and 1960s would be dominated by a combination of shady-dealing Christian Democrats and former Fascists, whose abuses of power quickly became notorious throughout Italy. Achille Lauro, one of the few Fascist hierarchs in Naples to have behaved badly enough to receive a proper punishment during the war, was mayor of Naples for most of the 1950s. He was followed by Nicola Sansanelli, a former member of the Grand Fascist Council and head of the Fascist militia. Under such people, much of the money that flowed southwards from Rome only ended up being misappropriated for political purposes. It is probably no coincidence that this was also the era when the Mafia and the Camorra really took a grip of the city and its hinterland for the first time.

All these problems stemmed at least partly from the failure of the Allies to stamp out corruption in the region when they had the chance. It was the short-sightedness of Allied administrators between 1943 and 1945 that stood in the way of desperately needed reforms, and paved the way for the further failures of the fifties and sixties.

The consequences for Naples and the south were dire. Given the choice between northern prosperity and southern corruption and stag-nation, the people of the south voted with their feet. Naples, once the largest city in Italy, now became a mere stopping-off place for peasants fleeing north to take up work in the factories of Turin and Milan.[14] There was little point in lingering: 'Nobody comes to Naples,' explained the demographers of the post-war era, 'because there are already more job applicants than actual employees.'[15]

The flight from the south was the logical conclusion of a century of neglect and under-investment, in which the Second World War and the short-sighted policies of the Allies also played their part. Southern Italy has never been the same since.

Neapolitan Memory of the War

For the people of Naples, the failure to convert the hopes and aspirations of 1943 into long-lasting reform and economic rebirth was an enormous disappointment – but never really a surprise. Naples has a long history of revolutions and uprisings that have ended in failure: there was no reason to suppose that the ousting of Fascism would be any different.

The disappointments began on day one. In the 1970s, one of the resisters of the Four Days told the story of his first encounter with the Allies on the day of liberation. Having seen the dead bodies of his comrades in Vomero laid out on tables in the local primary school, he descended to the city below to welcome the army that promised a new dawn. 'Via Roma was flooded with a blinding light,' he wrote.

> A stream of people was heading towards Piazza Municipio, and we too headed in the same direction. At the top of the royal gardens we encountered the first English tank. It was a huge, monstrous machine, covered in leafy branches. The Allied soldiers, among branches and strange carnival make-up, looked at us from above, without expression. All around, a sea of people was applauding, crying, laughing.

Carried away by the emotion of the moment, Paolo Ricci fought his way to the front of the crowd and reached up to offer a cigarette to the nearest English soldier. 'I threw it to him, but though he had followed my action, he didn't move. The cigarette ended up between the tracks of the tank. It was the only one I had.' Looking back, it seemed like an omen of what was to come.[16]

In the coming years, many Neapolitan activists from the war years would campaign for better recognition, for fairer distribution of resources, for political and economic reform and for an end to crime and corruption. On the whole, they were ignored and sidelined – first by the Allies and later by the Italian authorities. The revolutionaries of the Four Days were dismissed as crackpots and delinquents. The various Communists, Socialists and Action Party members who had led the charge for reform were always kept at arm's length from any real opportunity to bring about change. When their efforts got nowhere, the vast majority of Neapolitans simply went back to their old lives and tried to forget about the war.

Since then, the story of Naples between 1943 and 1945 has been told in a variety of ways. There were those who saw this as a time of heroes. Journalists like Aldo De Jaco and filmmakers like Nanni Loy portrayed wartime Naples as a tight-knit and inherently noble community, which rose up as one to defend itself from the twentieth century's most evil power. De Jaco's bestselling chronicle of the Naples uprising, *Le Quattro Giornate di Napoli: La città insorge*, has never been out of print; while Loy's film *Le Quattro Giornate di Napoli* won several awards and was nominated for an Oscar as best foreign film. Such stories do not concern themselves with what went before, or what came after – they are only interested in the moment of glory when Naples showed the whole world what it could do.

Then there are those who tell the story of the war years as a tragedy. The novelist Curzio Malaparte described wartime Naples as a vision of hell, filled with nothing but plague and corruption. Carlo Levi described the desperate poverty in the countryside south of Naples in his post-war classic *Christ Stopped at Eboli*; while Alberto Moravia described the similar poverty in the countryside north of Naples, followed by the wholesale rape of its women by Allied soldiers, in his 1957 novel *La Ciociara* (translated into English as *Two Women*). It is interesting that all three writers were outsiders from Tuscany, Turin and Rome. As such, they were perhaps able to broach subjects that were too sensitive or traumatic for local writers.

Finally, there were those who viewed the war years as a farce. The people of Naples are famous for their sense of humour. This city was one of the original birth places of the *commedia dell'arte* and all its caricatures of human follies and vices – many of which were on full display during the war years. For those who felt powerless to change their circumstances, it was often a relief simply to shrug their shoulders and laugh at them instead.

It is instructive that the most iconic Neapolitan actor of the 1940s and early 1950s was not a heart-throb or an action hero but a clown. Antonio De Curtis, better known as Totò, starred in dozens of films during those years and is still revered in Naples to this day: there are at least fifteen streets named after him in the city and its satellite towns. He almost always played the same character: a streetwise, self-centred trickster who is ready to take advantage of any opportunity, no matter how bizarre (or how illegal).

Sophia Loren, who acted alongside Totò in the 1954 comedy *Poverty and Nobility*, explained why this character appealed so much to Neapolitans in the aftermath of the war:

> In *Poverty and Nobility*, Totò has a famous scene that has gone down in the history of cinema, where he stuffs his pockets with spaghetti. It speaks volumes about the hunger of our people, of the ravenousness of Pulcinella, the character in our commedia dell'arte who represents the Neapolitan essence, and of the starvation I saw with my very own eyes in Pozzuoli during the war. Hunger that you can only fend off with a smile, with the lightness of spirit that we Neapolitans are filled to overflowing with.[17]

The character of Pulcinella – better known to English audiences as the puppet character Mr Punch – has been a favourite here ever since the early seventeenth century. By the eighteenth and nineteenth centuries Pulcinella could be found everywhere: not only on the stage, but on street signs, in children's books and toys, and even in nativity scenes.[18] And yet there is nothing admirable about this character. He is a darkly comic creation, selfish, lazy, dishonest, proud, vainglorious and devoted to his own bodily pleasures – all of the things that Neapolitans have so often been accused of over the years. What endears him to Neapolitan audiences is that he always comes out on top – and along the way, quite accidentally, he usually ends up rescuing other characters, too.

In the aftermath of the war, Neapolitans understood something that people in other, more fortunate parts of the world often forgot – that characteristics like virtue and dignity are luxuries reserved for those who can afford them. Between 1940 and 1945 Neapolitans suffered every type of indignity possible: they were bombed by both sides, occupied by both sides, and ruled by a succession of brutal and incompetent governments whose priorities always lay elsewhere. As at many other times in their history, the only way for Neapolitans to survive was by bending and breaking the rules, by prostituting themselves, or by relying on the charity of their neighbours. In such a crowded city, there was no way of hiding their infidelities, compromises and misdemeanours, all of which had to be carried out in plain sight of the whole community. This atmosphere of indignity and moral squalor has been the bittersweet essence of Neapolitan comedy for hundreds of years; but in the aftermath of the Second World War it gained a new and immediate poignancy.

Perhaps the most famous depiction of wartime life in Naples was Eduardo De Filippo's 1950 comedy *Napoli milionaria*, which tells the story of a Neapolitan father who is seized by German soldiers and taken away to work as a forced labourer. When he returns to the city a few months later he finds it filled with Allied soldiers spending money like water. His wife has become rich as a black market trader; his son has become a thief who spends every night stealing wheels from Allied jeeps; and his daughter has become a good-time girl, who whiles away all her time drinking with Allied soldiers, eventually falling pregnant by one of them. In the hands of a Roman writer like Alberto Moravia, or a Tuscan one like Curzio Malaparte, these might be despicable characters, filled with the shame of corruption and moral defeat – but in De Filippo's hands they are just ordinary people trying to navigate their way through the absurdities thrown up by the extraordinary times in which they are living. The truth of what went on during the war is buried beneath layers of Neapolitan humour.

All these stories of Neapolitan life are mythical in their own way, and the truth of those years probably lies somewhere in the gaps between them. Ever since the 1980s, historians have been trying to delve into those gaps: this book is merely the latest attempt of many. There is still much work to be done. The history of Neapolitan women during the war – the hardship they suffered, and the extraordinary lengths they went to in order to feed their families – is a particular blind spot. The subject of wartime prostitution is still taboo in Naples.

Meanwhile, the city itself has moved on. There is still poverty here, as there is in all European cities, but Naples is no longer the squalid, desperate place that it was in the post-war years. There is corruption here, too, but no longer on the scale of the 1950s and 1960s, and the activities of the Mafia and the Camorra are also, thankfully, in decline. Football crowds still taunt the Napoli fans when they play in other cities with chants about their hygiene – but the slurs seem old and outdated now. The days of cholera outbreaks are long gone. Crime has been decreasing ever since the start of the twenty-first century: there is now far less crime here than in Florence, Rome, Turin and Milan.[19] Prosperity is, slowly, returning. Naples is no longer a paradise inhabited by devils.

Acknowledgements

There have been times when I believed that this book would never be finished. Shortly after I began my research, the global Covid pandemic shut down all international travel, as well as access to archives and libraries everywhere. Three and a half years later, as I was in the final stages of writing up my discoveries, my mother died. Throughout all these months of delay and bereavement I have relied heavily on the love of my family, the patience of my publishers, and the kindness and resourcefulness of archivists and researchers on both sides of the Atlantic.

With this in mind, I would like to thank the following people, without whom this book would never have been completed.

In the United States I received a huge amount of help from museum staff and volunteers who gave their time to me quite selflessly. The Texas Military Forces Museum was particularly helpful, and I am indebted to Lisa Sharik, Rebecca Gandara and Audrey Griffen for scanning and transcribing dozens of previously unpublished personal testimonies for me. Rafael Alvarez at the 82nd Airborne Division Museum was similarly generous, as was Eric Reinert, curator of the US Army Corps of Engineers office of history. I am also grateful to Elijah Palmer of the US Army Quartermaster Museum, Vicki Archileti of the US Army Women's Museum, and Ms A. Howard of Tuskegee Airmen Inc. Last but not least, I received a huge amount of help from several researchers at the US National Archives: Satu Haas-Webb, Orrin Konheim, Alex Cira and Joe P. Harris.

In Italy, I was greatly helped in the initial stages of my research by my nephew and brother-in-law Giacomo and Antonio Gazzellone. All of the staff and volunteers at the Istituto Campano per la Storia della Resistenza were incredibly welcoming, but special mention must go to its director, Giulia Buffardi, and two extraordinarily knowledgeable and enthusiastic volunteers at the centre, Sara De Carlo and Valeria De Gennaro. Martina Magliacano and all of the staff at the Naples State Archives were similarly helpful and efficient. Jocelyn Vincent showed me behind the scenes at the Scugnizzo Liberato youth centre in Naples, one of the famous sites of resistance during the Four Days. I am also deeply grateful to Gabriella Gribaudi, Isabella Insolvibile, Carlo Gentile, Francesco Benigno and Paolo Masini, each of whom helped me with specific queries about the text.

In Germany, Sebastian Remus gave me invaluable help at the Bundesarchiv-Militärarchiv. In the UK, the staff of the National Archives, the National Army Museum, the Imperial War Museum and the British Library never once let me down.

As always, I am indebted to my agents, Simon Trewin and Jay Mandel; but also to all those at William Collins, St Martin's Press and my various international publishers. Special mention must go to Arabella Pike and Michael Flamini, who originally commissioned this book, but also to their teams of editors, designers, publicists, marketers and sales people who have helped to create and promote it. As a former editor myself I know how much work goes into publishing a book, and I am deeply grateful to them all.

Lastly, I would like to thank my family and friends, to whom this book is dedicated. Their support during a very difficult time was very much appreciated, even if I did not always remember to tell them so. To my wife, Liza, especially, and also to my children, Gabriel and Grace, I have only this to say: thanks for putting up with me.

Notes

Abbreviations Used in the Notes

82d ADM – 82nd Airborne Division War Memorial Museum, Fort Liberty, North Carolina

ACS – Archivio Centrale dello Stato, Roma

ANPI – Associazione Nazionale Partigiani d'Italia, Naples

ASN – Archivio di Stato di Napoli

BA-MA – Bundesarchiv-Militärarchiv, Freiburg

CEHO – US Army Corps of Engineers, Office of History, Unit Histories Collection, Alexandria, Virginia

FBIS – Foreign Broadcast Information Service. All references to FBIS, unless otherwise specified, relate to the daily reports on European affairs and official British broadcasts, available electronically through the Newsbank/Readex database (available at the British Library)

Hume report – NARA, RG 331, Allied Control Commission Italy Subject Files, Entry UD 1978, Box 939, 10000/129/167, 'AMG Report, Region III (Fifth Army) 8 Sept–15 Dec 1943'.

ICSR – Istituto Campano per la storia della resistenza, dell'antifascismo e dell'età contemporanea 'Vera Lombardi', Naples. Unless otherwise indicated, all references are to the 'Quattro Giornate' collection.

IWM – Imperial War Museum, London. All references are either to the oral history collection (IWM Sound) or the document collection (IWM Docs).

JAMHC – Japanese American Military History Collective, online archive

NARA – US National Archives and Records Administration, College Park, Maryland. The vast majority of reports come from ACC Italy Headquarters Subject Files, RG 331, Entry UD 1978.

PWB report – Series of weekly reports by the British Psychological Warfare Bureau, held in the UK National Archives. All reports are referred to by number and by date. Reports 1–12 (13 April–2 August 1944) are held in UKNA, WO 204/6313. Reports 13–24 (10 August–26 October 1944) are in WO 204/6314. Reports 25–36 (2 November 1944–19 January 1945) are in WO 204/6315.

S&S – the *Stars and Stripes*, US forces newspaper. Unless otherwise indicated, all references are to the Italian edition.

TMFM – Texas Military Forces Museum, Camp Mabry, Austin, Texas

UKNA – UK National Archives, London

UNRRA – Archive of the United Nations Relief and Rehabilitation Administration, New York City

VHP-LoC – Veterans History Project, American Folklife Center, Library of Congress – online video and audio archive.

Introduction
1. Hume report, pp. 12–13.
2. Norman Lewis, *Naples '44* (London: Eland, 2002), 4 Oct and 5 Nov 1943, and 26 Mar 1944, pp. 24, 50–1, 100.
3. Alan Moorehead, *Eclipse* (London: Granta, 2000), p. 66.
4. John Horne Burns, *The Gallery* (London: Hogarth Press, 1988), pp. 259–60.
5. John Huston, *An Open Book* (London: Macmillan, 1981), p. 106.
6. Curzio Malaparte, *The Skin* (New York: New York Review of Books, 2013), trans. David Moore, pp. 31, 32–3.
7. For the history of this particular stereotype see Benedetto Croce's essay 'Un paradiso abitato da diavoli', published in a collection with the same title by Adelphi in Milan (2006), pp. 11–27.

Chapter 1: Dreams of Naples
1. '"See Naples and Live," That's How This Reporter Heard It', *S&S* (African edition), 11 Sep 1943, p. 5.
2. Iacopo Sannazaro, *Arcadia* (Rome: Carocci, 2013), Canto XI, line 4, pp. 260–1.
3. Stendhal, *Rome, Naples et Florence en 1817* (Paris: Chez Delaunay, 1817), p. 116, entry for 8 Mar 1817.
4. Percy Bysshe Shelley, 'Ode to Naples', *Posthumous Poems of Percy Bysshe Shelley*, ed. Mary Wollstonecraft Shelley (London: J. & H. L. Hunt, 1824), p. 115.
5. Stendhal, *Rome, Naples et Florence*, 3rd edn (Paris: Delaunay, 1826), Vol. II, p. 166, entry for 9 Feb 1817.

6. Johann Wolfgang von Goethe, *Goethes italienische Reise* (Leipzig: Insel, 1913), 28 May 1787, p. 355.

7. Ibid., 16 Mar 1787, p. 220.

Chapter 2: Salerno

1. Quoted in Carlo D'Este, *Fatal Decision: Anzio and the Battle for Rome* (London: HarperCollins, 1991), p. 30.

2. See for example Alexandre Dumas, *Sketches of Naples* (Philadelphia: E. Ferrett & Co., 1845), trans. A. Roland, pp. 75–9.

3. Dumas quoted in Peter Gunn, *Naples: A Palimpsest* (London: Chapman & Hall, 1961), p. 206.

4. Mark Clark, *Calculated Risk* (London: George Harrap & Co., 1951), p. 180.

5. Douglas Porch, *Hitler's Mediterranean Gamble* (London: Cassell, 2004), p. 498.

6. Samuel Eliot Morison, *Sicily-Salerno-Anzio*, Vol. IX, *History of the United States Naval Operations in World War II* (Boston: Little, Brown & Co., 1964), p. 253.

7. Robert Wallace, *The Italian Campaign* (Alexandria, Va.: Time Life Books, 1978), p. 53; Rick Atkinson, *The Day of Battle: The War in Sicily and Italy, 1943–1944* (New York: Henry Holt, 2007), p. 200; Atkinson, *The Day of Battle*, p. 201.

8. Major Warren A. Thrasher, quoted in Martin Blumenson, *Salerno to Cassino: United States Army in World War II* (Washington DC: Center of Military History United States Army, 1993), p. 55.

9. Jack Maher, quoted in Atkinson, *The Day of Battle*, p. 201.

10. Fred L. Walker diary, *From Texas to Rome* (Dallas TX: Taylor Publishing Co., 1969), entry for 8 Sep 1943, p. 230.

11. 'Engineer History, Mediterranean Theater, Fifth Army', CEHO, Vol. I, p. 7; Clark, *Calculated Risk*, p. 184.

12. Correspondence James E. Taylor to Walter H. Beck, 2 Mar 1944, TMFM; quoted Atkinson, *The Day of Battle*, p. 204.

13. Quoted by Atkinson, *The Day of Battle*, p. 204.

14. Blumenson, *Salerno to Cassino*, p. 77.

15. Lt Col. John H. Hougen, *The Story of the Famous 34th Infantry Division* (n.p., 1949), chapter 12: https://archive.org/details/StoryOfTheFamous34thInfDiv/page/n77/mode/2up

16. Blumenson, *Salerno to Cassino*, p. 79.

17. D'Este, *Fatal Decision*, p. 39.

18. Brig. C. J. C. Molony et al., *The Mediterranean and the Middle East*, Vol. V, *The Campaign in Sicily 1943 and the Campaign in Italy 3rd September 1943 to 31st March 1944* (London: HMSO, 1973), p. 280.

19. Atkinson, *The Day of Battle*, p. 207.

20. Lewis, *Naples '44*, p. 12 , entry for 9 Sep; Atkinson, *The Day of Battle*, p. 207.

21. Albert Kesselring, *The Memoirs of Field Marshal Kesselring*, trans. Lynton Hudson (London: Greenhill, 2007), p. 183.

22. Ibid., p. 182.

23. James R. Safrit journal, Sep 1943: http://www.45thdivision.org/Veterans/Safrit179.htm

24. Hugh Pond, *Salerno* (Boston: Little, Brown, 1991), pp. 111–12.

25. Indeed, it had been predicted by General Patton early on in the planning process: see Porch, *Hitler's Mediterranean Gamble*, p. 494.

26. Dwight D. Eisenhower, *Crusade in Europe* (London: William Heinemann, 1948), pp. 206–7. In his memoirs Clark claimed that he quickly dismissed such ideas, but in reality he was still contemplating them the following evening. See Clark, *Calculated Risk*, pp. 192–3; and Atkinson, *The Day of Battle*, pp. 226–7.

27. Clark, *Calculated Risk*, pp. 196–7; Porch, *Hitler's Mediterranean Gamble*, pp. 500–1.

28. Lewis, *Naples '44*, pp. 17–18, entry for 14 Sep.

29. Harold Horning, 'Army Years: 20 November 1941–27 June 1945', TMFM, p. 36.
30. Lewis, *Naples '44*, pp. 16–18, entries for 12 and 14 Sep.
31. Clark, *Calculated Risk*, pp. 194–5.
32. Account by Cordino Longiotti, D Coy, 179th Regt, 45th Inf Div, 'Remembering "The way it was"', reproduced at http://www.45thdivision. org/Veterans/Longiotti.htm
33. Kesselring, *The Memoirs of Field Marshal Kesselring*, p. 186.
34. 'Nazis Win Out in Battle for Naples', Berlin Press (15 Sep 1943), FBIS-FRB-43-221, p. D1.
35. Saul David, *Mutiny at Salerno: An Injustice Exposed* (London: Brassey's, 1995), passim.
36. 'Allied Tanks Lead Drive on Naples', BBC to Overseas Forces, 30 Sep 1943, FBIS-FRB-43-234, p. 12.
37. Clark, *Calculated Risk*, p. 202.
38. Blumenson, *Salerno to Cassino*, p. 144. For varying statistics over varying periods of time, see Atkinson, *The Day of Battle*, pp. 236, 646.
39. Captain J. E. Williams, manuscript diary, entry for 9 Sep 1943, IWM Docs 11631.
40. Kesselring order 15 Sept 1943, quoted in Lutz Klinkhammer, *L'occupazione tedesca in Italia 1943–1945* (Turin: Bollati Boringhieri, 2016), p. 42.
41. Mark W. Clark war diary, Vol. IV, p. 89, entry for Aug 15; and Vol. V, p. 9, entry for Sept 6, 1943: https:// citadeldigitalarchives.omeka.net/items/ show/1567 and https:// citadeldigitalarchives.omeka.net/items/ show/1561
42. Hume report, pp. 6–7. For a chronology of AMG's progress towards Naples, see NARA, RG 331, Allied Control Commission Italy Subject Files, UD 1978, Box 939, 100000/129/168, 'AMG Naples Province activities report 14th September to 15th December 1943'.

43. 'Naples Suffering Famine, Nazi Bullets', delayed report in *S&S* (Oran edition), 30 Sep 1943.
44. 'The Fall of Naples', *The Times*, 2 Oct 1943, p. 5.
45. This and other similar German reports quoted in Klinkhammer, *L'occupazione tedesca in Italia 1939–1945* (Turin: Bollati Boringhieri, 1993), pp. 45 and 458.

Chapter 3: Liberation

1. Stanley Gladstone, IWM Sound 3954, Reel 4.
2. 'British Correspondents Killed', *The Times*, 1 Oct 1943; 'Naples Goes Mad with Joy as Grim Allied Push Ends', *New York Times*, 2 Oct 1943.
3. Stanley Gladstone, IWM Sound 3954, Reel 4.
4. 'First in Naples', *Daily Herald*, 12 Oct 1943. Clark himself conceded this in his memoirs, *Calculated Risk*, p. 207.
5. 'Hysterical Crowds in the City; Patrols Overwhelmed', *The Times*, 2 Oct 1943.
6. *Roma*, 2 Oct 1943, quoted in Maria Porzio, *Arrivano gli alleati!* (Rome and Bari: Laterza, 2011), p. 27.
7. Hume report, p. 8.
8. For an expansion of the theme of liberators being equated with 'messiahs' in Europe and Asia, see my previous works, *The Fear and the Freedom* (London: Viking 2017), pp. 28–36; and *Prisoners of History* (London: William Collins, 2020), pp. 35–6, 39–40.
9. Atkinson, *The Day of Battle*, p. 240.
10. Aldo De Jaco, *Le Quattro Giornate di Napoli: La città insorge* (Rome: Riuniti, 2016), pp. 216–17.
11. Citadel Archive and Museum, South Carolina, Mark Clark War Diaries, Vol. V, p. 67: https://citadeldigitalarchives. omeka.net/items/show/1562
12. Clark, *Calculated Risk*, p. 207.
13. See for example Richard M. Burrage, 'See Naples and Die', TMFM, p. 32. For criticism of Clark's leadership style, see Porch, *Hitler's Mediterranean Gamble*, pp. 488–90.

14. Ronald Herbert Hickman, IWM Sound 23368, Reel 3.

15. Moorehead, *Eclipse*, pp. 65–6.

16. Walker, *From Texas to Rome*, entry for 1 Oct 1943, p. 267.

17. 82d ADM, 'Sicily After Action Report', p. 80.

18. O'Reilly's article is reproduced in *S&S* (Algiers edition), 4 Oct 1943: 'City Wrecked, People Crazed From Hunger'.

Chapter 4: The Destruction

1. UKNA, WO 204/4092, C-in-C to Fifteenth Army Group, 1 Oct 1943, Ref. 1926.

2. Ibid., Fifth Army to C-in-C AFHQ, 6 Oct 1943, Ref. 875.

3. UKNA, WO 204/549, Port Commandant Naples to D.Q.M.G., 'Report on the Port of Naples', 11 Oct 1943, AFHQ, Ref. 1004.

4. '1051st Engineers Port Construction and Repair Group Unit History', CEHO, p. 12. See also UKNA, ADM 1/17183, Rear Admiral on duty to C-in-C Mediterranean, 23 Apr 1944, 'Report on Salvage Operations, Western Italy, October 1943–March 1944', which details the removal of 170 of these vessels.

5. UKNA, ADM 1/17183, Rear Admiral on duty to C-in-C Mediterranean, 23 Apr 1944, 'Report on Salvage Operations, Western Italy, October 1943–March 1944', pp. 1–2.

6. NARA, RG 331, UD 1978, Box 4826, 10260/143/210, AMG Province of Avellino 'Monthly report', 11 Jan 1944, p. 4; UKNA WO 204/4092, Pence to Eisenhower, 31 Oct 1943, Ref. PBS 265.

7. UKNA, WO 204/549, 'Rail situation – Salerno Area 7 Oct 1945'; and WO 204/4092, Pence to Eisenhower, 31 Oct 1943, Ref. PBS 265. Also 'Engineer History, Fifth Army, Mediterranean Theater', CEHO, p. 21.

8. 'Engineer History, Fifth Army, Mediterranean Theater', CEHO, p. 21.

9. UKNA, WO 204/12335, 'I.S.T.D. "C" Report on the Port and Town of Naples', 17 Jul 1943, pp. 11–12, 76.

10. '696 Pipeline Company Unit History', CEHO, p. 19.

11. '1051st Port Construction and Repair Group Unit History', CEHO, p. 15.

12. See for example 'Germans Burned Library in Naples', *New York Times*, 12 Oct 1943, p. 3; and 'Archives of Naples burned by Germans', 3 Nov 1943, p. 3. See also 'Engineers Restoring Naples' Public Works', *S&S* (Algiers edition), 18 Oct 1943.

13. 'Roosevelt to Hear of Naples Plunder', *New York Times*, 24 Oct 1943, p. 31; *The Times*, 26 Nov 1943, 'German Vandalism in Naples'.

14. 'Treasures of Italy', *The Times*, 2 Feb 1944.

15. 'German Vandalism in Naples', *The Times*, 26 Nov 1943.

16. According to the detailed 'Zerstörungsliste' distributed to troops on 21 Sept 1943, works of art and of historical value were expressly not to be looted or destroyed: BA-MA RH 24-14/81.

17. 'Treasures of Italy', *The Times*, 2 Feb 1944.

18. 'Engineers Restoring Naples' Public Works', *S&S* (Algiers edition), 18 Oct 1943.

19. '1051st Engineers Port Construction and Repair Group Unit History', CEHO, p. 13.

20. UKNA, ADM 1/29486, Ref. FOWIT 618, Report by Rear Admiral John A. V. Morse, 8 Dec 1943, p. 1.

21. UKNA, ADM 1/17183, 'Report on Salvage Operations, Western Italy, October 1943–March 1944', p. 4.

22. UKNA, ADM 1/29486, Report by Rear Admiral John A. V. Morse, p. 1; 'Engineer History, Fifth Army, Mediterranean Theater', CEHO, p. 12; 'Tornado in Italy Fails to Halt Medical Heroes', *S&S* (Africa), 9 Oct 1943.

23. '1051st Engineers Port Construction and Repair Group Unit History',

CEHO, p. 13; UKNA, ADM 1/17183, 'Report on Salvage Operations, Western Italy, October 1943–March 1944', pp. 5–6.

24. Forrest A. Hartley testimony, VHP-LoC: www.loc.gov/item/afc2001002.34475

25. UKNA, WO 204/7740, DQMG memo to AFHQ on 'Port Capacity Naples Area', 5 Nov 1943, Ref. Mov.5/542/5.

26. 'Naples Emerges as Top Allied Port', *New York Times*, 3 Sep 1944. See also NARA, RG 331, UD 1978, Box 939, 10000/129/167, 'Report on Activities of Labor Division, Region III AMG to 15 December 1943', p. 5.

27. UKNA, ADM 1/17183, C-in-C Med to Secretary of the Admiralty, 12 May 1944; and Director of Local Defence endorsement, 3 Jul 1944.

28. 'Engineer History, Fifth Army, Mediterranean Theater', CEHO, p. 30; Blumenson, *Salerno to Cassino*, p. 167.

29. NARA, RG 331, UD 1978, Box 67, 10000/100/1091, 'Public Safety Report for the month of December 1943', p. 5; Hume report, p. 30.

30. Ibid., Box 939, 10000/129/167, HQ AMG Region III report dated 18 Jan 1944, 'Report on Activities to 15 December 1943', pp. 10–11; Hume report, p. 22.

31. NARA, RG 331, UD 1978, Box 939, 10000/129/167, HQ AMG Region III report dated 18 Jan 1944, 'Report on Activities to 15 December 1943', pp. 7–9.

32. Hume report, p. 27.

33. O'Reilly's article is reproduced in *S&S* (Algiers edition), 4 Oct 1943: 'City Wrecked, People Crazed From Hunger'.

34. Stanley Anthony Fennell testimony, IWM Sound 4895, Reel 1.

35. UKNA, WO 204/6023, 'Narrative by Chief Advisor AFHQ on PAD, Fire Fighting and Civil Defence Arrangements before and after the Occupation of Naples, October 1943', p. 4.

36. UKNA, WO 204/4092, Pence to Eisenhower, 31 Oct 1943, Ref. PBS 265.

37. Francis Lucas testimony, IWM Sound 28653, Reel 8.

38. NARA, RG 331, UD 1978, Box 939, 10000/129/167, HQ AMG Region III report dated 18 Jan 1944, 'Report on Activities to 15 December 1943', pp. 3–4; 405th Engineer Water Supply Battalion activities described in 'Engineer History, Fifth Army, Mediterranean Theater', CEHO, p. 23; 'New Naples Emerges from Ravage of War', *S&S* (Oran edition), 13 Oct 1943; Hume report, p. 28.

39. Lewis, *Naples '44*, entry for 6 Oct, p. 25.

40. Stanley Anthony Fennell testimony, IWM Sound 4895, Reel 1.

41. UKNA, WO 204/4092, Pence to Eisenhower, 31 Oct 1943, Ref. PBS 265; 'Engineer History, Fifth Army, Mediterranean Theater', CEHO, p. 30.

42. UKNA, ADM 1/29486, Report by Rear Admiral John A. V. Morse, p. 4.

43. UKNA, WO 204/4092, Pence to Eisenhower, 31 Oct 1943, Ref. PBS 265.

44. Ibid.; and NARA, RG 331, UD 1978, Box 939, 10000/129/167, HQ AMG Region III report dated 18 Jan 1944, 'Report on Activities to 15 December 1943', p. 4.

Chapter 5: Underground

1. Jordan Lancaster, *In the Shadow of Vesuvius* (London: Tauris Parke, 2009), p. 90.

2. Eleonora Puntillo, *Grotte e caverne di Napoli: La città sotto la città* (Rome: Newton Compton, 1994), pp. 11, 16, 46.

3. Ibid., p. 31.

4. Ibid. p. 42.

5. Ibid., pp. 18–24.

6. Matilde Serao, *Il ventre di Napoli* (Naples: F. Perrella, 1906), p. 35; Carminie Allocca and Giuseppe Errico, *O Munaciello: Storia e storie di uno*

spiritello napoletano (Naples: Pironti, 2003).

7. For example the *monaciello* appears in Paolo Sorrentino's Oscar-nominated drama about life in the city during the 1980s, *È stata la mano di Dio* (2021).

8. Paolo De Marco, *Polvere di piselli* (Naples: Liguori, 1996), p. 56. See also Lewis, *Naples '44*, p. 32, entry for 13 Oct.

9. Carlo Celano, *Notizie del bello dell'antico e del curioso della città di Napoli*, ed. Giovanni Battista Chiarini (Naples: Edizioni dell'Anticaglia, 2000), Vol. V, Pt I, *Giornata Settima*, pp. 309–11.

10. Lewis, *Naples '44*, p. 34, entry for 13 Oct.

11. 'Delayed Action Mine in Naples', *The Times*, 8 Oct 1943; Noel Monks quoted in 'German Mine Kills Hundreds in Naples', *S&S* (Africa), 9 Oct 1943. In Monks' own article for the *Daily Mail* he toned down his remarks – see 'One More Naples Atrocity', *Daily Mail*, 8 Oct 1943.

12. 'Fifty Killed in Naples Blast', *S&S* (Oran Daily), 12 Oct 1943.

13. UKNA, WO 204/6023, 'Narrative by Chief Advisor AFHQ on PAD, Fire Fighting and Civil Defence Arrangements before and after the Occupation of Naples, October 1943', p. 5.

14. De Marco, *Polvere di piselli*, p. 23.

15. Ibid.; on 21 October the *New York Times* was still reporting that 100 had been killed on this date, even though the actual total had already been revised down to about fifty.

16. '10 More Killed in Naples by Time Bomb Explosion', *New York Times*, 21 Oct 1943. Those killed belonged to Coy B, 307th Airborne Engineer Btn; and Coy H, 36th Engineer Combat Regt: see 'Engineer History, Fifth Army, Mediterranean Theater', CEHO, p. 35. Colonel Hume reported slightly different figures to the Secretary of State: 24 killed and 47

wounded: see De Marco, *Polvere di piselli*, p. 23.

17. *Il Risorgimento*, 21 Oct 1943; '10 More Killed in Naples by Time Bomb Explosion', *New York Times*, 21 Oct 1943; 'German Time Bomb Kills Ten in Naples', *S&S* (Algiers Daily), 22 Oct 1943.

18. NARA, RG 331, UD 1978, Box 939, 10000/129/168, Naples City Police Dept, 'Report on Activities to 15th December 1943', p. 4.

19. 'Naples Emerging from Chaos', *S&S* (Algiers Daily), 12 Oct 1943.

20. Stanley Anthony Fennell testimony, IWM Sound 4895, Reel 1.

21. Lt Col. Lester J. Hensley's report, NARA, RG 331, UD 1978, 10000/129/167, HQ Region III, Transportation Communications and Public Utilities, 'Report on Activities to 15 December', p. 5. See also 'Half Naples Evacuated in Fear of Mines as Power Is Restored', *New York Times*, 2 Nov 1943; and '400,000 in Hills Watch as Naples Turns On Lights', *S&S* (Africa), 6 Nov 1943.

22. Hensley report, ibid.; Lewis, *Naples '44*, p. 40, Aldo Stefanile, *I cento bombardimenti di Napoli: I giorni delle Am-Lire* (Naples: Alberto Marotta, 1968), p. 184.

23. Lewis, *Naples '44*, p. 40. Lewis, who often got dates wrong, recorded this event as happening on 23 Oct 1943.

24. NARA, RG 331, UD 1978, Box 4826, 10260/143/209, HQ Region III, Public Safety Office, 'Report for the week ending 6th February 1944', p. 3.

25. Ibid., 10260/143/210, HQ Region III, 'Public Safety Report for the month of December 1943', p. 12.

26. Ibid., 10260/143/209, HQ Region III, Public Safety Office, 'Report for the week ending 1 Jan 1944', pp. 1–2.

Chapter 6: Allied Military Government

1. For a brief biography of Hume see De Marco, *Polvere di piselli*, p. 29.

2. Hume report, p. 7.

3. For different accounts of these first encounters, see Hume report, pp. 7–8; and Filippo Caracciolo di Castagneto, *'43–'44: Diario di Napoli* (Florence: Vallecchi, 1964), pp. 56–7, entries for 1 and 2 Oct 1943.

4. 'Political, Month of December 1943', p. 1; and 'Public Safety Report for the month of December 1943', p. 4, NARA, RG 331, UD 1978, Box 67, 10000/100/1091. See also Hume report, p. 40.

5. Caracciolo di Castagneto, *'43–'44*, pp. 56–7, entry for 2 Oct 1943.

6. Theodore J. Shannon testimony, VHP-LoC: www.loc.gov/item/afc2001001.68906

7. Ibid. See also Thomas R. Fisher, 'Allied Military Government in Italy', *Annals of the American Academy of Political and Social Science*, Vol. 267 (Jan 1950), p. 121, who confirms such impressions.

8. NARA, RG 331, UD 1978, Box 939, 10000/100/168, 'Activities Report for AMG Naples Province from 14th September to 15th December 1943', pp. 9–10.

9. Ibid., Box 4826, 10260/143/210, HQ Region III, 'Public Safety Report for the month of December 1943', p. 4.

10. Ibid., Box 67, 10000/100/1091, 'Monthly Report – Public Health and Welfare Department, Region III' (month of December), p. 5.

11. Ibid., Box 62, 10000/100/1040, HQ AMG, 'Sub-Commission Public Health and Welfare Report – Month of December 1943', p. 2.

12. George C. S. Benson and Maurice Neufeld, 'American Military Government in Italy', in Carl J. Friedrich (ed.), *American Experiences in Military Government in World War II* (New York: Rinehart & Co., 1948), p. 120.

13. C. R. S. Harris, *Allied Military Administration of Italy 1943–1945* (London: HMSO, 1957), p. 98.

14. NARA, RG 331, UD 1978, Box 62, 10000/100/1040: 'Forward Echelon of Subcommission for Monuments, Fine Arts and Archives, AMG HQ report for December 1943', pp. 1–2; 'Report covering the activities of the Public Safety Division, HQ AMG, for the month of December 1943', p. 2; HQ AMG Education Subcommission, 'Monthly Report for December 1943'.

15. Hume report, pp. 16–18; NARA, RG 331, UD 1978, Box 62, 10000/100/1040, 'Forward Echelon of Subcommission for Monuments, Fine Arts and Archives, AMG HQ report for December 1943', p. 1.

16. Quoted in Harris, *Allied Military Administration of Italy 1943–1945*, p. 114.

17. Adlai Stevenson, 'Report of FEA Survey Mission to Italy', 5 Feb 1944, Princeton University Library, pp. x–xiv.

18. Benson and Neufeld, 'American Military Government in Italy', pp. 111–12, 117, 119–22.

19. Fisher, 'Allied Military Government in Italy', pp. 117, 122.

Chapter 7: City of Pleasure

1. Eisenhower, *Crusade in Europe*, p. 223.

2. 'Equipment Blunders in Italy', *Daily Mail*, 10 Dec 1943.

3. 'This Campaign is Really Up-Hill', *S&S*, 15 Nov 1943.

4. Ibid.

5. Fred Majdalany, *The Monastery* (London: John Lane The Bodley Head, 1945), p. 52.

6. Private Harold Josephson, quoted in 'Rest Camp', *S&S*, 26 Nov 1943, p. 3.

7. Majdalany, *The Monastery*, p. 52.

8. 'Rest Camp', *S&S*, 26 Nov 1943, p. 3.

9. Ibid.

10. NARA, RG 331, UD 1978, Box 1088, 10000/136/417, 'Economic Facts and Factors', Jul 1944, p. 5.

11. 82d ADM, 'Sicily After-Action Report', p. 80.

12. Arthur Shaw testimony, HMS *Calder*, IWM Sound 22091, Reel 11.

13. 'Here's Situation on Beer in Italy', *S&S*, 16 May 1944.

14. NARA, RG 331, UD 1978, Box 4818, 10260/143/36, Police report, R. Questura di Napoli, File No. 1010104, Div. Gabinetto.

15. Ibid., Lt Col. Doherty memo to Provost Marshal Peninsula Base Section, 19 Nov 1943.

16. Ibid., Enrico Moreno letter to Lt Col. Doherty, 1 Dec 1943.

17. For various anecdotes about such brawls, see IWM Sound testimonies by Rolf Julius Weinberg (19912, Reel 5) and Arthur Edward Sean Crampton (17352, Reel 4). For Italians who got caught in the crossfire, see NARA, RG 331, UD 1978, Box 4818, 10260/143/36, R. Questura di Napoli report 103738I, Div. 2P. G., 16 Nov 1943; and R. Questura di Napoli report 4228, Div. 2A, 25 Nov 1943.

18. PWB report 1, 13 Apr 1944, p. 7 (item 13).

19. NARA, RG 331, UD 1978, Box 4826, 10260/143/210, 'Monthly Report', Allied Province of Avellino, 11 Jan 1944, p. 3

20. Ibid., Box 4818, 10260/143/36, 'Report from questura of 15-12-1943'.

21. See for example the testimony of Anthony John Spencer, who witnessed the savage beating of a black GI after curfew by four MPs, just 100 yards from where the GI was billeted: IWM Sound 20459, Reel 7.

22. PWB report 12, 2 Aug 1944, p. 28 (item 63).

23. NARA, RG 331, UD 1978, Box 4826, 10260/143/210, 'Public Safety Report for the Month of December 1943', 17 Jan 1944, p. 2.

24. Ibid., Box 4818, 10260/143/36, untitled lists of incident reports received 14–18 Dec 1943.

25. Ibid., Box 939, 10000/129/168, 'Report on the activities of Regional Headquarters Public Safety Division to 15th December 1943', p. 8.

26. 'Allied Police Raid "Poison Liquor" Plant', *S&S*, 1 Dec 1943.

27. 'Allied Police Make Another Arrest in Liquor Racket' and 'Four More Stills Closed in Drive', *S&S*, 4 and 6 Dec 1943.

28. Otha Lee Johnson testimony, VHP-LoC: https://www.loc.gov/item/afc2001001.87945

29. See for example the 'Mail Call' section of *S&S*, 17 May 1944.

30. Bill Mauldin, *The Brass Ring* (New York: W. W. Norton & Co., 1971), p. 195.

31. 82d ADM, 'Sicily After-Action Report', p. 82.

32. Richard Stephen Edward Harris testimony, IWM Sound 23432, Reel 7.

33. Wilfred George Beeson testimony, IWM Sound 4802, Reel 28.

34. Peter Francis testimony, IWM Sound 26741, Reel 1.

35. 'Yank About Italy' column, *S&S*, 17 Nov 1943.

36. For musical programmes see the 'Entertainment' section of *S&S*; for Caruso's school friend and *Jealousy* see especially editions for 11 Feb and 30 Jun 1944.

37. 'Entertainment', *S&S*, 18 Apr 1944.

38. Hugh David Richardson testimony, IWM Sound 28743; 'Entertainment', *S&S*, 12 May 1944; Atkinson, *The Day of Battle*, p. 446. Gracie Fields especially, who owned a villa on Capri, performed scores of times.

39. 'Local Entertainment', *S&S*, 11 Feb 1944 and 18 Apr 1944.

40. 'PBS Floor Tourney Attracts Total of 224 Teams for Opening Games', *S&S*, 8 Mar 1944.

41. PWB report 2, 20 Apr 1944, p. 9 (item 25); 'Woods Wins Main Event', *S&S*, 24 Apr 1944.

42. 'Vesuvius Funicolare Open for Business', *S&S*, 27 Jan 1944.

43. Herbert Matthews, 'Vesuvius' Anger Dwarfs War Fury', *New York Times*, 9 Oct 1943.

44. Moorehead, *Eclipse*, p. 68.
45. Alexander Clifford, 'Capri, Isle War Forgot, Still Unchanged', *Daily Mail*, 18 Oct 1943.
46. Moorehead, *Eclipse*, p. 68.
47. PWB report 22, 12 Oct 1944, p. 13 (item 31).
48. NARA, RG 331, UD 1978, Box 62, 10000/100/1040, Memo from Maj. Paul Gardner to Brig. Gen. Arthur W. Pence, 20 Dec 1943.
48. UKNA, WO 204/6264, PWB Information and Censorship Section, Unit No. 8, 'Activities Report for Week Ending 19 August 1944'.
50. PWB report 12, 2 Aug 1944, p. 24 (item 48).
51. NARA, RG 331, UD 1978, Box 4818, 10260/143/36, Giuseppe Puoti affidavit, 21 Nov 1943.
52. PWB report 1, 13 Apr 1944, pp. 6–7 (item 12).
53. Malaparte, *The Skin*, p. 42.

Chapter 8: Epidemic
 1. Priorities for requisitioning property are laid out in 'Administrative Instructions No. 11', 29 Sep 1943 UKNA, WO 204/4388.
 2. Ibid.
 3. Guido Dorso, 'Derequisire le industrie campane', *L'Azione*, 4 Sep 1945.
 4. Summary Report of the UNRRA Observers' Mission to Italy, 15 Sep 1944, UNRRA, S-1245-0000-0273-00001, p. 6.
 5. NARA, RG 331, UD 1978, Box 4826, 10260/143/209, 'Weekly Report' by Office of Commissioner of Public Safety, 10 Jan 1944, p. 3.
 6. Ibid., Box 67, 10000/100/1091, 'Monthly Report – Public Health & Welfare Department, AMG Region III' (Dec), p. 1.
 7. 'Yank About Town' column, *S&S*, 19 Nov 1943.
 8. NARA, RG 331, Box 67, 10000/100/1091, 'Monthly Report – Public Health & Welfare Department, AMG Region III' (Dec), pp. 3–4.
 9. Ibid.
10. UKNA, WO 204/414, 'Typhus Control Board, Minutes of Meeting 24 Jan 1944'.
11. Hume report, p. 13. For a fuller description of conditions, see Chapter 15.
12. For official population figures c. 1650 see Celano, *Notizie del bello dell'antico e del curioso della città di Napoli*, Vol. I, pp. 308–9. For similar figures in the 1880s, see Frank M. Snowden, *Naples in the Time of Cholera, 1884–1911* (New York: Cambridge University Press, 1995), p. 18, and Axel Munthe, *Letters from a Mourning City*, trans. Maud Valérie White (London: John Murray, 1887), p. 75. For figures in 2016 see Comune di Napoli, 'La struttura demografica della popolazione residente nella città di Napoli al 31 dicembre 2016: Dati comunali' on the Comune di Napoli website: https://www.comune.napoli.it/statistica particularly population statistics for municipalities I to V (pp. 78, 84, 90, 96, 102), or quarters 1–14 (pp. 138–9). Specific site for the document:https://www.comune.napoli.it/flex/cm/pages/ServeBLOB.php/L/IT/IDPagina/34362. According to the EU's Eurostats website, in 2022 Naples (NUTS 3 region ITF33) had a population density of 2,545 persons per km2, at least 400 more than its nearest rival (Milan, regions ITC4C and ITC4D): see https://ec.europa.eu/eurostat/databrowser/view/demo_r_d3dens/default/table?lang=en
13. Snowden, *Naples in the Time of Cholera, 1884–1911*, p. 20.
14. Munthe, *Letters from a Mourning City*, p. 76; Snowden, *Naples in the Time of Cholera, 1884–1911*, p. 20.
15. Jessie White Mario, *La Miseria in Napoli* (Naples: Quarto potere, 1978), originally published 1878. See also her shorter essay in English, 'The poor in Naples', in *The Poor in Great Cities* (London: Kegan Paul, Trench, Trübner & Co., 1896), p. 300.

16. Pasquale Villari, *Lettere meridionali*, ed. Luigi Marseglia (Bari: Palomar, 2007), pp. 61–74.

17. Serao, *Il ventre di Napoli*, pp. 9–10.

18. John Santore, *Modern Naples: A Documentary History 1799–1999* (New York: Ithaca, 2001), p. 211.

19. Maria Antonietta Macciocchi, *Letters from Inside the Italian Communist Party to Louis Althusser*, trans. Stephen M. Hellman (London, 1973), p. 91.

20. Celano, *Notizie del bello dell'antico e del curioso della città di Napoli*, Vol. IV, *Quinta Giornata*, pp. 316–17. See also Lancaster, *In the Shadow of Vesuvius*, pp. 68, 98.

21. Snowden, *Naples in the Time of Cholera, 1884–1911*, pp. 15, 374.

22. Ibid., p. 29.

23. Ibid., pp. 252, 329–30.

24. Mauldin, *The Brass Ring*, p. 188.

25. UKNA, WO 220/414, Lt Col. Herbert D. Chalke, 'Notes on the Civil Typhus Outbreak Italy 1943–1944', pp. 1–2; and Appendix B: Telegram from Naples Prefettura to Italian Director Public Health, 6 Sep 1943. See also F. L. Soper et al., 'Typhus Fever in Italy, 1943–1945, and its Control with Louse Powder', *American Journal of Hygiene*, Vol. 45, No. 3 (May 1947), p. 308.

26. UKNA, Chalke, 'Notes on the Civil Typhus Outbreak Italy 1943–1944', pp. 1–2.

27. Soper et al., p. 306.

28. UKNA, Chalke, 'Notes on the Civil Typhus Outbreak Italy 1943–1944', p. 1.

29. UKNA, WO 220/360, Algiers to Etousa, 2 Oct 1943, Ref. 2522; and Brief on Public Health Division AMGOT, 5 Oct 1943.

30. Hume report, p. 29.

31. UKNA, WO 220/414, AMG to AFHQ, 26 Nov 1943.

32. Hume report, p. 27.

33. UKNA, WO 220/414, AMG to AFHQ, 27 Nov 1943; and AFHQ Adv. Admin. Ech. letter, Ref. 3821M, 27 Nov 1943; and Algiers to AGWAR 4 Dec 1943, Ref. W-6853/9634 (NAF 538).

34. UKNA, WO 220/414, AFHQ Adv. Admin. Ech. letter, Ref. 3821M, 5 Dec 1943; Soper et al., p. 309.

35. Soper et al., p. 309.

36. NARA, RG 331, UD 1978, Box 67, 10000/100/1091, 'Report of Region 3 for December 1943', p. 2; and 'Monthly Report – Public Health & Welfare Department, AMG Region III' (Dec), p. 2.

37. UKNA WO 220/414 'Typhus in Naples', conference report.

38. Soper et al., pp. 308, 311; Chalke, 'Notes on the Civil Typhus Outbreak Italy 1943–1944', p. 8.

39. NARA, RG 331, UD 1978, Box 67, 10000/100/1091, 'Report of Region 3 for December 1943', p. 2; and Box 4393, 10241/163/49 'Typhus – Restrictions in Naples', 6 Jan 1944.

40. *Il Risorgimento*, 18 Jan 1944; De Marco, *Polvere di Piselli*, p. 33.

41. WO 220/414, minutes of Typhus Control Board meetings, 17 and 24 Jan 1944.

42. Soper et al., p. 316; UKNA, WO 220/414, minutes of Typhus Control Board meeting 24 Jan 1944; Herbert Chalke, 'DDT: Experience of Its Use During the Italian Campaign', *Proceedings of the Royal Society of Medicine*, Vol. XXXIX, No. 4 (Feb 1946), p. 166.

43. Soper et al., p. 317.

44. NARA, RG 331, UD 1978, Box 4393, 10241/163/49, Crichton to Regional Director Public Health, Region II, 9 Jan 1944.

45. John Miles testimony, IWM Sound 20538, Reel 2.

46. UKNA WO 220/414, 'Minutes of a Meeting of the Local Typhus Committee', 28 Jan 1944, p. 3; Soper et al., p. 309.

47. Soper et al., pp. 328–33; De Marco, *Polvere di piselli*, p. 33.

48. Basil Reeve testimony, IWM Sound 19674, Reel 4. The wider dangers of

DDT would not be discovered until the 1960s. In the meantime, its mass use in Naples without any ill effects was used as evidence of its safety: see Chalke, 'DDT: Experience of Its Use During the Italian Campaign', p. 168.

49. Summary Report of the UNRRA Observers' Mission to Italy, 15 Sep 1944, UNRRA, S-1245-0000-0273-00001, p. 8.

50. Soper et al., pp. 309, 319–20.

51. UKNA, WO 220/414, Cowell to Chief of Staff AFHQ, 18 Jan 1944, on 'Reuters Cable'.

52. Ibid., Brigadier Parkinson (Public Health Subcommission, ACC) to AFHQ 21 Feb 1944.

53. PWB report 12, 2 Aug 1944, p. 21 (item 36).

54. PWB report 9, 30 Jun 1944, p. 15 (item 28).

55. UKNA WO 220/414, 'Minutes of a Meeting of the Local Typhus Committee', 28 Jan 1944, p. 2.

Chapter 9: Hunger

1. Graham Lusk, *Food in Wartime* (London and Philadelphia: W. B. Saunders & Co., 1918), pp. 31–4. Lusk's calorie scale was taken up by the Commission Scientifique Interalliée de Ravitaillement at its Paris conference in October 1918, and later modified by the Health Committee of the League of Nations in 1936. On the basis of scales like this, the US Army medical manual recommended 3,000 calories as the standard ration needed by soldiers in order to maintain their health. All these documents became influential in decision-making about Italy in 1943–44: see NARA, RG 331, UD 1978, Box 1088, 10000/136/417, Economic Facts and Factors March 1944, p. 3; and 10000/132/190, Ellery Stone memorandum, 'Food Ration Scales in Italy', 21 Oct 1944.

2. Alan S. Milward, *War, Economy and Society, 1939–1945* (Berkeley and Los Angeles: University of California Press, 1977), p. 283.

3. Ibid., p. 281; Lizzie Collingham, *The Taste of War* (London: Penguin, 2012), p. 366.

4. 'La carta annonaria realizza per tutti i citadini piena equità e giustizia', *Il Mattino*, 30 Jan 1940.

5. NARA, RG 331, UD 1978, Box 4829, 10260/143/258, 'Combined Report of Market Study for Naples City and Province with special attention to "Black Market" problems', 21 Nov 1943, pp. 1–2.

6. Ibid., UD 1978b, Box 4876, 10260/146/96, report on 'Campania – Agriculture', 16 Jun 1943, p. 3.

7. De Marco, *Polvere di piselli*, p. 93: precise figures are 2,577 calories in 1940, 2,269 in 1941 and 2,238 in 1942.

8. NARA, RG 331, UD 1978, Box 4829, 10260/143/258, 'Combined Report of Market Study for Naples City and Province with special attention to "Black Market" problems', 21 Nov 1943.

9. Ibid., Box 1088, 10000/136/417, 'Economic Facts and Factors', Jul 1944, Fig. 1, p. 5.

10. John Marsh Holness testimony, describing the nearby town of Benevento, IWM Sound 18614, Reel 6.

11. Luther E. Hall testimony, VHP-LoC: www.loc.gov/item/ afc2001001.04994302:33:35

12. Leonard L. Neely testimony, website of the 45th US Infantry Division: http:// www.45thdivision.org/Veterans/Neely. htm

13. Henry William Moore testimony, IWM Sound 22129, Reel 2.

14. Lewis, *Naples '44*, pp. 28–9, entries for 8–9 Oct 1943.

15. Ibid.; and Bert Scrivens testimony, IWM Sound 29536, Reel 16.

16. Carroll John Reber testimony, VHP-LoC: www.loc.gov/item/ afc2001001.64925

17. Laurence James Rector testimony, VHP-LoC: www.loc.gov/item/ afc2001001.103109

18. Philip H. Fischer testimony, VHP-LoC: www.loc.gov/item/afc2001001.05500

19. Berchard Lamar Glant testimony, VHP-LoC: www.loc.gov/item/afc2001001.33801

20. UKNA, WO 220/362, 'Basic Documents Establishing Allied Military Government of Occupied Territory – AMGOT', Appendices, Proclamation No. 8.

21. UKNA, WO 220/333, 'AMGOT Plan for Italy', p. 15, paragraph 72.

22. Ibid., 'AMGOT Plan for Italy' and 'Revised AMGOT plan'.

23. NARA, RG 331, UD 1978b, Box 4876, 10260/146/96, report on 'Campania – Agriculture', 16 Jun 1943, p. 3.

24. UKNA, WO 204/2161, Whaley-Eaton Newsletter, 17 Aug 1943.

25. UKNA, WO 204/12335, 'Inter-Service Topographical Department "C" Report on the Port and Town of Naples', 17 Jul 1943, pp. 83–4. Also NARA, RG 331, UD 1978, Box 4876, 10260/146/96, 'Campania – Agriculture', 16 Jun 1943, p. 1; and Box 939, 10000/129/168, 'Agricultural Division – Region III – Report of Activities up to 15 December', p. 11.

26. UNRRA, S-1245-0000-0272-00001, Italy 1944 – Observers' Mission – General: 'Intelligence Memorandum no. 6', 20 Jun 1944, p. 8.

27. NARA, RG 331, UD 1978, Box 939, 10000/129/1968, 'Agricultural Division – Region III – Report of Activities up to 15 December', p. 4.

28. Propaganda leaflet quoted in full in Hume report, pp. 5–6.

29. NARA, RG 331, UD 1978, Box 939, 10000/129/168, Economics and Civilian Supply report, 'Oct. 1st to Nov. 16th 1943', p. 4.

30. Ibid., HQ AMG Region III, Agricultural Section, 'Wheat Situation Meridional Italy', p. 2; and Economics & Supply Section, 'Activities of Supply Branch to 15 Dec 1943', Appendix F.

31. NARA, RG 331, UD 1978, Box 67, 10000/100/1091, 'Economics and Supply Region III – Report for December 1943'.

32. Ibid., p. 1.

33. UNRRA, S-1245-0000-0272-00001, Italy 1944 – Observers' Mission – General: 'Intelligence Memorandum no.5', 13 Jun 1944, p. 4: the report quoted is from March 1944.

34. NARA, RG 331, UD 1978, Box 4830, 10260/143/260, 'Riots and Demonstrations'.

35. Ibid., Box 67, 10000/100/1091, 'Monthly Report – Public Health & Welfare Department, AMG Region III', p. 3.

36. Mario Palermo, *Memoria di un comunista napoletano* (Parma: Guanda, 1975), p. 171.

37. NARA, RG 331, UD 1978, Box 67, 10000/100/1091, 'Monthly Report – Public Health & Welfare Department, AMG Region III', p. 3.

38. Hume report, p. 24.

39. UNRRA, S-1245-0000-0272-00001, Italy 1944 – Observers' Mission – General: 'Intelligence Memorandum no.5', 13 Jun 1944, p. 5.

40. NARA, RG 331, UD 1978, Box 62, 10000/100/1040, HQ AMG Industry & Commerce Sub-Commission, 'Monthly Report – December 1943', pp. 4–5.

41. Ibid., Box 4829, 10260/143/258, 'Combined Report of Market Study for Naples City and Province with special attention to "Black Market" problems', 21 Nov 1943, p. 2.

42. Ibid., Box 939, 10000/129/168, 'Agricultural Division – Region 3 – Report on Activities up to 15 December', p. 8.

43. Ibid., pp. 9–10.

44. Ibid., p. 13.

45. Ibid., Box 67, 10000/100/1091, 'Economics and Supply Region III – Report for December 1943'; and Agricultural Section 'Activities Report for the Month of December 1943'.

46. Ibid., 'Monthly Report – Public Health & Welfare Department, AMG Region III', p. 3.

47. Ibid., Box 939, 10000/129/168, Economics and Civilian Supply report, 'Oct. 1st to Nov. 16th 1943', p. 5.

48. Benson and Neufeld, 'American Military Government in Italy', pp. 138–9; Harris, *Allied Military Administration of Italy 1943–1945*, p. 217.

49. Eva Erminia Denson testimony, VHP-LoC: www.loc.gov/item/afc2001001.55454

50. Benson and Neufeld, 'American Military Government in Italy', pp. 140–1.

51. Ibid., p. 140; Stevenson, 'Report of FEA Survey Mission to Italy', p. 27; Harris, *Allied Military Administration of Italy 1943–1945*, pp. 381–2.

52. Benson and Neufeld, 'American Military Government in Italy', p. 140.

53. 'They See Naples and Buy', *Daily Mail*, 25 Nov 1943.

54. Laurence James Rector testimony, VHP-LoC: www.loc.gov/item/afc2001001.103109

55. Harold G. Horning, 'Army Years: 20 November 1941–27 June 1947', TMFM, p. 40.

56. PWB report, 3 May 1944, p. 4 (item 5).

57. NARA, RG 331, UD 1978, Box 4826, 10260/143/209, weekly report for week ending 30 Jan 1944, p. 1; for the ease and frequency of evading typhus restrictions see also William Broderick personal account, TMFM.

58. Julian H. Philips, 'Hunger Flourished', TMFM, pp. 3–4.

59. NARA, RG 331, UD 1978, 10000/129/167 'Report on Activities of Labor Division, Region III AMG to 15 December 1943', p. 5; see also figures in De Marco, *Polvere di piselli*, pp. 204–5.

60. NARA, RG 331, UD 1978, Box 1088, 10000/136/417, 'Economic Facts and Factors, March 1944', Fig. 3, p. 6.

61. UNRRA, S-1245-0000-0272-00001, Italy 1944 – Observers' Mission – General: 'Intelligence Memorandum no. 6', 20 Jun 1944, p. 4; NARA, RG 331, UD 1978, 10260/143/258, 'Report on the Black Market in Naples by Maj. B. Mattei', p. 2.

62. Maurice Crowther testimony, IWM Sound 19093, Reel 2.

63. Hugh Powell testimony, IWM Sound 10351, Reel 4.

64. Ibid., Box 1088, 10000/136/417, 'Economic Facts and Factors, July 1944', Fig. 1, pp. 5–6.

65. NARA, RG 331, UD 1978B, Box 4876, 10260/146/92, Morse to Eisenhower, 'Treatment of Civilian Labour and Civilians Generally – Naples Area', 8 Jan 1944; and 'Supply of Food to Employees, Contractors and Workmen', 20 Jan 1944.

66. Ibid., 10260/146/95, Labor Division AMG Region 3, 'Weekly Report – Labor Supply', 25 Jan 1944.

67. Ibid., 10260/146/95, Labor Division AMG Region 3, 'Weekly Report – January 23 to 29, 1944', p. 2.

68. Ibid., 10260/146/95, Labor Division AMG Region 3, Pottle letter to Lane, 22 Feb 1944, p. 3.

69. PWB report 8, 23 Jun 1944, p. 1 (item 1).

70. PWB report 10, 19 Jul 1944, pp. 15–18 (item 29).

71. Hume report, p. 13.

72. NARA, RG 331, UD 1978, Box 4829, 10260/143/260, documents on 'Riots and Disturbances' in Region III.

73. AFHQ message to CCS in Washington, 14 Dec 1943, quoted in Harris, *Allied Administration of Italy 1943–1945*, p. 89, n. 1.

74. US Consulate General, Naples, 3 Jun 1944: quoted in UNRRA, S-1245-0000-0272-00001, Italy 1944 – Observers' Mission – General: 'Intelligence Memorandum no. 6', 20 Jun 1944, p. 3.

75. Lewis, *Naples '44*, p. 105, entry for 5 Apr.

Chapter 10: Prostitution

1. Lancaster, *In the Shadow of Vesuvius*, pp. 9–11; Gunn, *Naples*, p. 49.
2. Malaparte, *The Skin*, p. 224.
3. Ibid., p. 221.
4. Lewis, *Naples '44*, pp. 55–6, entry for 25 Nov.
5. Malaparte, *The Skin*, pp. 220–1.
6. Atkinson, *The Day of Battle*, p. 246.
7. Keith Lowe, *Savage Continent* (London: Viking, 2012), p. 39.
8. For an analysis of this and other related myths, and their cost, see Lowe, *The Fear and the Freedom*, pp. 15–80.
9. Malaparte, *The Skin*, p. 34.
10. Burns, *The Gallery*, p. 206.
11. Paul W. Brown, *The Whorehouse of the World: Tales of Wartime Italy – Casablanca, Algiers and Sicily* (Bloomington, Indiana: Authorhouse, 2004), pp. 1–2.
12. Jack Duncan testimony, IWM Sound 12985, Reel 5.
13. Burns, *The Gallery*, p. 208.
14. Brown, *The Whorehouse of the World*, p. 268.
15. Gunn, *Naples*, p. 242.
16. Harold Horning, 'Army Years: 20 Nov 1941–27 June 1945', TMFM, pp. 41–2.
17. Leland O. Carmany testimony, VHP-LoC: https://www.loc.gov/item/afc2001001.01502
18. Burns, *The Gallery*, p. 211.
19. Jack Duncan testimony, IWM Sound 12985, Reel 5.
20. Lewis, *Naples '44*, p. 175, entry for 8 Oct.
21. Brown, *The Whorehouse of the World*, p. 267.
22. Eva Erminia Denson testimony, VHP-LoC: https://www.loc.gov/item/afc2001001.55454
23. PWB report 19, p. 12 (item 14).
24. Brown, *The Whorehouse of the World*, p. 406.
25. Lewis, *Naples '44*, p. 100, entry for 26 Mar.
26. John Evelyn, *The Diary of John Evelyn* (London: Macmillan, 1906), Vol. I, entry for 6 Feb 1645, p. 226.
27. S. Di Giacomo, *La prostituzione in Napoli nei secoli XV, XVI e XVII: Documenti inediti* (Naples: Riccardo Marghieri, 1896), pp. 175–6.
28. NARA, RG 331, UD 1978, Box 4830, 10260/143/279, HQc3 District report on 'Venereal Disease', 26 Feb 1944, p. 2.
29. *Il Giornale*, 11 Jan 1943, quoted in PWB report 36, 19 Jan 1945, p. 18 (Item 11).
30. UKNA, WO 204/1265, PWB report 49, 19 Apr 1945, p. 18 (item 9). See also Lewis, *Naples '44*, who quotes similar but slightly different figures, entry for 5 Apr 1944, p. 105.
31. Brown, *The Whorehouse of the World*, p. 258.
32. PWB report 26, 9 Nov 1944, p. 9 (item 11).
33. PWB report 18, 14 Sept 1944, p. 8 (item 5).
34. PWB report 26, 9 Nov 1944, p. 10 (item 11); for average wages for women, see PWB report 10, 19 Jul 1944, p. 18 (item 29).
35. Jack Duncan testimony, IWM Sound 12985, Reel 5.
36. Laurence James Rector testimony, VHP-LoC: https://www.loc.gov/item/afc2001001.103109
37. Brown, *The Whorehouse of the World*, p. 409.
38. PWB report 26, 9 Nov 1944, pp. 9–10 (item 11).
39. Frank Stanley Luff testimony, IWM Sound 27267, Reel 5.
40. Julian H. Philips, 'Hunger Flourished', TMFM, pp. 3–4.
41. Bill Harr, *Combat Boots* (New York: Exposition Press, 1952), p. 52.
42. Wilfred George Beeson testimony, IWM Sound 4802, Reel 29.
43. Lewis, *Naples '44*, p. 24, entry for 4 Oct.
44. Ray Hunting, typescript memoir, IWM Docs 10519 P339, pp. 273–4.
45. Vere L. Williams, typescript memoir, part 3: https://www.45thdivision.org/Veterans/VWilliams2.htm

46. Elvin E. Thomas testimony, VHP-LoC: https://www.loc.gov/item/afc2001001.33621

47. NARA, RG 331, Entry 1978, 10260/143/36, CC.RR. report San Giovanni a Teduccio, 29 Nov 1943.

48. 82d ADM, 'Sicily After Action Report', p. 83.

49. Vere L. Williams, typescript memoir, part 2: https://www.45thdivision.org/Veterans/VWilliams_1.htm

50. Ibid.

51. PWB report 19, 21 Sept 1944, p. 12 (item 14).

52. PWB report 26, 9 Nov 1944, p. 12 (item 11).

53. PWB report 19, 21 Sept 1944, pp. 12–13 (item 14).

54. For a more detailed discussion of this topic on a Europe-wide scale, see Lowe, Savage Continent, pp. 40–4, 51–7, 163–78.

55. PWB report 20, 28 Sept 1944, p. 14 (item 23).

56. Mary Louise Roberts, 'The Price of Discretion: Prostitution, Venereal Disease, and the American Military in France, 1944–1946', American Historical Review, Vol. 115, Issue 4, p. 1004.

57. Quoted by Roberts, ibid.

58. NARA, RG 331, UD 1978, 10260/143/210, 'Public Safety Report for the month of December 1943', p. 3.

58. For comparative rates of VD in the US Fifth Army, see the official history of the US Army in World War II, The Medical Department, Part II by Charles M. Wiltse, Medical Service in the Mediterranean and Minor Theaters (Washington DC: US Army Center for Military History, 1987), p. 259. For the 82nd Airborne's hedonism, see 82d ADM, 'Sicily After Action Report', p. 80.

69. NARA, RG 331, Entry 65, Box 7, memo dated 22 Apr 1944, quoted by Roberts, 'The Price of Discretion', p. 1008.

61. War Office, Statistical Report on the Health of the Army 1943–1945 (London: HMSO, 1948), pp. 30, 63, 89.

62. 252 out of 338 cases: see NARA, RG 331, Entry 1978, Box 4830, 10260/143/279, 'Minutes of a Meeting on Venereal Disease Held in the Office of the Regional D. P. H. & W., AMG Region III, on 10 January 1944', p. 2.

63. War Office, Statistical Report on the Health of the Army 1943–1945, p. 91; Medical Dept, US Army, Preventive Medicine in World War II, Vol. V: Communicable Diseases Transmitted Through Contact or by Unknown Means (Washington DC: Office of the Surgeon General, Dept of the Army, 1960), pp. 474–5, 477.

64. NARA, RG 331, UD 1978, 10000/100/1091, 'Report of Region 3 for December 1943', p. 12.

65. Ibid., 'Monthly report, Public Health & Welfare Department', December 1943, AMG Region III', p. 6; and Box 4830, 10260/143/279, memo on 'Venereal Disease', 26 Feb 1944.

66. Surgeon's annual report, 3rd Division, quoted in Wiltse, Medical Service in the Mediterranean and Minor Theaters, p. 258.

67. NARA, RG 331, UD 1978, Box 4394, 10241/163/49, 'Typhus – Restrictions in Naples', 6 Jan 1944; for typhus as a type of VD, see 'Special Warning' notice to be published in Union Jack in Jan 1944, UKNA, WO 220/414.

68. For posters directed at women, see PWB report 6, 18 May 1944, p. 6 (item 11); for VD posters directed at soldiers, see Brown, The Whorehouse of the World, p. 295, and James Aulich, War Posters: Weapons of Mass Communication (London: Thames & Hudson, 2007), p. 199.

69. James Robinson, Jr, oral history, part 2 of 4, JAMHC: https://ndajams.omeka.net/items/show/1051641

70. NARA, RG 331, UD 1978, Box 4830, 10260/143/279, 'Minutes of a Meeting on Venereal Disease Held in the Office of the Regional D.P. H. & W., AMG Region III, on 10 January 1944', p. 2.

71. Ibid., Box 4830, 10260/143/279, memo on 'Venereal Disease', 26 Feb 1944, p. 4.

72. Ibid., Box 4830, 10260/143/279, 'Minutes of a Meeting on Venereal Disease Held in the Office of the Regional D.P. H. & W., AMG Region III, on 10 January 1944', p. 2.

73. Ibid., Box 4826, 10260/143/210, 'Public Safety Report for the Month of Feb 1944', pp. 1–2.

74. PWB report 26, 9 Nov 1944, p. 9 (item 11).

75. NARA, RG 331, UD 1978, Box 67, 10000/100/1091, 'Public Safety Report for the Month of December 1943', p. 2.

76. Lewis, *Naples '44*, pp. 180–5, entries for 16 and 20 Oct.

77. Susan Zeiger, *Entangling Alliances: Foreign War Brides and American Soldiers in the Twentieth Century* (New York: New York University Press, 2010), pp. 94–102.

78. Ibid., p. 96.

79. For graphic descriptions of these processes, see Brown, *The Whorehouse of the World*, pp. 253, 274, 290–2; and Burns, *The Gallery*, pp. 269–97.

80. Lewis, *Naples '44*, pp. 175–6, entry for 8 Oct 1944.

81. PWB report 6, 18 May 1944, p. 7 (item 17).

82. PWB report 6, 19 Jul 1944, p. 32 (item 53).

83. See my earlier work on this subject, Lowe, *Savage Continent*, pp. 163–72.

84. 'Nella scia della Guerra: bimbi neri nascono …', *L'Azione*, 8 Dec 1945, quoted in Patrizia Salvetti (ed.), *La Campania dal Fascismo alla Repubblica* (Naples: Edizioni Scientifiche Italiane, 1977), Vol. I: *Società e politica*, pp. 699–700. Perhaps the most famous example was the jazz-rock saxophonist James Senese, whose story is told in Andrea Della Monica's 2020 film documentary on Senese's life, *James*.

85. See for example Mieke Kirkels and Chris Dickon, *Dutch Children of African American Liberators* (Jefferson, NC: MacFarlane, 2020); and the film documentary *Brown Babies: The Mischlingskinder Story* (Dir. Regina Griffin, 2011). For illegitimate children with German fathers, see Lowe, *Savage Continent*, pp. 172–8.

Chapter 11: Africans

1. Alexandre Dumas, *Impressions de Voyage: Le Corricolo*, Vol. I (Paris: Michel Lévy Frères, 1865), p. 92.

2. Metternich quoted in Santore, *Modern Naples*, p. 117.

3. Quoted in Benedetto Croce, *History of the Kingdom of Naples*, trans. Frances Frenaye (Chicago and London: Chicago University Press, 1970), p. 242.

4. Constantino Nigra and Luigi Farini, quoted in Denis Mack Smith, *The Making of Italy 1796–1866* (London: Macmillan, 1988), pp. 330–1, 366–7.

5. Renato Fucini, *Napoli a occhio nudo* (Rome: Avagliano, 2004), p. 51.

6. Quoted in Antonino De Francesco, *La palla al piede: una storia del pregiudizio antimeridionale* (Milan: Feltrinelli, 2012), p. 84.

7. George Belfitt Plowman, IWM Sound 20469, Reel 7.

8. Raymond J. Hunting, IWM Docs 10519, 'The Second World War Memoirs of Lieutenant R.J. Hunting', p. 272.

9. Lewis, *Naples '44*, p. 40, entry for 23 Oct.

10. Ernie Pyle, *Brave Men* (Lincoln: University of Nebraska Press, 2001), p. 124.

11. Zeiger, *Entangling Alliances*, p. 95.

12. Edoardo Pansini, *Goliardi e scugnizzi nelle Quattro Giornate napoletane* (Naples: Cimento, 1945), p. 55; PWB report 1, 13 Apr 1944, pp. 6–7 (item 12).

13. PWB report 13, 10 Aug 1944, p. 22 (items 68 & 71).

14. PWB report 20, 28 Sep 1944, p. 12 (item 16).

15. For barriers that were placed in the way of inter-racial marriage between African

American soldiers and white European women, see Zeiger, *Entangling Alliances*, pp. 94–101, 169–73.

16. A. William Perry testimony, VHP-LoC: www.loc.gov/item/afc2001001.51117

17. Leo Longanesi, *Parliamo dell'elefante: Frammente di un diario* (Milan: Longanesi, 1957), pp. 172–3, entry for 1 Nov 1943.

18. Elena Canino, *Clotilde tra due guerre* (Milan: Longanesi, 1957), p. 590, entry for 3 Oct 1943.

19. Ibid., p. 609, entry for 30 Oct 1943.

20. Lowe, *Savage Continent*, pp. 51–7, 164–72.

21. PWB report 10, 19 Jul 1944, p. 32 (item 52); Roy Heber Ridgway testimony, IWM Sound 10350, Reel 3. See also Gabriella Gribaudi, *Guerra totale* (Turin: Bollati Boringhieri, 2005), p. 552.

22. French reports quoted in Gribaudi, *Guerra totale*, p. 552.

23. NARA, RG 331, UD 1978, Box 4826, 10260/143/209, 'Report of Public Safety Division for Week Ending 4 March 1944', p. 3.

24. Ibid., 10260/143/210, 'Monthly Report for May 1944 – Region 3 Public Safety Division', pp. 5–7.

25. PWB report 12, 2 Aug 1944, p. 28 (item 62).

26. NARA, RG 331, UD 1978, Box 4826, 10260/143/210, 'Monthly Report', Public Safety Section for Avellino Province, 31 July 1944', p. 1.

27. PWB report 15, 24 Aug 1944, p. 22 (item 50).

28. NARA, RG 331, UD 1978, Box 4826, 10260/143/210, 'Monthly Report for May 1944 – Region 3 Public Safety Division', p. 4.

29. Service Historique de l'Armée de Terre documents, quoted in Gribaudi, *Guerra totale*, pp. 561–2.

30. UKNA WO 204/9765 'Goums trouble', 25 May 1944.

31. Anonella A., quoted in Gribaudi, *Guerra totale*, p. 526.

32. Silvana R., quoted in ibid., pp. 525–6.

33. Maria P., quoted in ibid., p. 517.

34. Ludovica L., quoted in ibid., p. 524.

35. Gribaudi, *Guerra totale*, pp. 539–41, 547–9.

36. Quoted in ibid., pp. 527–8.

37. Quoted in ibid., p. 529.

38. Quoted in ibid., p. 530.

39. NARA, RG 331, UD 1978, Box 4826, 10260/143/210, 'Monthly Report for May 1944 – Region 3 Public Safety Division', p. 6; and Box 4818, 10260/143/37, 'Report' to Officer Commanding 510 Provost Company, 5 Aug 1944.

40. PWB report 10, 19 Jul 1944, prelims.

41. Lowe, *Savage Continent*, p. 52.

Chapter 12: A Brief History of Resentment

1. Private Jane McGovern, T-5 Jean Bambeck and T-5 Jean Prazek, quoted in 'Camera Comments', *S&S*, 22 Dec 1943.

2. Private Jane McGovern, T-5 Jean Bambeck, T-5 Jean Prazek, Pvt Yolanda Alcuri and PFC Harriett Barker, quoted in 'Camera Comments', *S&S*, 22 Dec 1943.

3. Thomas Lister oral testimony, IWM Sound 12825, Reel 12.

Chapter 13: Dreams of Revolution

1. Johann Andreas Bühel, *Proverbium Italorum: Regnum Neapolitanum Paradisus Est, Sed a Diabolis Habitatus* (Altdorf: Meyer, 1707), p. 19; https://www.digitale-sammlungen.de/en/details/bsb11074055. For a summary in Italian, see Benedetto Croce, *Un paradiso abitato da diavoli* (Milan: Adelphi, 2006), p. 18.

2. For descriptions of Masaniello's revolt see Michelangelo Schipa, *Masaniello* (Bari: Giuseppe Laterza & Figli, 1925); Rosario Villari, *The Revolt of Naples* (Cambridge: Polity Press, 1993); and Silvana D'Alessio, *Masaniello: La sua vita e il mito in Europa* (Rome: Salerno, 2007).

3. Marino Verde, quoted in Schipa, *Masaniello*, p. 86.

4. For the myth of Masaniello as a prototype for rebellion in Naples, see especially Aurelio Musi, *Masaniello: 'Il masaniellismo' e la degradazione di un mito* (Soveria Mannelli: Rubbettino, 2019).

5. According to actor and playwright Raffaele Viviani, who took part in the play as a child. See 'Masaniello, ieri e oggi', *Il Mattino*, 12 Jul 1941, quoted in Giovanna Percopo and Sergio Riccio (eds), *La Campania dal fascismo alla repubblica*, Vol. II: *Società e cultura* (Naples: Edizioni Scientifiche Italiane, 1977), p. 151.

6. Antonio Tarsia in Curia, *La verità sulle Quattro Giornate di Napoli* (Naples: Edizioni Scientifiche Italiane, 1993), p. 45; the satirical weekly newspaper *Loggione* also carried Leftist poems by an author calling himself 'Masaniello': see Percopo and Riccio (eds), *La Campania dal fascismo alla repubblica*, Vol. II, pp. 348, 359.

7. Raffaele Viviani, 'Masaniello, ieri e oggi', *Il Mattino*, 12 Jul 1941, quoted in Percopo and Riccio (eds), *La Campania dal fascismo alla repubblica*, Vol. II, p. 152.

8. Croce, *History of the Kingdom of Naples*, pp. 38–9: originally published in 1925. Italian edition: Benedetto Croce, *Storia del Regno di Napoli* (Milan: Adelphi, 1996), ed. G. Galasso, p. 61.

Chapter 14: Queen of the Mediterranean

1. Mussolini speeches at San Carlo Theatre, and afterwards in Piazza del Plebiscito, in Edoardo and Duilio Susmel, *Opera Omnia di Benito Mussolini* (Florence: La Fenice, 1951–62), Vol. XVIII (1956), pp. 457, 459.

2. See for example Pietro Nenni, *Sei anni di Guerra civile* (Milan: Rizzoli, 1945); Renzo De Felice, *Mussolini il fascista*, Vol. I: *La conquista del potere 1921–1925* (Turin: Einaudi, 1966); Emilio Gentile, *Storia del partito fascista 1919–1922: Movimento e milizia* (Rome-Bari: Laterza, 1989); Mimmo Franzinelli,

Squadristi: Protagonisti e techniche della violenza fascista 1919–1922 (Milan: Feltrinelli, 2003); Michael R. Ebner, *Ordinary Violence in Mussolini's Italy* (New York: Cambridge University Press, 2011).

3. P. A. Allum, *Politics and Society in Post-War Naples* (Cambridge: Cambridge University Press, 1973); Dahlia Sabina Elazar, 'Electoral democracy, revolutionary politics and political violence: the emergence of Fascism in Italy, 1920–21', *British Journal of Sociology*, Vol. 51, Issue 3 (Sep 2000), pp. 461–88.

4. Giacomo De Antonellis, *Napoli sotto il regime* (Milan: Donati, 1972), pp. 48–51.

5. Antonio Barone, *Piazza Spartaco: Il movimento operaio e socialista a Castellammare di Stabia 1900–1922* (Rome: Riuniti, 1974), pp. 126–63.

6. De Antonellis, *Napoli sotto il regime*, pp. 61–2.

7. Barone, *Piazza Spartaco*, p. 176.

8. Gloria Chianese, 'Movimento operaio e sindacato a Napoli dall'armistizio allo sciopero generale del dicembre 1946', in Pietro Laveglia (ed.), *Mezzogiorno e fascismo: Atti del convegno nazionale di studi promosso della Regione Campania* (Naples: Edizioni Scientifiche Italiane, 1978), Vol. I, pp. 95–6; Pasquale Villani, *Gerarchi e fascismo a Napoli (1921–1943)* (Bologna: Mulino, 2013), pp. 20–7.

9. Elazar, 'Electoral democracy, revolutionary politics and political violence', p. 472.

10. See for example Carlo Cassola's description of the Fascist takeover of Nocera in his letter to Giovanni Amendola, 26 Feb 1923: in Eva Amendola-Kühn, *Vita con Giovanni Amendola, Epistolario, 1903–1926* (Florence: Parenti, 1961), doc. 474, pp. 488–91.

11. Gentile, *Storia del Partito Fascista 1919–1922*, p. 499.

12. For the aesthetics and iconography of Fascist violence, see Gentile, *Storia del*

Partito Fascista 1919–1922, pp. 499–503; and Christopher Duggan, *The Force of Destiny: A History of Italy since 1796* (London: Allen Lane, 2007), pp. 425–6.

13. Roberto Farinacci, *Un period aureo del partito nazionale fascista* (Foligno: Franco Campitelli, 1927), p. 31, speech at Portoferraio, 22 Feb 1925.

14. Mussolini's speech to Chamber of Deputies, 3 Jan 1925, in Edoardo and Duilio Susmel, *Opera Omnia di Benito Mussolini*, Vol. XXI (1956), p. 240.

15. Duggan, *The Force of Destiny*, p. 494.

16. Ibid., p. 496. For the horrific conditions in these camps see Giorgio Rochat, *Guerre Italiane in Libia e in Etiopia: Studi military 1921–1939* (Paese/Treviso: Pagus, 1991), pp. 80–7.

17. Quoted in Rochat, *Guerre Italiane in Libia e in Etiopia*, p. 158.

18. Quoted in Galeazzo Ciano, *Ciano's Diary 1937–1938* (London: Methuen, 1952), trans. Andreas Mayor, p. 92, entry for 20 Mar 1938.

19. Piero Bellanova, 'To the Soldiers' Woman', in his collection *Bombarded Naples Sings* (Leicester: Troubador, 2018), trans. Christopher Adams.

20. Piero Bellanova, 'Joy', in ibid., p. 97.

21. Vittorio Mussolini, quoted in Duggan, *The Force of Destiny*, p. 504.

22. See the photograph of students carrying placards calling for the invasion of Tunisia, Corsica and Nice in Attilio Wanderlingh, *Storia Fotografica di Napoli 1939–1944* (Naples: Intra Moenia, 1998), p. 39.

23. 'Il Sovrano a Napoli', *Il Mattino*, 10 May 1940. For details of the many construction projects of this era, see De Antonellis, *Napoli sotto il regime*, pp. 186–93; and Villani, *Gerarchi e Fascismo a Napoli (1921–1943)*, pp. 78–84.

24. 'Opere per la potenza d'Italia iniziate a Napoli dal Duce' *Il Mattino*, 2 Apr 1939.

25. De Antonellis, *Napoli sotto il regime*, p. 189.

26. Wanderlingh, *Storia Fotografica di Napoli 1939–1944*, p. 20.

27. Laura Guidi, 'Le condizioni abitative e lo sviluppo edilizio a Napoli tra le due guerre', in Laveglia (ed.), *Mezzogiorno e Fascismo*, Vol. II, pp. 564–8.

28. Ibid., pp. 558–9, 564.

29. Ibid., p. 574.

30. Frank Snowden, *The Conquest of Malaria: Italy 1900–1962* (New Haven: Yale University Press, 2006), pp. 155–7.

31. Carlo Levi, *Christ Stopped at Eboli* (New York: Farrar, Straus & Giroux, 1947), pp. 45–6.

32. Villani, *Gerarchi e Fascismo a Napoli (1921–1943)*, p. 82.

33. *Il Mattino*, 10 May 1940.

34. Canino, *Clotilde tra due guerre*, p. 483, entry for 9 May 1940; Brian L. McClaren, 'Architecture During Wartime: The Mostra d'Oltremare and Esposizione Universale di Roma', in Andrew Herscher and Anooradha Siddiqi (eds), *Spatial Violence* (London: Routledge, 2017), pp. 299–318.

35. Canino, *Clotilde tra due guerre*, p. 469, entry for 10 Nov 1939.

36. Amadeo Maiuri, *Taccuino napoletano* (Naples: Vajro, 1956), p. 17, entry for 16 Jun 1940.

37. 'La replica degli intellettuali non fascisti al manifesto di Giovanni Gentile', *Il Popolo*, 1 May 1925.

38. 'La conversione', *Il Mondo*, 1 Apr 1923, quoted in Emilio Gentile, *E fu subito regime: Il fascismo e la Marcia su Roma* (Bari: Laterza, 2012), p. 276.

39. Teresa Ciciliano quoted in Gribaudi, *Guerra totale*, p. 279.

40. Francesco Russo, quoted in ibid., p. 278.

41. Rocco D'Ambra testimony in Pasquale Schiano, *La resistenza nel Napoletano* (Naples, Foggia and Bari: CESP, 1965), p. 153; and Salvatore Cacciapuoti, *Storia di un operaio napoletano* (Rome: Riuniti, 1972), pp. 55–76.

42. Pansini, *Goliardi e scugnizzi nelle Quattro Giornate napoletane*, p. 33.

For dozens of examples of other acts, see the many official reports on subversion in and around Naples, and supporting documents, reproduced in Salvetti (ed.), *La Campania dal Fascismo alla Repubblica*, Vol. I, pp. 124–54.

Chapter 15: Descent to War

1. 'Patriottismo ed entusiasmo di Napoli guerriera', *Il Corriere di Napoli*, 11 Jun 1940.
2. 'Il discorso dell'intervento accolto in provincia tra vibranti manifestazioni al Duce', *Il Mattino*, 12 Jun 1940.
3. De Jaco, *Le Quattro Giornate di Napoli*, pp. 165–6.
4. For eyewitness testimonies, see Gribaudi, *Guerra totale*, pp. 46–8.
5. Delia Tafuri, quoted in Gribaudi, *Guerra totale*, p. 8.
6. Stefanile, *I cento bombardimenti di Napoli*, p. 15.
7. Maiuri, *Taccuino napoletano*, p. 17, entry for 16 Jun 1940.
8. See *Il Mattino*, 12 Jun 1940.
9. Sergio Lambiasse and G. Battista Nazzaro, *Napoli 1940–1945* (Milan: Longanesi, 1978), pp. 43–7.
10. Ibid., pp. 32–7, 53–66.
11. Canino, *Clotilde tra due guerre*, p. 488, entry for 30 Jun 1940.
12. 'Alla ricerca di grotte e caverne per ricoveri', *Il Mattino*, 1 Jan 1943.
13. Maiuri, *Taccuino napoletano*, p. 17, entry for 11–15 Jun 1940.
14. Quoted in Canino, *Clotilde tra due guerre*, p. 494, entry for 31 Jul 1940.
15. Air raid 13 Jul 1940, ASN, Prefettura, Gabinetto, busta 1221/1
16. Stefanile, *I cento bombardimenti di Napoli*, p. 15.
17. Maiuri, *Taccuino napoletano*, p. 23, entry for 1 Nov 1940.
18. Air raids 1 Nov, 4 Nov, 2 Dec and 14/15 Dec 1940; ASN, Prefettura, Gabinetto, busta 1221/1; ACS, Ministero dell'Interno, Gabinetto, Cat. A5G, Seconda guerra mondiale, busta 88, fasc. 40-2-50.

19. Air raid 20–21 Jul 1941, ASN, Prefettura, Gabinetto, busta 1221/1. See also ACS, Ministero dell'Interno, Gabinetto, Cat A5G, Seconda guerra mondiale, busta 88, fasc. 40-2-50.
20. Air raid 21–22 Oct 1941, ASN, Prefettura, Gabinetto, busta 1221/1.
21. ASN, Prefettura, Gabinetto, busta 1221/1.
22. Report of 54th Corps Fire Brigade, 28 Oct 1941, ASN, Prefettura, Gabinetto, busta 1221/1.
23. UNPA report, 22 Jul 1941, ASN, Prefettura, Gabinetto, busta 1221/1. See also ACS, Ministero dell'Interno, Gabinetto, Cat A5G, Seconda guerra mondiale, busta 88, fasc. 40-2-50.
24. Telegram Albini to Ministry of Interior, 4 Dec 1942, ASN, Prefettura, Gabinetto, busta 1224/1; raid of 4 Apr 1943, Report of 54th Corps Fire Brigade, ASN, Prefettura, Gabinetto, busta 1226/1.
25. Quoted in Stefanile, *I cento bombardimenti di Napoli*, p. 126.
26. Maiuri, *Taccuino napoletano*, pp. 46–9.
27. Report of 21 Nov 1941, ASN, Prefettura, Gabinetto, busta 1221/1.
28. Report of 27 Mar 1941, 'Relazione sulla situazione politico-economica della provincia', ACS, Min. Int., Dir. Gen. P. S., Div AA.GG.RR 1920–45, Cat. K1-B15, busta.53.
29. Naples police chief to Minister of the Interior, report of 27 Dec 1941, in 'Relazione sulla situazione politico-economica della provincia', ACS, Min. Int., Dir. Gen. P. S., Div AA.GG.RR 1920–45, Cat. K1-B15, busta 53.
30. Police report of 31 Mar 1942, quoted in Salvetti (ed.), *La Campania dal Fascismo alla Repubblica*, Vol. I, pp. 182–4.
31. Police report 31 Dec 1942, quoted in Salvetti (ed.), *La Campania dal Fascismo alla Repubblica*, Vol. I, p. 207.
32. Mussolini speech, Palazzo Venezia, 10 Jun 1940, in Edoardo and Duilio Susmel, *Opera Omnia di Benito Mussolini*, Vol. XXIX (1958), pp. 403–5.

33. Giorgio Rochat, *Le guerre italiane 1935–1943*, p. 216.

34. Ciano, *Diario* (Milan and Rome: Rizzoli, 1948), Vol. 1, pp. 167–8, entry for 18 Sep 1939.

35. Rochat, *Le guerre italiane 1935–1943*, pp. 249–51.

36. Duggan, *The Force of Destiny*, p. 518.

37. R. Ernest Dupuy and Trevor N. Dupuy, *The Harper Encyclopedia of Military History* (New York: HarperCollins, 1993), pp. 1173, 1178; Duggan, *The Force of Destiny*, pp. 519–20; Rochat, *Le guerre italiane 1935–1943*, pp. 292–3.

38. Air Historical Group, *The Army Air Forces in World War II, Vol. II: Europe: Torch to Pointblank* (Chicago: University of Chicago Press, 1949, p. 511. See also Rochat, *Le guerre italiane 1935–1943*, pp. 233–4.

39. Lambiasse and Battista Nazzaro, *Napoli 1940–1945*, pp. 48–50.

40. Scholl's reply to Prefect Marcello Vaccari, 26 Mar 1943, quoted in Giovanni Cerchia, *La Seconda Guerra Mondiale nel Mezzogiorno* (Milan: Luni editrice, 2019), p. 148. For Neapolitan documents on traffic accidents and civil disturbances, see ASN, Gabinetto, busta 1248 (particularly the report on 'Disciplina di guerra: Tedeschi'); and busta 53, fasc. 'Relazioni mensili 1943'.

41. Cerchia, *La Seconda Guerra Mondiale nel Mezzogiorno*, pp. 149–50.

42. For contemporary accounts of the explosion, see Gribaudi, *Guerra totale*, pp. 109–24; Stefanile, *I cento bombardamenti di Napoli*, pp. 85–92; De Antonellis, *Napoli sotto il regime*, pp. 224–6.

43. Prefect Vaccari's report to the Minister of the Interior, 31 Mar 1943: ASN, Prefettura, Gabinetto, busta 1330/45.

44. According to the official report of the shipping company, quoted in Stefanile, *I cento bombardamenti di Napoli*, p. 87.

45. Maiuri, *Taccuino napoletano*, pp. 83–4; see also corroborating accounts in Gribaudi, *Guerra totale*, pp. 117–18; and Stefanile, *I cento bombardimenti di Napoli*, p. 89.

46. Inspector of civil engineering report to prefect, 29 Mar, ASN, Prefettura, Gabinetto, busta 1330/45.

47. Quoted in Gribaudi, *Guerra totale*, p. 116.

48. ASN, Prefettura, Gabinetto, busta 1330/45; see also Gribaudi, *Guerra totale*, p. 116.

49. Stefanile, *I cento bombardimenti di Napoli*, p. 90.

50. Masaniello's poem 'Ricordi (di un diario intimo)', quoted in Percopo and Riccio (eds), *La Campania dal Fascismo alla Repubblica*, Vol. II, p. 359.

51. See Antonio Ghirelli, *Napoli sbagliata* (Naples: Edizioni di Delfino, 1975), II, pp. 97–103.

52. Quoted in De Jaco, *Le Quattro Giornate di Napoli*, p. 39; Issue 1, Dec 1942, lays out the newspaper's political stance: reproduced in Salvetti (ed.), *La Campania dal fascismo alla repubblica*, Vol. I, pp. 202–3.

53. Anti-fascist leaflet of 12 Feb 1943, quoted in Salvetti (ed.), *La Campania dal fascismo alla repubblica*, Vol. I, p. 210.

54. 'La Fiaccola', No. 1, Jan 1943, quoted in ibid., pp. 203–4; examples of other similar leaflets are also reproduced on pp. 210, 211.

55. Mario Riccio testimony, quoted in ibid., pp. 199–201.

56. Rocco D'Ambra testimony, quoted in ibid., p. 186. For more on the national rebirth of the PSI see also Oreste Lizzadri, *Il regno di Badoglio e la resistenza romana* (Rome: Napoleone, 1974), pp. 94–5, 137–48.

57. Gennaro Rippa testimony, quoted in ibid., pp. 230–4.

Chapter 16: The Forty-Five Days

1. Air Historical Group, *The Army Air Forces in World War II, Vol. II: Europe: Torch to Pointblank*, pp. 463–4.

2. For a detailed analysis of the events on 24 and 25 Jul see Philip Morgan, *The*

Fall of Mussolini: Italy, the Italians, and the Second World War (Oxford: Oxford University Press, 2007), pp. 11–33.

3. Salvetti (ed.), *La Campania dal fascismo alla repubblica*, Vol. I, pp. 252–9; De Antonellis, *Napoli sotto il regime*, pp. 233–5; Cerchia, *La Seconda Guerra Mondiale nel Mezzogiorno*, p. 200.
4. De Jaco, *Le Quattro Giornate di Napoli*, p. 42.
5. Paul Ginsborg, *A History of Contemporary Italy 1943–1980* (London: Penguin, 1990), p. 12.
6. Cerchia, *La Seconda Guerra Mondiale nel Mezzogiorno*, p. 200. See also Giorgio Candeloro, *Storia dell'Italia moderna* (Milan: Feltrinelli, 1956–86), Vol. X: *La Seconda Guerra Mondiale, il crollo del fascismo, la Resistenza* (1984), p. 194.
7. De Antonellis, *Napoli sotto il regime*, p. 236.
8. Ibid., p. 234.
9. Prefect of Naples to Interior Minister, 13 Aug 1943, ASN, Gabinetto, busta 1254, 'Disciplina di guerra'.
10. Cerchia, *La Seconda Guerra Mondiale nel Mezzogiorno*, p. 201; De Antonellis, *Napoli sotto il regime*, p. 237.
11. Ibid., pp. 202, 206–7; ibid., p. 237.
12. For the text of this flier and the events surrounding it see Cerchia, *La Seconda Guerra Mondiale nel Mezzogiorno*, pp. 204–6.
13. De Jaco, *Le Quattro Giornate di Napoli*, p. 45.
14. Marco Gioannini and Giulio Massobrio, *Bombardate l'Italia: Storia della Guerra di distruzione aerea 1940–45* (Milan: Rizzoli, 2007), appendix.
15. NARA, RG18 Army Air Force, WWII Combat Operation Reports, Entry NM6 7A, Box 754, 301st Bomber Group Mission Reports, mission no. 131, 4 Aug 1943, 'Operations order, 3 August 1943'.
16. Ibid., mission no. 131, 4 Aug 1943, 'Narrative mission report'.
17. Account dated 5 Aug 1943 by the Comitato Provinciale di Protezione Antiaeria, ASN, Prefettura, Gabinetto, busta 1226/1. See also accounts in Gribaudi, *Guerra totale*, pp. 147–8; and Stefanile, *I cento bombardimenti di Napoli*, pp. 125–40.
18. 'La 96 incursione nemica su Napoli', *Roma*, 6 Aug 1943.
19. *Corriere della Sera*, quoted in De Antonellis, *Napoli sotto il regime*, p. 236. Gribaudi, *Guerra totale*, p. 148, quotes figures from ASN of 278 killed and 447 wounded; Stefanile, *I cento bombardimenti di Napoli*, p. 14.
20. Report of Comitato Provinciale di Protezione Antiaerea, 24 Aug 1943, ASN Prefettura, Gabinetto, busta 1226/1.
21. 'Per questa Grande Mutilata', *Il Mattino*, 31 Jul 1943; 'La 96 incursione nemica su Napoli', *Roma*, 6 Aug 1943.
22. Maiuri, *Taccuino napoletano*, pp. 105–6.
23. De Jaco, *Le Quattro Giornate di Napoli*, p. 47.

Chapter 17: The Germans Seize Control
1. Klinkhammer, *L'occupazione tedesca in Italia 1943–1945*, pp. 30–1.
2. For an excellent summary of the Armistice negotiations see Morgan, *The Fall of Mussolini*, pp. 88–92.
3. US National Archives, T-77, film 893, fo.644.108 sg.: report of 23 Jul 1943. Also quoted in Klinkhammer, *L'occupazione tedesca in Italia 1943–1945*, p. 27.
4. By the beginning of July there were already seven German divisions in southern Italy alone: see Klinkhammer, *L'occupazione tedesca in Italia 1943–1945*, p. 29.
5. Ibid., pp. 29–32.
6. Kesselring, *The Memoirs of Field Marshal Kesselring*, p. 184.
7. Elena Agarossi, *A Nation Collapses: The Italian Surrender of September 1943* (Cambridge: Cambridge University Press, 2000), p. 60.
8. Ibid., p. 62.
9. Ibid., p. 88.

10. For contradictory orders, see Agarossi, *A Nation Collapses*, p. 97; and Morgan, *The Fall of Mussolini*, pp. 92–6.

11. Morgan, *The Fall of Mussolini*, pp. 98–101, 107–8; Rochat, *Le guerre italiane 1935–1943*, pp. 434–6; Marco De Paolis and Isabella Insolvibile, *Cefalonia: Il processo, la storia, I documenti* (Rome: Viella, 2017), pp. 7–35.

12. 'Piombino città di eroi', *La Repubblica*, 8 Oct 2000: https://ricerca.repubblica. it/repubblica/archivio/repubblica/ 2000/10/08/piombino-citta-di-eroi. html

13. Walker, *From Texas to Rome*, entry for 1 Oct 1943, p. 267.

14. Cerchia, *La Seconda Guerra Mondiale nel Mezzogiorno*, p. 221; Klinkhammer, *L'occupazione tedesca in Italia 1943– 1945*, pp. 39–40; Morgan, *The Fall of Mussolini*, p. 102.

15. Lorenzo De Felice, quoted in Giulio Bedeschi (ed.), *Fronte italiano: c'ero anch'io* (Milan: Mursia, 1987), Vol. I, p. 609.

16. Alberto Liguoro, *Nola, cronaca dall'eccidio* (Formigine Modena: Infinito 2013). For a brief summary of these events, see Cerchia, *La Seconda Guerra Mondiale nel Mezzogiorno*, pp. 265–69; De Jaco, *Le Quattro Giornate di Napoli*, pp. 57–8.

17. Cerchia, *La Seconda Guerra Mondiale nel Mezzogiorno*, pp. 260–2.

Chapter 18: The Terror Begins

1. UKNA, WO 204/12335, Inter-Service Topographical Department report 'The Port and Town of Naples', 17 Jul 1943, pp. 39–46.

2. Del Tetto himself estimated the number around 7,250, but had a vested interest in underestimating his forces. See UKNA WO 204/12067, 'General Del Tetto's Report', 29 Oct 1943.

3. De Jaco, *Le Quattro Giornate di Napoli*, pp. 49–50.

4. Carolina Nobile Fiore diary, 8 Sep 1943, ICSR, B6, Fasc. 18, Sottofasc. 1.

5. Report of 57th Artillery Regiment, BA-MA, RH 24-14/81; Gribaudi, *Guerra totale*, p. 177. Gribaudi quotes this report at length.

6. Major Alfonso Ciavarella letter to Minister of War, 7 Apr 1944, ICSR, B5, Fasc. 8, Sottofasc. 1.

7. Report of 57th Artillery Regiment, BA-MA, RH 24-14/81; Gribaudi, *Guerra totale*, p. 178.

8. Ibid.

9. De Jaco, *Le Quattro Giornate di Napoli*, pp. 52–3.

10. Ibid., p. 56.

11. Mario Orbitello, *Napoli alla riscossa ovvero le Quattro Giornate* (Napoli: Treves, 1963), p. 13.

12. Giuseppe Aragno, *Le Quattro Giornate di Napoli: Storie di Antifascisti* (Naples: Intra Moenia, 2017), p. 150.

13. Paolo Caterina, '8 settembre 1943: I carabinieri difendono Roma e Napoli', in *Rassegna dell'Arma dei Carabinieri*, Vol. LXIV, No. 3 (Jul–Sep 2016), pp. 291–3.

14. De Jaco, *Le Quattro Giornate di Napoli*, pp. 50–2; Cerchia, *La Seconda Guerra Mondiale nel Mezzogiorno*, pp. 274–5.

15. Report of 57th Artillery Regiment, BA-MA, RH 24-14 vol. 81, p. 266.

16. De Jaco, *Le Quattro Giornate di Napoli*, pp. 48–9.

17. Report of 57th Artillery Regiment, BA-MA, RH 24-14, vol. 81, p. 267.

18. De Jaco, *Le Quattro Giornate di Napoli*, p. 49; Cerchia, *La Seconda Guerra Mondiale nel Mezzogiorno*, p. 277.

19. Gribaudi, *Guerra totale*, p. 188.

20. Cerchia, *La Seconda Guerra Mondiale nel Mezzogiorno*, pp. 279–80; De Jaco, *Le Quattro Giornate di Napoli* pp. 67–9.

21. De Jaco, *Le Quattro Giornate di Napoli*, pp. 70–1; Mariano Petino testimony, quoted in Gribaudi, *Guerra totale*, p. 183.

22. M. Bakunin testimony in anonymous collection *L'università di Napoli incendiata dai tedeschi* (Naples: Gaetano

Macchiaroli, 1944), pp. 19–20; the story is corroborated by a friend of Professor Bakunin, Carolina Nobile Fiore, who recorded Bakunin's story in her diary: ICSR, B6, Fasc. 18, Sottofasc. 1.

23. Mariano Petino testimony in *L'Università di Napoli incendiata dai tedeschi* (Naples: G. Macchiaroli, 1944), p. 24.

24. Petino's son, Gennaro Petino, quoted in Gribaudi, *Guerra totale*, p. 187. A separate testimony by Professor Guido della Valle confirms their account: ACS, Allied Military Command, bobina 618, scatola 228, German Atrocities, Oct 1943.

25. ACS, Allied Military Command, bobina 618, scatola 228, German Atrocities, Oct 1943. For descriptions of the fire in the Allied press, see 'Naples Library Fire Tops Art Destruction' in *S&S*, 11 Nov 1943; 'German Vandalism in Naples', *The Times*, 26 Nov 1943.

26. Mariano Petino testimony in *L'Università di Napoli incendiata dai tedeschi* (Naples: G. Macchiaroli, 1944), p. 25.

27. Enrico Ferrante account, ICSR, B6, Fasc. 12.

28. Mariano Petino testimony in *L'Università di Napoli incendiata dai tedeschi*, p. 25. See also Enrico Ferrante account, ibid.

29. Mariano Petino testimony in *L'Università di Napoli incendiata dai tedeschi*, p. 25; Gennaro Petino account in Gribaudi, *Guerra totale*, p. 188. For examples of other humiliations filmed see Ernesto Minino account in Gribaudi, *Guerra totale*, p. 200.

30. Personal correspondence with Carlo Gentile, 29 Feb 2024. Gentile conducted a study of German wartime films for a photographic exhibition in Naples in 2023.

31. Luigi De Rosa testimony, quoted in De Jaco, *Le Quattro Giornate di Napoli*, p. 75. See also Caterina, '8 settembre 1943: I carabinieri difendono Roma e

Napoli', pp. 296–7. For a list of names of those killed, see https://www.straginazifasciste.it/?page_id=38&id_strage=1277

32. BA-MA, RH 24-14, Vol. 81, p. 177: Gen Kdo XIV Panzer Korps, Ia, 531/43 g.Kdos. to Oberstleutnant Wolfgang Maucke, commander of Grenadier Regiment 115 of 15th Panzer Grenadier Div, 11 Sep 1943.

33. Report of 57th Artillery Regiment, BA-MA, RH 24-14, Vol. 81, p. 267.

34. Ibid., p. 269.

35. Enrico Ferrante account, ICSR, B6, Fasc. 12.

36. This order is reproduced in full in De Jaco, *Le Quattro Giornate di Napoli*, p. 80.

37. Giuseppe Sanges testimony, ICSR, B6, Fasc. 15.

38. See Vincenzo Sacco testimony, ICSR, B5, Fasc. 8, Sottofasc. 1; Federico Zvab, *Il prezzo della libertà* (Naples: Junior, 1988), pp. 81, 98; Giuseppe Riccio testimony in Gribaudi, *Guerra totale*, p. 263. See also Aragno, *Le Quattro Giornate di Napoli*, pp. 33–6.

39. Report of 57th Artillery Regiment, BA-MA, RH 24-14, Vol. 81, p. 270.

Chapter 19: Countdown to Revolution

1. De Jaco, *Le Quattro Giornate di Napoli*, pp. 82, 96.

2. Gioia Prinzi testimony, ICSR, B6, Fasc. 18, Sottofasc. 2: the testimony is clearly written by an unknown man, even though it is signed by Gioia Prinzi, presumably because she donated it to the archive.

3. De Jaco, *Le Quattro Giornate di Napoli*, p. 96; Gribaudi, *Guerra totale*, pp. 206–7.

4. Gribaudi, *Guerra totale*, pp. 199–207; see in particular Rosario Rega testimony, p. 205.

5. Ernesto Minino, quoted by Gribaudi, *Guerra totale*, pp. 199, 255.

6. BA-MA RH 24-14, Vol. 81, telegram from XIV Pz KorpsIa to Chief of Gen. Staff, 14 Sept 1943.

7. Ibid., Vol. 81, p. 384, Oberfehlshaber Süd to Italian Interior Ministry, 22 Sep 1943. See also Klinkhammer, *L'occupazione tedesca in Italia 1943–1945*, pp. 134–5.

8. BA-MA RH 24-14, Vol. 81, p. 441, XIV Pz Korps to Army High Command, 26 Sep 1943; *Roma*, 24 Sep 1943. Soprano's order is quoted in full in Salvetti (ed.), *La Campania dal fascismo alla repubblica*, Vol. I, p. 364.

9. For statistics see De Jaco, *Le Quattro Giornate di Napoli*, p. 92; and Gribaudi, *Guerra totale*, p. 191.

10. Caracciolo di Castagneto, *'43–'44*, p. 46, entry for 24 Sep 1943.

11. For a comprehensive list of facilities ordered destroyed, see BA-MA RH 24-24, Vol. 81, pp. 32–5, Army High Command 10 Abt.1a to XIV Pz Korps and other units, 21 Sep 1943 'Zerstörungsliste'. See also Nino Aversa, *Napoli sotto il terrore tedesco*, quoted in Salvetti (ed.), *La Campania dal fascismo alla repubblica*, Vol. I, pp. 372–3); and Cerchia, *La Seconda Guerra Mondiale nel Mezzogiorno*, pp. 287–8.

12. Aversa, *Napoli sotto il terrore tedesco*, quoted in Salvetti (ed), *La Campania dal fascismo alla repubblica*, Vol. I, p. 372–3; De Jaco, *Le Quattro Giornate di Napoli*, pp. 84–5.

13. De Jaco, *Le Quattro Giornate di Napoli*, p. 91.

14. Udo von Alvensleben, *Lauter Abscheide: Tagebuch im Kriege*, ed. Harald von Koenigswald (Frankfurt: Propyläen, 1971), pp. 333–4, entry for 23 Sep 1943.

15. Carolina Nobile Fiore diary, 26 Sep 1943, ICSR, B6, Fasc. 18, Sottofasc. 1.

16. Caracciolo di Castagneto, *'43–'44*, p. 45, entry for 23 Sep 1943.

17. Maiuri, *Taccuino Napoletano*, p. 123, undated entry for Sep 1943.

18. Ibid.

19. BA-MA 24-14, Vol. 81, p. 386 XIV Pz Korps to QU.Abt. 23 Sep 1943 and p. 403, 'Besprechungspunkte 16 Panzer-Division 24.9.43'. For statistics

see Klinkhammer, *L'occupazione tedesca in Italia 1943–1945*, pp. 133, 501.

20. The text of the decree was published in *Roma*, 24 Sep 1943.

21. Decree of 26 September, published in *Roma* the following day.

22. For these and other eyewitness stories of escaping the German round-ups, see Gribaudi, *Guerra totale*, pp. 209–15.

23. Gen. Kdo. XIV Panzer Korps war diary no. 5, BA-MA RH 24-14, Vol. 72, p. 52, 27 Sep 1943.

24. Alfredo Parente quoted in Camillo Albanese, *Napoli e la Seconda Guerra Mondiale* (Modena: Infinito, 2014), p. 116.

25. Gribaudi, *Guerra totale*, p. 194. German accounts corroborate the Italian point of view: see for example von Alvensleben, *Lauter Abscheide*, p. 339, entry for 28 Sep 1943.

26. Rosa Fusaro testimony in Gribaudi, *Guerra totale*, pp. 215–16.

27. Gribaudi, *Guerra totale*, p. 194; Klinkhammer, *L'occupazione tedesca in Italia 1943–1945*, pp. 133–5.

28. Caracciolo di Castageto, *'43–'44: Diario di Napoli*, p. 49, entry for 29 Sep 1943.

29. Antonio Amoretti testimony in Gribaudi, *Guerra totale*, p. 193.

39. Giuseppe Iaccarino testimony in ibid., p. 193.

Chapter 20: The Four Days of Naples

1. Federico Zvab, *Il prezzo della libertà* (Santa Maria Capua Veter: Edizioni Spartaco, 2003), p. 119.

2. Tarsia in Curia, *La verità sulle 'Quattro Giornate di Napoli'*, p. 40.

3. Zvab, *Il prezzo della libertà*, pp. 79, 84, 119–20.

4. Ibid., p. 81.

5. Ibid., p. 119.

6. Poster quoted in full in Zvab, *Il prezzo della libertà*, p. 120.

7. Zvab, *Il prezzo della libertà*, p. 119.

8. For a description of this battle and the one on the following day, see Zvab, *Il prezzo della libertà*, pp. 123–30.

9. Orbitello, *Napoli alla riscossa ovvero le Quattro Giornate* pp. 92–3.

10. Maiuri, *Taccuino napoletano*, p. 125.

11. Zvab, *Il prezzo della libertà*, pp. 122–5; Orbitello, *Napoli alla riscossa ovvero le Quattro Giornate*, pp. 109–11, 117–19, 194–5; De Jaco, *Le Quattro Giornate di Napoli*, p. 121; Aragno, *Le Quattro Giornate di Napoli*, pp. 127–44.

12. Orbitello, *Napoli alla riscossa ovvero le Quattro Giornate*, p. 93; corroborated by Vincenzo Pinto testimony, ICSR, B5, Fasc. 8, Sottofasc. 1.

13. Cacciapuoti, *Storia di un operaio napoletano*, pp. 122–3.

14. Vincenzo Pinto testimony, ICSR, B5, Fasc. 8, Sottofasc. 1.

15. De Jaco, *Le Quattro Giornate di Napoli*, pp. 121–2, 137, 156.

16. Antonio Ghirelli, *Storia di Napoli* (Turin: Einaudi, 2015), p. 168; Italo Ferraro, *Atlante della città storica* (Naples: Oikos, 2002–17), Vol. 5: *Stella, Vergini, Sanità* (2007), pp. 247–8.

17. For biographical sketches of this remarkable woman see Gaetana Morghese, *La Guerra di mama: Maddalena 'Lenuccia' Cerasuolo nelle Quattro Giornate di Napoli* (Naples: Massa 2010); Pietro Gargano, *Lenuccia di Vico Neve a Materdei* (Naples: Tulio Pironti, 2015); and Gribaudi, *Guerra totale*, pp. 242–5. For her SOE file see UKNA, HS 9/284/7, where she is misnamed 'Maria Cerasuolo'.

18. For contemporary mentions of these events, see Alfredo Parente's account of the first day of the uprising in *La Barricata*, No. 4, 4 Oct 1943. For later reconstructions, see also De Jaco, *Le Quattro Giornate di Napoli*, pp. 132–4; Zvab, *Il prezzo della libertà*, pp. 133–4.

19. Zvab, *Il prezzo della libertà*, pp. 134–5; Gribaudi, *Guerra totale*, p. 195.

20. De Jaco, *Le Quattro Giornate di Napoli*, p. 138.

21. Roberto Piccirella testimony, ICSR, B6, Fasc. 14; medal citations for Filippo Illuminato and Pasquale Formisano, B8, Fasc. 19, Sottofasc. 2.

22. Gennaro Capuozzo medal citation, Italian presidential website, https://www.quirinale.it/onorificenze/insigniti/14587

23. Maddalena Cerasuolo TV interview, reproduced in ICSR 68th anniversary booklet, Giulia Buffardi (ed.), *'Libertà … ch'è sì cara …': Le Quattro Giornate Testimoni e protagonist ricordano e raccontano* (Naples: ICSR, 2011), pp. 57–8.

24. He was caught in northern Italy and probably shot by the Germans in 1945: see Gaetano Barbarulo, *Una vita al cardiopalma* (Naples: Edizioni Scientifiche Italiane, 2019), pp. 121–3.

25. Barbarulo, *Una vita al cardiopalma*, p. 40.

26. Vincenzo Sacco testimony, 12 Jul 1944, ICSR B5, Fasc. 8, Sottofasc. 1.

27. Eduoardo Salvatore testimony in Simon Pocock, *Campania 1943*, Vol. II, Pt 3: *Città di Napoli* (Naples: Three Mice Books, 2018), Tomo I, p. 453; and Barbarulo, *Una vita al cardiopalma*, p. 41.

28. See Vincenzo Sacco testimony, ICSR, B5, Fasc. 8, Sottofasc. 1. See also Barbarulo, *Una vita al cardiopalma*, p. 41; De Jaco, *Le Quattro Giornate di Napoli*, p. 125; Albanese, *Napoli e la Seconda Guerra Mondiale*, p. 119.

29. Mario Puleio testimony, ICSR, Fondo 'La mia guerra', B59, Fasc. 71.

30. De Jaco, *Le Quattro Giornate di Napoli*, p. 126.

31. Tarsia in Curia, *La verità sulle 'Quattro Giornate' di Napoli*, pp. 87–8.

32. Giovanni Aiello testimonies in ICSR, Corrado Prosperini file, B5, Fasc. 8, Sottofasc. 1; and B6, Fasc. 15.

33. Giovanni Aiello testimony, ICSR, B6, Fasc. 15; see also Barbarullo, *Una vita al cardiopalma*, p. 44; De Jaco, *Le Quattro Giornate di Napoli*, p. 154.

34. Francesco Pintore testimony, 8 Sep 1973, ICSR, B6, Fasc. 11, Sottofasc. 2.

35. Ezio Berti, *Wehrmacht, 1943 Napoli-Salerno* (Udine: Carlo Lorenzini, 1988), p. 164. Berti's book has many demonstrable errors in it, is full of invented dialogue, and must therefore be treated with caution.

36. Mario Sepe testimony, 6 Oct 1943, ICSR, B6, Fasc. 11, Sottofasc. 2, Giovanni Abbate file.

37. ANPI Naples, B1, Fasc. 'Baiano Pietro' testimony.

38. See Francesco Pintore testimony and Giovanni Abbate medal citation in 6 Oct 1943, ICSR, B6, Fasc. 11, Sottofasc. 2, Giovanni Abbate file.

39. For a good summary of the conflicting sources, see Barbarulo, *Una vita al cardiopalma*, pp. 46–7, n. 27.

40. Alfonso Ciavarella testimony, ICSR, B5, Fasc. 8, Sottofasc. 1.

41. Mario Marisco testimony, ICSR, B5, Fasc. 8, Sottofasc. 1.

42. Caracciolo di Castagneto, *'43–'44*, p. 49: entry for 29 Sep; Francesco Penna testimony, ICSR, B6, Fasc. 15.

43. Alfonso Baldaro, 'Relazioni sugli eventi delle giornate insurrezionali del settembre scorso', in Orbitello, *Napoli alla riscossa ovvero le Quattro Giornate*, pp. 181–6.

44. Antonio Amoretti testimony in Gribaudi, *Guerra totale*, p. 290.

45. Tarsia in Curia, *La verità sulle Quattro Giornate di Napoli*, p. 41.

46. De Jaco, *Le Quattro Giornate di Napoli*, p. 143.

47. Gribaudi, *Guerra totale*, pp. 233–35.

48. See especially Aragno, *Le Quattro Giornate di Napoli*, pp. 75–98.

49. Zvab, *Il prezzo della libertà*, p. 140. Fiorillo was subsequently released without charge.

50. Giuseppe Sanges testimony, ICSR, B6, Fasc. 15.

51. Antonio Amoretti interview, printed in Buffardi (ed.), *'Libertà ... ch'è sì cara...'*, p. 53.

52. Zvab, *Il prezzo della libertà*, p. 132.

53. Ibid., p. 138.

54. Maiuri, *Taccuino napoletano*, p. 125: entry for 28 Sep–1 Oct 1943.

55. Orbitello, *Napoli alla riscossa ovvero le Quattro Giornate*, pp. 117–18; Zvab, *Il prezzo della libertà*, pp. 137–8.

56. Alfonso Ciavarella testimony, ICSR, B5, Fasc. 8, Sottofasc. 1.

57. Zvab, *Il prezzo della libertà*, p. 139.

58. Ibid., p. 140.

59. Alfonso Baldaro testimony, Orbitello, *Napoli alla riscossa ovvero le Quattro Giornate*, p. 185.

60. Orbitello, *Napoli alla riscossa ovvero le Quattro Giornate*, pp. 118–19. See also Giulio Schettini testimony, ICSR B5, Fasc. 7, Sottofasc. 1.

61. Orbitello, *Napoli alla riscossa ovvero le Quattro Giornate*, pp. 118–19; Giuseppe Sanges testimony, ICSR, B6, Fasc. 15; Ricompart, Scheda 554, Fasc. 'Martone Marcello'.

62. Franco Vassetti interview reproduced in Gribaudi, *Guerra totale*, pp. 265–6.

Chapter 21: Parting Shots

1. Report by Hans Habe-Békessy, Psych. Warfare Branch, quoted in Carlo Gentile, *I crimini di guerra tedeschi in Italia 1943–1945* (Turin: Einaudi, 2015), p. 110.

2. De Jaco, *Le Quattro Giornate di Napoli*, p. 166.

3. Ibid., p. 168; see also Gerardo M. testimony, quoted in Gribaudi, *Guerra totale*, 2005), pp. 225–6.

4. For the full story of the resistance in Ponticelli during the war, see Andrea D'Angelo, Giorgio Mancini and Luigi Verolino, *Guerra di periferia: Resistenza, vita quotidiana e stragi dimenticate nell'area Orientale di Napoli 1940–1943* (Naples: Il Quartiere, 2005), pp. 115–95. See also Francesco Soverina, 'Le Quattro Giornate di Napoli e l'antifascismo', in Felice Corvese (ed.), *Mezzogiorno tra Tedeschi e Alleati* (Naples: Edizioni Scientifiche Italiane, 2017), pp. 156–7. For Casu's involvement, see also ACS, MD, Ricompart Campania, B38, Fasc. 2601.

5. See the many eyewitness reports gathered by Naples territorial military tribunal between March and Apr 1945, many of which are quoted in D'Angelo, Mancini and Verolino, *Guerra di periferia*, pp. 136–43; and in Gribaudi, *Guerra totale*, pp. 222–6.

6. Francesca Esposito testimony, 8 Apr 1945, quoted in Gribaudi, *Guerra totale*, p. 227. See also the testimony of Carmela Milone, whose son was likewise beheaded, quoted in D'Angelo, Mancini and Verolino, *Guerra di periferia*, p. 155

7. Nino Ascione testimony, quoted in Gribaudi, *Guerra totale*, p. 228.

8. Testimonies of Pasquale Sannino, Teresa Sannino and Aniello Borrelli, quoted in Gribaudi, *Guerra totale*, pp. 228–9.

9. Armando Sorrentino testimony, quoted in Gribaudi, *Guerra totale*, p. 229.

10. For a list of their names and biographical details, see the summaries written by Dr Isabela Insolvibile at http://www.straginazifasciste.it/?page_id=38&id_strage=5372 and http://www.straginazifasciste.it/?page_id=38&id_strage=5376

11. D'Angelo, Mancini and Verolino, *Guerra di periferia*, pp. 176–81; Gribaudi, *Guerra totale*, pp. 26–9.

12. De Jaco, *Le Quattro Giornate di Napoli*, p. 190.

13. For a summary of events in Acerra, based on German documentation, see the study by Carlo Gentile commissioned by the Naples Military Tribunal in July 2002, in support of case no. 1860/99 R.G.N.R. against Gerhard Tschierschwitz, the leader of the German unit responsible for the massacre. Gentile's paper is at https://www.academia.edu/44434083/ProcNapoli_Acerra

14. De Jaco, *Le Quattro Giornate di Napoli*, pp. 190–91. See also 'L'eccidio di Acerra', *L'Unità*, 5 Feb 1955, which tells the same story, but consistently gets the names of local protagonists wrong.

15. Gentile, *I crimini di guerra tedeschi in Italia 1943–1945*, pp. 109–10; see also the memorial stone in Acerra, which lists the names of all eighty-eight dead. Isabella Insolvibile has slightly different figures, but gives biographical details of those who died: see http://www.straginazifasciste.it/?page_id=38&id_strage=1285

16. Most of these stories appear in De Jaco's *Le Quattro Giornate di Napoli*, pp. 196–9; but it is unclear whether they refer to killings that took place within the town or at other locations, and perhaps other dates, in the surrounding countryside. They have been repeated many times in the local press and community websites. See for example the article in the Acerra city newspaper, 'Acerra, Medaglia d'Oro al Valore Civile', *Tablò*, Vol. XXV, No. 9, Oct 2018, p. 12; and 'La Resistenza ad Acerra' online at https://www.marigliano.net/articolo.php?ru_id=2&sr_id=36&ar_id=17791

17. BA-MA, RL 32, Vol. 115, War diary No. 1, Panzer-Regiment 'Hermann Göring'.

18. Testimony of the mother of Gennaro Sapio, quoted in 'L'eccidio di Acerra', *L'Unità*, 5 Feb 1955.

19. Local tradition has all thirteen killed at once on 30 Sep, but actually they were killed over several days. See the details assembled by Isabella Insolvibile online at http://www.straginazifasciste.it/?page_id=38&id_strage=1287. Carlo Gentile puts the number of dead as thirteen: *I crimini di guerra tedeschi in Italia 1943–1945*, p. 107.

20. Gentile, *I crimini di guerra tedeschi in Italia*, p. 107; Isabella Insolvibile, http://www.straginazifasciste.it/?page_id=38&id_strage=5312: a fifth priest managed to escape.

21. Rosanna de Cunzo, 'Per una storia della resistenza in Campania', *Politica e Mezzogiorno*, Jan–Mar 1962, pp. 84–5; ICSR, B8, Fasc. 21. See also http://www.straginazifasciste.it/?page_id=38&id_strage=287

22. Gentile, *I crimini di guerra tedeschi in Italia*, p. 107; see also http://www.straginazifasciste.it/?page_id=38&id_strage=3088

23. Testimony of the mayor of Bellona, Gaetano Rossi, 15 Mar 1947, ICSR, B8, Fasc. 21. See also Gribaudi, *Guerra totale*, pp. 381–2; and Giuseppe Angelone's summary at http://www.straginazifasciste.it/?page_id=38&id_strage=356

24. Testimonies of Maria Zuppa, Elemerina Nobile and Elisabetta Canciello, made before the inquest carried out by the Carabinieri in 1945: quoted in Gribaudi, *Guerra totale*, pp. 374–5. See also http://www.straginazifasciste.it/?page_id=38&id_strage=641

25. NARA, RG 153, Entry 143, Box 527, CPI 10/29, Case Caiazzo. See also 'Germans pose as Yanks to massacre 23', *Chicago Daily News*, 20 Oct 1943; *Risorgimento*, 24 Oct 1943.

26. 'Kriegesverbrechen: Die Enttarnung des Biedemanns', *Focus*, 20 Dec 1993; 'Erklär mir, warum', *Der Spiegel*, 5 Mar 1995. See also http://www.straginazifasciste.it/?page_id=38&id_strage=371

27. Gribaudi, *Guerra totale*, pp. 352, 421–32; and relevant pages on the online Atlas of Nazi and Fascist Atrocities in Italy, http://www.straginazifasciste.it

28. Gentile, *I crimini di Guerra tedeschi in Italia 1943–1945*, pp. 115–16.

29. Ibid., p. 114.

Chapter 22: The Price of Myth

1. Von Alvensleben, *Lauter Abscheide*, p. 340, entry for 29 Sep 1943.

2. See Gentile, *I crimini di guerra tedeschi in Italia, 1943–1945*, pp. 107, 214.

3. Ibid.; Gribaudi, *Guerra totale*, p. 198.

4. See especially the reports gathered by Corrado Barbagallo in *Napoli contro il terrore nazista* (Naples: Maone, 1943), and those published in *Roma* and *Risorgimento* in the immediate aftermath of the uprising.

5. See the files on individual fighters in ACS, MD, Ricompart Campania.

6. For a critical bibliography of the Four Days, see Guido D'Agostino, *Le Quattro Giornate di Napoli* (Rome: Newton Compton, 1998), especially his chapter 'La questione storiografica'.

7. Gentile, *I crimini di guerra tedeschi in Italia, 1943–1945*, p. 214, n. 87.

8. Tarsia in Curia, *La verità sulle Quattro Giornate di Napoli*, p. 44. This was broken down as follows: 178 fighting partisans (including 26 killed on 10, 11 and 12 September), 140 civilians and 19 unknown.

9. Gribaudi, *Guerra totale*, p. 198.

10. See for example my earlier work, *Savage Continent*, pp. 141–3.

11. ICSR, B5, Fasc. 8, Sottofasc. 1. For more on Pansini's thoughts about the Four Days see his book, *Goliardi e scugnizzi nelle Quattro Giornate napoletane*; see also Aragno, *Le Guattro Giornate di Napoli*, pp. 185–9, 199–214.

12. Abbate, *Le Quattro Giornate di Napoli vissute, descritte e documentate dai protagonist: 1943–1983 (La Resistenza continua)* (Naples: Edizioni in Proprio, 1984), pp. 165, 171; and p. 466.

13. Barbagallo, *Napoli contro il terrore nazista*, p. 90; Tarsia in Curia, *La verità sulle Quattro Giornate di Napoli*, pp. 88–9; Tarsia in Curia, *Napoli negli anni di Guerra*, p. 46. See also Barbarullo, *Una vita al cardiopalma*, pp. 48–9.

14. Enzo Erra, *Napoli 1943: Le Quattro Giornate che non ci furono* (Milan: Longanesi, 1993).

15. Orbitello, *Napoli alla riscossa ovvero le Quattro Giornate*, p. 86.

16. Tarsia in Curia, *La verità sulle Quattro Giornate di Napoli*, p. 45.

17. Schipa, *Masaniello*, pp. 27–64

18. Roberto Battaglia, *Storia della Resistenza italiana* (Turin: Einaudi, 1953), p. 122.

19. Alfonso Baldaro testimony, quoted in

Orbitello, *Napoli alla riscossa ovvero le Quattro Giornate*, pp. 183–4.

20. Aragno, *Le Quattro Giornate di Napoli*, pp. 285–327.

21. Cerchia, *La Seconda Guerra Mondiale nel Mezzogiorno*, pp. 307–8.

22. *Life* magazine, 8 Nov 1943; Pansini, *Golliardi e scugnizzi nelle Quattro Giornate napoletane*, pp. 5–6; Aragno, *Le Quattro Giornate di Napoli*, p. 11. Aragno wrongly asserts that the photos in *Life* were credited to Robert Capa.

23. For their citations, see the honours page of the website of the Italian presidency: https://www.quirinale.it/onorificenze/insigniti/14587 and https://www.quirinale.it/onorificenze/insigniti/14058; https://www.quirinale.it/onorificenze/insigniti/14588 and https://www.quirinale.it/onorificenze/insigniti/14326

24. The prison is now a youth centre called 'Scugnizzo Liberato'. I am grateful to Jocelyn Vincent, a volunteer at the centre, who showed me around it in 2021.

25. Sophia Loren quoted in James Owen and Guy Walters (eds), *The Voice of War: The Second World War Told by Those Who Fought It* (London: Viking, 2004), pp. 360–1.

26. See for example Aragno, *Le Quattro Giornate di Napoli*, pp. 11–21; Cerchia, *La Seconda Guerra Mondiale nel Mezzogiorno*, pp. 297–301; Gribaudi, *Guerra totale*, pp. 302–8.

27. Aragno, *Le Quattro Giornate di Napoli*, p. 11.

28. Cerchia, *La Seconda Guerra Mondiale nel Mezzogiorno*, p. 301.

29. 'The Fall of Naples', *The Times*, 2 Oct 1943, p. 5: the article speaks of 'the conquest of a city of nearly a million inhabitants'.

30. 82d ADM, 'Sicily After Action Report', p. 82.

31. 'Italy Tough, Toilsome from Start', *S&S*, 8 May 1945, p. 7.

Chapter 23: Vesuvius

1. Maiuri, *Taccuino napoletano*, p. 158, entry for 18 Mar 1944.

2. UKNA WO 220/439, ACC HQ Naples Province, 'Final Report on the Vesuvius Emergency Operation', 12 Apr 1944, p. 18; NARA, RG 331, UD 1978, Box 1059, 10000/136/147 'Civilian War Relief: American Red Cross', report 26 Mar 1946, p. 42. For an hour-by-hour account of the emergency, see also UKNA AIR 29/840, HQ to No3 Base Area RAF, 'Hour to hour diary on eruption of Vesuvius'. Unless otherwise stated, the following account is based on these three reports.

3. 'Final Report on the Vesuvius Emergency Operation', p. 11; 'Large Lava Streams Threatening Towns on Vesuvius Slopes', *S&S*, 21 Mar 1944.

4. Eric Griffin testimony, National Army Museum London, 9708-46-1, 'An Interlude from Battle Casualties – Naples – 1944'.

5. John Miles testimony, IWM Sound 20538, Reel 3; Lewis, *Naples '44*, p. 93, entry for 19 Mar.

6. William James Dilworth testimony, IWM Sound 18435, Reel 4.

7. NARA, RG 331, UD 1978, Box 1059, 10000/136/147 'Civilian War Relief: American Red Cross', report 26 Mar 1946, p. 42.

8. 'Final Report on the Vesuvius Emergency Operation', p. 18. This report has the initial explosion on 22 March; but the RAF 'Hour to hour diary' and newspaper reports show that the first explosion was on 21 March.

9. John Miles testimony, IWM Sound 20538, Reel 3.

10. Kenneth Milton Roth testimony, VHP-LoC: https://www.loc.gov/item/afc2001001.05060, Reel 2.

11. Lewis, *Naples '44*, p. 93, entry for 19 Mar.

12. See for example the descriptions by Toyofumi Ogura, quoted in my

earlier work *The Fear and the Freedom*, p. 15.

13. Joseph Blair Brown testimony, VHP-LoC: https://www.loc.gov/item/afc2001001.30110

14. Reginal Gooch testimony, VHP-LoC: https://www.loc.gov/item/afc2001001.90042

15. Maiuri, *Taccuino napoletano*, p. 159, entry for 18 Mar 1944.

16. Robert Knox testimony, VHP-LoC: https://www.loc.gov/item/afc2001001.41081; see also Reginald Gooch testimony; and Maiuri, *Taccuino napoletano*.

17. UKNA, WO 204/2225, MacFarlane to MGS, Ref. FATIMA 2481, 23 Mar 1944.

18. 'Toll of Vesuvius', *The Times*, 27 Mar 1944.

19. UKNA, WO 204/2225, MacFarlane to MGS, Ref. 2526, 24 Mar 1944; 'Vesuvius returning to normal', *The Times*, 25 Mar 1944.

20. UKNA, WO 204/2225, MacFarlane to MGS, Ref. 2584, 25 Mar 1944; 'Final Report on the Vesuvius Emergency Operation', pp. 2–5; 'Old Vesuvius Finally Quiets Down after Six Days of Violent Belching', *S&S*, 25 Mar 1944.

21. Lewis, *Naples '44*, p. 93, entry for 19 Mar; see also testimonies by Kenneth Milton Roth (VHP-LoC), John Arthur Carteret Maule and John Miles (IWM Sound).

22. Kenneth Milton Roth testimony, VHP-LoC: https://www.loc.gov/item/afc2001001.05060, Reel 2.

23. Eric Griffin testimony, National Army Museum London, 9708-46-1, 'An Interlude from Battle Casualties – Naples – 1944'.

24. 'Mt Vesuvius Lets Loose Loudest Belch In 15 Years', *S&S*, 20 Mar 1944.

25. 'San Sebastiano Destroyed by Mt. Vesuvius Lava Flow', *S&S*, 22 Mar 1944.

26. Benson and Neufeld, 'American Military Government in Italy', p. 112.

Chapter 24: The *Epurazione*

1. UKNA, WO 220/362, 'Basic Documents Establishing AMGOT', Proclamation No. 2.

2. A. Baldaro testimony, reproduced in Salvetti, *La Campania dal Fascismo alla repubblica*, Vol. I, pp. 400–2.

3. Aragno, *Le Quattro Giornate di Napoli*, pp. 202–7; Pansini, *Golliardi e scugnizzi nelle quatrro giornate napoletane*, pp. 50–60.

4. Zvab, *Il prezzo della libertà*, pp. 154–9.

5. Richard M. Burrage, 'See Naples and Die', TMFM, p. 33.

6. UKNA, WO 220/333, 'AMGOT Plan for Italy', Proclamation No. 1.

7. For example, when Count Pellegrini was forced to resign as president of Società Esercizi Telefonici because his workforce refused to work for him any longer, AMG stepped in to force his reinstatement. He was finally arrested on charges of collaboration less than a month later. See PWB report 10, 19 Jul 1944, p. 10 (item 22).

8. De Marco, *Polvere di piselli*, p. 81.

9. *Roma*, 24 Sep 1943. Soprano's orders are quoted in full in Salvetti (ed.), *La Campania dal fascismo alla repubblica*, Vol I, pp. 362–4.

10. NARA, RG 331, UD 1978, Box 939, 10000/129/167, 'Removal of Fascist Officials', p. 4; De Marco, *Polvere di piselli*, p. 72; *Il Corriere* (Salerno), 25 Jun 1944; PWB report 23, 19 Oct 1944, prelims, p. 1.

11. De Marco, *Polvere di piselli*, p. 71.

12. NARA, RG 331, UD 1978, Box 939, 10000/129/167, 'Removal of Fascist Officials', p. 7; De Marco, *Polvere di piselli*, p. 71.

13. NARA, RG 331, UD 1978, Box 67, 10000/100/1091, 'Number changes in officials up to 31 December 1943'.

14. Benson and Neufeld, 'Allied Military Government in Italy', p. 122.

15. NARA, RG 331, UD 1978, Box 939, 10000/129/167 'Removal of Fascist Officials'.

16. Benson and Neufeld, 'Allied Military Government in Italy', pp. 122–5.
17. Ibid., p. 123.
18. NARA, RG 331, UD 1978, Box 939, 10000/129/167, 'Activities of Intelligence Division (G-2), Region 3, HQ, During the Period 21 September to 15 December 1943, inclusive', p. 2.
19. De Marco, *Polvere di piselli*, pp. 77–80.
20. UKNA FO 660/371, report on Frignani, 21 Dec 1943.
21. De Marco, *Polvere di piselli*, pp. 80–1.
22. NARA, RG 331, UD 1978, Box 939, 10000/129/167, Finance Division, 'Report', p. 14.
23. UKNA FO 660/371.
24. De Marco, *Polvere di piselli*, pp. 69–83.
25. NARA, RG 331, UD 1978, Box 4826, 10260/143/209, weekly 'Report on the Activity of the Public Safety Division Region III', 23 Nov 1943; and 10260/143/210, 'Report on the Activities of Regional Headquarters Public Safety Division to 15th December 1943', p. 16.
26. CGL statement issued in *Battaglie sindicali*, 16 Apr 1944; reproduced in Salvetti (ed.), *La Campania dal Fascismo alla repubblica*, Vol. I, p. 529.
27. NARA, RG 331, UD 1978, Box 939, 10000/129/167, 'Removal of Fascist Officials', pp. 4–12, lists names and positions of all those removed. See also Box 67, 10000/100/1091, 'Removal of officials – Naples Province', which has slightly different figures, but less detail.
28. De Marco, *Polvere di piselli*, p. 71.
29. Reproduced in *Gazzetta Ufficiale del Regno d'Italia*, 29 Dec 1943: https://www.gazzettaufficiale.it/ricerca/pdf/postRsi/foglio_ordinario1/1/0/0?reset=true
30. The first High Commissioner was Tito Zaniboni, a Socialist who had spent years in jail for an attempted assassination on Mussolini. He would be replaced at the end of April by Count Sforza. See Harris, *Allied Military Administration of Italy 1943–1945*, p. 150.
31. Harris, *Allied Military Administration of Italy 1943–1945*, pp. 150, 206–9. For Royal Decree Law no. 134 of 26 May 1944 and Lieutenant-General Legislative Decree no. 159 of 27 July 1944, see *Gazzetta Ufficiale del Regno d'Italia*, 31 May 1944 and 29 Jul 1944: https://www.gazzettaufficiale.it/eli/gu/1944/05/31/32/sg/pdf and https://www.gazzettaufficiale.it/eli/gu/1944/07/29/41/sg/pdf
32. The satisfaction was mixed with disappointment that they did not receive the death sentence: see PWB report 33, 28 Dec 1944, p. 22 (item 18).
33. PWB report 23, 19 Oct 1944, prelims.
34. PWB report 27, 16 Nov 1944, pp. 10–11 (item 13); *La Voce*, 1 Apr 1945, reproduced in Salvetti (ed.), *La Campania dal Fascismo alla repubblica*, Vol. I, p. 629.
35. Interview with Eugenio Mancini in PWB report 36, 19 Januarty 1945, p. 7 (item 4). Mancini became Naples Epuration Commissioner in Nov 1944.
36. Lowe, *Savage Continent*, pp. 149–53, 276–94.

Chapter 25: A New National Politics

1. Sergio Viggiani speech, Norman Lewis conference 2004, IWM Sound 27088, Reel 2.
2. So much so that Neapolitans regularly told Allied officers that they did not want AMG to hand back power to Badoglio because 'once the Allies have gone things will be just the same as before the war'. See NARA, RG 331, UD 1978, Box 4826, 10260/143/210, 'Monthly Report for May 1944 – Region 3, Public Safety Division', p. 14.
3. NARA, RG 331, UD 1978, Box 67, 10000/100/1091, 'Political, Month of December 1943', pp. 2–3.
4. Ibid., 10260/143/260, ACC HQ Region 3 proclamation 'Labour demonstrations, work stoppage and strikes', 2 Jul 1944; PWB report 10, 19 Jul 1944, p. 13 (item 22).

5. Ibid., Box 4826, 10260/143/210, 'Report on the Activities of Regional Headquarters Public Safety Division to 15 December 1943', p. 13; and Box 4829, 10260/143/260, memo on the 'Disturbance at Qualiano', 4 Feb 1944.

6. Carlo Sforza, *L'Italia dal 1914 al 1944 quale io la vidi* (Rome: Mondadori, 1945), p. 191.

7. Benedetto Croce, *Croce, the King and the Allies: Extracts from a diary by Benedetto Croce July 1943–June 1944* (London: George Allen & Unwin, 1950), entries for 15 and 20 Sep, pp. 16, 18. See also Harry Hargreaves, SOE account of rescuing Croce, IWM Sound 12158, Reel 3.

8. For documents on the Gruppi Italiani Combattenti see Croce, *Croce, the King and the Allies*, appendix, pp. 141–52; and Salvetti (ed.), *La Campania dal Fascismo alla repubblica*, Vol. I, pp. 444–6.

9. Croce, *Croce, the King and the Allies*, p. 38, entry for 13 Nov.

10. After the Gruppi Italiani Combattenti were dissolved, Pavone retired. He died in 1944. Ironically, the ACC replaced Pavone with General Antonio Basso, a much more controversial figure who had collaborated with the Germans during their evacuation from Sardinia.

11. Morgan, *The Fall of Mussolini*, pp. 159–63.

12. Caracciolo di Castagneto, *'43–'44*, p. 47, entry for 28 Sep 1943.

13. NARA, RG 331, UD 1978, Box 4826, 10260/143/210, 'Public Safety Report for the month of December 1943', p. 6; and Box 67, 10000/100/1091, 'Political, Month of December 1943', p. 1.

14. Ibid., Box 67, 10000/100/1091, 'Political, Month of December 1943', pp. 1, 4.

15. *Risorgimento*, 20 Oct 1943.

16. Ibid., 2 Dec 1943.

17. NARA, RG 331, UD 1978, Box 4826, 10260/143/210, report by Lauricella to Prefect of Naples, 29 Dec 1943; and

CCRR report 2 Feb 1944, letter file no. 14/43-1943; and the various reports of riots and disturbances listed in Box 4829, 10250/143/260. See also Salvetti (ed.), *La Campania dal Fascismo alla repubblica*, Vol. I, pp. 475–80.

18. NARA, RG 331, UD 1978, Box 67, 10000/100/1091, 'Political, Month of December 1943', p. 4.

19. Ibid.; CLN letter to Roosevelt, Churchill and Stalin, in ICSR, B1, Fasc. 2, Sottofasc. 1 and 5.

20. For Churchill's speech on 22 Feb 1944 see Hansard, Vol. 397, Col. 691, https://hansard.parliament.uk

21. Caracciolo di Castagneto, *'43–'44*, p. 129, entry for 28 Feb 1944. A copy of the telegram see UKNA WO 204/2167, MacFarlane to AFHQ, 1 Mar 1944, Ref. 1476.

22. Pamphlet quoted in UKNA WO 204/2167, MacFarlane to AFHQ, 2 Mar 1944, Ref. 1523.

23. According to AMG Proclamation No. 2: see UKNA, WO 220/362, 'Basic Documents Establishing AMGOT'.

24. For the following account, see MacFarlane correspondence with AFHQ, Feb to Mar 1944, UKNA WO 204/2167; and Caracciolo di Castagneto, *'43–'44*, pp. 129–38, entries for 28 Feb to 3 Mar 1944,

25. UKNA WO 204/2167, MacFarlane to AFHQ, 2 Mar 1944, Ref. 1523.

26. Rene 'Mac' Kisray testimony, IWM Sound 12325, Reels 4 and 5.

27. Caracciolo di Castagneto, *'43–'44*, p. 138, entry for 3 Mar 1944. According to Kisray (IWM Sound 12325, Reel 5) it was British behind-the-scenes diplomacy that convinced party leaders, particularly the Communist Velio Spano, to call it off.

28. See statements by DC and DL reproduced in Salvetti (ed.), *La Campania dal Fascismo alla repubblica*, Vol. I, pp. 494–6.

29. Togliatti testimony, quoted in Salvetti (ed.), *La Campania dal Fascismo alla repubblica*, Vol. I, pp. 505–8.

30. 'Party Moves in Italy', *The Times*, 3 Apr 1944.

31. Minutes of CLN executive committee meeting, 18 Apr 1944, quoted in Salvetti (ed.), *La Campania dal Fascismo alla repubblica*, Vol. I, pp. 524–5. See also Caracciolo di Castagneto, '43–'44, pp. 152–62, entries for 18–21 Apr 1944.

32. Caracciolo di Castagneto, '43–'44, p. 163, entry for 24 Apr 1944; Schiano, *La resistenza nel napoletano*, p. 104.

33. Croce, *Croce, the King and the Allies*, entry for 13 Nov, footnote to entry for 8 Jun 1944, p. 140.

34. Schiano, *La resistenza nel napoletano*, p. 104.

35. PWB report 20, 28 Sep 1944, p. 1 (prelims); and 23, 19 Oct 1944 (prelims). See also Palermo, *Memorie di un comunista napoletano*, pp. 271–3.

36. David W. Ellwood, *Italy 1943–1945* (New York: Holmes & Meier, 1985), pp. 96, 120.

Chapter 26: Political Corruption

1. Desmond Seward, *Naples: A Traveller's Reader* (London: Robinson, 1984), pp. 13–14; Denis Mack Smith, *Italy and Its Monarchy* (London and New Haven: Yale University Press, 1989), pp. 17–18.

2. Croce, *History of the Kingdom of Naples*, p. 241.

3. Allum, *Politics and Society in Post-War Naples*, pp. 67–71.

4. Giolitti and Saredo quoted in Allum, *Politics and Society in Post-War Naples*, p. 67.

5. For a description of these events, see Barone, *Piazza Spartaco*, pp. 126–64.

6. Ibid., p. 176; De Antonellis, *Napoli sotto il regime*, pp. 61–2.

7. Padovani quoted in De Antonellis, *Napoli sotto il regime*, pp. 105–7.

8. The historian Michele Fatica argues that, despite his words, Padovani promised repeatedly and vigorously to uphold the interests of the establishment. See his essay, 'Appunti per una storia di Napoli nell'età del Fascismo' in Laveglia (ed.), *Mezzogiorno e fascismo*, Vol. I, pp. 96–8.

9. Although De Nicola later repented of his collaboration with Mussolini, and didn't take up his seat on being re-elected in 1924, by then the damage had already been done. See Allum, *Politics and Society in Post-War Naples*, pp. 72–4.

10. Carlo Cassola letter to Giovanni Amendola, 26 Feb 1923, from Amendola-Kühn, *Vita con Giovanni Amendola, Epistolario, 1903–1926*, doc. 474, pp. 488–91.

11. Allum, *Politics and Society in Post-War Naples*, pp. 72–3.

12. See for example Croce's comments about Innocenti in *Croce, the King and the Allies*, pp. 121–2, entry for 27 Apr.

13. PWB report 9, 30 Jun 1944, pp. 4–5 (item 10).

14. Antonio Palma accusation against Don Nicola Ciccarelli, quoted in PWB report 12, 2 Aug 1944, p. 26 (item 56).

15. 'Una provincial in balia del fascismo', *L'Unità*, 4 Jun 1944; and 'Da Benevento. Come prima?', *L'Azione*, 22 Jul 1944; both reproduced in Salvetti (ed.), *La Campania dal Fascismo alla repubblica*, Vol. I, pp. 561–2, 585–6. See also PWB report 15, 24 Aug 1944, p. 2 (item 6).

16. Ibid., (item 5).

17. PWB report 20, 28 Sep 1944, p. 2 (item 2).

18. PWB report 10, 19 Jul 1944, pp. 1–2 (item 3); and PWB report 21, 5 Oct 1944, p. 6 (item 10).

19. PWB report 10, 19 Jul 1944, p. 2 (item 4).

20. PWB report 21, 5 Oct 1944, p. 7 (item 14).

21. Ibid.

22. PWB report 10, 19 Jul 1944, p. 2 (item 4).

23. PWB report 17, 7 Sep 1944, preamble, p. 1.

24. 'Da Benevento. Come prima?', *L'Azione*, 22 Jul 1944; reproduced in

Salvetti (ed.), *La Campania dal Fascismo alla repubblica*, Vol. I, pp. 585–6.
25. Allum, *Politics and Society in Post-War Naples*, pp. 274–92.

Chapter 27: Organized Crime

1. NARA, RG 331, UD 1978, Box 4829, 10260/143/258, 'Report on the Black Market in Naples by Maj. B. Mattei'.
2. See the various Carabinieri reports from 20 Apr 1944 (Torre Annunziata), 5 and 11 Jun (Torre del Greco) and 18 Jun (Arenaccia) in NARA, RG 331, UD 1978, Box 4818, 10260/1443/37. See also Box 4826, 10260/143/210, report by ACC Naples Province, Public Safety Division, 1 Aug 1944.
3. Lewis, *Naples '44*, pp. 116–19, entry for 3 May 1944.
4. UKNA, WO 204/1265, PWB report 19 Apr 1945, 'Conditions and Developments in Naples Area – No. 49', p. 18 (item 9).
5. NARA, RG 331, UD 1978, Box 4826, 10260/143/209, HQ Region 3, AMG, Commissioner of Public Safety, 'Weekly Report', 28 Dec 1943, p. 3.
6. Ibid., Box 939, 10000/129/168, Economics and Civilian Supply report, 'Oct. 1st to Nov. 16th 1943', p. 5.
7. Ibid., Box 4826, 10260/143/210, AMG Province of Avellino, 'Monthly Report', 11 Jan 1944, p. 1.
8. Agostino Degli Espinosa, *Il regno del Sud* (Florence: Parenti, 1955), pp. 353–4.
9. NARA, RG 331, UD 1978, Box 4826, 10260/143/210, HQ Region 3, 'Public Safety Report for the Month of January 1944', p. 3.
10. Ibid., Box 4826, 10260/143/210, HQ Region 3, 'Monthly Report for May 1944 – Public Safety Division', p. 5; and Box 4829, 10260/143/260, 'Riots and Demonstrations', 14 Jan 1944.
11. PWB report 10, 19 Jul 1944, p. 30 (item 46).
12. Gianluca Barneschi, *Balvano 1944* (Milan: Mursia, 2005), pp. 168–222.

For varying statistics on the number of dead, see pp. 152–4.
13. NARA, RG 331, UD 1978, Box 4829, 10260/143/258, 'Rapporto sul tasporto illicito di olio, 18 Apr 1944.
14. Domenico Colasanto, 18 Dec 1943, quoted in De Marco, *Polvere di piselli*, p. 163.
15. NARA, RG 331, UD 1978, Box 4829, 10260/143/258, Lt Col. James L. Kincaid memo, 'Causes of black market activities and increased cost of living in Naples Province', 23 Nov 1943.
16. Ibid., Box 4826, 10260/143/210, 'Public Safety Report for the Month of February 1944', p. 2; and 'Region 3 Public Safety Report for March 1944', p. 5.
17. Ibid., Box 4829, 10260/143/258, Lt Col. James L. Kincaid memo, 'Causes of black market activities and increased cost of living in Naples Province', 23 Nov 1943, p. 2.
18. Ibid., Box 4826, 10260/143/210, ACC Salerno Province, 'Report for Month of July 1944', p. 2.
19. Ibid., 'Region 3 Public Safety Report for March 1944', p. 5.
20. PWB report 21, 5 Oct 1944, p. 10 (item 16).
21. De Marco, *Polvere di piselli*, pp. 163–6.
22. Ibid., p. 164; NARA, RG 331, UD 1978, Box 4826, 10260/143/210, 'Monthly Report for May 1944 – Region 3, Public Safety Division', p. 5.
23. Mauldin, *The Brass Ring*, p. 191.
24. Graham Martin Rowntree testimony, IWM Sound 28758, Reel 5.
25. 'Carry Your Wallet in Shirts, Gents', *S&S* (Mediterranean), 2 Jun 1944.
26. Charles Cobraith Grinder testimony, VHP-LoC: www.loc.gov/item// afc2001001.05021
27. See for example Elvin E. Thomas testimony, VHP-LoC: www.loc.gov/ item/afc2002002.33621
28. PWB report 24, 26 Oct 1944, preamble.
29. Sam Cawdron testimony, IWM Sound 17106, Reel 9.

30. Lewis, *Naples '44*, pp. 91–2, entry for 14 Mar.

32. Bert Scrivens testimony, IWM Sound 29536, Reel 16.

32. Julian H. Philips, 'Hunger Flourished', TMFM, pp. 3–4.

33. Lewis, *Naples '44*, pp. 91–2, entry for 14 Mar.

34. Mervyn Thomas James Stockham, IWM Sound 25544, Reel 2; NARA, RG 331, UD 1978, Box 4818, 10260/1443/37, Questura di Napoli, 'Lesioni riportate da Polinaro Carmela', 15 Mar 1944.

35. Lewis, *Naples '44*, pp. 78–80, entry for 5 Feb.

36. Brown, *The Whorehouse of the World*, p. 241.

37. NARA, RG 331, UD 1978, Box 4826, 10260/143/210, 'Region 3 Public Safety Report for April 1944', pp. 3–4.

38. Lewis, *Naples '44*, p. 78, entry for 5 Feb.

39. Wilfred George Beeson testimony, IWM Sound 4802, Reel 28.

40. Stefanile, *I cento bombardimenti di Napoli*, p. 207. His description is corroborated by Charles Cobraith Grinder testimony, VHP-LoC: www.loc.gov/item/afc2001001/05021

41. PWB report 23, 19 Oct 1944, p. 8 (item 11).

42. NARA, RG 331, UD 1978, Box 4826, 10260/143/210, 'Region 3 Public Safety Report for April 1944', p. 4.

43. Ibid., 'Monthly Report for May 1944 – Region 3, Public Safety Division', p. 4.

44. UNRRA, S-1242-0000-0103-00003, Leo Gerstenzang memo to Mikhail Menshikov, 26 May 1944, 'Report of Operations of Allied Control Commission and AMGOT in Italy', p. 15.

45. NARA, RG 331, UD 1978, Box 4821, 10260/143/64, Special Detachment G-2 memo 15 Feb 1944, Lieutenant Colonel Warner to Maor. Papurt, 'Black Market – Alimentation'.

46. UNRRA, S-1242-0000-0103-00003, Leo Gerstenzang memo to Mikhail Menshikov, 26 May 1944, 'Report of Operations of Allied Control Commission and AMGOT in Italy', p. 1; and Office of War Information press release NB 2737, 3 Sep 1944, pp. 12–13. Gerstenzang claims the reduction in ration cards was only 240,000.

47. Dave Lingard testimony, IWM Sound 23045, Reel 8.

48. Matelon Eugene Chrestman testimony, VHP-LoC: www.loc.gov/item/afc2001001.86935

49. Stanley Gladstone testimony, IWM Sound 3954, Reel 4.

50. NARA, RG 3312, UD 1978, Box 4818, 10260/143/36, Questura di Napoli report, 27 Nov 1943.

51. James Robinson, Jr, oral history, part 2 of 4, JAMHC: https://ndajams.omeka.net/items/show/1051641

52. Harold Fine testimony, IWM Sound 21082, Reel 9.

53. PWB report 20, 28 Sep 1944, p. 3 (item 6).

53. PWB report 4, 3 May 1944, pp. 5–6 (item 8). See also the report for the following week (11 May), p. 2 (item 4).

55. 'Naples Emerges as Top Allied Port', *New York Times*, 3 Sep 1944.

56. Brown, *The Whorehouse of the World*, p. 410.

57. UNRRA, Reports on Naples, S-1242-0000-0103-00003, Gerstenzang to Menshikov, 'Report on Operations of Allied Control Commission and AMGOT in Italy', 26 May 1944, p. 5.

58. NARA, RG 331, UD 1978, Box 4829, 10260/143/258, 'Combined Report of Market Study for Naples City and Province with special attention to "Black Market" problems', p. 5; and 'Exhibit 1' by Captain Cecil H. Owen, 12 Nov 1943.

59. UKNA, WO 204/9846, Colonel John W. Chapman report to regional commissioner Region III, 'Conditions in Port of Naples', 16 Jun 1944, p. 1; NARA, RG 331, UD 1978, Box 4821,

10260/143/64, 'Causes of AMG Supply Losses and Recommended Corrective Measures', 22 Jan 1944; ibid., John A. Warner memo to Regional Public Safety Officer, Region III ACC HQ, 'Black Market etc.', p. 2.

60. UKNA, WO 204/9846, Colonel John W. Chapman report to regional commissioner Region III, 'Conditions in Port of Naples,' 16 Jun 1944, p. 2.

61. Ibid.

62. PWB report 4, 3 May 1944, pp. 5–6 (item 8).

63. Brown, *The Whorehouse of the World*, p. 266.

64. Lewis, *Naples '44*, p. 109, entry for 18 Apr.

65. NARA, RG 331, UD 1978, Box 4821, 10260/143/64, 'Causes of AMG Supply Losses and Recommended Corrective Measures', 22 Jan 1944.

66. Mauldin, *The Brass Ring*, p. 193.

67. NARA, RG 331, UD 1978, Box 4826, 10260/143/210, ACC HQ Region 3, 'Public Safety Report for the month of February 1944', p. 2; and 'Public Safety Report for March 1944', p. 3.

68. Ibid., Box 4826, 10260/143/210, 'Monthly report for July, 1944 – Region 3, Public Safety Division', p. 3.

69. For nineteenth-century views of the Camorra, see Marc Monnier, *La Camorra: Notizie Storiche* (Florence: G. Barbera, 1863; Liborio Romano, *Memorie politiche* (Naples: Marghieri, 1873); and Munthe, *Letters from a Mourning City*, pp. 187–233. For modern histories of the origin of the Camorra see Francesco Benigno, *La mala seta: Alle origini di mafia e camorra 1859–1878* (Turin: Einaudi, 2015); Gigi di Fiore, *La Camorra e le sue storie* (Milan: UTET, 2021), pp. 3–127. For Giuseppe Saredo letter to Giovanni Giolitti, see Allum, *Politics and Society in Post-War Naples*, p. 67. For the demise of the Camorra at the start of the twentieth century, see Marcella Marmo, 'Citta camorrista e i suoi confini: Dall'Unità al processo cuocolo' in Gabriella Gribaudi (ed.), *Traffici criminali: Camorra, mafia e reti internazionale dell'illegalità* (Turin: Bollati Bollinghieri, 2009).

70. Alison Jamieson, *The Antimafia: Italy's Fight against Organized Crime* (Basingstoke: Macmillan Press, 2000), pp. 14–16.

71. NARA, RG 331, UD 1978, Box 4826, 10260/143/210, ACC Commune of Naples, 'Monthly report Public Safety City of Naples', 4 Aug 1944, p. 1.

72. Tom Behan, *See Naples and Die* (London: I. B. Tauris, 2009), p. 54; di Fiore, *La Camorra e le sue storie*, p. 139. For obvious reasons, much of the history of the Mafia is based on rumour and speculation rather than witness testimony and documentary evidence.

73. Holmgreen quoted by Tim Newark, *The Mafia at War: Allied Collusion with the Mob* (London: Greenhill, 2007), p. 215.

74. Lewis, *Naples '44*, p. 110, entry for 18 Apr.

74. Behan, *See Naples and Die*, p. 54; di Fiore, *La Camorra e le sue storie*, pp. 138–9.

75. NARA, RG 331, UD 1978, Box 4826, 10260/143/209, HQ Region 3, AMG Office of Commissioner of Public Safety, 'Weekly Report', 3 Jan 1944, p. 4.

77. PWB report 13, 10 Aug 1944, p. 13 (item 31).

78. Between the 1940s and the 1980s the bulk of this smuggling trade was concerned with cigarettes – yet another legacy of the wartime black market in Naples. See di Fiore, *La Camorra e le sue storie*, p143.

70. Di Fiore, *La Camorra e le sue storie*, pp. 142–3; Gribaudi, *Guerra totale*, p. 619.

Chapter 28: The Last Crisis of the War

1. John Miles, Friends Ambulance Unit, IWM Sound 20538, Reel 1.

2. NARA, RG 331, UD 1978, Box 67, 10000/100/1091, 'Report of Region 2 for December 1943', p. 12; UNRRA, Italy – Displaced Persons, S-1245-0000-0254-00002, 'A likely UNRRA responsibility: Displaced Persons', p. 18.

3. Gribaudi, *Guerra totale*, pp. 448–72

4. UNRRA, Italy 1944 Observers' Mission, S-1245-0000-0272-00001, 'Intelligence memorandum no. 2', 19 May 1944.

5. UNRRA, Italy – Displaced Persons, S-1245-0000-0254-00001, Xanthaky memo to Whelk, 22 May 1945, 'Notes on the Displaced Person Problem in Italy', p. 3; estimated figures for Naples in *Il Domani d'Italia*, 8 Jun 1945, quoted in Salvetti (ed.), *La Campania dal Fascismo alla Repubblica*, Vol. I, p. 650.

6. NARA, RG 331, UD 1978B, Box 4876, 10260/146/95, Labor Division AMG Region 3, 'Weekly Report for the Period 8–15 October 1943'; for earlier figures see De Marco, *Polvere di piselli*, p. 176.

7. PWB report 22, 12 Oct 1944, p. 5 (item 8).

8. PWB report 30, 7 Dec 1944, p. 9 (item 7).

9. Adlai Stevenson, 'Report of FEA Survey Mission to Italy', p. 65.

10. Ibid., p. 99.

11. Ibid., pp. 66, 100.

12. PWB report 23, 19 Oct 1944, Appendix A: Report on the Industrial Position in Naples Province.

13. Adlai Stevenson, 'Report of FEA Survey Mission to Italy', pp. xii–xiv, 121.

14. PWB report 14, 16 Aug 1944, p. 10 (item 17).

15. PWB report 15, 24 Aug 1944, pp. 6, 9 (item 19).

16. UKNA, WO 204/12625, CIC Zone 6 memo, 'Public Opinion and Political Parties as of 20 August 1945', p. 2.

17. 'A Napoli si cerca di sostituire con prigionieri tedeschi i lavoratori del Porto', *La Voce*, 29 Jun 1945; and 'Nell'anniversario delle "Quattro Giornate"*: Migliai di lavoratori napoletani sostituiti da prigionieri tedeschi!', *La Voce*, 19 Sep 1945.

18. UKNA, WO 204/12626, 'Extract from HQ Allied Commission Security Div, Public Safety Sub Commission Monthly Report for September 1945, Ref. No. SD/615'; and CIC report, 'The Reaction to the Use of German POW Labor', 20 Sep 1945.

19. UKNA, WO 204/12626, CIC report, '21 September Demonstration at Naples', 23 Sep 1945, pp. 1–5. For Italian police and newspaper accounts, see p. 5 of the CIC report; and Salvetti (ed.), *La Campania dal Fascismo alla Repubblica*, Vol. I, pp. 674–80.

20. UKNA, WO 204/12626, CS report dated 16 Sept 1945, 'Situazione politica e organizzazione comunista a Napoli', p. 1; and Meldrum letter to Colonel Stepanovich, 23 Sep 1945.

21. Early in 1946, for example, riots broke out across Naples involving former soldiers campaigning for 'bread and work'. See 'Le dimostrazioni dei reduce turbate da tumulti e violenze', *Risorgimento*, 11 Jan 1946; and 'Unemployed riots spreading through Italy', *Canberra Times*, 14 Jan 1946.

22. Lowe, *Savage Continent*, pp. 276–94.

23. UKNA WO 204/12626, extract from CIC report, 27 Dec 1945, 'Political Parties and Public Opinion'.

24. UKNA WO 204/12625, CIC report, 'Public Opinion and Political Parties as of 20 August 1945', p. 2.

25. Ibid., p. 3; *Risorgimento*, 19 Aug 1945.

26. Ellwood, *Italy 1943–1945*, p. 227.

27. Epicarmo Corbino editorial, 'Il Ministero Parri ed il Mezzogiorno', *Il Giornale*, 23 Jun 1945.

28. Ibid.

29. 'Consigli al Mezzogiorno', *Il Paese*, 14 Jun 1945.

30. 'Saluto a Ferruccio Parri', *L'Azione*, 15 Jul 1945.

31. 'Perché Napoli ha votato per il re', *L'Unità*, northern Italian edition, 8 Jun 1946, quoted in Salvetti (ed.), *La*

Campania dal Fascismo alla Repubblica, Vol. I, pp. 735–7.

32. For precise numbers and voting trends, see Salvetti (ed.), *La Campania dal Fascismo alla Repubblica*, Vol. I, pp. 758–64.

33. 'Sette morti e oltre sessanta feriti durante le agitazioni monarchiche di ieri', *La Voce*, 13 Jun 1946.

Conclusion: Legacy

1. Giorgio Amendola quoted in Ginsborg, *A History of Contemporary Italy, 1943–1980*, p. 98.

2. UKNA, WO 204/12625, CIC Zone 6 memo, 'Public Opinion and Political Parties as of 20 August 1945', p. 4.

3. Guido Dorso, 'Derequisire le industrie campane', *L'Azione*, 4 Sep 1945, quoted in Salvetti (ed.), *La Campania dal fascismo alla repubblica*, Vol. I, p. 671.

4. Ben Shephard, *The Long Road Home* (London: Bodley Head, 2010), pp. 38, 46–7.

5. NARA, RG 331, UD 1978, Box 963, 10000/132/190, HQ Allied Commission to Eisenhower, 'Food Ration – Italy', 12 Dec 1944.

6. William I. Hitchcock, *Liberation: The Bitter Road to Freedom, Europe 1944–1945* (London: Faber & Faber, 2008), pp. 107, 120.

7. Lowe, *Savage Continent*, pp. 149–58.

8. Tony Judt, *Postwar* (London: Pimlico, 2007), p. 56; Giles MacDonogh, *After the Reich* (London: John Murray, 2007), pp. 355–6; Lowe, *Savage Continent*, p. 153.

9. Judt, *Postwar*, pp. 87–8.

10. Adlai Stevenson, 'Report of FEA Survey Mission to Italy', p. xiv.

11. Ginsborg, *A History of Contemporary Italy, 1943–1980*, pp. 60–3, 106;

Jonathan Dunnage, 'Policing and Politics in the Southern Italian Commmunity, 1943–1948' in Jonathan Dunnage (ed.), *After the War: Violence, Justice, Continuity and Renewal in Italian Society* (Market Harborough: Troubadour, 1999), pp. 32–47.

12. Ginsborg, *A History of Contemporary Italy, 1943–1980*, pp. 230–1; Allum, *Politics and Society in Post-War Naples*, pp. 25–6.

13. For shoddy building practices, see Allum, *Politics and Society in Post-War Naples*, pp. 35–6.

14. Ginsborg, *A History of Contemporary Italy 1943–1980*, pp. 216–20.

15. Michel Cocquery, 'Aspects démographiques et problems de croissance d'une ville "millionaire": le cas de Naples', *Annales de Géographie*, Vol. 72, No. 393 (Sept–Oct 1963), p. 585.

16. Paolo Ricci testimony in Percopo and Riccio (eds), *La Campania dal fascismo alla repubblica*, Vol. II, pp. 234–5.

17. Sophia Loren, *Yesterday, Today, Tomorrow* (New York: Atria, 2014), p. 72.

18. Benedetto Croce, *Pulcinella e il personaggio del Napoletano in commedia* (Rome: Ermanno Loescher, 1899), pp. 53–4.

19. According to a statistical list produced by the financial newspaper *Il Sole 24 Ore*, Naples ranked tenth on the list of crimes per capita in Italian cities. Florence was seventh, Rome fifth, Turin third. The highest crime rate was in Milan. See 'Indice criminalità nelle città italiane: la classifica del Sole 24 Ore', 3 Oct 2022, https://tg24.sky.it/cronaca/2022/10/03/indice-criminalita-2022-citta-italiane-classifica

Index